Arthur Griffiths

Memorials of Millbank, and chapters in prison history

Arthur Griffiths

Memorials of Millbank, and chapters in prison history

ISBN/EAN: 9783744756532

Printed in Europe, USA, Canada, Australia, Japan

Cover: Foto ©ninafisch / pixelio.de

More available books at **www.hansebooks.com**

Memorials of Millbank.

General View of Millbank Prison, from the River.

MEMORIALS OF MILLBANK

AND

CHAPTERS IN PRISON HISTORY.

BY

ARTHUR GRIFFITHS.

*Major, H.P., 63rd Regiment, one of H.M. Inspectors of Prisons,
and Author of "The Chronicles of Newgate," etc. etc.*

WITH ILLUSTRATIONS BY R. GOFF AND THE AUTHOR.

NEW EDITION.

LONDON: CHAPMAN AND HALL,
LIMITED.
1884.

PREFACE TO FIRST EDITION.

A FEW lines are perhaps needed to explain how I came to write this book.

Having filled since 1872 the post of Deputy Governor of Millbank Prison, I have had, ex-officio, custody of the archives and records of the place. Casual reference to these led me to suppose that extracts from them might prove readable, and I therefore began to collect anecdotes and ana, meaning to publish a small volume of them. As my task proceeded, however, I found my subject growing with it. Millbank has since its erection been so closely connected with all that concerns prisons and penal legislation generally, that the history of one naturally embraced the other. My work has, therefore, become wider and more pretentious in its aim than was originally intended. It may also have become drier and more dull; but what the narrative loses in merely amusing qualities will, I trust, be compensated for by the more comprehensive treatment of the subject.

I cannot allow these volumes to go to press without expressing my thanks to those who have assisted me with advice and information; more especially to WM. MORRISH, ESQ., Governor, R. M. GOVER, ESQ., Medical Officer, and MR. DENIS POWER, Chief Warder of Millbank Prison.

CONTENTS.

A *

X

CONTENTS.

LIST OF ILLUSTRATIONS.

MEMORIALS OF MILLBANK.

CHAPTER I.

PRELIMINARY HISTORY.

MILLBANK no longer attracts the wide attention it did in former days; and yet the very name contains in itself almost an epitome of our whole penal legislation. With it one intimately associates the names of men like Howard and Jeremy Bentham; an architect of eminence, Sir Robert Smirke, superintended its erection; while statesmen and high dignitaries, dukes, bishops, and members of parliament, were to be found upon its committee of management, exercising a control that was far from nominal or perfunctory, not disdaining a close consideration of the minutest details, and coming into intimate personal communion with the criminal inmates, whom, by praise or admonition, they sought to reward or reprove. Millbank has been doomed to demolition again and again; its site, valued now at nearly a quarter of a million, has been promised for other edifices—now for a barrack, now for aristocratic squares. Ten years ago a new prison, intended to replace it, was commenced in the western suburbs of London. The new prison is completed and occupied, yet Millbank still survives. Only within the last few months the penitentiary has passed into a new phase of its long and chequered existence. The female prison in Tothill Fields has been closed, under the power of the Prisons' Act of 1877, and Millbank has taken its place. It is now the sole metropolitan prison for females, just as once

it was the sole reformatory for promising criminals, the first
receptacle for military prisoners, the great *depôt* for convicts
en route to the Antipodes. A prison with such a history has
a right to its historian, and I have endeavoured, therefore,
to record in the following pages its origin, and the causes that
brought it into being; its object, and the success or otherwise of those who ruled it; its annals, and the curious
incidents with which they are filled.

The pictures painted by Howard of the horrors of prison
life are known to have been by no means over-coloured, but
familiarity with the revolting details has bred in us a certain
indifference to the frightful story they told. It was naturally
far otherwise when Howard's indignant protests were first
made public. They appealed then with a voice that was
trumpet-tongued to all in whom the instincts of humanity
were not quite dead, and woke even the most apathetic to
activity. Interest once evoked, sympathy followed, and from
that time forth the question of prisons and prison management
attracted daily greater attention.

Nor was it much too soon. The condition of our prisons,
as disclosed in Howard's reports, was a disgrace to civilisation.
The mere aspect of the prisoners was most miserable; when
visited they were found of thin and sallow visage, in form
emaciated, oftentimes dying of pestilential diseases as they lay on
the foul dungeon floors quite untended and destitute of the
commonest necessaries of life. They had no regular allowance of
food : perhaps a pennyworth or two of bread, and that reduced
in weight by petty thefts before it reached the prisoner. No
wonder that they looked half-starved when they came up for
trial; that they were clothed in rags; and they carried with
them, wherever they went, the seeds of deadly infection. The
" Gaol Fever," a disease now happily unknown, was the
product of these terrible times. " By it," says Howard,
" more people perished than were put to death by all the
public executions in the kingdom." At one court held at
Oxford Castle, in 1577, and still known as the " Black Assize,"
all who were present died within forty hours—the Lord Chief
Baron, the sheriff, and about three hundred more.* Again at

* Baker's Chronicle, p. 353.

Taunton, in 1730, some prisoners from the Dorchester Gaol infected the court so that the Lord Chief Baron Pengelly, the sergeant, Sir James Sheppard, the sheriff, and some hundreds besides, died of the distemper. It was common for released prisoners to take back contagion into their own homes; and later, in 1750, the Lord Mayor of London, two judges, an alderman, and many of inferior rank, fell victims to the fever. That such a terrible visitant should be ever present within the prison walls was indeed not strange. Sanitary precautions and rules, which are to-day deemed indispensable, were then almost altogether a dead letter.

Overcrowding was practised to a frightful extent. Cleanliness and good ventilation were words without meaning. The wretched inmates were lodged in "close rooms, cells, and subterraneous dungeons, for fourteen or fifteen hours out of the four-and-twenty. In some of these caverns the floor is very damp; in others there is sometimes an inch or two of water; and the straw or bedding is laid on such floors, seldom on barrack bedsteads."* But in few places was there any allowance of bedding: a little straw was sometimes issued, but left unchanged for months; and in the interval it became filthy, or was ground to dust. As often as not the prisoners lay on rags, or on the floors. No attention was paid to water supply. In most prisons there was no water at all; in others it was kept under lock and key, and given out in stinted quantities, the allowance being sometimes as low as three pints per head, daily, for all purposes. Sewers were generally unknown; and both inside and out the accumulations of filth were offensive beyond expression. It would have been a mockery to mention fresh air in such loathsome dens as these: it was conspicuous only by its absence.

So poisonous and pestiferous was the atmosphere the prisoners were compelled constantly to breathe, that Howard tells us the gaolers often would not accompany him into the felon ward; and that he himself, on leaving them, found his clothes smelt so offensively that he could not travel in a post chaise with the windows shut, and that he therefore made his journeys subsequently on horseback; the leaves of

* Howard : State of Prisons, i. p. 7.

his memorandum book were often tainted so that he could
not use it till it had been exposed to heat; and in the same
way the vinegar he carried as a preventive became "in-
tolerably disagreeable." The want of ventilation was greatly
increased by the rapacity of the gaolers, who, rather than
pay the window tax, preferred to stifle their prisoners.
For those who survived the horrors of such an existence,
other evils were superadded hardly less atrocious. The
indiscriminate herding together of all classes was one of
the most flagrant of these; yet it surely was sinful to
associate in this way the innocent with the guilty, male
and female, debtor and felon, youth and hardened offender.
A rapid spread of demoralisation and wickedness was the
natural and immediate result; and prisons, meant to punish
and deter, acted rather as hot-beds for the growth and multi-
plication of offenders. Lunatics, again, and persons of weak
understanding, were suffered to go at large in the midst of
the rest, sometimes serving for idle sport, often terrifying and
disturbing the other prisoners.

Practices the most objectionable flourished without let or
hindrance. Gaming in various forms : cards, dice, skittles,
mississipi, fives, tennis, billiards, portobello ; * drunkenness,
which was quite unchecked, and at the expense of the new
comers. For this purpose blackmail, styled "garnish," was
levied by the old hands. To pay or strip was the penalty,
and thus the poor became poorer, and the needy half naked.
In all matters the prisoners were at the tender mercies of
their gaolers, of whom in those days Sir William Blackstone
asserts that they were "frequently a merciless race of men,
and, by being conversant with scenes of misery, steeled against
any tender sensation." † Their chief aim was to make their office
profitable. Salaries that were often infinitesimal had to be
eked out by the iniquitous system of "gaol fees." Innocent
men, acquitted in court, were haled back to prison till they
paid the gaoler's dues. Extortion in every shape was openly
practised. The keepers sold spirituous liquors, and bartered
and trafficked with the inmates. Some gaols were private

* Howard : State of Prisons, i. p. 13.
† Blackstone, iv. ch. 22.

property, and, the funds meant for their maintenance being misappropriated, the establishments were left to prosper as best they could.

It was the custom to load all prisoners with irons so heavy that "walking, or even lying down to sleep, was difficult and painful."* Women even were not exempt from this barbarous infliction; and though gaolers pleaded safe custody as their excuse, Howard was convinced that avarice was the probable reason, "because county gaolers do sometimes grant dispensations, and indulge their prisoners, men as well as women, with what they call 'choice of irons' if they pay for it;" yet a learned judge, King, afterwards Lord Chancellor, would by no means admit of the pleading of "safe custody" as an excuse for "ironing" unconvicted men, declaring that prisoners should be secured by "raising higher the prison walls." One instance alone will show what were a gaoler's views of safe custody. Howard mentions that in 1768, at Ely, the prisoners were secured "by chaining them down on their backs upon a floor, across which were several iron bars, with an iron collar with spikes about their necks, and a heavy bar over their legs. An excellent magistrate, James Collyer, Esquire, presented an account of the case, accompanied by a drawing, to the King; with which His Majesty was much affected, and gave immediate orders for a proper inquiry and redress."†

A few items more, and the summary will be complete. Chaplains were appointed to most prisons, but they were never too zealous, and often failed miserably in the due discharge of their sacred office. There was little or no employment for convicted prisoners. Lastly, gaol deliveries were of rare occurrence, so that for ages, as it seemed, the innocent languished in prison awaiting trial. At Hull the assize was held but once in seven years; and in one case a murderer, after being confined for three years, was eventually released, because in the interval the principal witness against him had died. So much for the gaols: idleness, drunkenness, vicious intercourse; sickness, starvation, squalor; cruelty, chains—what need to mention more?

Yet side by side with all this worked a sanguinary code

* Howard: State of Prisons, i. p. 13.   † Ibid. p. 291.

of laws whereby capital punishment was inflicted for even
trivial offences. Death indeed was preferable to the living
miseries that overtook the respited criminal. For those who
had escaped the gallows, or passed scathless through the
accumulated dangers of incarceration, the plantations remained.
Since the time of Elizabeth, vagabonds under the Vagrancy
Act had been adjudged liable to banishment from the realm.
The first actual record of transportation is in the reign of
James I., when that monarch ordered 100 " dissolute persons "
to be sent out to Virginia; and Cromwell sent his political
captives to work as slaves or indented servants to America or
the West Indies: but in 1717 it was regularly introduced into
our criminal law. An Act passed in that year commented on
the inefficiency of the punishments in use, and pointed out
that in many of His Majesty's colonies and plantations in
America there was a great want of servants, who by their
labour and industry would be the means of improving and
making the said colonies more useful to the nation.* Persons
sentenced, not really but nominally, to death were henceforth
handed over to contractors, who engaged to send them across
the Atlantic. These contractors became vested with a right
in the labour of the convicts for terms of seven or fourteen
years, and this property was sold by public auction when the
exiles arrived at the plantations. There was much competition
for this labour at a date prior to the existence of negro slavery.
To meet the demand the pernicious practice of kidnapping came
into vogue, and flourished till the middle of the eighteenth
century, when it was put down by law. The price paid,
according to the mercantile returns of sale, appears to have
been about £20 a head; but Howard publishes receipts showing
that for two guineas a felon could purchase his freedom from
the contractor or captain of the ship.

Prisons being what they were, it was hardly likely that
the condition of places where felons awaited deportation would
be much better; accordingly we find Howard animadverting
strongly on the treatment of the wretched transports. At
several prisons he had found them chained to the floor. For
those in the hulks on the Thames he spoke in such terms,

* Heath: Paper on Secondary Punishments. Appendix to Parl. Rep. 1837.

when examined at the bar of the House, that a parliamentary inquiry was set on foot, which elicited, among other facts, that 176 deaths occurred in twenty months among 672 prisoners. Again he quotes from a letter of certain "transport convict" contractors, that their cargoes (of human beings) reached them in such a state, and the subsequent mortality was so great, that they had serious misgivings about embarking again on similar ventures. Howard further remarks that he had taken "some pains to make inquiries concerning the state of transports, with regard to whom many cruelties and impositions were practised, and whose condition was in many respects equally contrary to humanity and good policy," but he refrained from making these observations public, because by "a recent Act of Parliament a new turn was given to the matter."

The condition of our prisons was in truth a standing disgrace to the country. But evidence is not wanting to show that even before Howard spoke they had begun to attract attention. As far back as the commencement of the century the Society for the Promotion of Christian Knowledge had taken up the question, which was further discussed by a parliamentary inquiry in 1728. No tangible results followed in either case. The Society was probably powerless, and the publication of Blue Books even now does not ensure the remedy of abuses. Yet, like straws in running water, the action here alluded to served to show the current in which men's minds were set. A general sense of uneasiness and dissatisfaction was widespread through the country, waiting to find voice and expression. The movement needed only an apostle to preach its doctrines, and it found one in Howard. In no other way can we account for the immediate attention which was attracted by his exposures. Even before he spoke, however, Mr. Popham, member for Taunton, had introduced a Bill into the House of Commons for the abolition of gaolers' fees, and the substitution of fixed salaries payable from the county rates. In 1774 this Bill, in an improved state, became law; and from that time forth the progress of amelioration, though not too rapid, was at least continuous.

The first person roused by Howard's revelations to the necessity for reform was the Duke of Richmond, Lord

Lieutenant of Sussex, who in 1776 built a new prison at Horsham, under Howard's advice and co-operation. The effects of the new system were so remarkable that twelve years afterwards a learned judge, Lord Mansfield, remarked that the number of prisoners for trial was reduced by half; whereupon the Governor of Horsham gaol replied, " Although in days of yore my prisoners were very frequent in their visits to me, discharged at one assize and in again within the old walls long before the next, yet such, my lord, has been the effect of separate confinement, and of making a rogue think a little, and become acquainted with himself, that in the course of the last twelve years I can solemnly declare that only one prisoner has been twice within these walls." " Good God!" replied the noble earl, "this language of experience is very forcible, and the fact ought to be more generally known."

Such satisfactory results said much, of course, for the discipline of Horsham Gaol, and its effect in diminishing crime in the particular district in which it was situated. But if Horsham were empty—other prisons were perhaps more full. A "tight" prison may often clear its immediate neighbourhood of offenders; but not necessarily because it reforms them—more probably because it drives them elsewhere. Thieves are quick to discover the localities that fright or favour them; and in those days they probably avoided Horsham as Europeans would the Gold Coast, or a Hindoo the Arctic regions.

Howard then saw his remonstrance followed by some immediate action. The subject was now taken up warmly. He was more than once called to the bar of the House of Commons and closely interrogated. A thorough revision of the existing law was now contemplated; not alone because he had spoken thus, but because it became imperative to find some substitute for transportation, which just at this time came suddenly to an end. The revolt of the American colonies had closed that outlet for our criminal sewage. The legislature, making a virtue of necessity, had discovered that "Transportation to His Majesty's colonies and plantations in America was found to be attended by various inconveniences, particularly by depriving the kingdom of many subjects whose labour might be useful to the community;" * and an Act was thereupon passed, providing that convicts sentenced, or liable to transportation, might be employed in certain kinds of hard labour until some other more effectual means could be found for disposing of them. The elaboration of this new method was left to Sir William Blackstone and Mr. Eden (afterwards Lord Auckland), in conjunction with Mr. Howard; and their joint labours produced the Act for the establishment of Penitentiary Houses, which is dated 1778, and is styled the 19th Geo. III., c. 74. We have here, of course, the first foreshadowing of Millbank Penitentiary, though the first stone of that prison was not to be laid for another five-and-twenty years. The new principles of action were indicated by the 5th section of this Act, wherein the hope is expressed that "if any offenders convicted of crimes for which transportation has been usually inflicted were ordered to solitary imprisonment, accompanied by well regulated hard labour, and religious instruction, it might be the means under Providence, not only of deterring others, but also of reforming the individuals, and turning them to habits of industry." † And this prescription of separate confinement as the basis of treatment was no doubt the main feature of the Act; but transportation was still permitted, and to other colonies beside the American, while hard labour at the hulks was provided for the most atrocious and daring offenders.

It has been customary always to credit the Quakers of Pennsylvania with the earliest efforts for the amelioration of prisons and their inmates. But though they doubtless led the way in softening the harshness of the penal code that was universally short and sanguinary, they were clearly forestalled in prison reforms. It was not until 1786 that they established the well-known Walnut Street prison,‡ and this was years after the erection of the new gaol at Horsham. But if we were really at the head of the Americans in this respect, the Dutch were even before us—for Howard relates in his first edition, how he found a *Maison de Force* at Ghent, half finished, in 1775, wherein all the principles of cellular accommodation

* 16 Geo. III., c. 43.
† 19 Geo. III., c. 74, sec. 5. ‡ See chapter viii. p. 141.

and constant employment, as they afterwards obtained, were already thoroughly recognised. And we ourselves did not get much beyond the mere enunciation of the theory. Practice on the part of the Government did not follow for many years, although in Sussex the same Duke of Richmond was instrumental in the erection of the new prison at Petworth, in 1871, while in other counties, notably at Oxford, Stafford and Gloucester, great efforts were made to keep pace with the new ideas. That the legislature was really anxious also to carry out the suggestions of the Penitentiary Houses Act is undoubted : the delay arose in this wise. Three supervisors had been appointed, under the Act, to purchase ground for the proposed buildings, and to superintend the erection of the prison which was to hold 600 male and 300 female prisoners. Mr. Howard was the first of these three, and with him were associated Dr. Fothergill, a great personal friend, and Mr. Whately. Unhappily differences of opinion arose among them as to the choice of site. Howard and Dr. Fothergill had selected a spot at Islington, Mr. Whately one at Limehouse. Both parties adhered obstinately to their own views. Mr. Whately's arguments are not now known, but Howard has made public the grounds on which he based his choice.

That it had a healthy situation, and an abundant water supply, were amongst the most salient advantages. He considered it indispensable that the new prison should be built in London or close to it, because, being the first of its kind, and designed as a model for others in different parts of the kingdom, the success of the institution would depend largely on the constant attention of the persons named for its government. There could be no spot so suitable as Islington, except perhaps one upon the banks of the Thames ; but here Howard could not find what he required. A curious statement this, seeing that only a year or two later Jeremy Bentham bought, and at a cheap price, the lands in Tothill Fields, whereon Millbank was subsequently built. The disputes between the supervisors continued for a couple of years. Persons were not indeed wanting to act as arbitrators, but their name was legion. Among them were included the Lord Chancellor, the Speaker of the House of Commons, the twelve judges, and the Lord Mayor. Naturally all hope of uniformity in action or opinion was quite out of the question. So Howard gave up the fight, and resigned his appointment. His friend Fothergill was now dead, and he begged therefore to "decline all further concern in, the business," though he had at one time thought that his observations upon similar institutions in foreign countries would have qualified him in some degree to carry out the scheme.*

It is indeed interesting to observe, at this distance of time, how thoroughly this great man understood the subject to which he had devoted his life. In his prepared plan for the erection of the prison he anticipates exactly the method we are pursuing to-day, after a century of experience. "The Penitentiary Houses," he says, "I would have built in a great measure by the convicts. I will suppose that a power is obtained from Parliament to employ such of them as are now at work on the Thames, or some of those who are in the county gaols, under sentence of transportation, as may be thought most expedient. In the first place, let the surrounding wall, intended for full security against escapes, be completed, and proper lodges for the gatekeepers. Let temporary buildings of the nature of barracks be erected in some part of this enclosure which will be wanted the least, till the whole is finished. Let one or two hundred men, with their proper keepers, and under the direction of the builder, be employed in levelling the ground, digging out the foundation, serving the masons, sawing the timber and stone; and as I have found several convicts who were carpenters, masons, and smiths, these may be employed in their own branches of trade, since such work is as necessary and proper as any other in which they can be engaged. Let the people thus employed chiefly consist of those whose term is nearly expired, or who are committed for a short term; and as the ground is suitably prepared for the builders, the garden made, the wells dug, and the building finished, let those who are to be dismissed go off gradually, as it would be very improper to send them back to the hulks or gaols again." †

Suggestions such as these may have seemed far-fetched to

* State of Prisons, i. p. 226.　　　　　† Ibid. p. 221.

those to whom they were propounded; but that his plan of
action was simple and feasible, is now most satisfactorily
proved. Elam Lynds, the celebrated governor of Sing-Sing
prison, in the State of New York, acted precisely in this
manner, encamping out on the open with his hundreds of
prisoners, and compelling them in this way to build their
own prison-house, cell by cell, as bees would build a hive.
De Tocqueville, commenting on this seemingly strange episode
of prison history, observes that "the manner in which Mr.
Elam Lynds built Sing-Sing would no doubt raise incredulity,
were not the fact quite recent, and publicly known in the
United States. To understand it we have only to realise
what resources the new prison discipline of America placed at
the disposal of an energetic man." *

But the practice is precisely similar to that which we
pursue now when new convict prisons are constructed in this
country, and an actual example may at this moment be seen
in the immediate neighbourhood of London.

In December, 1875, the writer of these pages commenced
operations in the new prison at Wormwood Scrubs. Free
labour had surrounded the site with a wooden palisading,
and the first half of a temporary prison to accommodate one
hundred had just been roofed in. But only a few cells were
completed; they were of corrugated iron, the external wall
being strengthened by a casing, one inch thick. The first
detachment consisted of six " special class " convicts, men who
had behaved uniformly well and had still but one year to serve.
These six took possession of the unfinished buildings and
gradually completed cell after cell; as each was ready, it was
occupied, and when one hundred convicts were collected, the
second building for another hundred was commenced. Meanwhile, clay was being dug for brick making, rough roads were
laid, and other necessary works were undertaken. By the beginning of summer the foundations of the first permanent block
were laid, and the first batch of prison-made "stock" bricks
had been burnt. From that time forth progress was continuous: within a couple of years the first block of three
hundred and fifty cells were completed, the second commenced,

* Beaumont and De Tocqueville's Visit to the States.

and so until now in 1884, the whole establishment is in full
working order. A similar enterprise has just been set on foot
at Dover, where vast harbour works will shortly be undertaken by convict labour. The preliminaries at Dover follow
precisely the same lines as those at Wormwood Scrubs.

The scheme for the national penitentiary was not suffered
to fall to the ground because Howard declined to act. New
supervisors were appointed—Sir Gilbert Eliot (afterwards
Lord Minto), Sir Charles Bunbury, and Mr. Bowdler—who
took up the task where their predecessors had left it. This
choice of a suitable site was surrounded by many difficulties.
A portion of Wandsworth Fields was at length selected as
seeming to fulfil the required conditions; but no sooner was
the spot reported to the Lord Chancellor for approval, than an
agitation was set up in the neighbourhood to protest against
the introduction of a prison into those parts. People possessing landed property thereabouts had sufficient influence to
secure the rejection of the site, and the supervisors, after
a further search, fixed upon certain lands at Battersea Rise,
seventy-nine acres in extent, which, as the proprietors held
out for terms, were eventually assessed by a jury at the sum
of £6600.

And now everything was in fair working order. Plans
for the new buildings were actually prepared, and operations
about to commence, when the Government suddenly decided
to suspend further proceedings. The principle of transportation had never been entirely abandoned. Western
Africa had indeed been selected for a penal settlement, and
a few convicts sent there in spite of the deadly character
of the climate. But the statesmen of the day had fully
recognised that they had no right to increase the punishment of imprisonment by making it also capital; and the
Government, despairing of finding a suitable place of exile,
were about to commit themselves entirely to the plan of
home penitentiaries, when the discoveries of Captain Cook in
the South Seas drew attention to the vast territories of
Australasia. Everything spoke in favour of the adoption
of this island continent as a penal colony; it was healthy,
remote, and it was believed to possess within itself undefined

but inexhaustible elements of wealth. There was no doubt
much to recommend the scheme of transportation. As it then
· presented itself it must have possessed irresistible attractions,
even to minds philosophic and acute. The criminal, removed
to a mysterious distance from old haunts and dangerous
associates, was to be punished by exile; but at the same time
he was encouraged to make a new start in life and in a new
country, where, safe from competition, reclaimed and industrious, he might win rich harvests from the virgin soil. It might
reasonably be expected that eventually a large and prosperous
community would arise in the antipodes, capable of absorbing
all the criminality of Britain. Of the varying fortunes of this
new settlement I shall have occasion to speak hereafter, and we
shall then be able to judge by practical results the dictum of a
learned writer, who years before had declared that "the effect
of banishment, as practised in England, is often beneficial to
the criminal, and always injurious to the community."*

Embarking hotly on the new project, the Government could
not well afford to continue steadfast to the principle of
penitentiaries, and the latter might have fallen to the ground
altogether, but for the interposition of Jeremy Bentham.
This remarkable man published, in 1791, his "Panopticon, or
the Inspection House," a valuable work on prison discipline,
and followed it, in 1792, by a formal proposal to erect a prison
on the plan he advocated. His scheme was so peculiar that it
deserves to be described, more especially as the present Millbank
Penitentiary is often supposed to have grown out of his proposal.
As a matter of fact, however, except in the selection of site
and the purchase of the ground on which the prison now
stands, Bentham was in no way connected with Millbank.
Bentham states in his proposal that, "having turned his
Thoughts to the Penitentiary System from its first origin,
and having lately contrived a Building in which any number
of Persons may be kept within Reach of being Inspected
during every moment of their lives, and having made out, as
he flatters himself, to Demonstration, that the only eligible
mode of managing an Establishment of such a Nature in a
Building of such a construction would be by Contract, has been

* Eden: Principles of Penal Law, p. 33.

induced to make public the following proposal for maintaining and employing convicts in general, or such of them as would otherwise be Confined on Board the Hulks, for twenty-five per cent. less than it costs Government to maintain them there at present; deducting also the Average Value of the Work at present performed by them for the Public; upon the Terms of his receiving the Produce of their Labour."* Upon these terms he engaged as follows:—

"1. To furnish the prisoners with a constant supply of wholesome food not limited in quantity, but adequate to each man's desires.

2. To keep them clothed in a state of tightness and neatness superior to what is usual even in the improved prisons.

3. To keep them supplied with beds and bedding competent to their situations, and in a state of cleanliness scarcely anywhere conjoined to liberty.

4. To ensure them a sufficient supply of artificial warmth and light.

5. To keep from them, in conformity with the practice so happily received, every kind of strong and spirituous liquor.

6. To maintain them in a state of inviolable though mitigated seclusion, in assorted companies, without any of those opportunities of promiscuous association which in other places disturb, if not destroy, whatever good effect can be expected from occasional solitude.

7. To give them an interest in their work by allowing them a share in the produce.

8. To turn the prison into a school; thereby returning its inhabitants into the world instructed in the most useful branches of vulgar learning, as well as in some trade or occupation whereby they may afterwards earn their livelihood."

These are a few of the engagements into which he entered; but there were others. He bound himself to provide his prisoners with spiritual and medical assistance; to ensure them work on discharge by fitting up a subsidiary establishment, where they would labour on at the trades they learnt in prison; and to lay by for them (out of their earnings) "the foundation-stone of a provision for old age upon the plan of the annuity societies." To the Crown and to the public he was equally profuse in his promises. For every prisoner who might escape from his custody he agreed to be mulcted a certain

* Report of Select Committee on Police and Convict Establishments, 26 June, 1798. Appendix E.

penal sum; and to compel him to be careful of their health he
bound himself to forfeit a sum of money for every one who
died over and above a certain rate, " grounded on an average
of the number of Deaths, not among imprisoned Felons, but
among persons of the same ages in a state of Liberty within
the Bills of Mortality." * He was ready, moreover, to be
personally responsible for the reformatory efficacy of his
management, and even to make amends, in most instances, for
any accident of its failure, by paying a sum of money for
every prisoner convicted of a felony after his discharge, at a
rate increasing according to the number of years he had been
under his (Jeremy Bentham's) care. For one year the fine
was £10, and £5 for every additional year up to £30, which
was the outside limit; but the money was to be paid immediately on conviction, and to be applied to the indemnification of the sufferers by the felony.

Finally, by "neatness and cleanliness, and Diversity of
Employment, by Variety of Contrivance, and above all by that
Peculiarity of Construction, which, without any unpleasant or
hazardous vicinity, enables the whole Establishment to be
inspected at a view from a commodious and insulated Room in
the centre, the Prisoners remaining unconscious of being thus
observed, it should be his study to render it a spectacle such
as Persons of all Classes would, in the way of amusement, be
curious to partake of ; and that not only on Sundays at the
time of Divine Service, but on ordinary Days at Meal Times or
Times of Work; providing thereby a System of Superintendence, universal, unchangeable, and uninterrupted, the most
effectual and indestructible of all securities against abuse."
The outlines of the plan on which this model prison was
to be constructed were also indicated in Mr. Bentham's
memorandum:—"A circular building, an iron cage, glazed,
a glass lantern as large as Ranelagh, with the cells on
the outer circumference,"—such was his main idea.†

* This was eventually arranged by a bargain of the nature of an
insurance, by which the Government promised to pay £4000 per annum
for 1000 persons, on condition that he should pay £100 for every death
which should take place within the year above 40.

† Bentham claimed for his plan that it would be found applicable to

Within, in the very centre, an inspection station was so
fixed that every cell and every part of a cell could be at
all times closely observed; but, by means of blinds and
other contrivances, the inspectors were concealed, unless
they saw fit to show themselves, from the view of the
prisoners; by which "a sentiment of a sort of invisible
omnipresence" was to pervade the whole place.   There
was to be "solitude or limited seclusion *ad libitum;*" but
unless for punishment, limited seclusion in assorted companies was to be preferred.   As we have seen, Bentham
proposed to throw the place open as a sort of public lounge,
and to protect the prisoners from ill-treatment they were to be
enabled, by means of tubes reaching from each cell to the
general centre, to hold conversations with the visitors.   "The
superintendence thus bestowed," says Mr. Bentham in his
evidence before the committee on Peniten. ary Houses, in 1811,
"by a promiscuous assemblage of unknown, and therefore unpaid, ungarbled, and incorruptible inspectors, or in a word, by
the public at large—that is, by such individuals as curiosity
and the love of amusement (the most universally operative
springs of action that apply to such a case), mixed with any
better and rarer motives, may happen to attract—this is what,
from first to last, I have all along spoken of as being among
my principal dependencies, viz., for security against abuse and
imperfection in every shape; but the banquet offered to
curiosity will be attractive in proportion to the variety, and, if
such a term may be here endured, to the brilliancy of the
scene."   Mr. Bentham intended, I believe, to light up the
prison at night by reflection.

In theory Bentham's project may read well; but it is to be

---

all kinds of establishments, no matter how different or even opposite
the purpose.   "Whether it be that of punishing the incorrigible, guard-
ing the insane, reforming the vicious, confining the suspected, employing
the idle, maintaining the helpless, curing the sick, instructing the
willing in any branch of industry, or training the rising race in the path
of education ; in a word, whether it be applied to the purposes of perpetual prisons in the room of death, or prisons for confinement before
trial, or penitentiary houses. or houses of correction, or workhouses, or
manufactories, or madhouses, or hospitals, or schools."—Bentham's
Works, iv. p. 40.

feared that in execution it would have been found impracticable. It met with an enthusiastic reception, however, and
was warmly embraced by Mr. Pitt, and Lord Dundas, the
Home Secretary. Nevertheless, secret influences hindered its
adoption,* and it was not till 1794 that an Act was passed
containing a draft of the contract between Bentham and the
Treasury. A prison to contain a thousand convicts, together
with the necessary chapel, storehouses, warehouses, and quarters
for officials, was to be built according to the agreement for
£19,000. The whole edifice Bentham contracted to run up
within twelve months of the time that he was put in possession
of the ground. For each convict in his charge up to a thousand
he was to receive £12 per annum, over that £18; but in addition
to this he was to become invested with the right to retain
and apply to his own use the produce of, and profit upon, the
labour of all the prisoners. He himself, or his brother, Samuel
Bentham, who was a general in the Russian service, was to be
nominated governor; and touching this appointment Bentham
writes, "The station of gaoler is not in common account a very
elevated one; the addition of contractor has not much tendency
to raise it. He (Bentham) little dreamt when he first launched
into the subject, that he was to become a suitor, and perhaps
in vain, for such an office. But Inventions unpractised might
be in want of the Inventor, and a situation thus clipped of
emoluments while it was loaded with obligation might be in
want of candidates. Penetrated therefore with the importance
of the end, he would not suffer himself to see anything unpleasant or discreditable in the means." Mr. Bentham seems
to have hoped to make his new business one of considerable
profit. His brother, the general, had invented a plan of
executing by machinery, "without the aid of either dexterity
or goodwill, the most considerable branches of wood work,
besides many branches of stone work, and metal work," † and
the two Benthams were "on the look-out for a steam engine,"
when it seemed to Jeremy that convict labour would form an

* It has been said that personal hostility towards Bentham, because
he was such a Radical, led George III. to throw cold water upon the
project of the Panopticon.
† Exam. of J. Bentham, Parl. Rep. 1811. Appendix G.

admirable substitute. "Neither goodwill nor dexterity" could be counted upon "when dealing with the prisoners."

According to this Act above mentioned the sum of £2000 was advanced to Mr. Bentham, in order that he might make the necessary preparations. Four years later we find the project still hanging fire.* The preparations had been made; cast iron work, intended for the framework of the Panopticon, had been ordered to the amount of the whole £2000, and a great portion of it had been delivered; and Bentham was otherwise out of pocket to the extent of £9000. In the interval, too, the capital that was to have set the new invention "agoing" was "gone." "My brother's whole time," Bentham states, "is engrossed by his official situation,† and at my time of life, and after my experience, it is now too late for me to return to a manufacturing speculation into which no prospect of ordinary advantage would even then have tempted me." He clearly looked for indemnification, but was yet indisposed to relinquish his scheme. Before the same committee he gave evidence as to the site he proposed to purchase, that decided upon by the first supervisors at Battersea Rise having been for some reasons, not now apparent, abandoned. The new situation was a part of Tothill Fields, lying on both sides of the present Vauxhall-bridge Road, and amounting in all to fifty-three acres. The advantages of the site were chiefly its vicinity to the metropolis, and to water carriage—two points, it will be remembered, that were insisted upon by Howard, prompt communication with markets and ready inspection being considered indispensable. Eventually this land was purchased from Lord Salisbury for £12,000, and conveyed to Jeremy Bentham as feoffee for the Crown. But the undertaking still languished on from year to year. These were stirring times, when amidst the bitter strife of political parties, invasion threatened, and the "Corsican" kept all the world in dread.

Still, in 1810, active steps were taken to reopen the question, thanks to the vigour with which Sir Samuel Romilly called public attention to the want of penitentiaries. Nothing now would please the House of Commons but immediate

* Exam. of J. Bentham, Parl. Rep. 1811. Appendix G.
† As Commissioner for the Navy.

action; and this eagerness to begin is in strange contrast
with the previous long years of delay. But Mr. Ryder, the
Home Secretary, gained his point that a committee should first
inquire fully into the matter. George Holford, Esq., M.P., was
chairman of this committee, and among its number were
Mr. Ryder, Sir Samuel Romilly, Mr. Wilberforce, Sir Charles
Long, and Sir Evan Nepean. Their report, which was laid upon
the table in May, 1811, fully recognised the importance of
attempting reformation by the seclusion, employment, and
religious instruction of prisoners, but disapproved of the Panopticon scheme, inasmuch as it depended upon the personal character of one man, and the favourable opinion entertained of the
construction of the building proposed by him, rather than upon
the principles on which prisons had hitherto been conducted;
and they pointed out that under its provisions the management
of the convicts might in course of time pass out of the hands of
the original contractor, while there was no guarantee of similar
good qualities, or of similar capacity, in the superintendent who
might from time to time be appointed to succeed him. The
committee therefore was disposed to follow rather in design
the original proposals of Howard than the later plans and
suggestion of Bentham.

These proposals having been developed with considerable
success, but on a small scale, first at the Gloucester Penitentiary
House, established in 1791, and later in the House of Correction
at Southwell, the committee recommended the immediate
erection of a penitentiary for the counties of London and
Middlesex. A part of the business of this committee had
been the settlement of Mr. Bentham's outstanding claims,
arising from the non-performance of the contract to which I
have already referred. It now appeared that the £19,000, which
had been considered quite sufficient by Mr. Bentham for the
whole of his Panopticon, was really far short of the mark.
Bentham stated that he grounded his estimate on the assurances
of an architect since deceased, and he was not disposed now to
carry out his bargain. Still less was he prepared to be satisfied
with £12 per annum for any prisoners of whom he might take
charge. These alterations in his original scheme are interesting as showing to some extent its theoretical and unpractical

character. But it was not contemplated to reopen negotiations with Bentham, except in so far as he was entitled to remuneration for his trouble and original outlay. Eventually his claims were referred, by Act of Parliament, to arbitration, and so settled. The same Act empowered certain supervisors to be appointed hereafter, to become possessed of the lands in Tothill Fields, which Bentham had bought on behalf of the Government. These lands were duly transferred to Lord Farnborough, George Holford, Esq., M.P., and the Rev. Mr. Becher, and under their supervision Millbank Penitentiary as it now stands was commenced and finished.

THE SITE OF MILLBANK IN 1803.

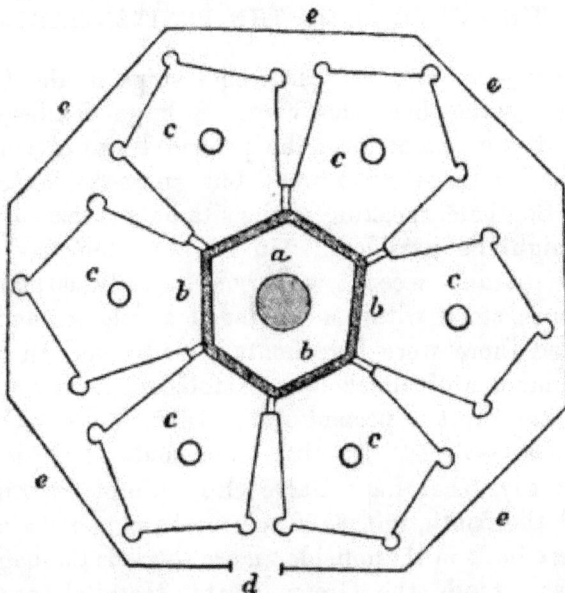

GROUND PLAN OF MILLBANK PENITENTIARY.

a Chapel.   b Hexagon.
c Pentagons.   d Entrance.
            e Boundary Wall.

CHAPTER II.

THE BUILDING OF THE PENITENTIARY.

THE lands which Bentham bought from Lord Salisbury were a portion of the wide area known then as Tothill Fields; speaking more exactly, they lay on either side of the present Vauxhall-bridge Road. This road, which was constructed after the purchase, intersected the property, dividing it into two lots of thirty-eight and fifteen acres respectively. It was on a slice of the larger piece that the prison was ultimately built, on ground lying close by the river. This neighbourhood, now known as an outskirt of Pimlico, was then a low marshy locality, with a soil that was treacherous and insecure, especially at the end towards Millbank Row. People were alive only a few years ago, who had shot snipe in the bogs and quagmires round about this spot. A large distillery, owned by a Mr. Hodge, stood near the proposed site of the prison; but otherwise these parts were but sparsely covered with houses. Bentham, speaking of the site he purchased, declared that it might be considered "in no neighbourhood at all." No house of any account, superior to a tradesman's or a public-house, stood within a quarter of a mile of the intended prison, and there were hereabouts already one other prison, and any number of almshouses, established at various dates. Of these the most important were Hill's, Butler's, Wicher's, and Palmer's—all left by charitable souls of these names; and Stow says, that Lady Dacre also, wife of Gregory, Lord Dacre of the south, left £100 a year to support almshouses which were built in these fields "more towards Cabbage Lane." Here, also, stands the Green Coats Hospital, erected by Charles I., but endowed by Charles II. for twenty-five boys and six girls with a schoolmaster to teach them. "Adjoining this hospital" (I am still quoting Stow) "is a bridewell, a place for the correction of such loose and idle livers as are taken up within the liberty of Westminister, and thither sent by the Justices of the Peace, for correction—which is whipping and beating of Hemp (a punishment very well suited for idlers), and are thence discharged by order of the Justices as they in their wisdom find occasion." Again, Stow remarks: "In Tothill Fields, which is a large spacious place, there are certain pest-houses; now made use of by twelve poor men and their wives, so long as it shall please God to keep us from the Plague. These Pest-houses are built near the Meads, and remote from people." Hospitals, bridewells, alms and pest-houses—these, the chief occupants of these lonely fields, formed no unfitting society for the new neighbour that was soon to be established amongst them.

As the prison, when completed, took its name from the Mill Bank, that margined the Thames close at hand, I must pause to refer to this embankment. I can find no record giving the date of the construction of this bank, which was no doubt intended to check the overflow of the river, and possibly, also, to act as one side of the mill-race, which served

the Abbot of Westminster's mill. This mill, which is in fact
the real sponsor of the locality, is marked on the plan of
Westminster from Nordon's survey, taken in Queen Elizabeth's
reign, in 1573. It stands on the bank of the Thames, almost
opposite the present corner of Abingdon and Great College
Streets; but it is not quite clear whether it was turned by
water from the river, brought along Millbank, or by the stream
that came from Tothill Street, which, taking the corner of the
present Rochester Row, flowed along the line of the present
Great College Street, and under Millbridge to the Queen's
slaughter-house. "The Millbank," says Stowe,* "is a very
long place, which beginneth by Lindsay House, or rather by
the Palace Yard, and runneth up to Peterborough House,.
which is the farthest house. The part from against College
Street unto the Horse Ferry hath a good row of buildings on
the east side, next to the Thames, which is mostly taken up
with large wood-mongers' yards, and Brew-houses; and here
is a water house which serveth this side of the town; the
North Side is but ordinary; except one or two houses by the
end of College Street; and that part beyond the Horse Ferry
hath a very good row of houses, much inhabited by the gentry,
by reason of the pleasant situation and prospect of the Thames.
The Earl of Peterborough's house hath a large courtyard
before it and a fine garden behind it, but its situation is but
bleak in the winter, and not over healthful, as being so near
the low meadows on the South and West Parts." But it was
on one edge of these low, well-wooded meadows that Millbank
Penitentiary was by-and-by to be built.

So much for the antiquities of the place. After careful
consideration of the various advantages and disadvantages of
the site, the new supervisors were content to abide by the choice
Bentham had made. It was something to have a place ready
to hand. The difficulty of making suitable selection had been
felt on previous occasions, and the supervisors were by no
means disposed to waste further time upon a new search.
Moreover, no opposition was to be feared from those who
resided near the spot. The dwellers round about were hardly
of a class to secure attention to their complaints, even if they

* Book vi. p. 66.

had been minded to resist the establishment of a prison in their midst—which they were not. Besides, it had been known for years that a prison was meant to occupy these lands; therefore those who had not objected already could hardly do so now after so great a lapse of time. The spot was deemed healthy, nothing to the contrary having then transpired; and in situation was convenient, lying as it did close to London and to the great highway of the Thames. Accordingly, upon the 12th of June, 1812, the three supervisors, having met at the State Paper Office, proceeded to business.

Their first act was to decide upon the plan for the new buildings. This had been thrown open to competition by public advertisement; and a reward was offered for the three best tenders. Forty-three were sent in, and the first prize was gained by Mr. William Williams, of No. 11, Tichborne Street, Golden Square. His design, however, was not considered perfect, and the supervisors reserved to themselves the right to make such changes as might appear desirable. The revised drawings, prepared by Mr. Williams, were subsequently submitted to Mr. Hardwicke, the appointed architect, a gentleman of reputation in his profession, who had already gained a prize for designing a female prison. This had happened at the time when the erection of penitentiaries under Geo. III., c. 19, had been in agitation. Mr. Hardwicke gained the prize for a female prison; that for a male prison was carried off by Mr. Blackburn, an architect of eminence, who had built or rebuilt half the county gaols in the kingdom. Mr. Hardwicke's remuneration was fixed at a commission of $2\frac{1}{2}$ per cent. on the value of all work done, or upon the estimated cost of the buildings. This estimate, according to a statement from Mr. Hardwicke,* amounted to £259,725, but a further sum of £42,690 was also required for the foundations. Accommodation was to be provided at this price for 600 prisoners, male and female, in equal proportions; and the whole building was intended solely for the confinement of offenders in the counties of London and Middlesex. It was at that time contemplated to erect a number of other similar prisons in various parts of the country, but the establishment of these " district " or, as

* Supervisors' Minute Book, 1812.

they were to be styled, "circuit" prisons, was ultimately abandoned on the score of expense. By subsequent decisions, arrived at after the work was first undertaken, the size of Millbank grew to greater proportions, till it was ultimately made capable of containing, as one great national penitentiary, "all such transportable convicts as were not sent abroad or confined in the hulks." Of course its cost increased *pari passu* with its size. By the time the prison was finally completed, the total expenditure had risen as high as £458,000. And over and above this enormous sum, the outlay of many additional thousands was needed within a few years, for the repairs or restoration of unsatisfactory work.

In order that future references and descriptions may be intelligible to the reader, and before proceeding to record the details of construction, it may be well to describe at once the appearance of the building when actually finished, and as it stands, in fact, at the present day.

"The Penitentiary," as it is still commonly called, looks on London maps like a six-pointed star-fort; built, say, against catapults and old-fashioned engines of war. The central point is the chapel, a circular building which, with the open space around it, covers rather more than half an acre of ground. A narrow building, three storeys high, and forming a hexagon, surrounds the chapel, with which it is connected at three points by covered passages. This chapel and its annular belt, the hexagon, forms the omphalos of the whole system. It is the centre of the circle, from which the several bastions of the star-fort radiate. Each of these salients is in shape a pentagon, and there are six of them, one opposite each side of the hexagon. They are built three storeys high, on four sides of the pentagon, having a small tower at each external angle; while on the fifth side a wall about nine feet high runs parallel to the adjacent hexagon. In these pentagons are the prisoners' cells, while the inner space in each, in area about two-thirds of an acre, contain the airing yards, grouped round a tall central watch-tower. The ends of the pentagons join the hexagons at certain points called junctions. The whole space covered by these buildings has been estimated at about seven acres; and something more than that amount is included between them and the boundary wall, which takes the shape of an octagon, and beyond which was a moat now filled up.

Such is a general outline of the plan of the prison. Any more elaborate description might prove as confusing as is the labyrinth within to those who enter without such clues to guide them as are afforded by familiarity and long practice. There was one old warder who served for years at Millbank, and rose through all the grades to a position of trust, who was yet unable, to the last, to find his way about the premises. He carried with him always a piece of chalk, with which he "blazed" his path as the American backwoodsman does the forest trees. Angles every twenty yards, winding staircases, dark passages, innumerable doors and gates—all these bewilder the stranger, and contrast strongly with the extreme simplicity of modern prison architecture. But indeed Millbank, with its intricacy and massiveness of structure, is suggestive of an order that has past. It is one of the last specimens of an age to which Newgate also belongs; a period when the safe custody of criminals could only be compassed, people thought, by granite blocks and ponderous bolts and bars. Such notions were really a legacy of mediævalism, bequeathed by the ruthless chieftains, who imprisoned offenders within their own castle walls. Many such keeps and castles still exist, and till very lately served as gaols or houses of correction for their immediate neighbourhood. They seem to us now-a-days clearly out of date; yet not a hundred years ago prison architects looked upon them as models of prison construction, and, not unnaturally, based all their designs on a similarly substantial style. In these matters modern experience has worked an entire revolution. Moral supervision has, to a certain extent, replaced mere physical restraint. It is found that prisoners can be more effectually guarded by warders of flesh and blood than by passive chains and huge senseless stones, provided only that there is above all the sleepless eye of a stringent systematic discipline.

But to return to the supervisors in the year 1812. I have said that the original estimate prepared by Mr. Hardwicke, the architect, amounted to £259,725. The following is a detail of the cost of each item :*

		£
Chapel in centre	...	9,671
Hexagon, three storeys high, with governor's, chaplain's, surgeon's, and other quarters	}	30,122
Six pentagons, with cells, work-rooms, towers, &c., at £28,422 each	}	170,532
Boundary wall, 17 ft. high from ground level and 10 ft. below	}	10,500
Lodge and gateway at entrance	...	4,500
Stoves for heating	...	8,400
Sewers and drains	...	5,000
Planking for foundations	...	5,000
Raising ground in all the courts... ...	...	6,000
Fitting up, and clerk of works	...	5,000
Unforeseen expenses	...	5,000
	Total	£259,725
Additional for the foundations ...	...	£42,690

The first part of the work set on foot was the boundary wall, which was commenced towards the end of 1812, the contractors being Messrs. Want & Richardson, who had already built the Military College at Sandhurst, and Covent Garden Theatre under Mr. Copeland. In the spring of 1813 contracts were entered into for the erection of the first pentagon, the foundations of which were in progress by June of that year. It was well known that the soil at Millbank was of such a nature as to render the establishment of a solid edifice thereon a matter of great difficulty and expense. The supervisors, fully alive to this, gave the matter their earliest and closest attention. The site was examined by them in January, 1812, when strong clay was discovered at no great distance from the surface. On the other hand, a Mr. Cook, temporary lessee of the ground, declared that Bentham had bored a distance of fourteen feet and found nothing but loose soil and peat, utterly unfit to support the proposed superincumbent weight of buildings, and that the ground had been condemned accordingly. Upon this the supervisors in May again examined for themselves, and had a deep hole dug, by which means they

* Supervisors' Minute Book.

came upon a bed of tenacious clay eight feet in thickness.
Mr. Cook then, to save his judgment, stated that the strata
were uncertain; in one place clay, in another peat or gravel;
and such, by new borings, was found to be the case. Planking
was now proposed as a "substruction;" but before finally
deciding, the supervisors visited Bethlehem Hospital ("Bedlam"),
just then in course of erection, in St. George's Fields, and
found that in uncertain spots the foundations were supported
on broad flags of Yorkshire stone.

About this time an architect of Blackheath, Mr. Alexander,
came forward and offered to contract for the foundations, on a
new and mysterious method of his own, which was to be
"independent of piles, planking, and brick piers or arches."
The supervisors declined to adopt a scheme which was veiled
in so much secrecy, notwithstanding Mr. Alexander's assurance
that his plan would not be "subject to any alteration by floods,
damp, heat, frost, or any failures by time; and that it should
be neither pervious to vermin (rats, etc.), nor liable to be
undermined by prisoners." Nevertheless, the supervisors were
honestly anxious to put this important preliminary on a
thoroughly satisfactory basis, and, having first experimented
for themselves with various materials, all heavily weighted
with from two to three hundred tons, they requested Mr.
Hardwicke to consult a number of eminent engineers and
architects.   These gentlemen — Messrs. Rennie, Lewis,
Cockerell, and Browne—having examined the site, reported
that by boring seven to twelve feet down below the existing
surface they had found the substrata to consist of alluvial
soil, made up of "vegetable earth, light clay, and more-log,"
after which came a sound bed of gravel. They were of opinion
therefore that the earth under the actual site of the proposed
buildings should be excavated down to this gravel, and that a
mass of puddled walling, of a breadth exceeding that of the
lines of buildings, should take the place of the excavated earth.
The puddled walling was to consist of "gravel or ballast only,
having perpendicular sides cast and mixed in lime-water, with
a small quantity of sand; and upon this foundation the prison
walls could be erected with security." No such precautions
were deemed necessary for the boundary wall; as the weight

was slight, a rubble foundation-wall of stone, rammed and two
feet deep, would be sufficient. The outer lodge and gateway
were to be built on a plan suggested by Mr. Hardwicke, partly
on an artificial rubble mound and partly on piles. All these
points are important, as will be seen later on.

Drainage and water supply were two questions that came
up early for decision. To provide the water, Mr. Braithwaite,
the engineer, was called in, who proposed two methods—either
to lay on Thames water through a six or seven-inch main,
storing it in a central reservoir to be filled every tide, or to
sink a deep well to a certain main-spring which he had discovered, and which was certain to furnish an ample supply of
the finest soft water. In both cases engines would be required
to raise the water to the level of the cisterns at the top of the
proposed buildings. The latter of these methods was adopted
in the first instance, but it was afterwards found necessary to
have recourse instead to the Thames, because Mr. Braithwaite
on analysis found the spring water impure. For the purposes
of drainage permission was given for the commissioners of
sewers for the city of Westminster to do away with all open
ditches, and substitute a main drain from the proposed site
through the embankment and into the river. Apprehension
was entertained lest the lowlands should be flooded when the
embankment was cut through, and a proviso in the agreement
ruled that no opening should be made till the ground area of
the new works had actually been raised.

It very soon became apparent that the ground on which
they were to build was too treacherous to be much depended
upon. The part of the boundary wall nearest the Thames,
which was now six feet high, sank, and was thrown out of the
upright. It had been built on a very thin substratum of clay,
and, like the rest of the wall, had very insufficient foundations.
This part had therefore to be taken down and rebuilt, care
being taken to dig first as far down as the gravel and fill up
with puddled walling,—gravel or ballast mixed with lime. All
the other portions of the boundary wall had to be similarly
treated. The lodge also, which was to be executed by Messrs.
Joliffe & Banks, as contractors, soon gave great trouble. The soil
being here extremely soft and boggy, the builders had pro-

ceeded by driving piles. On these the walls were raised a
height of five feet all round, the boundary wall being built at
the same time and regularly tied into each course at either end
of the lodge. Just at this time, however, the other portions of
the work were drained of water by a steam pump, and the
peat thus deprived of water, all the surface of the marsh sank
some nine inches. The masonry between the piles intended to
carry the lodge walls sank also, and the building rested only
on the bare piles. These might have sufficed to support the
lodge, but the boundary wall which was tied in it also sank,
as we have seen, and the lodge was bound to go too. This
was the contractors' story; but on examination it was found
that the piles had not been driven deep enough, and others of
greater length and more numerous were substituted. Notwithstanding the pains thus taken, the lodge continued for
years after it was built to be in an unsatisfactory state, and it
had eventually to be in part taken down, when all the piles and
planking were found to be entirely decayed.

Towards the end of 1813 Mr. Hardwicke resigned his
appointment, giving as his ostensible reason that the
management of this extensive concern took up more time
than he could spare from his regular business; but it was
really because he was dissatisfied with the remuneration
originally agreed upon, which was at the rate of 2½ per cent.
on all sums that passed through his hands. Mr. Hardwicke
wanted 5 per cent., as did another eminent architect to whom
the supervisors applied as soon as the place became vacant.
Eventually a Mr. Harvey fell in with the terms proposed: "a
person of less note in his profession, but who had been employed
in some works on unsound ground, and was supposed to possess
more experience on that subject that many architects of greater
general knowledge." * Mr. Harvey's first proposition was to
give greater security to the foundations by laying strong flat
stones under all walls; but later, three courses of brickwork,
laid in Parker's cement, were used for this purpose,
because stone was not easily procured. It was now the spring
of 1814; a full year had elapsed since the commencement
of the work, and already, although no part of the prison

* Holford's General Penitentiary, p. 29.

house was as yet begun, and the lodge and boundary walls were
still unfinished, £26,000 had been disbursed in one way or
another.

While fully crediting the supervisors with every desire
to do justice to the work in hand, it is impossible to read
their minutes without observing that they proceeded in
a liberal open-handed fashion, as gentlemen do who are
dealing with money supplied from a liberal purse. They
were evidently anxious to do their job well; and the
stout substantial building they erected is the best testimony,
as it stands to this day, to the pains they took. But
the article was dear; and long before it reached completion the tax-payers grumbled not a little at its cost. In
the earlier years, however, the Treasury issued money with a
readiness that accords little with modern notions of economy.
In May, 1814, replying to Mr. Lushington, the supervisors
announced that they had spent £30,000, and would want
£45,000 more before the next session of Parliament; expressing
a hope, however, that by the following spring the works would
be sufficiently advanced to admit of the confinement of one
hundred convicts in the prison. In the following November
they notified that an additional £60,000 would be required
during the ensuing years, when the total expenditure would
include the building of the lodge, boundary wall, and
two pentagons, with their corresponding parts of the hexagon.
It is but just to state that the details of disbursements show
that there was no great increase in the actual cost of building
the lodge and outer walls over the original estimate. All the
money went in the pentagons, which must have cost quite
£50,000 apiece. However, in March, 1816, when the first was
completed and nearly ready for occupation, the supervisors
found they would have more room than was anticipated, and
that with but little variation in the plans, the buildings when
completed could be made to contain eight hundred prisoners.
A fresh Act of Parliament was issued giving the necessary
authority, but already it would appear as if the House
of Commons was turning restive about the expenditure
on Millbank. More than two years had elapsed since the
commencement of the work, and so far the only apparent

results were continual demands for money. Accordingly, we find that in May the House ordered that an account of all sums already spent, and of all that would hereafter be required, should be laid upon the table. By this statement it appears that £128,304 had been already spent, and that a further sum of £228,813 would still be required.*

This total of £350,117 is indeed considerably in excess of the original estimate made by Mr. Hardwicke, which amounted to £259,420. But when people take to building the bill runs up often beyond all previous calculation. The supervisors were now paying the penalty for dabbling in bricks and mortar. No one who has waded through their lengthy minutes and the voluminous correspondence which record the history of their proceedings, can under-estimate their devotion or doubt their integrity. But their work, so to speak, ran away with them. It was as impossible to foresee all requirements as it was to forbid indispensable outlay. Bramah locks, patent foundations, iron bedsteads for the prisoners, heating apparatus and water closets on the newest and most approved patterns—all these were in turns experimented upon, and generally, if found suitable, ordered regardless of expense. Moreover other works beyond the prison walls fell upon the supervisors. For instance, they had to contribute to the embankment, and to the road that was to lead to the New Vauxhall Bridge from the end of Millbank Row. In this way the expenditure grew like a snowball, and, as we shall see, even this increased sum of £350,000 by no means sufficed to complete the whole affair.

On the 9th February, 1816, however, the supervisors reported† to Lord Sidmouth, the Home Secretary, that the Penitentiary was now partly ready for the reception of offenders, and begged that a committee might be appointed to take charge of the prison, under the provisions of the 52 Geo. III., cap. 44. By this Act the King in Council was empowered to appoint "any fit and discreet persons, not being less than ten or more than twenty, as and for a Committee to Superintend the Penitentiary House for the term of one

* House of Commons' Journals, 23rd May, 1816.
† Minute Book, 9th Feb., 1816.

D

year, then next ensuing, and until a fresh nomination or appointment shall take place." Accordingly, at the Court at Brighton, on the 21st Feb., 1816, His Royal Highness the Prince Regent in Council nominated the Right Hon. Charles Abbot, Speaker of the House of Commons, and nineteen others to serve on this committee, and it met for the first time at the prison on the 12th March following. The proceedings of the Committee of Management from the first meeting I reserve for another chapter, it being enough to record here the fact of its appointment. The Right Hon. Charles Long, George Holford, Esq., and the Rev. J. J. Becher, were among the members of the new committee, but they continued their functions as supervisors distinct from the other body, until the final completion of the whole building in 1821.

On the 27th June, 1816, the first batch of convicts—thirty-six females from Newgate—arrived. Others followed, and it seemed probable that by the end of the year the two first pentagons would both be fully occupied. In September, however, alarming symptoms of failure and settlement appeared in the building. Serious cracks and fissures opened in the walls of Pentagon No. 1, and the safety of the whole edifice was for a moment in question. This occurrence is thus recorded in the Governor's Journal :—

"September 21, 1816.—Arose at six o'clock in the morning in consequence of being informed that the passage gates of Pentagon No. 1, next the angle towers, were all fast and incapable of being unlocked by the turnkeys. Went there and found it was so, and that it was occasioned by all the three angle towers having sunk a little lower, which had cracked the arches and wall in several places. Gave immediate notice to the clerk of works, who came and inspected the places, and sent for Mr. Harvey the architect.

"Went again into the pentagon and found all the prisoners of Mrs. Todd's division under considerable fear and alarm, and that Ann Turner had just recovered from a fit, which I understood she is subject to. Talked to the prisoners and assured them there was no danger, and succeeded in pacifying them and quieting all further apprehension."

As soon as Mr. Harvey made his appearance he gave it as

his opinion that the fractures were caused by the admission of the tide from the Thames, which had been let in a day or two previous to cleanse the prison drains. This was checked, and the effect closely watched. In the three following weeks there was no perceptible increase in the cracks; but for a time the reception of new prisoners was stopped, and advice sought of two eminent engineers and architects, Messrs. Rennie and Smirke. It is not now apparent whether these failures in the pentagons came on suddenly and without warning; but there must have been every reason for apprehension from the first, for the shifty, uncertain character of the site had been proved by the necessity for taking down and rebuilding both lodge and boundary walls; and even as early as February, 1815, when the pentagon walls were as yet only a few feet high, cracks had appeared which could only be remedied by iron ties stretching quite across the building. The result of Messrs. Rennie and Smirke's examination of the site was to condemn the main sewer and the artificial foundations; the former had been negligently built, and the latter were too meagre to guarantee security. When the tide rose a large body of water made its way through imperfections in the sewer walls in among the loose strata below the buildings, and affected of course the superstructure. Besides this, the artificial foundation walls had been built so narrow—unwise economy in this one instance getting thus the better of safety—that they afforded no sufficient support for the weight of building above. It appeared to be immediately necessary to take down three of the pentagon towers, and to set on foot works to secure the other foundations, both in the pentagons erected and those to come, by considerably increasing the brickwork footings to the main walls, and more effectually digging over and puddling the ground excavated to receive them. Taking into consideration, too, the importance of all these works, the supervisors resolved to appoint Mr. Robert Smirke to carry them into effect.

From this time forth the works progressed steadily. During 1817 the second pentagon was occupied by prisoners notwithstanding the settlement of its walls. In 1818 no further accommodation was rendered available, but a further statement of the expenditure incurred was in that year presented to the House of Commons. It now appeared that the total outlay had increased to £221,788; that a further sum of £64,000 would be required to complete the third and fourth pentagons, £4,500 to rebuild the shaky towers, and an additional £90,000 for the remaining two pentagons and other contingencies. The grand total for all executed and projected works was now represented at £380,288, a rise of £30,000 over the second estimate of 1816, and of £130,000 over the first of 1812. But it was now estimated by Mr. Smirke that the buildings when completed could hold 1000 prisoners instead of 800. Next year the two new pentagons, the third and fourth, were finished and filled, so that the total prison population amounted in December, 1819, to 325. At the end of 1820 the numbers rose to 551, though no fresh pentagon was opened; but in 1821 the fifth and sixth were finished, and the prison was practically completed. But other works lingered on for some time later. There were plumbers, painters, glaziers, paviors, locksmiths, and coppersmiths, busy inside till the middle of the following year; the kitchen ranges had to be fixed, iron flues also, steam pipes, hot air stoves, and so forth. But on the 24th July, 1822, the supervisors closed their accounts, and the bill for the whole outlay was sent in to the Treasury. It amounted to £450,310, a further increase of £70,000 on the last estimate of 1819. It is to be regretted that the official records contain no allotment of the grand total to the various portions of the building. It would be interesting to observe how far the cost of each pentagon exceeded the estimate for it, but as all the bills and accounts are lumped together in the supervisors' minute book, it is impossible to separate the items. Undoubtedly the undertaking grew with its years, till at last the total cost seemed quite disproportioned to its first promise or intention.

But Millbank Penitentiary was the first building of its kind, and those who erected it had to contend with many serious difficulties. Not the least of these was the insecure character of the site. As we have seen, from first to last the foundations were a source of constant anxiety and exacted the closest attention. They were continually being doctored, and to an extent sufficient to justify the familiar saying, "that there is more stuff below than above ground at Millbank." But indeed every part of the prison, visible or invisible, is a mine of building wealth. Hidden amongst its hundreds of cells, its length of corridor and passage, beneath its acres of roof, are, without exaggeration, miles of lead piping, hundreds of tons of iron, immense iron girders, gates in dozens,—some of wrought iron, some of cast,—flagstones without end, shiploads of timber, millions of bricks. If ever the old place comes to be pulled down, the curious inquirer may perhaps understand why it was that it cost half a million of money. But it will be less easy to explain why such an enormous outlay was rendered necessary in the face of the fact that the new buildings which have in a measure replaced it have cost hardly a fifth of that sum.

CHAPTER III.

THE Penitentiary Committee was appointed on the 12th February, 1816, by the Prince Regent in Council, but the first instalment of prisoners did not arrive till the 27th of July following. In the interval, however, there was plenty of work to be done. The preparation of rules and regulations, the appointment of a governor, chaplain, matron, and other officials, were among the first of them; and the committee took up each subject with characteristic vigour. It was necessary also to decide upon some scale of salaries and emoluments; * to arrange with the Treasury as to the receipts, custody, and payments of the public moneys; and to ascertain the "sorts of manufactures best suited to the establishment, and the best method of obtaining work for the convicts, without having to purchase the materials." †

On the 10th of March, Mr. John Shearman was appointed governor. This gentleman was strongly recommended by Lord Sidmouth, who stated in a letter to the Speaker that, having been induced to make particular inquiries respecting his qualifications and character, he had found them "well calculated for the office in question." Mr. Shearman's own account of himself was, that he was a native of Yorkshire, but chiefly resident in London; that he was aged forty-four, was married, had eight children, and that he had been brought up to the profession of a solicitor, but for the last four years had been second clerk in the Hatton Garden police office. Before

* See Appendix A.   † Minute Book of Committee, p. 14.

actually entering upon his duties, the committee sent Mr.
Shearman on a tour of inspection through the provinces, to
visit various gaols, and report on their condition and management. In this way he inspected the prisons at Dorchester,
Gloucester, Shrewsbury, Chester, Manchester, Liverpool,
Lancaster, Southwell, and Lincoln, and the result of his
inquiries appeared to be :—

> "1. That the system of Individual Separation was not carried into
>   effect except at the Gloucester Penitentiary.
> 2. That the habit of Industry tended much to the reformation of
>   offenders.
> 3. That the labour of prisoners, though to a certain extent profitable,
>   was not sufficient to defray the cost of their victualling.
> 4. That Solitary Confinement and the deprivation of food were
>   found to be the usual and best punishment for prison offences.
> 5. That prisoners ought not to be permitted to associate, or to be
>   brought together in large numbers, without being ironed or
>   effectually secured.
> 6. That the agency of Females as to the government of Female
>   Prisoners had not yet been tried."

Mr. Shearman eventually resigned his appointment, because he thought the pay insufficient, and because the committee found fault with his frequent absences from the prison.
He seems to have endeavoured to carry on a portion of his old
business outside, as solicitor, concurrently with his governorship. His journals show him to have been an anxious, painstaking man, but neither by constitution nor training was he
exactly fitted for the position he was called upon to fill as head
of the Penitentiary.

At the same time, on the recommendation of the Bishop of
London, the Rev. Samuel Bennett was appointed chaplain.
Touching this appointment the bishop wrote, "I have found a
clergyman of very high character for great activity and
beneficence, and said to be untainted with fanaticism. . . .
His answer is not yet arrived; but I think he will not
refuse, as he finds the income of his curacy inadequate to the
maintenance of a family, and is precluded from residence on
a small property by want of a house and the unhealthiness of
the situation."

Mr. Pratt was made house-surgeon, and a Mr. Webbe, son to a medical man, and bred himself to that profession, was appointed master manufacturer; being of a "mechanical turn of mind, he had made several articles of workmanship, and he produced to the committee specimens of his shoemaking, paper screens, etc."

There was more difficulty in finding a matron. "The committee," writes Mr. Morton Pitt, "was fully impressed with the importance of the charge, and of the difficulty of finding a fit person to fill this most essential office." Many persons were of opinion that it would be "impracticable to procure any person of credit or character to undertake the duties of a situation so arduous and so unpleasant," and the fact that no one had applied for it was "strong proof of the prevalence of such opinions." Mr. Pitt goes on: "The situation is a new one. I never knew but two instances of a matron in a prison, and those were the wives of turnkeys or porters. In the present case it is necessary that a person should be selected of respectability as to situation in life. How difficult must it be to find a female educated as and having the feelings of a gentlewoman, who would undertake a duty so revolting to every feeling she has hitherto possessed, and even so alarming to a person of that sex."

Mr. Pitt had, however, his eye on a person to suit. "Mrs. Chambers appears to me to possess the requisites we want; and I can speak of her from a continued knowledge of her for almost thirty years, since she was about fifteen. Her father was in the law, and clerk of the peace for the county of Dorset from 1750 to 1790. He died insolvent, and she was compelled to support herself by her own industry, for her husband behaved very ill to her, abandoned her, and then died. She has learned how to obey, and since that, having kept a numerous school, how to command. She is a woman, forty-three years of age, of a strong sense of religion and the most strict integrity. She has much firmness of character with a compassionate heart, and I am firmly persuaded will most conscientiously perform every duty she undertakes to the utmost of her power and ability." * Accordingly, Mrs. Chambers was duly appointed.

* Letter to Com., Min. B. i. 27.

The same care was exhibited in all the selections for the minor posts of steward, turnkeys male and female, messengers, nurses, porters, and patrols; and most precise rules* and regulations were drawn up for the governance of everybody and everything connected with the establishment. All these had, in the first instance, to be submitted for the approval of the Judges of the Court of King's Bench, and were subsequently reported to the King in Council and both Houses of Parliament.

The supreme authority in the Penitentiary was vested in the superintending committee, who were required to make all contracts, examine accounts, pay bills, and make regular inspection of prison and prisoners. A special meeting of the committee was to be convened in the second week of each session of Parliament, in order to prepare the annual report. Under them the governor attended to the details of administration. He was to have the "same powers as are incident to a sheriff or gaoler—to see every prisoner on his or her admittance; to handcuff or otherwise punish the turbulent; to attend chapel; and finally, to have no other employment, other than such as belong to the duties of his office." The chaplain was to be in priest's orders, and approved by the bishop of the diocese, and to have no other profession, avocation, or duty whatsoever. Besides his regular Sunday and week-day services, he was to "endeavour by all means in his power to obtain an intimate knowledge of the particular disposition and character of every prisoner, male and female; direct them to be assembled for the purposes of religious instruction in such manner as may be most conducive to their reformation." He was expected also to "allot a considerable portion of his time, after the hours of labour, to visit, admonishing and instructing the prisoners," and to keep a " Character-Book," containing a " full and distinct account from time to time of all particulars relating to the character, disposition, and progressive improvement of every prisoner." Intolerance was not encouraged, for even then the visitation of ministers other than those of the Established Church was permitted on special application by the prisoners. Such ministers were only required to give

* Printed by Luke Hansard & Sons, near Lincoln's Inn Fields, 20th July, 1816.

in their names and descriptions, and "were admitted at such hours and in such manner as the Governor shall think reasonable, confining their ministrations to the persons requiring their attendance." * No remuneration was, however, to be granted to these additional clergymen. The duties prescribed for the house-surgeon were of the ordinary character, but in cases of difficulty he was to confer with the consulting physician and other non-resident medical men. The master manufacturer was to act as the governor's deputy if called upon, and was charged more especially with the control and manufacture of all materials and stores. It was his duty to make the necessary appraisement of the value of work done, and to enter the weekly "per-centage." The total profit was thus divided: three-fourths to the establishment, or 15s. in the pound; one twenty-fourth to the master manufacturer, the task-master of the pentagon, and the turnkey of the ward; leaving the balance of one-eighth, or 2s. 6d. in the pound, to be credited to the prisoner.

For the rest of the officers the rules were what might be expected. The steward took charge of the victualling, clothing, etc., and superintended the cooking, baking, and all branches of the domestic economy of the establishment; the task-masters overlooked the turnkeys, and were responsible for all matters connected with the labour and earnings of the prisoners; and the turnkeys, male and female, each having charge of a certain number of prisoners, were to observe their conduct, extraordinary diligence, or good behaviour. The turnkey was expected to "enforce his orders with firmness, but shall be expected to act with the utmost humanity to all prisoners under his care. On the other hand, he shall not be familiar with any of the prisoners, or converse with them unnecessarily, but shall treat them as persons under his authority and control, and not as his companions or associates." The prisoners themselves were to be treated in accordance with the aims and principles of the establishment. On first arrival they were carefully examined by the doctor, cleansed, deprived of all money, and their old clothes burned or sold. Next, entering the first or probation class, they remained therein

* Minute Book, p. 586.

for half the whole period of their imprisonment. Their time in prison was thus parcelled out : at daybreak or 5.30, according to the time of the year, they rose; cell doors opened, they were taken to wash, for which purpose "soap and round towels were provided;" after that to the working cells till 9 a.m., when they got their breakfast—one pint of hot gruel. At half-past nine to work again till half-past twelve; then dinner—for four days of the week six ounces of coarse beef, the other three a quantity of thick soup, and always daily a pound of bread made of the whole meal. For dinner and exercise an hour was allowed, after which again to work, leaving off in summer at six, and in winter at sunset. They were then again locked up in their cells, having first, when the evenings were light, an hour's exercise, and last of all supper—another pint of gruel, hot.

The turnkeys were to be assisted by wardsmen and wardswomen, selected from the more decent and orderly prisoners. These attended chiefly to the cleanliness of the prison, and were granted a special pecuniary allowance. "Second Class" prisoners were appointed also, to act as trade instructors. Any prisoners might work extra hours on obtaining special permission. The general demeanour of the whole body of inmates was regulated by the following rule: "No prisoner shall disobey the orders of the governor or any other officer, or shall treat any of the officers or servants of the prison with disrespect; or shall be idle or negligent in his work, or shall wilfully mismanage the same; or absent himself without leave from Divine Service, or behave irreverently thereat; or shall be guilty of cursing or swearing, or of any indecent expression or conduct, or of any assault, quarrel, or abusive words; or shall game with, defraud, or claim garnish, or any other gratuity from a fellow-prisoner; or shall cause any disturbance or annoyance by making a loud noise, or otherwise; or shall endeavour to converse or hold intercourse with prisoners of another division; or shall disfigure the walls by writing on them, or otherwise; or shall deface, secrete, or destroy, or pull down the printed abstracts of rules; or shall wilfully injure any bedding or other article provided for the use of prisoners." Offences such as the foregoing were to be met by punishment,

at the discretion of the governor, either by being confined in
a dark cell, or by being fed on bread and water only, or by
both such punishments; more serious crimes being referred to
the committee, who had power to inflict one month's bread
and water diet and in a dark cell. Any extraordinary diligence
or merit, on the other hand, was to be brought to the notice of
the Secretary of State, in order that the prisoner might be
recommended as an object for the Royal mercy. When finally
discharged, the prisoners were to receive decent clothing, and
a sum of money at the discretion of the committee, in addition
to their accumulated per-centage, or tools, provided such
money or such tools did not exceed a value of £3. Moreover, if any discharged prisoner, at the end of twelve months,
could prove on the testimony of a substantial householder,
or other respectable person, that he was earning an honest
livelihood he was to be entitled to a further gratuity not
exceeding £3.

The early discipline of the prisoners in Millbank, as designed by the committee, was based on the principle of constant
inspection and regular employment. Solitary imprisonment
was not insisted upon, close confinement in a punishment cell
being reserved for misconduct. All prisoners on arrival were
located at the lodge, and kept apart, without work, for the
first five days; the object in view being to "awaken them to
reflection, and a due sense of their situation." During this
time the governor visited each prisoner in the cell for the
purpose of becoming acquainted with his character, and ex-
plaining to him the spirit in which the establishment had been
erected. No pains were spared in this respect. The governor's
character-books, which I have examined, are full of the most
minute, I might add trivial, details. After the usual preliminaries of bathing, hair-cutting, and so forth, the prisoners
passed on to one of the pentagons and entered the first class,
remaining therein for half their total sentences. The only
difference between first and second class was, that the former
worked alone, each in his own cell; the latter in company, in
the work rooms. The question of finding suitable employment
soon engaged the attention of the committee. At first the
males tried tailoring, the females needlework. Great efforts

were made to introduce various trades. Many species of industry were attempted, skilled prisoners teaching the unskilled.
Thus, at first, one man who could make glass beads worked at
his own trade, and had a class under him; another, a tinman,
turned out tin-ware, in which he was assisted by his brother, a
"free man" and a more experienced workman; and several
cells were filled with prisoners who manufactured rugs under
the guidance of a skilful prison artizan. But Mr. Holford,
one of the committee, in a paper laid before his colleagues, in
1822, was forced to confess that all these undertakings had
failed. The glass-bead blower misconducted himself; the
"free" tinman abused the confidence of the committee, probably by "trafficking," and the rug-maker was soon pardoned
and set at large. By 1822 almost all manufactures, including
flax-breaking, had been abandoned, and the prisoners' operations were confined to shoemaking, tailoring, and weaving.
Mr. Holford, in the same pamphlet, objects to the first of these
trades, complaining that shoemakers' knives were weapons too
dangerous to be trusted in the hands of prisoners. Tailoring
was hard to accomplish, from the scarcity of good cutters, and
weaving alone remained as a suitable prison employment. In
fact, thus early in the century, the committee were brought
face to face with a difficulty that even now, after years of
experience, is pressing still for solution.

I have now described at some length the system pursued
at the Penitentiary. Beyond doubt—and of this there is
abundant proof in the prison records—the committee sought
strenuously to give effect to the principles on which the establishment was founded. Nevertheless their proceedings were
more or less tentative, for as yet little was known of so-called
"systems" of prison discipline, and those who had taken
Millbank under their charge were compelled to feel their way
slowly and with caution, as men still in the dark. The Penitentiary was essentially an experiment—a sort of crucible into
which the criminal elements were thrown, in the hopes that they
might be changed or resolved by treatment into other superior
forms. The members of the committee were always in earnest,
and they spared themselves no pains. If they had a fault,
it was in over-tenderness towards the felons committed

to their charge. Millbank was a huge plaything; a toy for a parcel of philanthropic gentlemen, to keep them busy during their spare hours. It was easy to see that they loved to run in and out of the place, and to show it off to their friends; * thus we find the visitor, Sir Archibald Macdonald, bringing a party of ladies to visit the pentagon, when " the prisoners read and went through their religious exercises," which edifying spectacle "gave great satisfaction to the persons present."† Again, at Christmas time the prisoners were regaled with roast beef and plum pudding, after which they returned thanks to the Rev. Archdeacon Potts, the visitor (who was present, with a select circle of ladies and gentlemen), "appearing very grateful, and sang 'God save the King.'"‡ With such sentiments uppermost in the minds of the superintending committee, it is not strange that the gaoler and other officials should be equally kind and considerate. No punishment of a serious nature was ever inflicted without a report to the visitor, or his presence on the spot. The whole of the female prisoners, who were first received, were found to be liable to fits, and the tendency gave Mr. Shearman great concern, till it was found that by threatening to shave and blister the heads of all persons so afflicted immediate cure followed. Two Jewesses, having religious scruples, refused to eat the meat supplied, whereupon the husband of one of them was permitted to bring in for their use " coarse meat and fish, according to the custom of the Jews;" and later we find the same man

* The following list of visitors who came to Millbank sight-seeing within a month or two of its opening, will give some idea of the public interest taken in the place. I have selected these from others in the governor's Journal:

The Grand Duke Nicholas of Russia; H.R.H. the Duke and the Duchess of York; Lady Louisa Connolly; the Saxon minister; Dr. Jenner and the Archbishop of York; the Earl of Fitzwilliam and Lord Clive; Sultan Hatimgary Krimgary; the Bishop of Bangor; Lord Gambier, Lord Prudhoe, the Dean of Westminster, and Lord Templetown; Mr. Shaw Lefevre, Miss Vansittart, and about eighteen other ladies; the Duke of Bedford and the Marquis of Tavistock; H.R.H. the Duke and Duchess of Kent, the Grand Duke Michael, Colonel D'Oyley, Lady Teignmouth, the Hon. Captain Waldegrave, etc., etc.

† Governor's Journal, i. p. 122.　　　　‡ Ibid. p. 116.

came regularly to read the Jewish prayers, "as he stated, out of the Hebrew book." Many of the women refused positively to have their hair cut short, and for a time were humoured. In February, 1817, all the female prisoners were assembled, and went through a public examination, before the Bishops of London and Salisbury, to show their progress in religious instruction, and "acquitted themselves greatly to the satisfaction of all present."

Judith Lacy, having been accused of stealing tea from a matron's canister, which had been put down, imprudently, too near the prisoner, was "so hurt at the charge, that it threw her into fits." She soon recovered, and it was quite evident she had stolen the tea. Any complaint of food was listened to with immediate attention. Thus the gruel did not give satisfaction and was repeatedly examined.

"A large number of the female prisoners still refuse to eat their barley soup," says the governor in his Journal* on the 23rd April, 1817, "several female prisoners demanding an increase of half a pound of bread," being refractory. Next day some of them refused to begin work, saying they were half-starved.

Mary Turner was the first prisoner released. She was supposed to be cured. Having equipped her in her liberty clothing, "she was taken into the several airing grounds in which were her late fellow-prisoners. The visitor (Sir Archibald Macdonald) represented to them in a most impressive manner the benefits that would result to themselves by good behaviour. The whole were most sensibly affected, and I think the event will have a very powerful effect on the conduct of many and prove an incentive to observe good and orderly demeanour."†

Next day the whole of the female prisoners were at their cell windows, and shouted vociferously as Mary Turner went off. This is but one specimen of the free and easy system of management. Of the same character was a petition presented by a number of the female prisoners, to restore to favour two other convicts who had been punished by the committee. Indeed, the whole place appears to have been like a big school,

* Page 198.　　　　† Governor's Journal, Sept. 2, 1817.

and a degree of license was allowed to the prisoners consorting little with their character of convicted criminals.

This mistaken lenity could end but in one way. Early in the spring the whole of the inmates broke out in open mutiny. Their alleged grievance was the issue of an inferior kind of bread. Change of dietary scales in prisons is always attended with some risk of disturbance, even when discipline is most rigorously maintained. In those early days of mild government riot was of course inevitable. The committee having thought fit to alter the character of the flour supplied, soon afterwards, at breakfast-time, all the prisoners, male and female, refused to receive their bread. The women complained of its coarseness; and all alike, in spite of the exhortations of the visitor, Mr. Holford, left it outside their cell doors. Next day, Sunday, the bread was at first taken, then thrown out into the passages. The governor determined to have Divine Service as usual, but to provide against what might happen, deposited within his pew "three brace of pistols loaded with ball."* To make matters worse, the Chancellor of the Exchequer arrived with a party of friends to attend the service. The governor immediately pointed out that he was apprehensive that "in consequence of the newly adopted bread the prisoners' conduct would not be orderly, as it had ordinarily been." At first the male prisoners were satisfied by raising and letting fall the flaps of the kneeling benches with a loud report, and throwing loaves about in the body of the chapel, while the women in an audible tone cried out, "Give us our daily bread." Soon after the commencement of the communion service, the women seated in the gallery became more loudly clamorous, calling out most vociferously, "Better bread, better bread!" The men below, in the body of the church, now rose and stood upon the benches; but again seated themselves on a gesture from the governor, who then addressed them, begging them to keep quiet. Among the females the confusion and tumult was continued, and was increased by the screams of alarm from the more peaceable. Many fainted, and others in great terror entreated to be taken away. "These were suffered to go out

* Journal, April 19, 1818.

in small bodies, in charge of the officers, and so we continued to remove them, till the whole of the females were withdrawn. About six of them, as they came to the place where they could see the males, made a halt and most boisterously assailed the men, calling them cowards, and other opprobrious names." After the women had gone the service proceeded without further interruption, after which the Chancellor of the Exchequer (who was present throughout) addressed the males, giving them a most appropriate admonition, but praising their orderly demeanour, which he promised to report to the Secretary of State. Afternoon service was performed without the female congregation, and was uninterrupted except by a few hisses from the boys.

Next morning the governor informed the whole of the prisoners, one by one, that the new brown bread would have to be continued until the meeting of the committee; whereupon many resisted when their cell doors were being shut, and others hammered loudly on the woodwork with their three-legged stools; and this was accompanied by the most hideous shouts and yells. In one of the divisions, four prisoners, who were in the same cell, were especially refractory, "entirely demolishing the inner door, every article of furniture, the two windows and their iron frames; and, having knocked off large fragments from the stone of the doorway, threw the pieces at, and smashed to atoms the passage windows opposite." One of them, Greenslade, assaulted the governor, on entering the cell, with part of the door frame; but "I parried the blow, and drove the prisoner's head against the wall; and I was also compelled, in my defence, to knock down Michael Sheen."* Such havoc and destruction were accomplished by the prisoners, that the governor repaired to the Home Secretary's for assistance. By him directed to Bow Street, he brought back a number of runners, and posted them in various parts of the building, during which a huge stone was hurled at his head by a prisoner named Jarman, but without evil consequences. A fresh din broke out on the ringing of the bell on the following morning, and neither governor nor chaplain could permanently allay the tumult; the governor

* Governor's Journal, April 20, 1818.

determined thereupon to handcuff all the turbulent males
immediately. "The effect was instantaneous. Although there
were still mumblings and grumblings, I felt that the storm
would soon be over. . . . In the course of the day I had
placed all the refractory in irons, and all was quiet in the male
pentagon." But many still muttered, and all was yet far from
over. There was little doubt at the time that a general rising
of the men was contemplated, and the governor felt it necessary to use redoubled efforts to make all secure, calling in
further assistance from Bow Street. The night passed, however, without any outbreak, and next morning all the prisoners
were pretty quiet and orderly. Later in the day the committee met and sentenced the ringleaders to various punishments, chiefly reduction in class, and by this time the whole
were humble and submissive. Finally five, who had been
conspicuous for good conduct, were pardoned.

It is satisfactory to find that the committee firmly resisted
all efforts to make them withdraw the objectionable bread, and
acted on the whole with spirit and determination. How far
the governor was to blame cannot clearly be made out, but the
confidence of the committee was evidently shaken, and a
month or two later he was called upon to resign. He refused;
whereupon the committee informed him that they gave him
"full credit for his capacity and talents in his former line of
life, but did not deem he had the talent, temper, or turn
of mind necessary for the beneficial execution of the office of
governor of the institution." There was not the slightest
imputation on his moral character, the committee assured him;
but they could not retain him. He would not resign, and they
were consequently compelled to remove him from his office.

There can be no doubt but that Millbank in these early
days was overmuch governed. The committee took everything into their own hands, and allowed but little latitude to
their responsible officers. The first governor complains *
that the visitors (members of the committee) "went to the
Penitentiary, and gave orders and directions for things to be
done by inferior officers, which I thought ought to come
through me. . . . Prisoners were occasionally removed

* Parliamentary Select Committee on Millbank, July, 1823.

from one ward to another, and I knew nothing of it—no communication was made to me; and if the inferior officers had a request to make, they got too much into the habit of reserving it to speak to the visitors; so that I conceived I was almost a nonentity in the situation." The prisoners, even, were in the habit of saying they would wait till the visitor came, and would ask him for what they wanted, ignoring the governor altogether. Indeed it appears from the official journals that the visitors were constantly at the prison. One (Mr. Holford) admits that "for a considerable time he did everything but sleep there." But their excuse was that they were not fortunate in their choice of some of their first officers; and knew therefore they "must watch vigilantly over their conduct, to keep those who answered expectations, and to part with those who appeared unfit for their situations." Besides which it was necessary to see from time to time how the rules first framed worked in practice, and what customs that grew up should be prohibited, and what sanctioned, by the committee, and adopted into the rules.

It must be confessed that the committee do not appear to have been well served by all their subordinates. The governors were changed frequently; the first "expected to find his place better in point of emolument, and did not calculate upon the degree of activity to be expected in the person at the head of such an establishment; the second was not thought by the committee to have those habits of mind— particularly those habits of conciliation—which are required in a person at the head of such an establishment;" the third was seized with an affection of the brain, and was never afterwards capable of exercising sufficient activity. The first master manufacturer, who as will be remembered was appointed because he was of a mechanical turn of mind, was removed because he was a very young man, and his conduct was not thought steady enough for the post he occupied. The first steward was charged with embezzlement, but was actually dismissed for borrowing money from some of the tradesmen of the establishment. The first matron was also sent away within the first twelve months, but she appears to have been rather hardly used, though her removal also proves

the existence of grave irregularities in the establishment.
The case against Mrs. Chambers was that she employed
certain of the female prisoners for her own private advantage.
Her daughter was about to be married; and to assist in
making up bed furniture a portion of thread belonging to the
establishment was used by the prisoners, who gave also their
time. The thread was worth a couple of shillings, and was
replaced by Mrs. Chambers. A second charge against the
matron was for stealing a Penitentiary Bible. Her excuse
was that a number had been distributed among the officers—
a present, as she thought, from the committee—and she had
passed hers on to her daughter. But for these offences, when
substantiated, she was dismissed from her employment.

Entries made in the Visitors' Journal, however, are fair
evidence that matters were allowed by the officials to manage
themselves in rather a "happy-go-lucky" fashion. One day
new prisoners were expected from Newgate; but nothing was
ready for them. "Not a table or a stool in any working cell;
and one of those cells where the prisoners were to be placed,
in which the workmen had some time since kept coals, was in
the dirty state in which it had been left by them. Not a
single bed had been aired." The steward did not know these
prisoners were expected, and had ordered no rations for them.
But he stated "he has enough, all but about two pounds."
Upon which the visitor remarks, "If sixteen male prisoners
can be supplied without notice, within two pounds, the
quantity of meat sent in cannot be very accurate." Again,
the visitor finds the doors from the prison into the hexagon
(where the superior officers lived) "not double-locked as they
ought to be. . . . Two prisoners together in the kitchen
without a turnkey." "The daily allowance of food issued to
the prisoners not the right weight." "29th.—Came at ten.
There are in the bathing-room at the lodge several bundles
of clothes belonging to male prisoners who have come in
between the 1st and 21st of this month; they are exactly
in the state in which they were when the subject was
mentioned to the committee last week; some of them are
thrown into a dirty part of the room—whether intended to
be burned I do not know; the porter thinks they are not.

I do not believe any of the female prisoners' things have been yet sold. I understand from the governor he has not yet made any entry in the Character-book concerning the behaviour of any male prisoner since he came into the prison, or relative to any occurrence connected with such prisoner." All this will fairly account for any extra fussiness on the part of the committee. Doubtful of the zeal and energy of those to whom they confided the details of management, they were continually stepping in to make up for any shortcomings by their own activity. But the direct consequence of this interference was to shake the authority of the ostensible heads. Moreover, to make the more sure that nothing should be neglected, and no irregularity overlooked, the committee encouraged, or at least their most prominent member did, all sorts of talebearing, and a system of espionage that must have been destructive of all good feeling among the inmates of the prison. Mr. Pitt, when examined by the Select Committee, said, " Mr. Holford has mentioned to me : ' I hear so and so; such and such an abuse appears to be going forward ; but I shall get some further information.' I always turned a deaf ear to these observations, thinking it an erroneous system, and that it was not likely to contribute to the good of the establishment." He thought Mr. Holford's being so ready "to lend a willing ear to such communications operated as an encouragement to talebearing; the consequences of which certainly have appeared to me to have been disputes, cabals, or intrigues." * Mr. Shearman, the governor, remarks on the same subject: " I certainly did think there was a very painful system going on in the prison against officers . . . by what I might term 'spyism.' I have no doubt it all arose from the purest motives, thinking it was the best way to conduct the establishment, setting up one person to look after another." The master manufacturer and the steward in this way took the opportunity of vilifying the governor ; and there is no doubt the matron, Mrs. Chambers, fell a victim to this practice. She was the victim of insinuation, and to the evil reports of busybodies who personally disliked her.

* Parliamentary Select Committee on Millbank, July, 1823, p. 165.

It is easy to imagine the condition of Millbank then. A
small colony apart from the great world; living more than
as neighbours, as one family almost—but not happily—under
the same roof. The officials, nearly all of them of mature
age, having grown up children, young ladies and young gentlemen, always about the place, and that place from its peculiar
conditions, like a ship at sea, shut off from the public, and
concentrated on what was going on within its walls. Gossip,
of course, prevalent—probably worse; constant observation of
one another, jealousies, quarrels, inevitable when authority
was divided between three people, the governor, chaplain, and
matron, and it was not clearly made out which was the most
worthy; subordinates ever on the look out to make capital of
the differences of their betters, and alive to the fact that they
were certain of a hearing when they chose to carry any slan-
derous tale, or make any underhand complaint. For there,
outside the prison, was the active and all-powerful committee,
ever ready to listen, and anxious to get information. One of
the witnesses before the committee of 1823 stated: "From
the earliest period certainly the active members of the Superintending Committee gave great encouragement to receive
any information from the subordinate officers, I believe with
the view of putting the prison in its best possible state; that
encouragement was caught with avidity by a great many,
simply for the purpose of cultivating the good opinion of
those gentlemen conducting it; and I am induced to think
that in many instances their zeal overstepped, perhaps, the
strict line of truth; for I must say that during the whole
period I was there, there was a continual complaint, one officer
against another, and a system that was quite unpleasant in an
establishment of that nature."

Of a truth, the life inside the Penitentiary must have been
rather irksome to more people than those confined there against
their will.

THE PRISON GRAVEYARD.

CHAPTER IV.

THE GREAT EPIDEMIC.

THE internal organisation of Millbank, which has been detailed in the last chapter, is described at some length in a Blue Book, bearing date July, 1823. But though Millbank was then, so to speak, on its trial, and its value, in return for the enormous cost of its erection, closely questioned, it is probable that its management would not have demanded a Parliamentary inquiry but for one serious mishap which brought matters to a crisis. Of a sudden the whole of the inmates of the prison began to pine and fall away. A virulent disorder broke out, and threatened the lives of all in the place. Alarm and misgiving in such a case soon spread; and all at once the public began to fear that Millbank was altogether a huge mistake. Here was a building upon which half a million had been spent, and now, when barely

completed, it proved uninhabitable! Money cast wholesale
into a deadly swamp, and all the fine talk of reformation and
punishment to give way to coroners' inquests and deaths by
a strange disease. No wonder there was a cry for investigation. Then, as on many subsequent occasions, it became
evident Millbank was fulfilling one of the conditions laid
down as of primary importance in the choice of site. Howard
had said that the Penitentiary House must be built near the
metropolis, so as to insure constant supervision and inspection.
Millbank is ten minutes' walk from Westminster, and from
the first has been the subject of continual inquiry and
legislation. The tons of Blue Books and dozens of Acts of
Parliament which it has called into existence will be sufficient
proof of this. It was, however, a public undertaking, carried
out in the full blaze of daylight, and hence it attracted more
than ordinary attention. What might have passed unnoticed
in a far-off shire, was in London magnified to proportions
almost absurd. This must explain State interference, which
nowadays may seem quite unnecessary, and will account for
the giving a national importance to matters oftentimes in
themselves really trivial.

But this first sickness in the Penitentiary was sufficiently
serious to arrest attention. The story of it is as follows.

In the autumn of 1822 (state the physicians appointed to
report on the subject)* the general health of the prisoners
in Millbank began visibly to decline. They became pale and
languid, thin and feeble; those employed in tasks calling for
bodily exertion could not execute the same amount of work as
before, those at the mill ground less corn, those at the pump
brought up less water, the laundry-women often fainted at their
work, and the regular routine of the place was only accomplished by constantly changing the hands engaged. Throughout the winter this was the general condition of the prisoners.
The breaking down of health was shown by such symptoms as
lassitude, dejection of spirits, paleness of countenance, rejection of food, and occasional faintings. Yet, with all this
depression of general health, there were no manifest signs of
specific disease; the numbers in hospital were not in excess

* Report of Drs. Roget and Latham.

of previous winters, and their maladies were such as were commonly incident to cold weather. But in January, 1823, scurvy—unmistakable sea-scurvy—made its appearance, and was then recognised as such and in its true form for the first time by the medical superintendent, though the prisoners themselves declared it was visible among them as early as the previous November. Being anxious to prevent alarm, either in the Penitentiary itself or in the neighbourhood, the medical officer rather suppressed the fact of the existence of the disease; and this, with a certain tendency to make light of it, led to the omission of many precautions. But there it was, plainly evident; first, by the usual sponginess of the gums, then by "ecchymosed" blotches on the legs, which were observed in March to be pretty general among the prisoners.

Upon this point, the physicians called in remark, that the scurvy spots "are at their first appearance peculiarly apt to escape discovery, unless the attention be particularly directed towards them, and that they often exist for a long time entirely unnoticed by the patient himself." And now with the scurvy came dysentery and diarrhœa, of the peculiar kind that is usually associated with the scorbutic disease. In all cases, the same constitutional derangement was observable, the outward marks of which were a sallow countenance and impaired digestion, diminished muscular strength, a feeble circulation, various degrees of nervous affections, such as tremors, cramps, or spasms, and various degrees of mental despondency.

With regard to the extent of the disease, it was found that quite half of the total number were affected, the women more extensively than the men; and both the males and females of the second class, and those who had been longest in confinement, were more frequently attacked than the newest arrivals. Some few were, however, entirely exempt; more especially the prisoners employed in the kitchen, while among the officers and their families, amounting in all to one hundred and six individuals, there was not a single instance of attack recorded.

Such then was the condition of the prisoners in the Penitentiary in the spring of 1823. To what was this sud-

den outbreak of a virulent disorder to be traced? There
were those who laid the whole blame on the locality, and
who would admit of no other explanation. But this argument was in the first instance opposed by Drs. Latham and
Roget. Had the situation of the prison been at fault, they
said, it was only reasonable to suppose that the disease
would have shown itself in earlier years of the prison's
existence; whereas, as far as they could ascertain, till 1822–3
it was altogether unknown. Moreover, had this been the real
cause, all inmates would alike have suffered; how then explain
the universal immunity of the officers in charge? Again, if
it were the miasmata arising upon a marshy neighbourhood
that militated against the healthiness of the prison, there
should be prevalent other diseases which marsh miasmata
confessedly engender. Besides which, the scurvy and diarrhœa
thus produced are associated with intermittent fevers, in this
case not noticeable; and they would have occurred during the
hot instead of the winter season. Lastly, if it were imagined
that the dampness of the situation had contributed to the
disease, a ready answer was, that on examination every part of
the prison was found to be singularly dry, not the smallest
stain of moisture being apparent in any cell or passage, floor,
ceiling, or wall. But indeed it was not necessary to search far
afield for the causes of the outbreak; they lay close at hand.
Undoubtedly a sudden and somewhat ill-judged reduction in
diet was entirely to blame. For a long time the luxury of the
Penitentiary had been a standing joke.* The prison was
commonly called Mr. Holford's fattening house. He was told
that much money might be saved the public by parting with
half his officers, for there need be no fear of escapes; all that
was needed was a proper guard to prevent too great a rush of
people in. An honourable member published a pamphlet in
which he styled the dietary at Millbank "an insult to honest
industry and a violation of common sense." And evidence
was not wanting from the prison itself of the partial truth of
these allegations. The medical superintendent frequently
reported that the prisoners, especially the females, suffered
from plethora, and from diseases consequent upon a fulness of

* Parl. Rep., p. 114, 1823.

habit. Great quantities of food were carried out of the prison
in the wash-tubs; potatoes, for instance, were taken to the pigs,
which Mr. Holford admitted he would have been ashamed to
have thus seen carried out of his own house. It came to such
a pass at last that the committee was plainly told by members
of the House of Commons, that if the dietary were not changed,
the next annual vote for the establishment would probably be
opposed. In the face of all this clamour the committee could
not hold out; but in their anxiety to provide a remedy, they
went from one extreme to the other. Abandoning the scale
that was too plentiful, they substituted one that was altogether
too meagre. In the new dietary solid animal food was quite
excluded, and only soup was given. This soup was made of
ox heads, in the proportion of one to every hundred prisoners;
it was to be thickened with vegetables or peas, and the daily
allowance was to be a quart, half at midday, and half in the
evening. The bread ration was a pound and a half, and for
breakfast there was also a pint of gruel. It was open to the
committee to substitute potatoes for bread if they saw fit, but
they do not seem to have done this. The meat upon an ox
head averages about eight pounds, so that the allowance per
prisoner was about an ounce and a quarter. No wonder then
that they soon fell away in health.

The mere reduction in the amount of food, however, would
not have been sufficient in itself to cause the epidemic of
scurvy. Scurvy will occur even with a copious dietary.
Sailors who eat plenty of biscuit and beef are attacked, and
others who are certainly not starved. The real predisposing
cause is the absence of certain necessary elements in the diet,
not the lowness of the diet itself. It is the want of vegetable
acids in food that brings about the mischief. The authorities
called in were not exactly right, therefore, in attributing the
scurvy solely to the reduced diet. The siege of Gibraltar was
quoted as an instance where semi-starvation superinduced the
disease. Again Mr. White traced the scurvy prevalent in the
low districts round Westminster to a similar deficiency and the
severe winter, adding, however, the want of vegetable diet also,
This last was the real explanation; of this, according to our
medical knowledge, there is not now the faintest doubt. Long

enforced abstinence from fresh meat and fresh vegetables is certain sooner or later to produce scurvy. At the same time it must be admitted that the epidemic of which I am writing was aggravated by the cold weather. It had its origin in the cold season, and its progress and increase kept pace with it. Those who suffered most were those who occupied uninterruptedly the coldest cells. Others, as I have said, who slept in the same parts, but were employed during the day in the kitchen, generally escaped attack.

I have been quoting so far from the report of two eminent physicians, Drs. Latham and Roget, who were called in by the committee at an early stage of the outbreak. The chief adviser of the committee had so far been Dr. Hutchinson, the medical superintendent; but he seems to have quite forfeited the confidence of the committee, rather by his impracticable attitude than by actual shortcomings in his professional duties. In April he was removed from his situation, and the task of grappling with the disorder fell upon the gentlemen above mentioned. Their plan of action from the first was just what might have been expected. A ration of fresh meat, four ounces in weight, was at once substituted for the peas or barley soup, with eight ounces of rice daily, white bread instead of brown, and, as the cheapest and best anti-scorbutic, three oranges were given to each prisoner every day, or one at each meal. Under this treatment the disease gradually declined, the prisoners gained strength daily, were more cheerful, and did more work.

The scorbutic marks had in all cases begun to disappear by the end of March, and together with them went the diarrhœa and dysentery, which throughout had been the most formidable part of the disease. The report from which I quote is dated the 5th of April, 1823, and after recommending strongly a new dietary nearer the original scale than that which caused all this mischief, it winds up with expressing "a firm conviction that there is now no obstacle to the entire re-establishment of the healthy state of the Penitentiary."

Unhappily this conclusion proved distinctly premature. The report above quoted had hardly been made public before disease reappeared in another form. By the middle of May it was general throughout the prison; before June was ended all were equally affected—those who had before suffered, those before exempt, and even new arrivals, admitted to the Penitentiary since the first outbreak.

Now, too, the remedies that had once proved successful, exercised no appreciable effect upon the disease: this it must be understood was no longer scurvy—the scorbutic spots and blotches never again showed themselves; the complaint was exclusively a species of "flux." "The disease was neither a diarrhœa nor a dysentery simply—nor did it belong exclusively to the bowels; but it belonged to the whole system, and was very extraordinary and (as I believe) * peculiar in its nature. There was every degree of flux that was ever seen or described. There were cases which corresponded with the description of the Indian cholera. The patients were seized with intolerable cramps at the pit of the stomach; . . . the pulse became feeble and frequent; they were pale and chilly; and a sudden anguish pervaded the whole frame. Again, there were cases which corresponded with the common autumnal cholera of this country. . . . Moreover, there was every kind and degree of dysentery. . . . Again, there were cases which differed very little from the diarrhœa of common casual occurrence, except that they were quite intractable by common remedies. . . . Lastly, there were cases which had no resemblance whatever either to cholera, or dysentery, or diarrhœa, or to any disorder that has obtained a name." A strange anomaly was that those attacked with the most serious forms of illness were not necessarily those who succumbed. Prisoners suffering from the extreme symptoms of cholera or dysentery were as likely to recover as those who had simple diarrhœa; while the mild disease was frequently as fatal as the most severe. The peculiar symptom, among others, which affected the great majority, was "a kind of perpetual uneasiness within the abdomen.† There was a general complaint of what was called sinking at the pit of the stomach. What this sinking is, only those know who have suffered it. All patients speak of it by the same name, but do

* Latham on the Diseases of the Penitentiary, p. 31, et seq.
† Ibid, p. 36.

not describe it further. From observation, I suspected it to
consist of a certain degree of actual pain combined with a
feeling which is akin to approaching syncope, and spreads
from the stomach as a centre over the whole frame. It is a
painful and overpowering sensation, as if animal life itself was
hurt and lessened." Apparently this sensation was the most
painful and distressing of all a patient's sufferings. "Patients
would continually endeavour to withdraw our attention from
the more tangible symptoms of their disorder, for the sake of
fixing it upon this. When we were interrogating them upon
circumstances apparently more urgent, they would interrupt
us, exclaiming, 'But this sinking, this sinking, pray do
something for this sinking.'"*

Many suffered severe pains, which came and subsided, and
came again, and were often aggravated into paroxysms of
most extreme torture. These pains partook chiefly of the
character of colic. Another feature curious in the disease was,
that whether the patient had diarrhœa, dysentery, cholera, or
flux, his tongue during the whole course of the complaint was
clean and moist, and of its natural colour. This struck every
medical man who came to the prison. In a few cases it might
be a little redder than usual; sometimes coated with mucus,
sometimes brown and dry; but in not a single instance was
there the red, glossy, smooth tongue peculiar to dysentery.
As has been stated already, the severity of the symptoms
were no criterion of the severity of the disease; indeed, the
most formidable form of the disorder was mild diarrhœa.

Two cases of this kind occurred early in the outbreak,
and progressed slowly and certainly to a fatal termination.
The patients had no other symptom but simple diarrhœa;
they were in no pain, no fever; pulse at sixty and no more.
"Never," says Dr. Latham, "did I witness the process of
dissolution so lingering." † Later on cases of this kind became
more and more numerous; and it was that form of the disease
which the physicians most feared. The patients thus affected
were generally given up for lost; they lay in bed without
fever, and without pain; no excitement of the pulse, no

* Latham on the Diseases of the Penitentiary, p. 37.
† Ibid. p. 41.

symptom but continuous diarrhœa. But this one symptom nothing whatever could restrain. They did not complain much, speaking only of "this terrible sinking at the stomach." * But soon their complaining ceased. "If roused then, they looked up for a moment, made no lamentation, then laid their heads down again in despair. It was a dismal office to watch over their tardy dissolution, and witness the frustration of every expedient for their relief. These were the cases in which we first put the efficacy of mercury to successful proof; and I cannot help mentioning the relief my mind experienced from a sense of responsibility which had now become truly awful, as soon as the salutary influence of this remedy was apparent." Mercury was then eventually tried, because the remedies formerly efficacious were now found to fail altogether even in the simplest cases. Neither chalk mixture nor tincture of opium afforded the slightest relief; nor had astringent bitters, aromatics, mucilaginous drinks, antimonials, and ipecacuanha.

So far we have dealt only with the bowel complaints; but other disorders showed themselves in those attacked by the Penitentiary epidemic. Principal among these were the disorders of the brain and nervous system. The physicians in their first report stated that all who suffered from scurvy were liable also to "various degrees of nervous affections, as tremors, cramps, or spasms, and various degrees of mental despondency." But for a long time after the epidemic re-appeared, there seemed to be no special reason for connecting these symptoms with the predominating disease. By-and-by the disorders of the brain became more and more frequent and of various kinds, including headache, vertigo, cramps and twitching of the limbs, delirium, convulsions, and apoplexy. Then it was that the doctors began to understand that these disorders were contingent on the flux. Fever also, of more rare occurrence, accompanied the other symptoms; so that the whole disease, taking it from its beginning, might be said to include four different classes of symptoms—those of scurvy, flux, brain disorders, and fever.

The following figures will show at a glance the character and extent of the disorder during the months of May, June,

* Latham on the Diseases of the Penitentiary, p. 43.

and July, 1823.—On May 15th, 345 were sick; on May 23rd,
386; next month the numbers rose to 454; but on July 3rd
they had fallen to 438. At this time the prison population .
amounted to about 800. There were in all 30 deaths.

By July a slight improvement for the better took place;
but it is easy to understand that the medical men in charge
were still much troubled with fears for the future. Granting even that the disease had succumbed to treatment,
there was the danger, with all the prisoners in a low state
of health, of relapse, or even of an epidemic in a new shape.
Hence it was felt that an immediate change of air and place
would be the best security against further disease. But
several hundred convicts could not be sent to the sea-side like
ordinary convalescents; besides which they were committed
to Millbank by Act of Parliament, and only by Act of Parliament could they be removed. This difficulty was easily met.
An Act of Parliament more or less made no matter to Millbank—many pages in the Statute Book were covered already
with legislation for the Penitentiary. A new Act was immediately passed, authorising the committee to transfer the
prisoners from Millbank to situations more favourable for the
recovery of their health. In accordance with its provisions
one part of the female prisoners were at once sent into the
Royal Ophthalmic Hospital in Regent's Park, at that time
standing empty; their number during July and August was
increased to 120, by which time a hulk, the *Ethalion*, had
been prepared at Woolwich for male convicts, and thither went
200, towards the end of August. Those selected for removal
were the prisoners who had suffered most from the disease.
This was an experiment; and according to its results the fate
of those who remained at Millbank was to be determined.
"The benefit of the change of air and situation," says Dr.
Latham, "was immediately apparent." Within a fortnight
there was less complaint of illness, and most of the patients
already showed symptoms of returning health. Meanwhile,
among the prisoners left at Millbank there was little change,
though at times all were threatened with a return of the old
disorder, less virulent in its character, however, and missing
half its former frightful forms. By September, a comparison

between those at Regent's Park or the hulk and those still in
Millbank was so much in favour of the former that the point
at issue seemed finally settled. Beyond doubt the change of
air had been extremely beneficial; nevertheless, of the two
changes, it was evident that the move to the hulks at Woolwich had the better of the change to Regent's Park. On
board the *Ethalion* the prisoners had suffered fewer relapses and
had gained a greater degree of health than those at Regent's
Park. On the whole, therefore, it was considered advisable to
complete the process of emptying Millbank. The males and
females alike were drafted into different hulks off Woolwich.
These changes were carried out early in December, and by
that time the Millbank Penitentiary was entirely emptied.

One remarkable circumstance attended the removal of the
prisoners. All alike, on arrival at Woolwich, experienced
an immediate improvement in health. For a time, indeed,
their disorder altogether disappeared. But this speedy
amendment was unhappily almost always completely fallacious.
The diarrhœa invariably returned, and though milder in
its form, it was still the same old Millbank complaint. Nor
was there even any security that those who became convalescent were entirely and completely cured. Sometimes
patients, after having been free from any symptoms of
complaint for even four or five months, again fell victims
to the disease. This fluctuation was necessarily embarrassing to the physicians in charge. At one visit they found,
perhaps, not five-and-twenty cases in a couple of hundred
men; at the next, half the whole number would be
afflicted with diarrhœa. The progress, therefore, to ultimate and complete restoration to health was altogether
uncertain. In all cases the females were those whose cure
seemed permanently postponed. Fresh attacks of a severe
character continually appeared among them. On the other
hand, women who had been pardoned came back, from time
to time, and showed themselves at the hulks, restored to
perfect health. It seemed, then, that the only chance of
preserving the lives of all, was to set all at liberty; and,
indeed, the sufferings they had undergone might well be
taken as an equivalent of many years' imprisonment. These

F

arguments prevailed, and eventually the whole of the female prisoners received the pardon of the Crown. But though all were thus made free, they were not turned adrift *en masse* to shift for themselves. The Home Secretary, in all cases, communicated first with the prisoners' friends throughout the kingdom; and no one was set at large till it was clear that she had a home to receive her. In this way the dismissal of the prisoners was protracted, and it was not till the 18th January, 1824, that the last woman had left the Penitentiary hulks. With the men it was different: their health had not, certainly, deteriorated nearly so much; and yet it was felt to be unsafe to send them back to the prison. On board the hulks, however, they were lapsing rapidly into utter anarchy and confusion. To extend a wholesale pardon to some 400 felons was a measure that rather frightened those who wielded the prerogative of clemency. These men must remain in durance, but where? After some discussion it was resolved to transfer the whole of the men to the regular hulk establishments, and accordingly another Act was passed, giving Government the necessary power. It was hoped that by thus distributing the Penitentiary prisoners, subjecting them to a new discipline and active occupation, their health would soon recover. The result verified the expectation. At the end of the year those who were in medical charge reported that the health of these men was quite as good as that of the other prisoners. In this manner the epidemic came to an end. Millbank was emptied, remained vacant for some months, and was eventually refilled, but with an entirely new class of inmates.

But though the epidemic ended thus, the question was not to die out with the flickering out of the disease. For some time to come the question how it originated and who was to blame, agitated many minds. As I have already pointed out, the physicians in the first instance (in April) attributed the disease to a sudden change from a full to a sparse diet, aided by the cold of an unusually severe winter. At that time they absolved the locality of all share in the noxious causes. But when in May the disease reappeared with renewed virulence, they had to reconsider their verdict, and issued a second report. They stated now that it was impossible that it could have sprung exclusively from the causes at first put forward. Cold and scanty nourishment would always suffice, of course, to produce scurvy; but here at Millbank these causes were not present in the most intense degree. The winter was cold, no doubt; but then the prisoners were not out of doors—they were sheltered under a warm roof. Again, the diet might be insufficient, still it was wholesome in its kind. Neither one nor other, nor both combined, might well be credited with producing a disorder so virulent and fatal. New facts had to be sought out; and these were to be found, the physicians thought, in contagion and an injurious influence peculiar to the place. Of the first there could be no reasonable doubt. The illness was no longer confined, as on the first outbreak, to the prisoners alone; the officers high and low were now equally attacked. The chaplain caught it from attending the sick, and his family suffered because he had taken as servant a convict who was not entirely recovered. New prisoners, too, upon whom the changed dietary had had little time to act, were quite as susceptible as the old. This showed the diet was not alone at fault; and as to the weather—why, it was already spring time, or indeed the early summer before the epidemic showed itself in its worst form. Undoubtedly, then, the inference was that the disease had grown contagious. And it was contagious in a manner peculiar to itself; convalescents were reinfected by it, which is quite unusual with ordinary diseases.

Again, as to the noxious influence peculiar to the place, the physicians asserted that, on a close examination of the prison apothecary's books, they now ascertained that for years past diarrhœa had been prevalent in the Penitentiary. Its existence was proved less by recorded cases than by the character of the prescriptions made up. The medicine commonest in use was chalk mixture, and this of itself was evidence enough. The inmates of Millbank must, they thought, have been always subject to attacks of this kind.

It was not to be supposed that this second report could be accepted by the committee without comment. Its conclusions were construed into a direct attack upon the prison situation

and its management generally. Mr. Holford, an active
member of the committee, took up the cudgels and replied
warmly. Pamphlet followed pamphlet on either side; but the
question at issue was never satisfactorily set at rest. Looking
back now, after a lapse of years, and with the light of acquired
experience, it is less difficult to decide the question. All the
causes quoted undoubtedly contributed their share, in a greater
or less degree. But it was the change of diet that actually
originated the disease. Conditions that might otherwise have
continued dormant or unnoticed, were by this agent called
into active existence. The inmates of the Penitentiary were
ripe for attack perhaps, but failing some spark to set the
mass aflame might have escaped altogether. This spark
was the ill-judged reduction of the dietary, accompanied
as it was by a complete change in the character of its con-
stituents. Not only was the supply of sustenance insufficient, but solid food was now altogether excluded. Gruel
for breakfast, soup for dinner, soup for supper; these were
the viands at the three meals. Everything was liquid but
the bread; yet even this might have passed without such
serious consequences but for another and more fatal error.
Vegetables were almost entirely omitted from the new
scale. In the first there had been a daily issue of a
pound of potatoes; in the second, potatoes might be substituted for bread at the discretion of the committee, but
practically this never occurred. Taking all these circumstances in conjunction, it is easy to understand that a body
of prisoners, not indisposed naturally to attack, fell an easy
prey to the epidemic. The spirit of evil once evoked
soon found allies all around, and could not easily be laid.
Now the situation and surroundings of the prison threw
their weight into the scale—the artificial ground on which
the building had been raised, the stagnant moat of dirty
water that encircled its walls, the bitter cold of an unusually
severe winter. Aided and abetted thus, the scurvy and its
sequelæ took fast hold of the place, and the disease ran its
course with the severity that has been described.

HOSPITAL HULKS AT WOOLWICH.

CHAPTER V.

PRISON LIFE BEFORE AND AFTER THE EPIDEMIC.

THE inner life of the Penitentiary went on much as usual
in the early days of the epidemic. There are at first only
the ordinary entries in the governor's journal. Prisoners
came and went; this one was pardoned, that received from
Newgate or some county gaol. Repeated reports of misconduct are recorded. The prisoners seemed fretful and
mischievous. Now and then they actually complained of
the want of food. One prisoner was taken to task for

telling his father, in the visiting cell, that "six prisoners
out of every seven would die for want of rations." But at
length the blow fell. "On the 14th of February, 1823, Ann
Smith died in the infirmary at half-past nine." On the 17th,
Mary Ann Davidson; on the 19th, Mary Esp; on the 23rd,
William Cardwell; on the 24th, Humphrey Adams; on the
28th, Margaret Patterson. And now, by order of the visitor,
the prisoners were ordered more walking exercise. Then
follow the first steps taken by Drs. Roget and Latham. The
governor records, on the 3rd March, that the doctors
recommend each prisoner should have daily four ounces of
meat and three oranges; that their bread should be divided
into three parts, an orange taken at each meal. Accordingly
"I sent the steward to Thames Street to lay in a week's
consumption of oranges."

An entry soon afterwards gives the first distinct reference
to the epidemic. "The medical gentlemen having begged for
the bodies of such prisoners as might die of the disorder now
prevalent in the prison, in order to make post-mortem
examinations, the same was sanctioned if the friends of the
prisoner did not wish to interfere." Deaths were now very
frequent, and hardly a week passed without a visit from the
coroner or his deputy.

On the 25th March the governor, Mr. Couch, who had
been ailing for some time past, resigned his charge into the
hands of Captain Benjamin Chapman. Soon afterwards there
were further additions to the dietary—on the 26th of April
two more ounces of meat and twelve ounces of boiled potatoes;
and the day after, it was ordered that each prisoner should
drink toast-and-water,—three half-pints daily. Lime, in
large tubs, was to be provided in all the pentagons for the
purpose of disinfection.

About this period there was a great increase of insubordination among the prisoners. It is easy to understand that
discipline must be relaxed when all were more or less ailing
and unable to bear punishment. The sick wards were
especially noisy and turbulent. One man, for instance, was
charged with shouting loudly and using atrocious language;
all of which of course he denied, declaring he had only said,

"God bless the King, my tongue is very much swelled." Upon this the turnkey in charge observed that it was a pity it was not swelled more, and Smith (the prisoner) pursued the argument by hitting his officer on the head with a pint pot. Later on they broke out almost into mutiny. Here is what the governor says:—"At a quarter to eight o'clock Taskmaster Swift informed me that the whole of the prisoners in the infirmary ward of his pentagon were in the most disorderly and riotous state, in consequence of the wooden doors of the cells having been ordered by the surgeon to be shut during the night; that the prisoners peremptorily refused to permit the turnkeys to shut their doors, and made use of the most opprobrious terms in speaking of Mr. Pratt, threatening destruction to whoever might attempt to shut their doors. Their shouts and yells were so loud as to be heard at a considerable distance. I immediately summoned the patrols, and several of the turnkeys, and making them take their cutlasses, I repaired to the sick ward. I found the wooden doors all open, and the prisoners, for the most part, at their iron gates, which were shut. The first prisoner I came to was John Hall. I asked him the reason he refused to shut his door when ordered. He answered in a very insolent tone and manner, 'Why should I do so?' I then said: 'Shut your door instantly,' but he would not comply. I took him away and confined him in a dark cell. In conveying him to the cell he made use of most abusive and threatening language, but did not make any personal resistance." Five others who were pointed out as prominent in the mutiny were also punished on bread and water and dark cell, by the surgeon's permission.

Nor were matters much more satisfactory in the female infirmary wards.

"Mrs. Briant, having reported yesterday, during my absence at Woolwich, that Mary Willson had 'wilfully cut her shoes,' and having stated the same verbally this morning, I went with her into the infirmary, where the prisoner was, and having produced the shoes to her (the upper-leather of one of them being palpably cut from the sole), and asked her why she cut them, she said she had not cut them, that they

had come undone whilst walking in the garden. This being
an evident falsehood, I told her I feared she was doing something worse than cutting her shoes by telling an untruth.
She answered in a very saucy manner, they were not her
shoes, and that she had not cut them. She became at length
very insolent, when I told her she deserved to be punished.
She replied she did not care whether she was or not. I then
directed the surgeon to be sent for; when not only the
prisoner, but several others in the infirmary, became very
clamorous, and evinced a great degree of insubordination. I
went out with the intention of getting a couple of patrols,
when I heard the crash of broken glass and loud screams. I
returned as soon as possible with the patrols into the infirmary.
The women generally attempted to oppose my entrance, and
a group had got Willson amongst them, and said she should
not be confined. I desired the patrols to lay hold of her, and
take her to the dark cell (I had met with Dr. Hugh when
going for the patrols, who under the circumstances sanctioned
the removal of the prisoner). In doing so, Betts and Stone
were assaulted with the utmost violence; I myself was
violently laid hold of, and my wrist and finger painfully
twisted. I had Willson, however, taken to the dark cell,
when, having summoned several of the turnkeys and officers
of the prison, I with considerable difficulty succeeded in
taking six more of them who appeared to be most forward
in this disgraceful riot. Several of the large panes in the
passage windows were broken; and the women seized everything they could lay their hands on, and flung them at the
officers, who, in self-defence, were at length compelled to
strike in return. I immediately reported the circumstance to
Sir George Farrant, the visitor, who came to the prison soon
after. I accompanied him, as did Dr. Bennett (the chaplain)
and Mr. Pratt, through the female pentagon and infirmary,
when a strong spirit of insubordination was obvious. Sir
George addressed them, and so did Dr. Bennett, and pointed
out the serious injury they were doing themselves, and that
such conduct would not pass unpunished. We afterwards
visited the dark refractory cells, where the worst were
confined; two of whom, on account of previous good conduct

and favourable circumstances, were liberated. For myself, I never beheld such a scene of outrage, nor did I observe a single individual who was not culpably active."

As a general rule, the prisoners in the Penitentiary were in these days so little looked after, and had so much leisure time, that they soon found the proverbial "mischief" of the hymnist. Having some suspicions, the governor searched several, and found up the sleeves of five of them, knives, playing cards (made from an old copy-book), two articles to hold ink, a baby's straw hat, some papers (written upon), and an original song of questionable tendency. The hearts and diamonds in the cards had been covered with red chalk, clubs and spades with blacking. "Having received information that there were more cards about, I caused strict search to be made, and found in John Brown's Bible, one card and the materials for making more, also a small knife made of bone. In another prisoner's cell was found another knife and some paste, ingeniously contrived from old bread-crumbs." But even these amusements did not keep the prisoners from continually quarrelling and fighting with one another. Any one who had made himself obnoxious was severely handled. A body of prisoners fell upon one Tompkins, and half killed him, "because he had reported the irreverent conduct of several of them while at Divine Service." The place was like a bear-garden. Insubordination, riots, foul language, and continual wranglings among themselves—it could hardly be said that the prisoners were making that rapid progress towards improvement which was among the principal objects of the Penitentiary.

But now the scene shifts to the Woolwich hulks, whither by this time the whole of the inmates were being by degrees transferred. The first batch of males were sent off on the 16th August, embarking at Millbank, and proceeding by launch to Woolwich. Great precautions were taken. All the disposable taskmasters, turnkeys, and patrols being armed and stationed from the outer lodge to the quay (River Stairs), the prisoners were assembled by six at a time, and placed without irons in the launch. The same plan was pursued from time to time, till at length the whole number were removed. The hulks were the *Ethalion, Narcissus, Dromedary*. A master was on board in charge of each, under the general supervision of Captain Chapman, the Governor of the Penitentiary. There was immediately a further great deterioration in the conduct of the prisoners. Not only were they mischievous, as appeared from their favourite pastime, which was to drag off one another's bed-clothes in the middle of the night, by means of a crooked nail attached to a long string,* but the decks which they occupied were for ever in a state of anarchy and confusion. "All the prisoners below," says the overseer of the *Ethalion*, " conducted themselves last night in a most improper manner, by singing obscene songs and making a noise. When summoned to appear on the upper deck, they treated the master with defiance and contempt, so that the ringleaders had to be put in irons." But it was a mere waste of time to confine prisoners below. There was no place of security to hold them. "A number of prisoners broke their confinement by forcibly removing the boards of the different cabins in which they were placed in the cockpit, and got together in the fore hold, where they were found by Mr. Lodge at half-past nine at night." Another prisoner, a day or two later, confined in the hold, broke out, and proceeded through the holds and wings of the ship till he arrived at the fore hold, where another prisoner, Connor, was confined for irreverent behaviour during chapel. Connor tore up the boards fastened on to the mast-hatch, and admitted Williams to him. " When Williams' escape was discovered," says the overseer, "I searched for him in the bottom of the ship. On my arriving at the bulkhead of the fore hold I inquired of Connor if Williams was with him. He declared he was not, calling on God to witness his assertion; but on opening the hatch, to my astonishment I found him there. I ordered him back to the place in which he was first confined; on which he used the most abusive language, saying, by God, when he was released he would murder me and every officer in the ship. I talked mildly to him, and desired him to return to the place in which he had been confined. He

---

* The prisoners called this in their own slang, " toeing and gooseing."

at last complied, using the most abusive and threatening language. When he had returned to the after hold, I put the leg-irons on him to prevent his forcing out a second time, giving him at the same time to understand, that if he would behave himself they would soon be taken off. But he was still turbulent, breaking everything before him. I then put hand-cuffs on him, notwithstanding which he broke out at 9 P.M., disengaged himself from the handcuffs, and got a second time to the fore [hold, where I again found him, and insisted on his returning. He kicked me very much in the legs, using, as before, threatening language. I then found it necessary to use force, and taking guards Wadeson and Clarke with the steward, we again removed him to his first place of confinement. He appeared so resolute and determined to commit depredations, that I fastened his leg-irons to a five-inch staple in the timber of the hold, which staple he tore up during the night, and again passed to Connor in the fore hold.

"The prisoners were assembled upon deck, and were expostulated with, both by Mr. Holford and Captain Chapman, and exhorted to avoid insubordination on pain of certain punishment." Mr. Lodge also reported five prisoners for highly improper and reprehensible conduct, by making use of profane expressions and shocking language when interrogated as to their knowledge of the catechism. These five men Mr. Holford individually addressed, and all promised they would endeavour to learn it, "except Isaac Squince, who appears a hardened wretch."

"Lieut. Goulding of the navy came on board to prefer a complaint against some of the prisoners for repeatedly insulting him as he passed the ship in his boat. It appears that the lieutenant using his glass to view the ship, some of the prisoners from the ports have imitated him, by putting something to their eyes as if to quiz, at which he was greatly incensed."

On the 6th November, Mr. Lodge, who was in charge of the *Ethalion*, was drowned in coming off to the ship. The tide was running very strong, and the boat in which Mr. Lodge was became unmanageable; the current taking it between the two hulks, Mr. Lodge used the boat-hook to keep clear of the

ship's sides, but missing his hold was precipitated backwards
into the river. Mr. Gould, who was with him, plunged in immediately to save him, but without effect, and with difficulty saved
himself. The prisoners are reported to have testified much good
feeling on hearing of Mr. Lodge's fatal accident, "with the
simple exception of John Lovatt, who, having expressed some
indecent exultation, was immediately laid hold of by the rest
of the prisoners and ducked in the water cistern, and had it
not been for the interference of the guards would have treated
him much worse." A day later the prisoners sent in the
following petitions, which the governor considers "so credit-
able, that he felt highly gratified in permanently recording
them" in his Journal.

"To the Honble. Committee managing the affairs of the
     General Penitentiary, per the favour of Benjamin
     Chapman, Esquire, the Governor. Given on board the
     Ethalion Hospital Ship, 7th Nov., 1823.

     "Gentlemen,—The undermentioned individuals, composing
the prisoners of the upper deck, with feelings of the deepest
commiseration for the melancholy fate of their late most
worthy Master Lodge, together with all the distressing circumstances attending it, are desirous of showing some mark of
gratitude for his uniform kindness; and the only means
within their power of doing so, is to contribute a small sum
out of their percentage (of earnings) as a reward for the
recovery of his body; and should there be any overplus, to be
presented to his disconsolate widow, if she will please to accept
it; but in case of non-acceptance, it is their wish that it be
applied towards erecting a tombstone on his grave, as a
lasting monument of his worth and a token of their unfeigned
respect to his memory."

The sums subscribed varied from 2s. 6d. to 5s. and 10s.,
even 25s. A second petition set forth that the following
prisoners "voluntarily subscribed the undermentioned sums
to be given to the watermen employed in searching the River
Thames for the body of their much lamented master, John
Lodge; or as a consideration for his unhappy wife, at the

discretion of the Honble. Committee, whom they humbly hope will allow their several donations to be deducted from their percentage profit, as a token of respect for this late excellent man while living, and now unfeignedly regretted dead."

In addition to the foregoing, Morgan Williams, a prisoner pretty familiar by name, told the governor: "If I had the money, sir, I would have cheerfully subscribed as much as any man; but I am in debt to the establishment already, and putting down my name would be pretending to what I know I could not perform."

These several petitions were received with much satisfaction by the committee.

Having aired their good feelings thus, the prisoners soon returned to their normal condition of savage turbulence. On the 18th a most tumultuous noise took place on the lower deck about eight in the evening; and reiterated cries of "Murder!" "You'll throttle me," were distinctly heard from one who appeared to be almost exhausted. "I immediately assembled the guards," says the overseer, "and armed them with cutlasses, and went into the lower deck, which was in the greatest state of uproar and confusion. The prisoners were congregated at the head of the deck, holding John Pryce, who was foaming at the mouth, and appeared to be in a complete state of madness." There had been a violent quarrel between this man and another named Robinson, and but for the prompt interference of the officers it is probable that murder would have been committed.

On the 27th it was found that some prisoners had made their escape from the *Ethalion* hulk. On mustering the prisoners in the morning three were missing. Search was immediately made, but they were not to be found. All the hatches on the lower deck were secure; but it was ascertained, on examination of the after hold, that the prisoners must have made their way into the steward's store-room, where they had taken out the window. One of them then swam off to the *Shear* hulk, secured the boat, brought it to the after windows, and by that means, assisting each other, the three effected their escape. The boat belonging to the *Shear* hulk was found at the Prince Regent's Ferry House, on the Essex coast.

After a close investigation it was not possible to bring the blame home to any one. All the guards proved of course that they were on the alert all night. The steward said he had had a blister on, and could not sleep a wink, but he never missed hearing the bell struck (by the watch) every quarter of an hour. Stevenson, one of those who had escaped, had always been employed in the steward's store-room, hence he knew his way about the ship. Being a sailor and a good swimmer, it was probably he who had gone to the *Shear* hulk and got a boat, taking with him one end of a rope made of hammock nettings, the other being fast to a beam in the store-room. By this rope the *Shear* hulk boat was hauled gently to the *Ethalion;* then the two other prisoners got into it, and it was allowed to drift down for some distance with the tide. No sound whatever of oars had been heard during the night by the sentries on board or on shore. The escape must have been made between 1 and 2 A.M., as at three the men were seen landing from a boat on the Essex coast.

Information of the escape soon spread among the other prisoners, and it was pretty certain that many would attempt to follow. They were reported to be ripe for any mischief. The fire-arms were carefully inspected by the governor, who insisted on their being kept constantly in good order and "well-flinted." At the same time a strict search was made through the ship, particularly of the lower deck, for any implements that might be secreted to facilitate escape. False keys were reported to be in existence, but none could be found ; only a large sledge-hammer, a ripping chisel, and some iron bolts which were concealed in the caboose. A few days afterwards the master of the *Ethalion* reported the discovery of a number of other dangerous articles in various parts of the ship, several more sledge-hammers, chisels, iron bars, spike nails, etc., all calculated to do much mischief, and endanger the safety of the ship. At the same time, four prisoners were overheard planning another escape. They were to steal the key of a closet on the deck, and alter it so as to fit the locks of the bulkheads into the infirmary wards, and pass by this means to the cabin, and out through one of the ports. The key was immediately impounded, and a strict watch kept all night. Between eleven and twelve the guard reported that he heard a noise like filing through iron bars; so the master got into a boat with two others and rowed round the ship. They were armed with a cutlass and blunderbuss, "which," says the master, "I particularly requested might be put out of sight." But everything was perfectly quiet on the lower deck, and on going through the upper deck the only discovery made was a prisoner sitting by a lamp, manufacturing a draught-board, which he refused to part with. They left the deck quite quiet; yet at half-past three the whole place was in an uproar. A regular stand-up fight took place between two prisoners, Elgar and Blore, in which the former got his eyes blackened and face damaged in the most shameful manner. This Elgar was the man who gave information of the projected escape, thereby incurring the resentment of the rest. It is improbable, however, that any attempt was actually intended this time, though "escape" was in every mouth, and had been since the event of the previous Thursday.

Speaking of the hulks at this time, the governor says: "It is but too true that little if any discipline exists among the prisoners, and that the state of insubordination is extremely alarming. This may in a great degree be attributed to the lamentable state of idleness, the facility of communicating with each other, concerting and perpetrating mischief, and the inadequate means of punishment when contrasted with the hulks establishment."

Four days afterwards the master of the *Ethalion* hulk reports that the disorderly conduct of the convicts in the upper deck still continued; their language to their officers was always contemptuous and insolent; they seldom or ever did what they were told; and if put under restraint or in close confinement, they generally managed to tear down the bulkhead and smash everything in their reach. The women were not much better. When a draft of male prisoners going to the *Ethalion* passed the females' hulk, the whole of the women commenced to shout and yell, and wave handkerchiefs. They abused the deputy matron with choice invectives, and appeared quite beyond control.

But by this time news had come of the missing three.
At nine o'clock one night a person called at the Penitentiary and asked to see the governor in private. He was
shown into the office. " You had three prisoners escape
from Woolwich lately? One of them is my brother, Charles
Knight. I am very anxious he should be brought back.
What is the penalty for escaping?" He was informed,
also, that there was a charge of stealing from the steward's
store. Knight's brother said he would willingly pay the
damage of that, and wished to make conditions for the
fugitive if he was given up. The governor would not
promise beyond an assurance of speaking in Knight's
favour to the committee; and said all would depend upon
his making a full and candid disclosure of all the circumstances connected with the escape, and to give all the
information in his power which would lead to the arrest
of the other two. The visitor then observed that his
brother was very young, and by no means a hardened
offender; that he was led into this act and was sorry for it;
that none of his relations would harbour him, and that he
was quite ready to return. Next morning he was brought
back by his mother and brother, and gave immediately a
full account of the affair. The escape had been concerted
a full week before it was carried into effect, and had
been arranged entirely by Stevenson, who having been
employed in the store-room, had purloined a key, filed out
the wards and made a skeleton key, with which he opened
the hatches. The rope was made out of spun yarn, found
in the hold by Stevenson, who also got there the sledge-
hammer, chisel, and iron spikes. There was not a soul
moving or awake on the lower deck, and no one knew of
their intention to escape. They then got away in a boat,
just as had been surmised. On landing at the new ferry
on the Essex coast, they went across the chain pier, Payne
changing a shilling to pay the toll. This was all the money
they had amongst them, and had been conveyed to Payne
by some person in the ship. They then proceeded to London,
and were supplied with hats by a Jew named Wolff, living in
Somerset Street, Whitechapel, to whose house they were taken

by Stevenson. Afterwards they went to the West End. Payne separated from them in Waterloo Place, saying he meant to go to a brother living at Stratford-on-Avon. Stevenson then took Knight to his brother's (Stevenson's), a working jeweller, who gave them money to buy clothes. They hid together for the night in a house in George Street, St. Giles; and then Knight went home to his aunt's in Hanover Street, Long Acre, but was refused admittance. The same happened with all his other relatives, and at last he was compelled to give himself up in the manner described. Through information which he gave the others also were apprehended.

It was now found that there must be some superior authority resident on the spot. "The visits of the governor to these hulks," say the committee in their report of 6th March, 1824, "though frequent, were not sufficient to preserve order in the ships, and it was quite necessary to have a person, with the full authority of the governor to inflict punishment, resident on board one of these vessels; and there appearing to be no power in the committee under the existing Act of Parliament either to appoint a second governor, or to authorise any person not being governor to inflict punishment, it was arranged between the committee and Captain Chapman that he should resign the situation of governor for a time, in order that the office might be exercised by a person who should continually reside on board one of these vessels." Accordingly Captain Chapman resigned his appointment *pro tem.* into the hands of a Mr. Kellock, a hulk master from Sheerness, who was said to have had great experience. This was on the 14th December, 1823, on which date his Journal, from which I shall frequently quote, takes up the story. No improvement in conduct marked the change in rulers. On the 21st Mr. Kellock reports: "I heard this morning an extraordinary noise on the upper deck. In a moment I called the guards and went below. All was quiet, but on searching, I found a prisoner lying almost lifeless, who had been most unmercifully beaten by his fellows. I interrogated them, but could not find the parties concerned."

The numbers on board the several ships were in all 634.

They were not classified; the distinctions of the Penitentiary, as well as the dress, were done away with. All alike were clothed in a coarse brown suit. They were kept in divisions of seventy-five, with a wardsman in charge of each division; besides which, a number of well-conducted prisoners were appointed to keep watch during the night, who were to report any irregularity that might occur during the watch. There was no employment for the prisoners; the making of great coats was tried, but it did not succeed. There was no work to be got on shore, and it was doubtful whether these prisoners could be legally employed on shore. In fact the whole establishment was considered a sort of house of recovery, and all the prisoners were more or less under hospital treatment throughout. The general conduct of the prisoners was "unruly to a degree, and in some instances to the extent of mutiny." This is one case, reported in writing by the master of the *Ethalion:* "This morning, soon after the lower-deck prisoners were let up to wash themselves, three of them attempted to make their escape, by getting down the ship's side, and then into the waterman's boat, which was alongside without oars. Being observed by the guard, two returned, whilst one strove to make his escape. He was pursued by two turnkeys, who took him and brought him back, when he was placed in confinement. Shortly afterwards, this man and another, who had previously been in confinement, were liberated by their fellow-prisoners on the lower deck, by forcibly entering into the hold and making their way through the bulkhead which separates the dark cells from the hold. They have the prisoners now in their possession, and will not deliver them up. They continue to be in a state of mutiny." Mr. Kellock was immediately summoned to the scene. He found the prisoners ranged on the deck, with the two men in their possession, and peremptorily refusing to give them up. The guard of marines was then sent for from the shore, while the chaplain and surgeon remonstrated with the prisoners, pointing out the dreadful consequences certain to follow military interference. But they spoke to no purpose, and were about to leave the ship, unwilling to witness the shedding of blood, when a last effort was more successful. The two prisoners

were given up by the rest, who now expressed sorrow for
their atrocious conduct. Nothing, however, came of all this,
beyond general exhortation. The prisoners were all mustered
and harangued, but as they promised to behave better in
future, the affair passed over.

The state of affairs was shortly this: if on deck, the
prisoners hallooed and jeered at all boats or passing ships;
if below, they massed together, disobeyed all orders, openly
hissed their officers and pelted them with coals. The crowd-
ing was so great that it was almost impossible to single out
offenders. The ill-conducted were when practicable placed in
irons, but generally without effect. The bad became worse, not
better. The governor's Journal continues to tell the same tale:

"*December 29th.*—At three o'clock this afternoon, when
the prisoners from the upper deck went up for air, I went
below with two guards to search for articles which prisoners
were said to have concealed for purposes of escape. We had
not been there for a few moments when the prisoners on deck
lowered all the ports to prevent us from seeing anything."
(They had previously torn off the locks on the hatchway, and
pursued the governor below in a body. Upon this occasion
nails, chisels, cards and dice were found secreted.) "Two
such unexpected instances of cool and deliberate insolence,
contempt, and mutiny I have never witnessed. I immediately
applied for a military guard. Those concerned are probably
the youngest, or those who have least time to serve.

"*January 2nd,* 1824.—The conduct of the prisoners has
been very refractory on board the *Dromedary.* In one
instance they pressed so very close on the sentinel, and
were so very disorderly and in some instances so abusive,
that he was under the necessity of giving the worst of them
a stab with his bayonet." Those on deck now tried to
tear off the hatches, and called upon those below to come
up and attack the sentry, but without effect. Charles Moore,
one of the twenty-eight removed from the *Dromedary* to the
Ethalion, got into the lower deck after being told off for
the upper, and refused to quit it when ordered, running
in among the other prisoners, and hoping they would protect him.

About this time Mr. Kellock wrote to the committee as follows:

"GENTLEMEN,—Since you were pleased to appoint me to the governorship of prisoners on board the hospital ships I turned my whole attention to the care and management of them, and had, until a few days ago, some faint hopes, with some good effect; but the very recent disorderly conduct of the prisoners on board the *Dromedary* has in a great measure damped my hopes. . . . I have now been ten years among men of a similar description, and have always found the London prisoners and the younger the worst: they possess very bad principles connected with bad habits, and wherever they are they are a pest to all with whom they are connected. I shall not relax in any part of my duty, and hope to effect the aim in my appointment."

Several of the prisoners next day refused to come up on deck to get their hammocks down, declaring they were afraid of the soldiers. "I went myself," says the governor, "accompanied with a number of men; but they still refused to come up and be mustered quietly, complaining still of the soldiers. The soldiers were then ordered to stand to their arms; upon which the prisoners gave way.

"*January 5th.*—At 7.30 A.M. the waterman of the *Dromedary* was lying alongside in his wherry, and saw the wherry belonging to the *Ethalion* drifting past with the tide. Thinking the other waterman was in it, he cried out, 'Holloa, Joe, is that you?' 'Whist! Hold your tongue,' said the man in the boat; and on closer inspection he proved to be a prisoner, Henry Smijick by name, of the *Ethalion.* The waterman gave the alarm, and promptly giving chase captured the fugitive. The prisoners had broken open the hatchways and set Smijick loose, who got away unperceived. When Smijick was sent back the other prisoners again broke open the black holes and set him loose, nor would they give him up till a military guard had been fetched from the shore. . . . I am sorry to say the ships are not fitted by any means in a secure way. Men determined to escape could very easily at any time make their way through the partitions, although I do not conceive they are so much bent on escape as on insolence and refractory conduct.

"*9th.*—Mr. Parr, master of the *Ethalion*, reports that he is three prisoners short of his muster. At 4 A.M., as soon as it was daylight, he saw the waterman's boat on the opposite side of the river, a little above the *Ethalion*. The guards relieving at 4 A.M. noticed the boat was gone. Some bars were found removed from the after port on the lower deck, and through this place the prisoners had doubtless got out. Officers were sent at once in search. The opposite shore was looked at, as it was possible the men were lying up close. The prisoners were, however, traced as far as the toll bar; and as they had no money to pay the toll they gave the toll keeper a small pen-knife instead of coppers. No further tidings being received, a guard named Richard Armstrong, who was well acquainted with all the places of resort for thieves in London, was sent to town in search of the fugitives.

"*13th.*—Prisoners on board the *Ethalion* much unsettled still, and showing great disposition to attempt further escape.

"*14th.*—The prisoners on board the *Dromedary* continue to be orderly and quiet. . . . I am disposed to think they have made up their mind to behave themselves well in future. . . . I attribute it in some measure to the attention and advice of the Rev. Dr. Bennett, and themselves being employed at school, and the determination I have made in the case of any disorder to have a military guard on board, whom the prisoners seem to be afraid of.

"*17th.*—Guard Armstrong returned with prisoner Dickenson, one of those who escaped on the 9th, and who had been apprehended at St. Albans."

On the 23rd the governor reports the prisoners, with some few exceptions, to have conducted themselves with some degree of order. "I allow them on deck for air and exercise, from sunrising to sunset, with the exception of one hour for dinner and half-an-hour for breakfast. I allow them all the exercise on deck and below which

the nature of their situation will admit of. There is a great
want of more, to promote health and make them sleep
and be still at night. I am continually amongst them in
the day time, from ship to ship, inquiring into their conduct,
and adjusting differences when any—and such will, and
do too often occur, amongst people of such a description, without employment, well fed, and to all appearance
improving.

"It has been observed that they wear out or destroy more
clothes than formerly.

"24th.—Elias Thompson behaved in a most mutinous
and contemptuous manner, cutting up his jacket. On being
ordered below to fetch it he refused to go. When ordered
into confinement he made a grab at a warder's watch-chain,
pulled the watch out of his pocket, and nearly succeeded in
throwing it overboard.

"29th.—At two o'clock P.M., I came out from the cabin,
and asked for the waterman to get his boat ready to take
me to the *Ethalion*. I was told by Richard Armstrong that
the boat was not alongside. I asked where she was. He
told me off at the moorings. I desired Samuel McGill, the
guard, to call the guard in the jolly-boat, which was on
shore for the milk, to bring the wherry alongside. When he
went forward to call for the jolly-boat he saw her coming.
While he was calling for the boat, Richard Armstrong
said the boat belonging to the workmen of the dockyard
had broke adrift. I said to Armstrong, 'Are you sure the
prisoners have not taken her?' I had hardly done speaking,
when Samuel McGill, guard, called to me and said, 'Look;
see, there are three prisoners in the dockyard boat, landing.'
I immediately got a boat passing, and sent after them, and
ordered all the prisoners to muster, and found three absent;
Thomas Nannody, Jabez Pickering, and Robert Hunter."
Six guards were sent in chase, and within a couple of
hours two were brought back. This escape occurred entirely
through the negligence of the guards, one of whom had left
his post at the time.

"29th.—There seems to be an increase of impatience
amongst the prisoners, both male and female, and they aim

at stratagem to accomplish what they suppose cannot be done otherwise; and there seems to be in them (with everything that's bad) a disposition to reflect, and very improperly, on their officers and guards; and always bringing forward their past sufferings, and holding out that their impaired constitutions will never be recovered; and on such they ground their hopes of success for mitigation of punishment, or to shorten their term of imprisonment. I am aware that gratitude is no part of their composition, and that they have been and are now very much indulged.

"*February 5th.*—At ten o'clock this morning, when passing the *Ethalion* in the wherry, I heard an unusual noise, and saw all the prisoners from the lower deck in the gangway on the main deck, and saw some rags thrown out of one of the lower deck ports; then saw one of the lower deck ports lowered down, and then all, and in another moment all the upper deck. . . . It appeared on inquiry that the officers were searching the lower deck, and the prisoners took this means of preventing their seeing anything. When the chief culprit was discovered, and was about to be confined, he assaulted an officer, and the others attempted to rescue him."

On the 6th the governor reports an increase of murmuring and dissatisfaction among the prisoners; and they pretended to feel an increase of bowel complaint, which was clearly assumed, as was proved by their manner, activity, and general appearance. "Their aim is by such means to obtain their liberty. I never experienced so much insolence and contempt as some of them from time to time evince. . . . The waste of clothes is three times more than when in the Penitentiary. Caps are lost or thrown overboard in great numbers, clothes destroyed by romping on deck and below with one another.

"*12th.*—So very wicked and wildly disposed are some of them at times, that I am under the necessity, when the hatches are unlocked, to have the hatch bar and the locks brought up to the quarter-deck, as, if left, they would certainly be thrown overboard." The bell had to be unhung always, as it was within their reach and " in danger of a watery grave."

"*16th.*—On going to the upper deck of the *Ethalion*, I saw a party of prisoners at a table with cards. They were

well executed (the cards), of writing-paper. I had a wish to
know what the inside was made of, and when examined, to my
astonishment found it was principally of Prayer-books cut to
pieces.

"18*th*.—An attempt was made by a body of prisoners to
rescue Anthony Beacham from the dark cell, and with this in
view had forced the lock of the hatchway leading there. They
were discovered in time, and retreated *en masse*. It was too
evident that two were the ringleaders, and these they refused
to give up. Mr. Goodfellow, the master, was desired to go
down with two guards, and bring them up instantly, still
without success. All the guards were then armed, and the
governor himself went down and captured the offenders,
carrying them off to the dark cells.

"As soon as we were gone up, the whole of the deck
—eighty-five prisoners—behaved in the most mutinous
manner, and unshipped the ladder to prevent our getting
into the deck that way. Some part of them broke open
a part of the hatchway, which prevents communication
between the upper deck and the after part of the lower
deck; another part of them made the attempt to break
down the bulkhead which divides the fore part of the lower
deck from the after part. They at the same time secured the
door on the after part of the deck which is intended for the
guards to go in at in the event of any disorder amongst them.
During this time I was apprehensive all the decks would be
thrown into one. I immediately sent to the office of the guards
at the dockyard for a guard of marines, which came in a few
minutes. When the guards came they were put in charge of
the deck, and then we proceeded to force our way with
our own guards to the lower deck aft. We found no
access there in the regular way by the hatchway or the door
aft; the ladder being unshipped and the door secured. I
ordered a blunderbuss without shot to be fired down the
hatchway to clear a way, and then made an attempt to ship
the ladder, but could not, they had got it so well secured; nor
could we get into the deck that way. I then had recourse to
the door aft, and was obliged to use the saw, axe, and crowbar
before I could force it open, and get into the deck amongst

them. With the assistance of the officers and guards, I selected some of the ringleaders, seven in number, and put them into the disorderly ward on bread and water, and ironed them on both legs. They continued disorderly. . . . When I visited the deck the whole of the prisoners were in a very great perspiration from the great exertions they had been making to force the bulkheads.

"*20th.*—The whole of the prisoners are evidently getting better in many respects. They came forward in a body this morning on behalf of their fellow-prisoners, acknowledging their own improper conduct, and promising to behave better in future."

For a time, indeed, the conduct of all improved. They were in hopes that they were about to get some remission of their sentences, and feared lest misconduct should militate against their release. "The whole are in full expectation that something will be done for them by Parliament, in consequence of their very great sufferings." The tenor of all their letters to their friends was to the same effect. They were, however, doomed to disappointment; for on the 14th April, Mr. Kellock states: "This morning I received information that the bill for the labour and removal of the male convicts under the Penitentiary rules, and at present on board the prison ships, had received the Royal assent. When informed that they were to be removed to labour at the hulks, they received the news with some degree of surprise and astonishment." But the same day the exodus took place, and they are reported to have gone away "very quietly and resigned."

THE INNER GATE.

CHAPTER VI.

THE PENITENTIARY RE-OCCUPIED.

No pains were spared to make the Penitentiary sweet and fit for re-occupation. A Parliamentary Committee—that great panacea for all public ills—had however already reported favourably upon the place. They had declared that no case of local unhealthiness could be made out against it; nor had they been able to find "anything in the spot on which the Penitentiary is situated, nor in the construction of the building itself, nor in the moral and physical treatment of the prisoners confined therein, to injure health or render them peculiarly liable to disease."

Yet to guard against all danger of relapse, they advised that none of the old hands should return to the prison, and recommended also certain external and internal improvements. Better ventilation was needed; to obtain this they called in Sir Humphrey Davy, and gave him *carte blanche* to carry out any alterations. Complete fumigation was also necessary; and this was effected with chlorine, under the supervision of a Mr. Faraday from the Royal Institution. To render innocuous the dirty ditch of stagnant water—dignified with the name of moat—which surrounded the buildings just within the boundary wall, it was connected with the Thames and its tides. Additional stoves were placed in the several pentagons, and the dietary reorganised on a full and nutritive scale, in quality and quantity equal to that in force before the epidemic. Provision was also made to secure plenty of hard labour exercise for the prisoners daily, by increasing the number of crank mills and water machines in the yards. More schooling was also recommended, as a profitable method of employing hours otherwise lost, and breaking in on the monotony and dreariness of the long dark nights. The cells, the committee thought too, should be lighted with candles, and books supplied " of a kind to combine rational amusement with moral and religious instruction." Indeed there was no limit to the benevolence of these commissioners. Adverting to the testimony of the medical men they had examined, who were agreed that cheerfulness and innocent recreation were conducive to health, they submitted for consideration, whether some kind of games or sports might not be permitted in the prison during a portion of the day. Fives-courts and skittle-alleys were probably in their minds, with cricket in the garden, or football during the winter weather. As one reads all this, one is tempted to ask whether the objects of so much tender solicitude were really convicted felons sentenced to imprisonment for serious crimes. Thus comfortably lodged and warmly clad, fed with so much wasteful luxury that daintiness soon supervened, their every want thus tenderly forestalled—the condition, but for one drawback, of these rogues was far superior to that of soldiers or sailors, or the honest poor who had done no wrong; that drawback was the loss of liberty, yet many would have

cheerfully sacrificed it for the ease and comfort of the
Penitentiary.

It must not, however, be forgotten that the inmates of
Millbank were people specially selected as capable of reformation. Whatever we may have come to think of the efficacy
of the power of persuasion to reform the criminal classes, it
was thoroughly believed in then. A modern writer who has
had much experience, says it is easier to tame a wolf into a
house dog, than make a thief into an honest man.* They
were more hopeful at the beginning of this century; probably
because the experiment was still new, and barely tried. It
was confidently expected then, that a year or two in Millbank
would cure the most confirmed criminal. Of the realisation
of such hopes, or their failure, I shall have to speak in a later
chapter. To give the system of the Penitentiary, then, every
chance of success, the most hopeful material only was committed to it, drawn from the following classes: 1. Young
persons; 2. Adults of both sexes convicted of first offences;
3. Persons "who from early habits and good character, or
from having friends or relations to receive them at their discharge, afford reasonable hope of their being restored to society
corrected and reclaimed by the punishment they had undergone." What kind of punishment it was, and how these
precious subjects bore it, we shall soon have abundant opportunity of observing.

The rule of Governor Chapman was essentially considerate
and mild. There was no limit to his long-suffering and
patience. Though by all the habits of his early life he must
have learnt to look at breaches of discipline with no lenient
eye, we shall find that he never punished even the most
insubordinate and contumacious of the ruffians committed to
his charge till he had first exhausted every method of exhortation or reproof; and when he had punished he was ever
ready to forgive, on a promise of future amendment, or even a
mere hypocritical expression of contrition alone. It is now
generally admitted that felons cooped up within four walls can
be kept in bounds only under an iron hand. Captain Chapman
acted otherwise; the committee which controlled him fully

* Convicts. By a Practical Hand.

endorsing his views. For a long time to come the prison was like a bear garden; misconduct was rife in every shape and form, increasing daily in virulence, till at length the place might have been likened to Pandemonium let loose. Then more stringent measures were enforced, with satisfactory results, as we shall see; but for many years there was that continuous warfare between ruffianism and constituted authority which is inevitable when the latter is tinged with weakness or irresolution.

Feigned suicides were among the earliest methods of annoyance. It is not easy to explain exactly what end the prisoners had in view, but doubtless they hoped to enlist the sympathies of their kind-hearted guardians, by exhibiting a recklessness of life. Those who preferred death to continued imprisonment must indeed be miserably unhappy, calling for increased tenderness and anxious attention. They must be talked to, petted, patted on the back, and taken into the infirmary, to be regaled with dainties, and suffered to lie there in idleness for weeks. So whenever any prisoner was thwarted or out of temper, often indeed without rhyme or reason, and whenever the fancy seized him, he tied himself up at once to his loom, or laid hands upon his throat with his dinner-knife or a bit of broken glass. Of course their last idea was to succeed. They took the greatest pains to ensure their own safety, and these were often ludicrously apparent; but now and then, though rarely, they failed of their object, and the wretched victim suffered by mistake. Happily the actually fatal cases were few and far between.

This fashion of attempting suicide was led by a certain William Major, who arrived from Newgate on the 8th October, 1824. A few days afterwards he confided to the surgeon that he was determined to make away with himself; "that, or murder some one here; for I'd sooner be hanged like a dog than stay in the Penitentiary." Such terrible desperation called of course for immediate expostulation, and Captain Chapman proceeded at once to Major's cell. The prisoner's knife and scissors were first removed; then the governor spoke to him. Major replied sullenly;

adding, "I've made up my mind: I'd do anything to get
out of this place; kill myself or you. I'd sooner go to the
gallows than stay here." "I reasoned with him," says Captain Chapman in his Journal, "for a length of time on the
wickedness of such shocking expressions; telling him there
was only one way of shortening his time, and that was by
good conduct. I told him his threats were those of a silly
lad, which I should however punish him for." So Major
was carried off to a dark cell, but not before the governor
had said all he could "think of, to reason him out of his
evil frame of mind." He remained in the dark two days,
and then, having expressed himself penitent and promising
faithfully better behaviour, he was released. For three
weeks nothing further occurred, and then, "Suddenly," says
the governor, "as I was passing through a neighbouring
ward, a turnkey called to me, 'Here, here, governor! bring
a knife. Major has hanged himself.'" He had made himself
fast to the cross-beam of his loom. The action of his
heart had not however ceased, though the circulation was
languid and his extremities cold. He was removed at
once to the infirmary, and as soon as animation was
restored, the governor returned to the prisoner's cell, and
then found that "the hammock lashing was made fast in
two places to the cross beam from the loom to the wall;
in one was a long loop, in which Major had placed his feet;
in the other a noose, as far distant from the loop as the
length of the beam would permit, in which he had put his
head; a portion of the rope between noose and loop he had
held in his hand." It was quite clear, therefore, that he
had no determined intention of committing suicide; besides
which he had chosen his time just as the turnkey was about
to visit him, and he had eaten his supper, "which," says the
governor, "was no indication of despair." Major soon
recovered, and pretended to be sincerely ashamed of his
wicked behaviour.

Not long afterwards a man, Combe, in the refractory cell,
tries to hang himself with a pockethandkerchief. Placing his
bedstead against the wall, he had used it as a ladder to climb
up to the grating of the ventilator in the ceiling of his cell.

To this he had made fast the handkerchief, then dropped; but he was found standing calmly by the bed, with the noose not even tight. Next a woman, Catherine Roper, tries the same trick, and is found lying full length on the floor. She was found to be quite uninjured too. Next, however, comes a real affair; and from the hour at which the act is perpetrated all doubt of intention is unhappily impossible. Lewis Abrahams, a gloomy, ill-tempered man, is punished for breaking a fly-shuttle; again for calling his warder a liar. That night he hangs himself. He is found quite dead and cold, partly extended on the stone floor, and partly reclining as it were against the cell wall. He had suspended himself by the slight nettles (small cords) of his hammock, which had broken by his weight. The prisoner in the next cell reported that between one and two in the morniug he had heard a noise of some one kicking against the wall; and then no doubt the deed was done.

After this unhappy example attempts rapidly multiplied, though happily none were otherwise than feigned. One tries the iron grating and a piece of cord; another uses his cell block as a drop, but is careful to retain the halter in his hands; a third, Moses Josephs, tries to cut his throat, but on examination nothing but a slight reddish scratch is found, which the doctor was convinced was done by the back of the knife. In all these cases immediate and anxious attention is given by all the officials of the Penitentiary. The governor himself, who never gave himself an hour's relaxation, and was always close at hand, was generally the first on the scene of suicide. If there was but a hint of anything wrong he was ready to spend hours with the intending *felo-de-se*. Thus in Metzer's—a fresh case: a man who would not eat, was idle too, morose and sullen, "though spoken to always in the kindest manner." No sooner was it known that he was brooding over the length of his confinement—his was a life sentence—and had hinted at suicide, than the governor spent hours with him in exhortation. Metzer, being a weaver by trade, had been placed in a cell furnished with a loom; from this he was to be changed immediately to another, lest the beam should be a temptation to him; but the governor, being uneasy, first visited him again, and found him, though late at night, in his clothes perambulating his cell. On this his neighbour was set to watch him for the rest of the night, and the doctor gave him a composing draught. Next morning, when they told him he was to leave his cell for good, he became outrageously violent, and assaulted every one around. He was now taken forcibly to the infirmary, and put in a strait-waistcoat; whereupon he grew calmer and promised to go to his new cell, provided he was allowed to take his own hammock with him. It struck the governor at once that something might be concealed in it, and it was searched minutely. Inside the bedclothes they found a couple of yards of hammock lashing, one end of which was made into a noose, "leaving," the governor remarks, "little doubt of his intention."

But to meet and frustrate these repeated attempts at suicide were by no means the governor's only trials. The misconduct of many other prisoners must have made his life a burthen to him. Thefts were frequent; these fellows' fingers itched to lay their hands on all that came in their way. The tower wardsman—a prisoner in a place of trust—steals his warder's rations; others filch knives, metal buttons, bath brick, and food from one another. Then there was much wasteful destruction of materials, with idleness and careless-ness at the looms, aggravated often by the misappropriation of time by the manufacture of trumpery articles for their own wear; one makes himself a pair of green gaiters, another a pair of cloth shoes, a third an imitation watch of curled hair, rolled into a ball, which hangs in his fob by a strip of calico for guard.

These were doubtless offences of a trivial character. The anxiety evinced by many to escape from durance was a much more serious affair. I shall have occasion further on to recount more than one instance of the surprising ingenuity and unwearied patience with which prisoners sought to compass this, the great aim and object of all who are not free. As yet, however, the efforts made were tentative only and incomplete. To break a hole in the wall, or manufacture false keys, was the highest flight of their inventive genius, and the

plot seldom went very far. One of the first cases was discovered quite by chance. On searching a prisoner's cell, some
screws, a few nails, and two pieces of thick iron wire were
found concealed in his loom; and in one of his shoes as it
hung upon the wall, a piece of lead shaped so as to correspond
with the wards of a cell key. This the prisoner confessed he
had made with his knife from memory, and altogether without
a pattern. " I have a very nice eye," he said, " and I have
always carefully observed the keys as I saw them in the
officers' hands." " And what did you mean to do with the
key ? " he was further asked. " To get away, of course."
" How ? " " I can open the wooden door when I please, and
then I should have unlocked my gate."* On examination a
hole was found in his door, just below the bolt and opposite
the handle; through this, by means of a narrow piece of wood,
a knitting needle in fact, he could move back the bolt whenever he pleased. Once out in the ward, he meant, with a file
he had also secreted, to get through the bars of the passage
window. The wards of this key were fastened into a wooden
handle, which was also found in his cell. Another prisoner,
having been allowed to possess himself of a large spike nail,
which had been negligently left about in the yard, worked all
night at the wall of his cell, and soon succeeded in removing
several bricks. The hole he made was large enough to allow
him passage. Besides this, from the military great coats, on
which he was stitching during the day, he had made himself
a coat and trousers. He might have actually got away
had not a warder visited his cell to inspect his work, and
taking up the great coats as they lay in a heap in the corner,
discovered the disguise beneath, also the spike nail, and the
rubbish of bricks and mortar from the hole. More adven-
turous still, a third prisoner proposed to escape by stealing
his warder's keys. Failing an opportunity, he too turned his
attention to making false ones; and for the purpose cut up
with scissors his pewter drinking can into bits. By holding
the pieces near the hot irons he used for his tailoring, he

* Every cell at Millbank has two doors: one of wood, next the
prisoner, the other a heavy iron trellis gate. The former is closed by a
running bolt; the gate has a double lock.

H

melted the metal and ran it into a mould of bread. Information of this project was given by another prisoner in
time to nip it in the bud. Another, again, had been clever
enough to remove a number of bricks, and would have passed
undetected, had not the governor by chance, when in his cell,
touched the wall and found it damp. A closer inspection
showed that the mortar around the bricks had been picked
out, and the joints filled in by a mixture of pounded mortar
and chewed bread. On the outside was laid a coating of
whiting, such as was issued to the prisoners to help them in
cleaning their cans.

In some mischief of this kind, one or other of the prisoners
was perpetually engaged. Cutting up their sheets to fabri-
cate disguises; melting the metal buttons, as the man just
mentioned had melted his pewter can; laying hold of files,
rasps, old nails, scissors, tin, copper wire, or whatever else
came handy; and working always with so much secrecy and
despatch, that their plans were discovered more by fortune
generally, than good management. In those days the best
methods of prison discipline were far from matured. We
know now that the surest preventives against escape are
repeated and unexpected searchings, with continuous vigilant
supervision. A prisoner to carry out his schemes must have
leisure, and must be left to himself to work unperceived. By
the practice of the Penitentiary, prisoners had every facility
to escape; and we shall find ere long, that they knew how to
make the most of their advantages. For the present, all the
good luck was on the side of the gaolers.

But at this juncture a new trouble threatened all the
peace and comfort of the place. The prisoners seem to have
grown all at once alive to the power they possessed of combination. It had been suspected for some time that a
conspiracy was in progress among the denizens of D Ward,
Pentagon 2, and a minute search of the several cells brought
to light a number of clandestine communications. These,
written mostly on the blank pages of Prayer-books, and spare
copy-book leaves, were all to the same effect: exhortations to
riot and mutiny. A certain George Vigers was the prime
mover; all the letters, which were very widely disseminated,

having issued from his pen. It had long been openly discussed among the prisoners that the hulks were pleasanter
places than the Penitentiary. Here, then, was an opportunity
of removal. All who joined heartily in the projected com-
motion would draw upon themselves the ire of the committee,
and would certainly be drafted to the hulks.

To explain what might otherwise appear unintelligible, it
must be mentioned here, that the punishment implied by a
sentence to the hulks was by no means of a terrifying
character. A year or two later, the report of the Parliamentary Committee on Secondary Punishments* laid bare the
system, and expressed their unqualified disapprobation of the
whole treatment of convicts on board the hulks. It being
accepted that the separation of criminals, and their severe
punishment, are necessary to make crime a terror to the evil
doer, the committee pointed out that in both these respects
the system of management of the hulks was not only necessarily deficient, but actually inimical. "All that has been
said of the miserable effects of the association of criminals in
the prisons on shore, the profaneness, the vice, the demoralisation that are its inevitable consequences, applies in the
fullest sense" to the hulks. The numbers in each ship vary
from eighty to eight hundred. The ships are divided into
wards of from twelve to thirty persons; in these they are
confined when not at labour in the dockyard, and the evil
consequences of such associations may easily be conceived,
even were the strictest discipline enforced. But this was far
from being the case. "The convicts after being shut up for
the night are allowed to have lights between decks, in some
ships as late as ten o'clock; although against the rules of the
establishment, they are permitted the use of musical instruments; flash songs, dancing, fighting, and gaming take place;
the old offenders are in the habit of robbing the new comers;
newspapers and improper books are clandestinely introduced;
a communication is frequently kept up with their old associates
on shore; and occasionally spirits are introduced on board.
It is true that the greater part of these practices are against
the rules of the establishment; but their existence in defiance

* 1832.

of such rules shows an inherent defect in the system. But the
indulgence of purchasing tea, bread, tobacco, etc., is allowed,
the latter with a view to the health of the prisoners; the
convicts are also allowed to receive visits from their friends,
and during the time they remain, are excused working, sometimes for several days. Such communications can only have
the worst effect. It is an improper indulgence to people in
the position of a convict, and keeps up a dangerous and improper intercourse with old companions. The most assiduous
attention on the part of the ministers of religion would be
insufficient to stem the torrent of corruption flowing from
these various and abundant sources; and but little attention
is paid to the promotion of religious feelings, or to the improvements of the morals of the convicts." It was plainly
seen that the convicts were also allowed to earn too much
money—threepence a day to convicts in the first class, three
halfpence to second; out of which the first got sixpence a
week, and the latter threepence, to lay out in the purchase of
tea, tobacco, etc., and the remainder was laid by to be given
to them on their release. They were supposed to work during
the day at the arsenals and dockyards, "but there was
nothing in the nature or severity of their employment which
deserves the name of punishment or hard labour." The work
lasted from eight to ten hours, according to season; but so
much time was lost in musters, and going to and from labour,
that the summer period was only eight hours and three
quarters, and winter six and a half. As common labourers
work ten hours, and when at task work or during harvest
much longer, the convicts could hardly be said to do
more than was just sufficient to keep them in health and
exercise; indeed, their situation "cannot be considered penal;
it is a state of restriction, but hardly of punishment."

Thus the committee described that the criminal sentenced
to transportation for crimes to which the law affixes the
penalty of death, passed his time, well fed, well clothed,
indulging in riotous enjoyment by night, with moderate
labour by day. No wonder that confinement on the hulks
failed to excite a proper feeling of terror in the minds of
those likely to come under its operation. The hulks were

indeed not dreaded ; prisoners describe their life in them as a "pretty jolly life." If any convict could but overcome the sense of shame which the degradation of his position might evoke, he would feel himself to be better off than large numbers of the working-classes, who have nothing but their daily labour to depend on for subsistence. At the dockyards, among the free men the situation of a convict was looked upon with envy; and "many labourers would be glad to change places with him, and would be much better off than they were before." *

It was not strange, then, that the discontented denizens of the Penitentiary found even the moderate rigour of that establishment too irksome, and that they were eager to be transferred to the hulks.

Towards the end of September, 1826, came the first indications of disturbance. A prisoner having smashed his bedstead, demolishes also the iron grating to his window, and thrust through it his handkerchief, tied to a stick, shouting and hallooing the while loud enough to be heard in Surrey. The same day, Hussey, another notorious offender, returning from confinement in the dark, is given a pail of water to wash his cell out, but instead, discharges the whole contents over his warder's head. Before he could be secured he had destroyed everything in his cell, and had thrown the pieces out of the window. Next, a number of prisoners during the night take to rolling their cell-blocks and rattling their tables about. By this time the dark cells have many occupants, who spend the night in singing, dancing, and shouting to each other.

Early next morning, about 5 A.M., in this same ward from which all the rioters came, Stephen Harman breaks everything he can lay hands on—the window-frame and all its panes of glass, his cell table, stool, shelf, trencher, salt-box, spoon, drinking-cup, and all his cell furniture. He had first barricaded his door, and could not be secured till all the mischief was done. Later in the day from another cell comes a long low whistle, followed by the crash of broken glass. The culprit here, when seized, confessed he had been persuaded by others ; all were to join after dinner, the whistle being the

* Evidence of Mr. Long, master shipwright of Woolwich dockyard.

signal to commence. The governor is now really apprehensive, anticipating something of a serious nature. He has
a strong force of spare warders and patrols posted in the
tower of the pentagon; but though the whistle* is frequently
heard during the night, nothing occurs further till next day,
at half-past eight, when George Vigers and another follow
Harman's lead and destroy everything in their cells. They
join their companions in the dark cells, all of whom, being
outrageously violent, are now in handcuffs. In the dark they
continued their misconduct; using the most shocking and
revolting language to all officials who approach them; assaulting them, deluging them with dirty water, resolutely refusing
to give up their beds, and breaking locks, door panels, and
windows, though they were restrained in irons, as we know.
These handcuffs having failed to produce any salutary effect,
they were now removed; though several of the prisoners did
not wait for that, and had ridded themselves of their bracelets.
For the next few days "the Dark," as these underground
cells were styled in official language, continued to be the scene
of the most unseemly uproar. When Archdeacon Potts, one
of the committee, visited it he was received with hoots and
yells; and this noise was kept up incessantly day and night.
But at length, after nearly a fortnight of close confinement,
the strength of the rioters broke down, and several of them
were removed to hospital, while the others went back to their
cells. But there was no lack of reinforcements: fresh
offenders took up the game, and the dark cells were continually full. As soon as those first punished were sufficiently
recovered they broke out again. The cases of misconduct
being generally of the same description, varied now and then
by a plot to break the water-mill by whirling round the
cranks too fast, continuous noise, insolence, dancing defiantly
the double shuffle, attempts to incite a whole ward, when in
the corridor at school, to rise against their warders, overpower
them, and take possession of their keys.

Throughout the long nights of the dreary winter months
these disturbances continued. A time of the utmost anxiety
and annoyance to worthy Captain Chapman, who was invariably the foremost in the fray. Nothing can exceed the

---

* Known as the "thieves' whistle."

pluck and energy with which he tackled the most truculent.
When a prisoner, mad with rage, dares any man to enter his
cell, it is Governor Chapman who always enters without a
moment's hesitation; when another, armed with a sleeveboard,* threatens to dash out everybody's brains, it is Captain
Chapman who secures the weapon of offence; when a body of
prisoners on the mill break out into open mutiny, and the
warder in charge is in terror for his personal safety, it is
Governor Chapman who repairs at once to the spot and collars
the ringleaders. Perhaps it would have been better if so
much resolute courage had not been tempered with too much
kindness of heart. No one can read of Captain Chapman's
proceedings without admitting that he was brave; but for his
particular duties he was undoubtedly also amiable to a
fault. Had he been more unrelenting it is probable that the
worst offenders would never have gone such lengths in their
insubordination. A word or two of contrition, often the
merest sham, was sufficient generally to secure his pardon.
Thus when a man has worked himself into a fury and appears
ready for any act of desperation, the mere appearance of the
governor calms him, and the prisoner, softened, says, " You,
sir, use me much better than I deserve. Put me in the dark."
" I left him," says Captain Chapman, " saying I trusted
my lenity would have a much better effect than a dark cell.
I therefore admonished and pardoned him." Had such kindness been productive of good results no one could have
questioned its wisdom. But it almost invariably was worse
than futile, and the recipients of it soon were worse than ever.

It was in this winter that the superintending committee
became convinced that the methods of coercion they possessed
were hardly so stringent as the case required. They report to
the House of Commons† that " there are among the prisoners
some profligate and turbulent characters for whose outrageous
conduct the punishments in use under the rules and regulations
of the Penitentiary are by no means sufficient." They have
found by experience that " confinement in a dark cell, though
in most cases a severe and efficacious punishment, operates
very differently on different persons. It appears to lose much

* Used in tailoring.
† Report of the Penitentiary Committee, 1827.

of its effect from repetition; it cannot always be carried far
without the danger of injuring health; and on some men, as
well as boys, it has no effect." Many of the ringleaders in the
disturbances we have just described were subjected to twenty-
five, twenty-eight, even thirty days of uninterrupted imprisonment in the dark, and certainly with little effect. In view of
this want of some more salutary punishment the committee
expressed a wish for power to flog. They were convinced
that "the framers of the statute under which the Penitentiary is now governed acted erroneously in omitting the
power to inflict corporal punishment when they re-enacted
most of the other provisions of the 19th Geo. III.* And they
are satisfied that a revival of this power (a power possessed in
every other criminal prison in this country) would be highly
advantageous to the management of this prison, provided such
power were accompanied by regulations adequate to control
the exercise of it, and to guard against its being abused."

Soon after these lines were in print, and presented to the
House, it became more than ever apparent that to tame these
turbulent characters some serious steps must be taken soon.
During the early months of 1827 there had been no cessation
of misconduct of the kind already described, but the cases
were mostly isolated, and generally succumbed to treatment.
But as March began a storm gathered which soon burst like a
whirlwind on the place. It was heralded by a riot in chapel
on Sunday, the 3rd March. Previous to the sermon, during
evening service, a rumbling noise was heard, as if the prisoners
assembled were stamping in unison with their feet. The
sound ceased with the singing of the psalm, and recommenced
during the sermon, and increased in violence. It was discovered
that the noise was made by the prisoners knocking with their
fists against the sheet iron that separated the several divisions.
As the uproar continued to increase to a shameful and alarming extent, the governor left the chapel to fetch the patrols,
and other spare officers, all of whom, with drawn cutlasses,
were posted near the chapel door. The prisoners were then
removed to their cells, and, in the presence of this exhibition
of force, they went quietly enough. The ringleaders were

* The Act passed to introduce the Penitentiary system.

afterwards singled out and punished : the chief among them being a monitor, long remarkable for his piety, who on this occasion had distinguished himself by mimicking the chaplain, and commenting in scandalous terms upon the sermon, and using slang expressions instead of responses.

After this, in all parts of the prison there were strong symptoms of mutiny. Loud shouts, laughter, and the thieves' whistle on every side. For the next few days there is much uneasiness; and at length, about midnight on the 8th, the governor is roused from his bed. Pentagon 6 is in an uproar. As Captain Chapman hurries to the scene he is saluted with the crash of glass, interspersed with loud cries of triumph and of encouragement. The airing-yard below is strewed with fragments; broken window-frames, fragments of glass, utensils, and tables smashed to bits. Two notorious offenders in B Ward, Hawkins and John Caswell, are busy at the work of destruction, and already everything is in ruins. The tumult is so tremendous, so many others contribute their shouts, and the thieves' whistle runs so quickly from cell to cell, that sleep is impossible to anyone within the boundary wall; and presently all officials, chaplain, doctor, manufacturers, and steward, have joined the governor, and are helping to quell the disturbance. It is quelled, but hardly has the governor got back to bed, at two in the morning, when the uproar recommences: the same noise and loud shouts from one side of the pentagons of prisoners, inciting each other to continue the riot. Next day, from various other wards, came reports that a spirit of insubordination is on the increase; and the offenders in the dark, ten in number, are violent in the extreme. Again, at midnight, the governor is aroused by a tremendous yelling from Pentagon 6, followed by the smashing of glass. The offenders were seized at once, and, remarks the governor, "from what I could learn, were pretty roughly handled by their captors." During this night, too, " in noise and violence the several prisoners in the dark exceeded, if possible, their accustomed mutinous conduct." One, by some extraordinary effort, broke the part of his door to which the lock was attached, and got it into his cell, swearing he would brain the first person who approached him.

There was much answering to and from the dark cells, and
the upper storeys of the pentagons opposite. There was
evidently discontent also in other parts of the prison. Those
prisoners who had no hopes of gaining any remission of their
sentences, having no inducement to behave well, were on the
point of insurrection. In addition to these alarms, on the
night of the 14th it was reported to the governor that the
prisoners were making their escape from the dark cells.
"The noise was so tremendous it could be heard all over the
prison."

And now mysterious documents emanating from the
prisoners are picked up, containing complaints mostly of the
treatment they receive, and full of terrible threats. As time
passed, the worst of these threats found vent in the hanging
of the infirmary warder's cat. The halter was a strip of
round towel from behind the door, and a piece of paper was
affixed to it, with these portentous words :

> "you see yor Cat is hung And
> you Have Been the corse of it
> for yoor Bad Bavior to Those
> arond you. Dom yor eis, yoo'l
> get pade in yor torn yet."

Next were several closely written sheets, full of inflamma-
tory matter, which give the authorities so much uneasiness
that several hundred prisoners are closely examined as to
their contents. As these letters afford curious evidence of the
importance prisoners arrogated to themselves, it may be interesting to publish one *in extenso*. It was found on the road
back from chapel. There was no signature to it.

"SIR,—Four instances of brutality have occurred in this
Establishment within the last week ; the which we, as men
(if we do our duty towards God and man), cannot let escape
our notice, and hope and trust you will not let them pass
without taking them into your serious consideration. We
will take the liberty of putting a few questions to you, which
we hope you will not be offended at. Who gave Mr. Bulmer
authority to strike a lad named Quick almost sufficient to have
broken his arm, indeed so bad that the lad could not lift his

hand to his head? and who gave Mr. Pilling the same authority to smite a lad to the ground, named Caswell, with a ruler,
the same as a butcher would a Bullock, without him (Caswell)
making the least resistance?   On Saturday night last there
was brutal and outrageous doings, Mr. Pilling as desperate as
ever, assisted by that villian Turner (we cannot give him a
better term—we wish we could).   Who would have thought a
man could have been so cruel as to lift a poker against a fellow-
creature?   A ruler, we have heard, was broken into two
pieces, a thing that is made of the hardest of wood.   Was
there ever, in the annals of treachery and oppression, facts
more scandalous than these!   No.   To hear their cries was
sufficient to make the blood run cold of any man, if he was
possessed of the least animal feeling ('For God's sake have
compassion, and do not quite kill me,' etc., etc.).   And we do
not hesitate to say, had not the wise Creator, that sees and
hears all, put it into the heart of a man to be there and stop
them in their bloody actions, homicide would have been committed: then God knows what would have been the result.
We will admit that these men committed themselves in the
most provoking manner; but still, who are, what are these
men, that they should take the law into their own hands?
You are the person they should have applied to, and we are
satisfied you would not have given them such authority.
Many men have committed as bad, or worse crimes than either
of these, and in less than one minute afterwards have been
sorry for it.   How did these men know but this was the case
here? but without speaking to them, as Christians would do,
knocks them down, as we have stated before, as a Butcher
would do an Ox—we cannot make a better comparison—Messrs.
Pilling and Turner in particular.   The governor, too, who
professes to fear God, we think if he would study the great
and principal commandment, that is, to do to others as he
would be done unto, it would be much more to his credit;
especially, sir, as you and other gentlemen of this establishment expect when there is a discharge of prisoners (and it is
to be hoped that soon will be the case) that they will give the
establishment a good name.   They cannot do it, unless there
is a stop put to such brutal actions; they will most likely

speak the sentiments of their hearts; they will say they have
seen some of their fellow-creatures driven like wrecks before
the rough tide of power till there was no hold left to save
them from destruction. That will be a pretty thing for the
public to hear. And, sir, we do not wish to be too severe,
but unless Pilling and Turner are dismissed from the Establishment, and that shortly, we will fight as long as there is a
drop of blood in us; for it is evident, many men have expired
from a much lighter blow than either of those received;
therefore necessity obliges us—we must do it for our own
safety; but depend upon it, sir, it is far from our wish to do
anything of the kind, for your sake, and for the sake of what
few good ones we have (and God knows it is but few). There
is 3 good men in the Pentagon—Messrs. Newstead, Rutter,
and Hall, and we wish we could speak well of the others—
but we cannot.

"N.B. We do not wish to give the last new warder a bad
name, for we have not seen sufficient of him to speak either
way, but what little we have seen leads us to believe he is a
good man. We hope, sir, you will excuse us, but we will ask
you another question. If you were in Mr. Pilling's situation,
and a man committed himself, would you not reason with him
on the base impropriety of what he had done? We know you
would. Instead of that, Mr. Pilling takes a delight in aggravating the cause with a grin, or a jeer of contempt, not only
before you see him (the prisoner), afterwards the same; which,
without the least doubt, makes a man commit acts of violence
which at other times he would tremble at the idea. We hope,
sir, you will take this into your worthy and serious consideration, and by so doing you will greatly oblige,

"Your obedient humble Servants,
"FRIENDS TO THE OPPRESSED."

But this was only of a piece with the prisoners' attitude
generally. On another occasion a body of them go to the
governor's office to remonstrate with him on one of his punishments. We might as well imagine—to compare great things
with small—a deputation from the criminal classes waiting on
a judge to complain of his sentence on a thief. As soon as

the protesters are ushered in, one says that Davis, the culprit,
is very sorry for what he has done; another says that he was
unwell at the time, and the whole unite in hoping the governor
will let him off. Fortunately the governor is not so weak as
they fancied. "On my remarking to them—which I did with
much indignation—their highly improper conduct in presuming to remonstrate with me in the execution of my duty,
Boak (one of the three) remarked, that by their rules they
were to apply to the governor or visitor if they had any
complaint. To which I answered, 'Most certainly,' but that
my confining Timothy Davis could not possibly be any
grievance to them; and repeated that their presuming to
dictate to me was of such a reprehensible and insubordinate
nature that I should confine them in the dark cells." But as
they were penitent, and promised for the future to mind their
own business, they were released the same day.

Meanwhile, the rioting and destruction proceeded without
intermission. A frequent device now was for prisoners to
barricade their cell doors, so as to work the more uninterruptedly. For this purpose the cell blocks or some of the
fragments from the demolished furniture served; and, as a
brilliant idea, one or two prisoners invented the practice of
filling their keyholes with sand and brick rubbish, or hamper-
ing the locks with their knives. But in March the riots
exceeded anything in previous experience. It was prefaced
by the usual exhibitions of defiance and insubordinate conduct,
and the uproar as before broke out in the middle of the night.
A dozen or more of the prisoners dressed themselves, barricaded their doors, and then set to work. By-and-by the
whole ward was in a tumult. The dark cells were already
full, and there was no other place of punishment. The shouting and yelling could not therefore be checked, and continuing
far into the day excited other prisoners at exercise, so that they
were on the point of laying violent hands upon their warders.
One scoundrel took off his cap and tried to cheer on his fellows
to acts of violence; and some followed the warder into a
corner, swearing they would have his life. The condition of
the whole prison was now so alarming that the governor, with
permission of the visitor, sought extraneous help. Application

was made to the Queen's Square police office for a force of
constables to assist in maintaining order, and ensuring the safe
custody of the prisoners. As soon as these reinforcements
arrived they were marched to the airing-yard of Pentagon 5—
the scene of the recent riots.

Here a large body of prisoners were at exercise. The
governor and the visitor in turn addressed them, pointing out
"the shame and disrepute they were bringing on themselves
and the institution by their mutinous conduct." Several in
reply were most insolent in speech and manner, declaring
they did not deserve to be treated with suspicion. One
attacked a warder close at hand with loud abuse, another the
taskmaster, swearing he was starved to death, and both had
to be removed. These constables remained on duty during
the night, and for several weeks to come continued to give
their assistance. On the return of the prisoners to their
wards, the governor spent four hours, from 7 to 11 P.M., in
going patiently from cell to cell, impressing on each man in
turn the necessity for orderly and subordinate conduct. "My
time and efforts," he says next day, "were, I regret to say,
quite thrown away, for the noise and shouting continued
during the night, though not quite to the same extent."
Nothing very serious, however, happened till 3 P.M. next day,
when Hickman, a prisoner in the infirmary, began to break
his windows, and with loud huzzahs endeavoured to incite the
others (from Pentagon 6) in the yards to "acts of violence
and insubordination." He was answered by many voices, and
the tumult soon became general. Meanwhile, the governor
and the visitor had repaired to Hickman's cell as soon as
the smashing of glass was heard, but the man had cunningly
made fast his door, and could not be interfered with. It
appeared that he had complained of want of exercise, and
had accompanied this complaint with so much contrition for
previous violent conduct, that the surgeon had allowed his
cell door to be unlocked, so that he might walk when he
liked in the passage. Directly the officers had gone to dinner
he got out, and, using his knife which had imprudently been
left in his possession, hampered the locks at both ends of the
passage. His next act was to slice into ribbons the whole of

his bedding and that of several cells adjoining his own, which were unoccupied and (a grave error) not locked. This business satisfactorily arranged, he began to shout and smash all the windows within his reach. Before he could be secured he had demolished eighty-two panes of glass and several sashes complete. He was found brandishing his broom, and offering to fight the lot of his captors, one of whom promptly knocked him down, when he was quickly handcuffed and carried back to his cell. But the noise he made that night, with others, was so great that the governor declares, "I never closed my eyes during the night." Night after night the misconduct of the prisoners continued, and grew worse and worse. Wards hitherto well-behaved became infected. In C Ward, Pentagon 6, "they commenced at 4 A.M. shouting and bellowing like the rest." The visitor on going to the dark is again most grossly insulted and abused. Another evening the noise and shouting that breaks out is so loud that many officers going off duty heard the disturbance at the other end of Vauxhall Bridge, and returned to the prison.

All through the months of April and May the violence of the malcontents continued unabated. They had found out their strength, no doubt, and laughed at all attempts to coerce them. Neither dark cells nor irons exercised the least effect, and the only remaining punishment—the lash, the committee were not as yet empowered to enforce. It must be confessed that one reads with regret that a parcel of unruly scoundrels should thus be allowed to make a mockery of the punishment to which they were sentenced by the law, and that they should be suffered unchecked to set all order and discipline at defiance. And all this deliberate insolence and open subordination could have but one end. They culminated at length in a murderous affray, in which a couple of prisoners fell upon the machine-keeper and half killed him. The plot had been well laid, and had been brewing for some time. About 7 A.M. one morning, while working quietly at the crank, prisoner Salmon rushed at Mr. Mullard, the machine-keeper, and knocked him off the platform by a tremendous blow, which caught him just behind the ear, and cut his head open.

Crouch, another prisoner, struck Mr. Mullard at the same moment. When on the ground he was kicked by Salmon in the mouth. No one but the wardsman, another prisoner, came to poor Mullard's assistance; but this man "acted with great spirit, and it was mainly owing to his prompt interference that the machine-keeper escaped with his life." *

At the moment the attack was made all the other officers were at a distance. One warder said he saw Mr. Mullard fall, but thought it was accidental, and that the prisoner Salmon had stooped over to pick him up. However, when the other prisoners crowded round, shouting, "Give it him! Give it him! Lay on," this warder, perceiving their evil intentions, took to his heels—to get assistance, for he afterwards "indignantly disclaimed all idea of quitting the yard through personal apprehension." At the tower he found the taskmaster coming out cutlass in hand; Rogan, the warder, got one also, and both hurried back to the yard. Smith, the wardsman, was fighting with Crouch, and Mr. Mullard, who had got again to his feet, with Salmon; the other prisoners looking on, being, as they afterwards asserted, afraid to stir, "particularly after seeing the warder, Rogan, run away." † Crouch now came at the taskmaster "with fury in his looks;" upon which the latter drew his cutlass and warned him to stand off, and then both Crouch and Salmon were secured. There was no doubt the greater part of the prisoners were concerned in this mutiny, for although Mullard called aloud for assistance, not a soul but Smith the wardsman stirred a finger to help him. These miscreants were subsequently tried at the Old Bailey, and sentenced to increased imprisonment.

But soon after this the new Act, authorising the committee to flog for aggravated misconduct, was passed, and then a clearance was made of the worst subjects by sending them from the Penitentiary to the hulks. This was really yielding to the prisoners. But it gained a certain lull of peace within the walls—no slight boon after the disturbances, and it was hoped that the new powers of punishment would check any further outbreak amongst those who remained.

"Governor's Journal," vol. vii.   † Ibid.

THE WAY TO THE "DARK."

CHAPTER VII.

GENERAL MISCONDUCT.

HARDLY had the exodus of the worst behaved been completed before irregularities of an entirely new character appeared. An intrigue was discovered to have been in progress for many months, between the women in the laundry and certain of the male prisoners. This had never gone further than the interchange of correspondence, and its existence is in some respects a proof of the laxity of the discipline maintained in the Penitentiary. It was customary to make up the clothes of the male prisoners sent to the wash in kits, or small parcels, which were opened in the laundry by a female prisoner, called the "kitter." One day the kitter, by name Margaret Woods, found among the clothes a slip of paper—a Prayer-Book leaf —on which some man had written that he came from Glasgow, and that he hoped the women were all well. Woods not being able to read, showed it to another woman, who showed it to a third, a Scotch girl, Ann Kinnear, who came also from Glasgow. "Yes," she said, "I know him well. It's John

I

Davidson—a very nice young man; and if you won't answer
it, I'll write myself." The acquaintance, on paper, soon
deepened between Kinnear and Davidson. One of her tributes
of affection was a heart, which she worked with gray worsted
on a flannel bandage belonging to Davidson. At another time
she sent him a lock of her hair.

It is easy to understand the flutter throughout the laundry
caused by this flirtation, which was known and talked of by all
the women. They were all eager to have correspondents too;
having husbands "outside" being no obstacle seemingly; nor
was age, for an old woman, with grown-up children, entered
herself as eagerly as the girls barely in their teens. John
Davidson was in all cases the channel of communication. He
promises to do his best for each of his correspondents: to find
out a nice sweetheart for Mary Ann Thacker, and to tell
Elizabeth Trenery how fares her friend Combs, with whom she
had travelled up from Cornwall. He expresses his regret to
his own friend Kinnear, that he is likely soon to be set at
large; but that before going he will "turn her over" to
another nice young man, in every way similar to himself.
How long this clandestine intercommunication might have
continued, it would be difficult to say; but at length the
wardswoman came to know of it, and she instantly reported it
to the matron. One fine morning the whole of the kits were
detained, and a general search made in the tower. Several
letters were discovered. They were written mostly with blue
ink made of the blue-stone used for washing, and contained
any quantity of rubbish: questions, answers, gossips, vows
of unalterable affection, promises to meet "outside" and
continue their acquaintance. About the same time a letter
from one of the men was picked up on the chapel stairs. As a
specimen of this prison correspondence I give it here *in extenso*.

"Last at Chapel.   "*June* 17*th*.

"From the young man that wrote first, to the
young woman that wrote last.

"My Dear,—It is with a pleasure produced from a mind
enduring the bitters of anxious suspense, that I set myself

down for the purpose of relating to you the candid feelings
I possess at the present hour; and I hope, my dear, that it
will find you enjoying the sweets of good health, as thank
God I am at present : and I must not omit to ask you to be
as candid with me as possible, without the slightest display of
deception; for by this time you must be very well acquainted
how I stand in present circumstances, and that it is not from
the pleasure received from our correspondence, that I venture to
commit myself to yours and your friend's generosity; but it is
from the real expectation of being joined to one of you by the
appointed precept of the Creator, to stick strong and constantly
to you, and to live an honest and industrious life, endeavouring to attain felicity in the world to come. So, my dear, if
you think me not unworthy of your attention; if that your
heart be disposed to acknowledge a sympathy with mine, con-
ditionally, that is to say by the blessing of God restored to
liberty, and becoming a spectator of my person, I myself am
not so very particular about having a handsome wife, for many
pretty girls are so sensible of their beauty that it makes their
manners rather odious; but, so as you are a tidy looking girl,
and industriously inclined, with a good disposition, and will
love me, and me only, you may depend upon it I should
gladly accept you, and be studious to comfort you all the rest
of our lives. But if there is any young man, at liberty or
anywhere else, who is your intended suitor, I beg of you to
give me a true answer in reply to this. And I hope, my dear,
that neither you, nor your two companions, show our notes to
any one; for I know well some women can never keep a
secret. They acquaint those whom they call their friends of
their affairs ; who, when friendship ceases, do not fail to let all
out. This is the only thing I fear, and that causes me to be
more distant in my expressions than I should otherwise be, for
I would not have this known for the best 10 pound that ever
was coined."

All this of itself would be sufficient proof of the laxity
that prevailed in the discipline of the Penitentiary. Harmless enough, the reader may say: and such it would have
been undoubtedly in a boys' school next door to some

seminary for young ladies, in the suburbs; but hardly in
accordance with the condition of prisoners, or the seclusion that was a part of their punishment. And no sooner
was this intrigue detected, and put an end to, than another of
similar character was discovered between the male convicts in
the kitchen and certain maid-servants kept by the superior
officers. The steward on searching the kitchen drawer of his
housemaid—it does not appear what led him to ransack the
hiding-places of his servants' hall—found a letter addressed
to the girl by the prisoner named Brown. Brown, when taxed
with it, admitted the letter, but declared that the first over-
tures had come from the maid. He had been cleaning the
steward's door-bell, when this forward young person nodded
to him from the passage, and he nodded back. At the same
time another prisoner was caught at the same game with the
female servant of the resident surgeon. On searching the
prisoner-cooks a letter from the girl was found in this man's
pocket, and a lock of long hair, neatly plaited. The first-
mentioned girl had not confined her smiles to Brown, for in
her possession was another letter from John Ratcliffe, a
prisoner who had been working in the starching yard close by
the steward's quarters. Betsy S., the surgeon's second maid,
had become also the object of the affections of a prisoner
named Roberts, who had thrown a letter to her through the
open window, But Betsy would not encourage his advances,
and took the letter at once to her master. Then the chaplain's
maid is always at her kitchen window, making signs.

Nor were these irregularities confined to the male side of
the prison. The maid-servant of the matron was discovered to
have long carried on clandestine communications with one of
the female prisoners. The gate-keeper at the inner lodge
caught them in the act. Having heard some one cough and
hem very loudly in the laundry, he was surprised to find the
signal answered by the matron's maid. Then he set a watch
on the latter, and tracked her to the iron grating of the coal-
hole of the female wash-house. As soon as she appeared a
hand thrust out a letter through the bars, which the girl snapt
up quickly and concealed in her dust box. The letter was of
course captured, and proved to be from a prisoner to her

father, praying him to intercede with the chaplain of Newgate to obtain a pardon for her.

The chief lesson to be learnt from these nefarious practices is, that it is a grave error to permit officers and their families to reside within the walls of a prison. In the old constructions the "gaoler's" house was always placed in the very centre of the buildings, from whence he was supposed to keep a watchful eye on all around. But the gain was only imaginary; and even if there had been any advantage it would have been more than nullified by the introduction of the "family," or "unprofessional" element within the walls. A prison should be like a fortress in a state of siege: officers on duty, guards posted, sentries always on the alert, everyone everywhere ready to meet any difficulty or danger that may arise. No one should pass the gates but officials actually on duty inside. In this way the modern practice of placing all residences and private quarters in close proximity to, but outside, the prison is a distinct improvement on the old. By it the moral presence of the supreme authority with his staff is still maintained, and no such irregularities as those I have just described could possibly occur.

So far I have made but little reference to the female convicts. Indeed, during the first years after the reopening of the Penitentiary, except in isolated cases, they appear to have conducted themselves quietly enough. But the contagion from the male pentagons could not but spread, sooner or later. The news of the removal of the worst men to the hulks no doubt acted as a direct incitement to misconduct. Had not this power of removal been accompanied, in the case of the males, with authority to inflict corporal punishment, we should have seen a great and continuous increase of the riotous disturbances described in the last chapter. A certain number had gained their ends; but if those who remained were ambitious to tread the same path, it was possible that sound flogging would be tried before removal to the hulks. With the women it was different—they could not be flogged, so they had it much their own way. It was the same then as now: the means of coercion to be employed against females are limited in the extreme, and a really bad woman can never be tamed, though she may in time wear herself out by her violence. We shall see more than one instance of the seemingly indomitable obstinacy and perversity of the female character, when all barriers are down and only vileness and depravity remains.

Long before the women broke out into open defiance of authority there were more than rumours that all was not right in the female pentagon. "Irregularities are on the increase there," observes the governor in his Journal. The object of the agitation is no secret. The women want to get away from the Penitentiary like the men did. One having abused a matron in the most insolent terms, swears, if not sent at once to the hulks, or abroad, she will have some one's life. Another, Nihill, sends for the governor, saying she had something particular to confide to him. "Well?" asked Captain Chapman. "You must send me to the hulks or to New South Wales." Another woman made the same request, pleading that they had not a friend on earth, and that when they were released they must return to their old vicious courses. "I told them," says the governor, "they could only be sent to the hulks when they were incorrigible, and to qualify for that they must pass months in the dark. Then I exhorted them to return to their work and better thoughts." But they both at once flatly refused either to work or to think better of it, demanding to be sent immediately to the dark, a wish which was gratified without further delay.

It now appears evident that the discipline of the female side is far from satisfactory. There has been great remissness on the part of the officers. It is discovered, too, among other things, that the religious exercises have been greatly neglected: the reading of the lesson in the morning service in the wards has been "either shamefully slurred over, or neglected altogether." For this, and other omissions, the visitor assembles the matrons in a body, and lectures them in plain terms.

That very afternoon occurs the first real outbreak. All at once the whole of one of the wards is found to be in an uproar. The shouts and yells of the women could be heard all over the prison, and for a great distance beyond. The-disturbance arose in this wise: there had been great misconduct that morning in chapel, but the offenders had eluded, as they thought, detection; when, however, the matron came and reprimanded, they concluded that one of their number had "rounded" or "put them away," in other words, had turned informer. Elizabeth Wheatley was suspected, and upon her the whole of her companions fell, tooth and nail, when let out for exercise. It was with the utmost difficulty she was rescued from their clutches. Then the ringleaders, having been again confined to their cells, commenced a hideous din and continued it for hours.

Soon after this a violent attack is made upon the chief matron; a woman assaults her, and deals her a blow that makes her nose bleed. This is the signal for a general disturbance. All the ward join in the uproar; those not under lock and key crowd round the matron with frightful yells and imprecations, and from those in their cells come shouts through the bars, such as, "Give it her! give it her! I'd make a matron of her, if I was out. I'd have her life." The unfortunate officer is only saved from serious injury by the prompt interposition of the wardswoman, a well-conducted prisoner.

The excitement now becomes tremendous. Let us take a scene enacted in another part of the prison that very evening.

It is towards dusk in the "Long Room," where there were beds for nearly forty.

Half a dozen women here, unattended by a turnkey, are discussing the topics of the day. One, Nihill, is lamenting in bitter terms the want of pluck exhibited by the others. None of the women were "game," she said. She was ready to do anything, but none of the others would give her a helping hand. There were men in the prison, too, who were willing and able to join in a mutiny if they only got a lead. It might be done in chapel, where the whole of the population of the Penitentiary collected together twice a day for prayers.

At this moment comes a new arrival, bearing the news of the murderous assault upon the matron, to which reference has been already made.

"How many were in it?" Nihill asked, she being the leading malcontent of those mentioned above.

"Five."

"That's three too many. I wish I'd been there. Wait till I get my green jacket,* I'll carry a knife, and I'll stick it into her" (the matron).

"She's a brute," adds another. "I'd serve her so too."

"If two or three well-behaved women were to hit her again and again, the gentlemen of the committee would say she wasn't respected, and wasn't the prisoners' friend. Then they'd send her away, and we'd be quit of her."

"What's happened now?" asks a woman, Roach, who had hitherto sat silent.

"The matron's been struck. Aren't you glad?"

"No; I'm not glad."

"You're a mean-spirited devil, then—that's what you are."

"And you're a——"

"Well? what am I? Yes. Tell me." Nihill was five or six yards off, taking the pins out of her dress; but on this provocation, she came forward and prepared to fight.

"You'd better strike me; just do it," said Roach.

"No, you strike me first."

"Shut up, Roach," interposed another woman, Price by name. "You ought to have more sense than to quarrel with that child."

"Child yourself!" replied Nihill, in great indignation. "I'm well able to take care of myself, which is more than you are."

"You're a regular bull dog, but you shan't bully me," said Roach.

"I tell you you ought to have more sense," Price repeated.

"Leave me alone, Price; you are a low blackguard."

"I'll blackguard you," cried Price, suddenly seizing the poker and rushing at Roach.

---

* The dress of women in the second or superior class consisted of dark green jacket and stuff petticoat; the first or lower class wore a yellow jacket.

"Yes," said Nihill, forming at once an offensive alliance with Price; "you say another word against Price and I'll split your skull open."

"Murder! murder!" yelled Roach, running for her life to the other end of the room, where she fell upon her bed in hysterics.

The other prisoners gave the alarm; assistance arrived; Nihill and Price were secured and carried off to the dark cells, the former expressing the utmost contempt for Roach. "Yes," she said to the matrons, "you think a lot of Roach, I suppose, because she can throw herself into hysterics. But she's not the only one. I can, and fits too. My blood's as hot as hers."

The next affair occurred at school time. A prisoner, Smith, was checked by the matron for quarrelling with the monitress, whereupon Smith, seizing her stool, swore she would make away with the matron. Two other prisoners came to the rescue, and, pushing the matron into a cell close by, got in with her, and pulled the door to. Smith in a fury raced after them, but the cell gate was locked before she arrived, and she had to be satisfied with the grossest abuse from the further side. But Sara Smith was now mistress of the ward, and ranged up and down with uplifted stool, and fury in her looks, till the governor, bold Captain Chapman, came to the spot with his patrols, and she was, but with some difficulty, secured.

So determined were the women to misconduct themselves, that they took in bad part the advice of the few who were well-disposed. When one Mary Anne Titchborne begged her companions to behave better, they turned at her *en masse*, pursuing her to her cell with horrid threats, brandishing their pattens over their heads, and swearing they would have her life. But the next feminine feat at first sight appeared more extraordinary than any. One of the female prisoners, it was declared, had in the night jumped out of her window, on the second floor, into the airing yard below, a height of seventeen feet; and the governor, who visited her about 7 A.M., four hours after the accident, found her sitting in her cell again, quietly at work, and "with the exception of a sprain, or a

contusion of the fingers of the right hand, quite unhurt."
According to this woman's story, she had got tired of life
about 10 P.M., and at once threw herself out of her window.
" It seems incredible," remarks Captain Chapman, "that she
could have effected this, as the sash of the window opens
from the bottom with the hinge, forming thus an acute
angle—in fact a V—having an aperture atop ten inches
wide. Not a single pane of glass was broken, and Miller,
for all her fall, was unhurt, beyond a scratch or two upon
her fingers." Miller (the prisoner) further stated that on
reaching *terra firma* she was at first quite stunned. By-and-
by she got up and walked about the yard for several hours ;
then, finding it cold, she returned to her ward, which she
accomplished easily, as all the external doors and passage
gates had been left unlocked. This carelessness with reference
to "security" locks, as they are called, or the gates that
interpose between the prisoners and fresh air, might easily
make the hair of a modern gaoler stand on end ; and even the
considerate Governor Chapman was forced to reprimand the
matrons for this gross neglect of duty. But by-and-by Miller
confesses her fraud. After school at night, she had managed
to secrete herself in an unoccupied cell. No one misses her ;
and about 'eleven, coming out, she commences to wander up
and down the ward, going from cell to cell knocking. "Who's
there?" "Miller." "Where have you come from?" "I
have jumped out of the window, and got through the gates,
which were left open." "Go back to your cell, for goodness'
sake." "I can't get in, the door is locked." "Call up the
matron then." "I daren't." Such was the conversation overheard by others. But about 3 A.M. Miller could stand it no
longer, and woke the matron of the ward.

One other case of misconduct among the females must be
mentioned here, and then we will for the present leave them.
Some months afterwards a conspiracy was discovered which at
first sight seemed of rather serious dimensions. Its apparent
object was to murder the chaplain, the matron, and a female
officer named Bateman, all of whom had incurred the rancour
of certain of the worst prisoners. One day in chapel an officer
noticed much nudging and winking between two or three of

the women, one of whom afterwards came up to her, as she stood by the altar rails, and said, "There's a conspiracy going on."

"Where?" asked the matron.

"In a bag."

"A bag? Who's got it?"

"Jones."

And in effect, upon Jones is found a bag of white linen, six inches by four, and inside it a strip of bright yellow serge, such as the "first-class" women wore. On this yellow ground was worked in black letters, as a sampler might be, the following :—

"Stab balling (bawling) Bateman, dam matron too, and parson; no justis now, may they brile in hell and their favrits too. God bless the governor; but this makes us devils. Shan't care what we do—20 of us sworn to drink and theve in spite—get a place—rob and bolt. Make others pay for this. Shan't fear any prison or hel after this. Can't suffer more. Some of us meen to gulp the sakrimint, good blind : they swear they'll burk the matron when they get out, and throw her in the river. No justis. Destroy this. No fear. All swer to die ; but don't split, be firm, stic to yor othe, and all of ye, stab them all. Watch yor time—stab am to the hart in chaple; get round them and they can't tell who we mean to stab."

This bag was akin somewhat to the mysterious *chuppaties*, which were the forerunner of the Indian Mutiny. It was passed from hand to hand, each prisoner opening, reading, and then sending it on. Jones, on whom it was found, declared she had picked it up in the passage. She was lame, and returning from exercise had put her crutch on something soft. "Why, here is some one's swag," she cried, and thereupon became possessed of it. But she had intended to give it up to the matron; "Oh yes, directly she had read it." However, another prisoner forestalled her, and Jones gets into trouble. Then, with the instinct of self-preservation, which is stronger, perhaps, among prisoners than in other human beings, Jones "rounds" at once, in other words, gives full information of the plot. Hatred to the matron was at the bottom of it. "She is a devilish bad one," said a prisoner, one day in public. "There's no justice in her religion. Pity she hasn't some one here to serve her as Matron Palmer was served."

"What d'ye say, Jane?"

"Ah! there's none of them staunch ones in here now. There's only you, and Cooper, and me, that's worth a pinch."

"But what did they do to Matron Palmer?"

"Why, they beat her, and knocked her cap off at school. I'd like to frighten this one too, now."

"Well, send her a letter."

"A letter? when there's no paper, no ink, no nuffink?"

"You can work a sampler—work the letters on a strip of cloth. You're a quick marker. Why, they say you covered a handkerchief with writing in a week."

"I'll do it; but what shall I say?"

"Everything that's bad—but say, 'God bless the old governor.'"

"Suppose we should be found out?"

"Pouf—found out! It can't be found out among so many. We'll drop it in chapel."

And with this beginning, the great conspiracy grew to the dimensions we have seen it. It was of a piece with many such plots in modern experience—mere empty threats and rank bombastic talk. Prisoners are very fond of bragging what they mean to do, both inside and when again free. In the present case there was supposed to be much more in store for the matron than the actual assault with which they threatened her. One of the conspirators swore that if she (the matron) escaped now, later on vengeance should overtake her. "As soon as I am free I'll do for that cat of destruction. I'll send her first a dead dog with a rope round its neck, made up into a parcel. That'll frighten her. Curse her, I'll give her a bitter pill yet. If it's ten years hence, I'll never forget her. I'll watch her, and track her outside; and I have friends of the right sort that'll help me." But threatened men and women live long, and nothing much happened to the matron then or afterwards.

Let us now return to the male side. Here the worries and

annoyances of the governor were still varied and continuous. Hardly had misconduct in one shape succumbed to treatment, than it broke out in another. Many attempts to escape—one of which, to be detailed hereafter, went very near complete success; a couple of very serious assaults, a fresh suicidal epidemic, still kept his energies fully on the stretch. It was his practice, as we know, to give his immediate attention to anything and everything, directly it occurred; and although he must by this time have been alive to the preponderance of imposture in the attempts prisoners made upon their own lives, still so kind-hearted a man could not but be greatly exercised in spirit, whenever the suicides seemed *bonâ fide* and real.

Here is a case which called at once for his most anxious interference. One Thomas Edwards was reported to have it in contemplation to do himself a mischief. Another prisoner detected him in the act of concealing a piece of hammock lashing in his bosom, gave information, and the halter was seized at once by the officer in charge. It was found to be nearly two yards in length. In Edwards' pocket was also a letter, an old letter from his brother, across which in red chalk was written the following :—

"To Captain Chapman. The last request of an innocent and injured man is, that this note may be delivered to a much loved brother.

"I can no longer bear my unfortunate situation. Death will be a relief to me, though I fain would have seen you once more; but I was fearful it might heighten your grief. The privations of cold and hunger, I can no more suffer. I now bid you an eternal farewell. God forgive me for the rash act I am about to commit—the hour is fast approaching when I must leave this troublesome world. Write to my dear sister, but never let her know the truth of my end, and comfort her as well as you can. God forgive me.

"Farewell for ever,

"Farewell."

"I immediately sent for Edwards," says Captain Chapman

in his Journal. "He appeared much distressed. The tears rolled down his cheeks, but he would not speak. I said everything I could think of to soothe and console him, and had him taken by the surgeon to the infirmary." The case seemed to require full investigation, which it received; and the result is recorded a little further on by the governor. "It appeared that up to three or four days before he had been remarkably cheerful. But one day some extra soup had disagreed with him, after which he hardly spoke, not even to his partner with whom he walked in the yard." Then, when he thought he was unobserved, he had secreted the hammock lashing which was to put an end to his wretched existence.

Bile or indigestion have doubtless driven many to desperation; but though the saying is common enough, that life under such afflictions is barely worth having, actual cases of suicide from stomachic derangements are comparatively rare. Perhaps the soup story opened the governor's eyes a little to the prisoner's real character, and then, later on, a second detection of fraud proved beyond doubt that Edwards was an impostor.

He is caught in a clandestine correspondence with his relatives outside, and for this he is transferred to "the dark." Fifteen minutes afterwards they find him suspended from the top of his cell gate by his pocket-handkerchief. They cut him down at once. He pretends to be unable to speak, yet it is clear that he has not done himself the slightest injury. Nevertheless, to keep him out of mischief, he is removed to the infirmary and put into a strait jacket. To escape from this restraint he embarks upon a new line of imposture. He sends an urgent message to the chaplain, having, as he asserts, a weighty sin upon his conscience, which he wishes at once to disclose.

"Some four years ago, sir, I murdered a young woman. She was the one I kept company with. I was jealous. I threw her into the New River. Sir, I have never had a happy moment since I committed the deed. My life is a burthen to me; and I would gladly terminate it upon the scaffold."

"Are you quite sure you are telling me the truth?" the chaplain asks.

"The truth, sir—God's truth. If I am not, may I," etc.

He detailed the circumstances of the murder with so much circumstantiality that it was thought advisable to take all down in writing, so as to make full inquiry; but both governor and chaplain are "fully convinced that the prisoner had fabricated the whole story in the hopes of getting himself removed to Newgate." No sort of corroboration is obtained outside, of course, and by-and-by the matter drops. I have merely quoted this as a sequel and commentary upon the conduct of Edwards, proving that he was clearly an impostor from first to last.

But not long after this a fatal case occurred. The suicide was a man long suspected of being wrong in his head. Early one morning he was found hanging to the cross-beam of his loom, from the frame-work of which he had jumped, and thereby dislocated his neck. It appeared on inquiry that the mental derangement of which this man showed symptoms had been kept quite a secret from the governor and medical officer; so also had his frequent requests to see the chaplain; and the officer in charge of the ward was very properly suspended from duty "for culpable neglect, as probably, with timely interference, the prisoner's life might have been saved." But whether it might or might not, the news of his death spread rapidly through the prison, and from having occurred but rarely, real or feigned suicides became again quite the fashion. The gossip of an incautious matron took the intelligence first into the female pentagon. That very evening, after the women had been locked up, one yelled to another in the next cell that she meant to hang herself directly, and had a rope concealed, which she dared anyone to discover. This woman was made safe at once; but next morning another was found tied up by her apron to the pegs of the clothes rack behind her cell door. She had failed to come out with the rest to wash, and as the officers approached to examine her cell they heard a noise of groaning within. A sort of feeble barricade had been made by the prisoner, with her mattress and pillows, to prevent entrance; but the door was easily opened, and behind it hung Hannah Groats by the neck, to one peg, while she carefully kept herself from harm by holding on by her

hands to the two pegs adjoining. She was instantly taken
down, when it was seen that she had not sustained the
slightest damage. She had of course chosen her time just
when she knew the cell doors were about to be opened, and
she was safe to be quickly discovered.

Next the men take up the contagion. One announces
that unless he be removed without delay from the cell he
occupies he shall forthwith make away with himself, as he
is tired of life. "He appeared so much dejected, and spoke
with so much apparent earnestness, that I ordered him to the
infirmary," says the governor. Another man writes on his
slate that the authorities treat him with such severity,
he shall certainly commit suicide. He is seen at once by
both chaplain and governor, but continues "dogged and
intractable." Then a certain impudent young vagabond,
notorious for his continual misconduct, is found one morning
seated at his table, reading the burial service aloud from
his Prayer-Book, and sharpening his knife on a bit of hearth-
stone. A woman with a piece of linen tied tightly round her
neck, and nearly producing strangulation; men, one after
another, found suspended, but always cut down promptly, and
proved to be unhurt in spite of pretended insensibility; cases
of this kind really occurred so frequently, that I should fill
many pages were I to recount a tithe of them.

But I will pass to describe the first instance in which it
was found necessary to inflict corporal punishment in Millbank.
It was as a punishment for a brutal assault. One of the
prisoners, David Sheppard, checked "mildly" by his officer
for walking in his wrong place, replied, "I'll walk as I have
always done, and not otherwise."

"You must walk with your partner."

Sheppard turned round most insolently and said, "What
is that you say? I'll partner you." An answer that is pretty
conclusive as to the sort of discipline maintained in the
prison.

The officer made no further remark, but walked away to
unlock a gate. Sheppard followed him quickly, and without
the least notice, caught him a tremendous blow behind the
ear, striking him again and again, till other officers came to

the victim's assistance. Many of the prisoners cried "Leave off!" but none offered to interfere. As soon as the prisoner had been secured, he was carried before the governor. The assault was brutal and unprovoked, and seemed to call for immediate example. Under the recent Act of 7 & 8 Geo. IV., it had become lawful to inflict corporal punishment in serious cases, and now for the first time this power was made available. The prisoner Sheppard was sent to the Queen's Square police office, and arraigned before the sitting magistrate, who sentenced him forthwith to "one hundred and fifty lashes on the bare back." The whole of the prisoners of the D ward, to which Sheppard belonged, were therefore assembled in the yard, and the culprit tied up to iron railings in the circle. "Having addressed the prisoner," says the governor, "on this disgraceful circumstance, I had one hundred lashes applied by Warder Aulph, an old farrier of the cavalry, and therefore well accustomed to inflict corporal punishment, who volunteered his services. The surgeon attended, and he being of opinion that Sheppard had received enough, I remitted the remainder of his sentence, on an understanding to that effect with Mr. Gregory (the sitting magistrate). The lashes were not very severely inflicted, but were sufficient for example. Sheppard, when taken down, owned the justice of his sentence, and, addressing his fellow-prisoners, said he hoped it would be a warning to them. He was then taken to the infirmary." A strong force of extra warders was present to overawe the spectators; but all the prisoners behaved well, except one who yelled "Murder" several times, which was answered from the windows above, whence came also cries of "Shame." Another, who had been guilty some months before of a similar offence, witnessed the operation. It affected him to tears. "He was much frightened, and promised to behave better for the future."

It is impossible to read this account of the infliction of what seemed a highly necessary chastisement without noticing the peculiar sensitiveness of the prison authorities on the subject. In these days there are crowds of thin-skinned philanthropists, ever ready to loudly rail against the use of the lash, even upon garrotters and the cowards who

K

beat their wives. But at the time at which I am writing now —in 1830 that is to say, when soldiers, for purely military offences, were flogged within an inch of their lives, and the "cat" alone kept the slave population of penal colonies in subjection—it is almost amusing to observe what a coil was raised about a single instance of corporal punishment. Were proof required of the exceeding mildness of the rule under which Millbank was governed, we should have it here. But, really, all milk-and-water tenderness is misplaced in the management of criminals. They are ever disposed to view leniency as weakness, ignoring altogether the kindness of heart which prompts the benevolent to treat them well. What ruffianism *in excelsis* can accomplish—when there is a mass of evilly-disposed villains, that is to say, almost uncontrolled, with the strength of associated numbers setting a childishly weak executive at defiance—we shall see in discussing events at Norfolk Island at a later date than this.

Between this and the next assault there was a long interval. But after a little more than twelve months had elapsed, the ferocity of these candidates for reformation again made itself apparent. This time it was a concerted affair between two prisoners who fancied themselves aggrieved by the stern severity of their officer, Mr. Young. These men, Morris and King, had been reported for talking to each other from cell to cell. Next day both were let out to throw away the water in which they had washed. They met at the trough, and recommenced conversation which had been interrupted the day before.

"At your old tricks, eh?" cried Mr. Young. "I shall have to report you again."

"You lie, you rascal," shouted Morris, suddenly drawing a sleeveboard which he had concealed behind his back. Holding this by the small end with both hands, he aimed several tremendous blows at Mr. Young's head, which the latter managed to ward off, partly, with his arms. But now King, armed with a pewter basin in one hand and a tailor's iron in the other, attacked him from behind. Soon Mr. Young's keys were knocked away from him, and he himself brought to the ground. However, he managed to regain his legs, and

then made off, closely pursued by his assailants, who, flourish-
ing their weapons and smashing everything fragile in their
progress, drove him at length into a corner, got him down,
beat him unmercifully, and left him for dead, King throwing
the basin behind him as a parting shot.

Mr. Young's cries of "Murder!" had been continuous.
They were re-echoed by the shouts of the many prisoners
who, standing at their open cell doors, were spectators of the
scene. One man, Nolan, climbing up to his window, gave
the alarm to the tower below. Assistance soon arrived—
the taskmaster followed by two others, who met first, Morris
and King, as they were returning to their cells. "What has
happened?" they asked. "I haven't an idea," Morris replied
coolly. King, too, is equally in the dark. The officers pass
on and come to other cells, in which the prisoners are seen
grinning as if in high glee, and when questioned they only
laugh the more. But at length Nolan is reached. "Oh, sir,"
says Nolan at once, through the bars of his gate, "they've
murdered the officer, Mr. Young, sir. There lie his keys,
and his body lies a little further on." At this moment,
however, Mr. Young is seen dragging himself slowly towards
them, evidently seriously injured and hardly able to walk.
He just manages to explain what has happened, and as the
governor has by this time also arrived, the offenders are
secured and carried off to the refractory cells.

Here was another case in which a prompt exhibition of the
"cat" would probably have been attended with the best
results. But for some reason or other this course was not
adopted; the prisoners Morris and King were remanded for
trial at the next Clerkenwell Assizes, where, many months
afterwards, they were sentenced to an additional year's imprisonment. Naturally, such a punishment, so tardily administered, must have altogether failed as an example. The
retribution that should attend flagrant insubordinate misconduct should be not only certain but immediate. The
cowardly brute who, for fancied wrongs, suffers his temper to
lead him into a treacherous attack upon his officer should be
flogged just as he is taken, red-handed and fresh from the
commission of his offence. No other form of punishment—

certainly not a prospective lengthening of sentence indefinitely delayed—can be expected to exercise an equally deterrent effect. But, as far as I can discover, in these times the power to inflict corporal punishment in the Penitentiary was very sparingly employed. No other case beyond that which I have just described appears recorded in the Journals till some four years afterwards, viz., in 1834, when a prisoner having attacked his officer with a shoe frame, the sitting magistrate ordered him to be flogged with as little delay as possible. For this purpose the services of the public executioner were obtained from Newgate, and one hundred out of the three hundred ordered were laid in "not very severely." A large gathering of the worst behaved prisoners witnessed the punishment; but all were very quiet. "Not a word was spoken, though many were in tears." "I fervently hope," goes on Captain Chapman, "that this painful discharge of my duty may be productive of that to which all punishment tends—the prevention of crime."

TOWER STAIRS.

CHAPTER VIII.

THE FIRST TIGHTENING OF THE REINS.

WE now come to another stage in the onward career of the Penitentiary. The committee, compelled to admit that the discipline was not sufficiently severe, resolved to tighten the reins. In order to understand this decision we must take into consideration certain influences at work outside the walls.

There was, about this time, a sort of panic in the country at the alarming prevalence of crime. Its continuous and extraordinary growth was certainly enough to cause uneasiness. In the years between December, 1817, and December,

1831, it had increased 140 per cent.* For this there was more than one reason, of course. One unquestionably was the transition from a state of war to one of peace, followed by a great increase of population with a diminution in the demand for labour. No doubt the prevalence of distress or plenty among the poorer classes must have an appreciable effect upon the statistics of crime. "It is so easy for rich people to be honest," says Becky Sharp. They know not the potent temptations that lure a starving wretch to theft, or worse. To them the dearness of food is only an inconvenience, while scarcity of work has no meaning at all. The nearer, then, that the masses approach a general level of comfort and ease, the more should offences decrease. Although they cannot be expected to disappear altogether while human nature is constituted as it is, they are certainly decreasing to-day, because the material prosperity of the country is removing many of the incentives to crime. At the time of which I am writing it was far otherwise: wide-spread distress swelled the ranks of the dangerous classes, and drove into evil ways many who would willingly have been honest, like Becky Sharp, if they had not been so poor. This, as I have said, was one reason. But another, and no insignificant cause, was the comparative immunity enjoyed by offenders. It came now to be understood that the lot of the transgressors was far from hard. The system of secondary punishments in force for their correction was felt to be inadequate, either to reform criminals or deter from crime.† Here was an explanation: evidently a screw was loose in the way in which the sentence of the law was executed. The judges and the juries did their duty, but the criminal snapped his fingers at the ordeal to which they subjected him. This discontent with our own system of imprisonment grew and gained strength, till at last the whole question of secondary punishments was referred to a Select Committee of the House of Commons.

All prisoners found guilty of crimes against the law were

* December 31, 1817,   Committed 56,308,   Convicted 35,259.
    December 31, 1824,   „   92,848,   „   62,412.
    December 31, 1831,   „   121,518,   „   85,257.
† Select Committee on Secondary Punishments, 1831-2.

at that time disposed of by committal for short periods to the
county gaols and houses of correction, or they were sentenced
to transportation for various terms of years. Those whose
fate brought them within the latter category were further
disposed of, according to the will of the Home Secretary, in
one of these ways:—either, 1st, by committal to Millbank
Penitentiary; or, 2nd, by removal to the hulks; or, finally, by
actual deportation to the penal colonies beyond the seas.
There were therefore four chances for a criminal. How he
fared in each case, according as his fate overtook him, I shall
proceed to describe.

The county gaols were in these days still faulty. They
made no attempt to reform the morals of their inmates, nor
could they be said to diminish crime by the severity of their
discipline. Indeed, they held out scarcely any terrors to the
criminal. Of one of the largest, Coldbath Fields, Mr. Chesterton, who was appointed its governor in 1829, speaks in the
plainest terms. "It was a sink of abomination and pollution.
The female side was only half fenced off from the male—
evidently with an infamous intention; all its corrupt func-
tionaries played into each others' hands to prevent inquiry
or exposure." * "None of the authorities who ruled the
prison had acquired any definite notion of the wide-spread
defilement that polluted every hole and corner of that Augean
stable."† "Shameless gains were promoted by the encouragement of all that was lawless and execrable."‡ The same
writer describes Newgate, which he visited, as presenting "a
hideous combination of all that was revolting."§ The thieves
confined therein smoked short pipes, gamed, swore, and fought
through half the night: the place was like a pandemonium.
Again, "The prisons of Bury St. Edmund's, Salford, and
Kirkdale created in my mind irrepressible disgust. I wondered
why such detestable haunts should be tolerated." Gaolers
and criminals were on the best of terms with each other.
At Ilchester the governor was in the habit of playing whist
with his prisoners, and at Coldbath Fields the turnkeys shook

---

* Chesterton, i. 108.   † Ibid.   ‡ Ibid.

§ Convicts frequently arrived at Millbank from Newgate drunk,
escort and prisoners having visited one or two public houses *en route.*

hands with new arrivals and promised to take "all possible care" of them. With all this there was such a deficiency of control that unlimited intercourse could not be prevented, and there followed naturally that corruption of innocent prisoners by the more depraved, which was a bugbear even in the time of Howard.

But, indeed, it was a wonder that Howard did not rise from his grave. Half a century had elapsed since his voice first was heard, and yet corrupt practices, idleness, and widespread demoralisation characterised the greater part of the small prisons in the country. Herein were confined the lesser lights of the great army of crime, and if they escaped thus easily, it could not be said that the more advanced criminals endured a lot that was much more severe. The reader has, perhaps, some notion by this time of the kind of punishment to be met with in the walls of the Penitentiary; of the hulks, too, I have already spoken. The third method of coercion, by transportation, that is to say, beyond the seas, remains to be described; but this I reserve for a later page,* recording only here the opinion of the committee of 1831, that as a punishment transportation held out to the dangerous classes absolutely no terrors at all. "Indeed, from accounts sent home, the situation of the convict is so comfortable, his advancement, if he conducts himself with prudence, so sure, as to produce a stray impression that transportation may be considered rather an advantage than a punishment."

After a long and careful investigation, the committee wound up their report with the following pregnant words: "Your committee having now passed in review the different modes of secondary punishment known to the practice of this country, wish once more to direct the attention of the House to their obvious tendency. If it is a principle of our criminal jurisprudence that the guilty should escape rather than the innocent suffer, it appears equally a principle, in the infliction of punishment, that every regulation connected with it, from the first committal of a prisoner to gaol to the termination of his sentence of transportation, should be characterised rather by an anxious care for the health and convenience of the

* See vol. ii., chapters i.-v.

criminal than for anything which might even by implication appear to bear on him with undue severity. It cannot then be deemed surprising that, in an over-peopled country, where a great portion of the community must necessarily be exposed to considerable privation, and where consequently the inducement to the commission of crime under any circumstances must be great, those who have been brought up with little attention to their moral improvement should, when urged by the pressure of want, yield to the temptation. On the one hand they trust to the uncertainty of the law and the chance of impunity it presents, while in the event of conviction they know that the worst that can befall them will be a change to a condition often scarcely inferior to that they were in before."*

It will be easily seen now why the authorities at Millbank wished to set their house in order. Not that the select committee had reported really unfavourably upon the Penitentiary; on the contrary, after close inspection they spoke of Millbank in the highest terms. "Nothing," they say, "can exceed the order and cleanliness which characterises every department." Again, "As a place of punishment, it possesses one great advantage over any other in the country—in being generally dreaded for the strictness of the discipline and the irksomeness of the confinement." Yet it had its faults, and doubtless it was the recapitulation of these that shook the self-complacency of its rulers.

But it was clear that up to this time they had been perfectly well satisfied with the place. Captain Chapman reported at the end of 1830, that it afforded him the greatest satisfaction to place on record the good order and regularity of the prison. "Serious reports rarely occur. At no period since the first opening of the institution has it been in so high a state of discipline and subordination." Of course this paragraph was penned in good faith; but it can hardly be said to agree with actual facts—at least opinions differ as to what constitutes serious misconduct. But the committee endorsed the statement, and for a time all went well. Then came the parliamentary inquiry, only a few months later, and the committee of Millbank awoke all at once to the true condition of

* Report of Select Committee on Secondary Punishments, 1831 and 1832.

the prison. On account of the repeated "irregularities" laid
before them, they now considered it necessary to "ascertain
whether any, and what abuses existed; and whether there
were any, and what defects in the system upon which the
prison was conducted." The whole subject was therefore
entrusted to a sub-committee, with full powers to examine
and report. All the officials resident in the place were, of
course, consulted in turn, and drew up statements of their
views upon the causes at work.

This sub-committee, after some months of patient investigation, were of opinion that all the irregularities arose from
"the too great intercourse which the present system permits
prisoners to hold with one another. The comparatively
ignorant are thus instructed in schemes and modes of vice
by the hardened and the depraved; and those upon whom
good impressions have been made are ridiculed and shamed
out of their resolutions by associating with the profligate."
We have here an admission that one of the old evils of prison
life — indiscriminate association — which was to have been
abolished by the Penitentiary system, was still in full vigour,
and that in fact it had never been interfered with.

The committee arrived therefore at the conviction "that
the prosperity and well-being of the establishment must depend upon effecting a *more strict seclusion of the prisoners,*
one from another." But as this increase of the solitary
hours must inevitably increase the rigour of imprisonment,
it was proposed now to shorten the term which every
prisoner was required to pass in prison, and under the
new rules.

In support of which they urged that in no case does the
work of amelioration "advance after a certain period."
Under the existing system no prisoner was found to improve
after 2½ or 3 years in the prison. "The monotony and
absence of stimulus, which are the invariable consequence of
long imprisonment, produce a languor even in the most
robust subjects, which is equally prejudicial to the bodily
exertion and the mental improvement of the prisoner."

The committee then proceeded to point out the evils of the
"classes" through which each prisoner passed.

At his first arrival at the Penitentiary a "partner" was appointed for him to walk with in the airing yard. The selection was the result of chance. No. 1 cell walked with No. 2, No. 3 with No. 4, and so on. According to the chance of which cell was vacant, the new prisoner found his companion. Thus it often happened that the new comer was thrown into constant association with an old hand, up to all the schemes and tricks of the prison; or a countryman fell in with a London thief, or a burglar long trained to housebreaking or the worst of crimes. To put a stop to all this, notwithstanding the hardships of it, it was proposed that exercise should in future be in single files.

But a still greater evil arose from the practice of employing the prisoners in the second class at associated labour. Being thus together for many hours during the day, communication between them could not be prevented. Cases were known of prisoners who had passed well through the first class becoming soon "entirely depraved by entering the second. Indeed some, on the point of promotion or just after it, begged to be kept in, or put back into the first class" as the only means of saving themselves from the seductions of their profligate comrades; and instances have been related of prisoners who had, after having quitted the Penitentiary, committed crimes and been convicted, having attributed their ruin to the evil of the second class."

This plan of working together must therefore be abolished. But what to substitute? Although so much money has been spent already, it was felt that more might well be employed in effecting so desirable a result; but happily a plan was suggested which would obviate fresh outlay.

One scheme was to throw a number of cells into one large working room, where the prisoners might work in company certainly, but under close supervision of officers. The insecurity of the foundations unfortunately forbade this. The other plan suggested was a simple re-arrangement of the wards, by which, as the Penitentiary was never quite full, a number of extra cells were given to the second-class wards, enough to allow every second-class prisoner one to himself, wherein to sleep at night and work all day.

It is to be hoped that the reader is not yet weary of these details. There is no doubt, and not unnaturally, a notion prevalent among many that the subject of prison discipline has been nearly done to death. What with native dryness, and added verbiage, a chapter about it is felt to be less interesting than one of Scuderi's romances, or a page in a dictionary of dates. Yet prison discipline at the date at which we have arrived was the topic of the hour. Its discussion filled the public prints and men's mouths wherever they talked, whether in the Houses of Parliament or in the world at large. As Millbank continued to be intimately connected with the subject throughout, I cannot omit from these pages a somewhat extensive review of the whole question.

There was no doubt in these days a very general impression with us, that in matters of prison discipline we had much to learn from the practice of the United States. This led to the despatch of Mr. Crawford, as special commissioner, to report upon the American penitentiaries. The results of his labours were embodied in a Blue Book,* which appeared in 1834, and which was thoroughly exhaustive of the subject. Having carefully inspected all the prisons, and compared them one with another, he was enabled to sum up decisively in favour of that which he thought most worthy of imitation. Taken broadly, the penitentiaries of the United States might be classed in two principal groups. There was the system of Pennsylvania, and there was the system of the State of New York. Of the first the leading characteristic was that the prisoners were subjected during all their sentence to solitude the most absolute and severe; in the second, the prisoners worked together in troops, but in silence, enforced by the strictest supervision and the lash. The first has been called the "separate" system; and the latter the "silent." By these titles they are still known to the student of social science, and to their respective champions in this country and elsewhere.

The quakers of Pennsylvania were undoubtedly early in the work of prison reform. At a time when Howard was

* Penitentiaries of the United States.

lifting up his voice against the state of the English prisons, they also were busy in softening the severity of their penal code. They abolished the punishment of death, and made more than one effort to discover some substitute. The first found was certainly a failure. It consisted in forced ignominious labour in the public streets. The convicts, with their heads shaved, shackled, and in a hideously distinctive dress, were turned out to work amidst the populace. Their conduct when thus exposed proved outrageous; drunkenness, profanities, and indecencies prevailed to such an extent that it was dangerous for the public to approach them. Every spark of right feeling and propriety was altogether extinguished in them. They begged openly from the passers-by; collected around them crowds of idle boys, and held with them the most disgraceful conversation; planned and carried out the most desperate escapes; and when again free were a terror to all from their violence and unrestrained depravity. This could not last long, and within four years the second experiment was tried. An old war-prison, in Walnut Street, Philadelphia, was appropriated for criminals. The sexes were separated, trades were taught, and a certain number of single cells built, "in the hope that the addition of unremitted solitude to laborious employment, as far as it can be effected, will contribute as much to reform as to deter." "The erection of these cells," says Crawford, "and the introduction of trades excited shortly afterwards considerable attention. Visitors struck by the manufacturing character of the establishment, and the apparent industry of its inmates, hastily assumed that the ends of punishment were at once accomplished; and the Walnut Street prison, great as were its defects, was pronounced to be a model for general imitation." This impression was strengthened by the fact, that about this period, crime (from other causes) sensibly diminished, and at first the gaol got all the credit. But its discipline was very far from perfect. In the main body of the prison indiscriminate association was permitted, and the prisoners could talk together as they chose during the hours of work. The separate cells were useless. They were too small, badly ventilated, and did

not "separate" people at all. So far from being a model,
the Walnut Street prison was in every way unsatisfactory
from the earliest date.

The next effort, the erection of the Pittsburg Penitentiary,
in 1818, also proved a failure. Here solitary confinement
without labour was to be the rule; but this, when the building was finished, was found impossible. The convicts were
indeed confined in separate cells, but they could, and did
freely communicate with each other. These facilities for
corrupt intercourse were greatly increased by the idleness in
which they spent their time; and the results generally
were so mischievous, that the legislature determined to
erect another prison, if possible, on better principles. The
result was the celebrated Eastern Penitentiary. No pains or
costs were spared on its construction. The cells were large,
and contained within them all necessary appliances; for here,
alone, the prisoners were condemned to remain for ages,
perhaps for ever. On arrival, the convict was taken into an
office at the entrance, examined, bathed, clothed in prison
dress, then blindfolded and marched to his cell. He was like
a live man entering his tomb; he was dead and buried to all
intents and purposes, for the world knew him no more, nor
he the world. The process of his reception recalls somewhat
the mysterious fate that overtook unfortunate offenders in the
dark ages. As he was led with bandaged eyes, by long
passages, he knew not whither, a solemn voice was heard
admonishing him, reminding him of his position, and requiring
implicit obedience for the future. On arriving at his cell the
hood was removed and he was left alone. There he might
remain for years, perhaps for life, without seeing any human
being but the inspectors, the warders, and his officers, and
perhaps occasionally one of the official visitors of the prison.
For the first day or two he was left entirely to his own
thoughts, without work and without even a Bible to read.
The hours of isolation were aggravated by his unbroken idleness, and the prisoner driven in on himself soon petitioned for
employment. But it was not "till solitude appears to have
effectually subdued him that employment of any kind is introduced into his cell. Under such circumstances labour is

regarded as a great alleviation; and such is the industry manifested, that with few exceptions has it been necessary to
assign tasks."

Mr. Crawford was greatly captivated by what he saw in
the Eastern Penitentiary. He found the deterring influence
greater, as he thought, than in any other system of gaol
management. The prisoners whom he examined were unanimous in their testimony that solitude was the most corrective
of all punishments. He was indeed "particularly struck by
the mild and subdued spirit which seemed to pervade the
temper of the convicts, and which is essentially promoted by
reflection, solitude, and the absence of corporal punishment."
There were few prison offences in the Eastern Penitentiary.
There was no scope for their commission. The caged-up
criminal could only be idle, or in a fit of sullenness and temper
destroy the materials at which he worked. "Solitary imprisonment," goes on Mr. Crawford, warming with his subject,
"is not only an exemplary punishment, but a powerful agent
in the reformation of morals. It inevitably tends to arrest
the progress of corruption. In the silence of the cell contamination cannot be received or imparted. A sense of
degradation cannot be excited by exposure, nor reformation
checked by false shame. Day after day, with no companion
but his thoughts, the convict is compelled to reflect, and
listen to the reproof of conscience. He is led to reflect on
past errors, and to cherish whatever better feelings he may
at any time have imbibed. These circumstances are in the
highest degree calculated to ameliorate the affections and re-
claim the heart." Of course Mr. Crawford from henceforth
became a consistent supporter of this method of prison management. He considered it safe and efficacious, without
unfavourable effect upon either mind or health; and when
accompanied by sufficient moral and religious instruction, it
might be rendered "powerfully instrumental," not only in
deterring but also in reclaiming the offender.

So much for the "separate system": let us turn now to
the "silent"—silent but not solitary, for the name is a slight
misnomer and calculated to mislead. The first-mentioned
system was also most essentially "silent," unless a prisoner

liked to talk to himself; but the latter has gained this special
epithet mainly because the prisoners, though congregated,
were absolutely forbidden to converse with each other.

The leading examples of this method were the prisons of
Auburn and Sing-Sing, in the State of New York, wherein
the prisoners were not caged up singly, and treated like dangerous beasts, to be tamed only by unbroken confinement,
but they were allowed to associate, partly, at least to see one
another.   They slept in separate cells, but by day they worked
together in gangs, under the eye of authority.   Large shops,
ateliers, were filled with the various tradesmen, who were
required to continue their labours with downcast eyes; if
detected at any time in looking off their work, communicating,
or attempting to catch another prisoner's eye, they were immediately flogged.   The punishment was summary: every
warder carried a "cat" of cowhide on purpose, and there was
no limit to the number of lashes laid on.   The power thus
confided to subordinate officers was unchecked, and led often
to outrageous excesses.   Horrible stories are told by Crawford,
of weak-minded persons beaten black and blue; of others
found bleeding from the head and face, with their shirts
sticking to their backs, and with old sores breaking out
afresh ; of prisoners knocked down for making gestures, or
for being slow in coming out of their cells, and kicked when
on the ground.   A more revolting case was that of a pregnant
woman, Rachel Welsh, who was nearly flogged to death by
one Cobb, an assistant keeper.   She was obstinate, violent,
and abusive; and for this she was held down by two negroes
while he beat her.   When examined afterwards by the doctor
she was found black and blue from the neck to the small of
the back, and the marks of the blows extended to her sides
and to the calves of her legs.   Having lain long in a dangerous state she partially recovered, but after her confinement
died, "under a succession of the most distressing sufferings."
Although the whipping was admitted to be a proximate cause
of death, Cobb escaped, and was not even removed from his
situation.   Such repressive measures could not fail to exercise
a powerful effect on the prisoners; but though otherwise well
disciplined, communication could not be entirely prevented

among them; notes passed notwithstanding, tending to incite to insurrection; and so far as they could safely venture they were found talking, laughing, singing, whistling, altercating, and quarrelling with each other and with the officers. "They *will* idle away their time in gazing; and will waste or destroy the stock they work upon," says one witness. Naturally, Mr. Crawford was hostile to the system here described. "In the permanent effects the Auburn discipline is alleged to produce, I have no faith. It is true that the discipline of the lash produces instantaneous submission; but this obedience is of but a temporary nature. It imparts no valuable feeling, and presents no motive that is calculated to deter eventually from the commission of crime and amend the moral character."

As compared with one another, he calls the discipline of Philadelphia moral, and that of Auburn physical. "The whip inflicts immediate pain; but solitude inspires permanent terror. The former degrades, while it humiliates; the latter subdues, but it does not debase. At Auburn the convict is uniformly treated with harshness, at Philadelphia with civility; the one contributes to harden, the other to soften the affections. Auburn stimulates vindictive feelings; Philadelphia induces habitual submission."

No wonder that after summing up thus, Mr. Crawford declared for the system that provided complete solitude for the prisoners. There were horrors in the method by which Auburn and Sing-Sing were managed sufficient to condemn it. On the other hand, cellular seclusion and the reformatory results that were to flow therefrom could not fail to constitute a plan attractive to every enlightened mind. Unfortunately, practice in this, as in numberless other cases, fell short of theory; and we know by the light of our modern experience that solitary imprisonment protracted beyond certain limits is impossible except at a terrible cost. This price is, that the prison becomes the ante-chamber of the madhouse, or leads even to the tomb. It has taken years to establish this now incontrovertible conclusion, but it is now so distinctly known that argument seems superfluous. We might quote here from the pages of a popular romance, which did much to expose the fatal effects of solitary confinement long continued, but

L

Mr. Reade's story is a little over-coloured. The language of
Charles Dickens is more to the point, because he speaks from
close personal observation. He thus gives his opinion of the
method in vogue at the Eastern Penitentiary when he visited
it in 1842:

"In its intention I am well convinced that it is kind,
humane, and meant for reformation; but I am persuaded that
those who devised this system of prison discipline, and those
benevolent gentlemen who carry it into execution, do not
know what it is they are doing. I believe very few men are
capable of estimating the immense amount of torture and
agony which this dreadful punishment, prolonged for years,
inflicts upon the sufferers. . . . I hesitated once, debating
with myself, whether, if I had the power of saying 'yes' or
'no,' I would allow it to be tried in certain cases when the
terms of imprisonment were short; but now I solemnly
declare, that with no rewards or honours could I walk a happy
man beneath the open sky by day, or lie me down upon my
bed at night, with the consciousness that one human creature
for any length of time, no matter what, lay suffering this unknown punishment in his silent cell, and I the cause, or I
consenting to it in the least degree."* This forcible language
is fully justified when animadverting upon absolute and long-
continued solitary confinement. This principle was for a time
established at Millbank, with what results we shall by-and-by
see. At Pentonville also, the model prison, constructed in
1841-2, solely to carry out this solitary imprisonment, the
term of confinement had to be reduced by degrees from two
years to nine months, the maximum period enforced to-day in
the case of convicts in government hands. Some prisoners are
still sentenced to two years' imprisonment, to be undergone in
the "local" prisons, but in this case the confinement is not
absolutely solitary. There are many breaks in on the loneli-
ness of the hours; attendance with others at church, associated
exercise, visits from chaplain, schoolmaster, and trade instructor.
As these are permitted in our modern method of separate confinement, the punishment, if it really be irksome—which is by
no means certain—is at least robbed of half its terrors.

* American Notes.

But to return to Crawford, in 1834. Having thrown in his lot with the advocates for complete solitary imprisonment, he fought bravely for his opinions. But he was vigorously opposed. There were not wanting advocates of the congregate, or "silent" system, partly, I apprehend, because it would have entailed enormous expense to supply separate cellular accommodation for every prisoner, in every gaol throughout the kingdom. Many who had the management of prisons naturally leant to the method which was capable of execution in the existing buildings. Where two plans of treatment have each certain merits of their own, and the superiority of neither is distinctly and finally proved, that which is the cheapest generally claims support. To enforce solitary confinement everywhere meant the reconstruction of almost every prison in the kingdom. Only now, after a lapse of nearly forty years, has this entire separation been universally provided. However much, in 1834, people went with those who advocated complete prison reform, few cared to countenance the expenditure of millions to attain it, especially if equal results could be otherwise obtained. There sprang up, therefore, a large class, officials and others, who, while admitting that reform in discipline was greatly needed, considered that it was sufficient to ensure separation of prisoner from prisoner by night, but that they might work together by day, provided only that silence was rigorously maintained. In other words, they became the partizans, openly acknowledged, of the Auburn system which Mr. Crawford had so loudly condemned. Its faults, they said, lay rather with the practice than with the principle. Eliminate the brutality, deprive subordinate officers of their cowardly cow-hide "cats," vest authority to punish in the supreme head of the prison alone, and the leading objections to that system were successfully removed. I do not wish to travel over all this ground again, or to reopen the dispute, which, for all the heat that animated it once, is long since dead and buried. In our practice to-day, by a simple compromise, we have nearly solved the problem : we subject our prisoners to solitary confinement for a time, for as long, in point of fact, as by our modern experience we find it feasible without

damage to life or understanding. Whenever the sentence
exceeds this limit of time, the prisoner passes into "association;" in other words, he works in company with others,
but in silence, as far as it is humanly possible to enforce
the rule.

But in 1834, and the years immediately following, the
question was in course of animated discussion. The Millbank committee undoubtedly leant to Mr. Crawford's side.
Already, as I have related in a previous chapter, they had
changed greatly the system of classes. Every prisoner was
lodged in a separate cell. They were exercised in single file,
at long intervals, circling round an officer, who stood in the
centre to check all attempts at conversation between them.
Then, at the end of 1836, the committee report that "great
and important changes are contemplated in the general
discipline of this institution, with a view to render the
punishment of prisoners more certain and severe. But by
far the most interesting subject, both as regards punishment
and reformation, is the experiment intended to be made in
the total separation of individuals, by confining them in cells
so constructed as to render all communication between them
impracticable. The committee are so fully sensible of the
evils resulting from communications between prisoners, that
they would hail as a great public benefit the introduction of
a plan which should effectually obviate these evils without
endangering the mental and bodily health of the prisoners."*
Next year we hear that the cells by which the complete separation of prisoners was to be ensured, were all but completed.
The committee go on to say, "Whether the separate system,
as it is called, is likely to be attended, either with the benefits
its supporters anticipate, or with the evils its opponents
denounce, it is not for the committee to decide. The merits
or demerits of the system can only be ascertained by actual
experiment."

Some notion of the results of the experiment will be
obtained from this narrative as it proceeds.

* Annual Report to the House of Commons.

THE CHAPEL.

CHAPTER IX.

THE CHAPLAIN'S REIGN.

WHEN the new system to be pursued at Millbank was under discussion, as described in the last chapter, one of the most important of the projected improvements was suggested by the new chaplain, Mr. Whitworth Russell. By it he hoped "to be enabled to afford to the prisoners generally, a regular course of religious instruction." He proposed that "the open part of the chapel should be provided with benches, so that he might assemble daily, large classes for religious instruction." To these classes he was to devote three hours every morning, the schoolmaster performing the same duty in the afternoon. During the morning instruction by the chaplain this schoolmaster had to visit the prisoners, cell by cell, either collecting information as to the previous habits and connections of the prisoners, or carrying on the instruction commenced at school or the lectures in chapel.

In this last paragraph we have struck the key-note of the system that was now to prevail with increasing strength, till by-and-by, as we shall see, it grew altogether supreme. Never since the opening of Millbank, in 1817, had the spiritual welfare of the prisoners been forgotten, nor the hope abandoned of reforming them by religious influences. But now, and for years to come, the chaplain was to have the fullest scope. Whether much tangible benefit followed from his increasing ministrations, will be best shown in these pages as my narrative proceeds; but it cannot be denied that the efforts of Mr. Whitworth Russell, and of his successor Mr. Nihil, who in himself combined the offices of governor and chaplain, were praiseworthy in the extreme. Speaking, however, with all due reverence, I cannot but think that their zeal was often misdirected; that conversion, such as it is, obtained by force almost, could never be either sincere or lasting; and in short, that the continued parade of sacred things tended rather to drag them into the mire, while the incessant religious exercises—the prayers, expositions, and genuflexions were more in keeping with a monastery of monks than a gaol full of criminals.

There are numberless instances scattered up and down among the records of the sort of spirit in which the prisoners received their sacred instruction. It was the custom for a monitor, specially selected from among the prisoners, to read aloud the morning and evening service in each ward. He was frequently disturbed. Once when "Balaam's" name appeared in the lesson, it was twisted into " Ba—a—Lamb !" and as such went echoing along with peals of laughter from cell to cell. The monitor was frequently called upon for a song just before he gave out the hymn; others mocked him as he sang, and sang ribald verses so loud as to drown the voices of the rest; many said they couldn't sing, and nothing should compel them; often they would not join in the Lord's Prayer —there was no law, they said, to make them say their prayers against their wills. Then a certain Joseph Wells, an old

offender, was reported for writing on his pint cup these
lines :

" Yor order is	but mine is
for me to go	that I'll go to
to chapel,	Hell first ; "

and when remonstrated with, he merely laughed in the
governor's face. There was constant antagonism between the
prisoners and their comrade the monitor, generally over the
church catechism, in which, as a species of chaplain's assistant,
the latter had to instruct the others. " What's your name ? "
he asks one. " George Ward; and you know it as well as I
do," replies the prisoner. Another reads his answers out of
the book. The monitor suggests that by this time he ought to
know the catechism by heart. " Ah, everyone hasn't got the
gift of the gab like you have. And look here, don't talk to
me again like that, or you'll be sorry for it." Again, as a
proof of the glibness with which they could quote scriptural language, I must insert here a strange rhapsody found
on a prisoner's slate. He himself pretends to be dumb.
When spoken to he merely shook his head and pointed to the
writing. It was as follows :

" MY KIND GOVERNOR,—I hope you will hearken unto me,
as your best friend; in truth I am no prophet, though I am
sent to bear witness as a prophet. For behold my God came
walking on the water, and came toward me where I stood, and
said unto me, Fear not to speak, for I am with you. Therefore I shall open my mouth in prophesies, and therefore do
not question me too much; but if you will ear my words, call
your nobles together, and *then* I will speak unto you of all he
has given me in power, and the things I shall say unto you
shall come to pass within 12 months; therefore be on your
guard, and mind what you say unto me, for there be a tremor
on all them that hear me speak, for I shall make your ears to
tingle. And the first parable I shall speak is this : Behold,
out of the mire shall come forth brightness against thee."

This man, when brought before the governor, continued

obstinately dumb. The surgeon consulted was satisfied he was shamming, but still the prisoner persisted in keeping silence. "Is there any reason why he should not go to 'the dark'?" the surgeon was asked. "Certainly not; on the contrary, I think it would be of service to him." And to the dark he goes, where he remains for six days, till he voluntarily relinquished the imposture.

The energy and determination of the new chaplain, who was appointed about the time the new rules were established, were very remarkable. He was a man of decided ability, and his influence could not fail to be soon felt throughout the prison. Perhaps in manner he was somewhat overbearing, and disposed to trench on the prerogative of the governor as to the discipline of the establishment. He soon came into collision with the prisoners. Many "tried it on," as the saying is, with him, but signally failed; and any who were guilty of even the slightest disrespect were immediately punished. Mr. Russell constantly reported cases of misconduct. Thus, having asked at school, whether any present had been unable to write on coming into prison, a man, Fleming, said, "Yes! I could not." "You have every cause to be thankful, then, at the opportunities afforded you here." "Not at all," replied Fleming. "I have reason to curse the Penitentiary and everybody belonging to it." "Be silent," said the chaplain. "I shall not stand by and listen to such reprehensible language." "I'll not be gagged. I shall speak the truth," persisted Fleming; and for this without loss of time he was transferred to the dark.

All the chaplain's professional feelings were also roused by another incident that transpired not long after his arrival. It was discovered that a prisoner, George Anderson, a man of colour, who had been educated at a missionary college, had through the connivance of a warder been endeavouring to sow the seeds of disbelief in the minds of many of the prisoners. He had turned the chaplain and his sacred office into ridicule, asserting that the services of the Church of England were nonsense from beginning to end, that the prayers contained false doctrine, that the Athanasian Creed was all rubbish, and that the church "went with a lie in her right hand." This man Anderson must have been a thorn in the chaplain's side, for they had more than once a serious scuffle in the polemics of the church. Mr. Russell got "warm" in the discussion of a certain passage in Scripture, and jumping up suddenly to reach his Bible, struck his leg against the table. After this Anderson had drawn a caricature of the scene, writing underneath, "Oh, my leg!" and from henceforth the chaplain went by the name of "Oh, my leg." At another time there was a long dispute as to the date of the translation of the Septuagint, and upon the service for "the Visitation of the Sick." Anderson on returning to his cell from Mr. Russell's office, had been in the habit of taking off his coat, and shaking it, saying always, "Peugh——I smell of fire and brimstone." One cannot refrain from observing here how much better oakum picking would have suited Anderson than theological controversy.

Fortunately among the prisoners were two—Johnson and Manister Worts—who were more than a match for the unorthodox black man. Though Anderson maintained that the Athanasian Creed was objected to by many able divines; though he took exception to the title "religious," given to the King in the prayer for the High Court of Parliament, whether he was religious or not; though he maintained that his animadversions upon the church were the very words used by his former pastor, the Reverend Silas Fletcher, from the pulpit—yet the knowledge and acquirements of Johnson and Worts enabled them "triumphantly to refute Anderson."

Nor were the women behindhand in giving the chaplain annoyance. In the middle of the service on one occasion a woman jumped up on to her seat, crying out, "Mr. Russell, Mr. Russell, as this may be the last time I shall be at church, I return you thanks for all favours." The chaplain replied gravely that the House of God was no place for her to address him, but the attention of the male prisoners in the body of the chapel below was attracted, and it was with some difficulty that a general disturbance was prevented. At another time there was actually a row in the church. Just as the sermon began, a loud scream or huzza was heard among the females. At first it was supposed that some woman was in a fit, but

the next moment half-a-dozen Prayer Books were flung at
the chaplain's head in the pulpit. With some difficulty the
culprits were removed before the uproar became general;
but as soon as the chaplain had finished his sermon, and said
"Let us pray," a voice was heard audibly through the building
replying, "No, we have had praying enough."   A more
serious affair was only prevented with difficulty a year or two
later when the women in the galleries above plotted to join
the men in the body of the church below in some desperate
act.

Mr. Whitworth Russell, however, through it all continued
to exhibit the same unwearied activity and zeal. He never
spared himself; and as the years passed by, he became
known as one experienced in all that concerned prisons
and their inmates.   Therefore it was that, when the cry
for prison reform echoed loudly through the land, he was
named one of Her Majesty's inspectors of prisons.   His
colleague was Mr. Crawford, who has been mentioned 'in
these pages already; and they divided the whole of Great
Britain between them.   How vigorously they applied
themselves to their task will be best seen by a reference
to their voluminous reports, which issued year by year, in
huge volumes, from the parliamentary printers.   They contributed in no slight degree to subsequent legislative action in
matters connected with prison discipline, and the reader will
meet with both names again in future pages of this book.

Mr. Russell was succeeded as chaplain at Millbank by the
Rev. Daniel Nihil, a gentleman who soon gave satisfactory
evidence that he was worthy to wear his predecessor's mantle.
All that Mr. Russell did, did Mr. Nihil also, and more. Ere
long he found himself so firmly established in the good graces
of the committee, that he was soon raised by them to wider, if
not exactly higher, functions.   In 1837 it was decided that he
should hold the appointment of both governor and chaplain
combined.

On the 15th of April in that year, the governor, Captain
Chapman, wrote to tender his resignation for various reasons.
" The changes that have taken place, those about to be intro-
duced by the new Bill, his advanced age and indifferent

health, induced him to consider it due to the public service to retire, for the purpose of enabling the committee to supply his place by the appointment of an officer who might begin the new system at its commencement." In reply came a gracious message from the committee, to the effect that they were aware of the "unwearied assiduity, zeal, and ability" with which he had discharged his arduous duties for fourteen years, and they recommended him "for the most liberal and favourable consideration of the Secretary of State, on account of his long and faithful services."* At the same meeting it was at once mooted that Mr. Nihil should succeed to the vacancy. But first the sanction of the bishop of the diocese was sought, and of the Secretary of State, to both of whom deputations were despatched, seeking their views on the subject.

The Rev. Mr. D'Oyley next meeting reported to the committee that "the Bishop of London, after much consideration, approved of the plan, thinking that the advantages would more than counterbalance any probable disadvantages from the office of governor being held by a clergyman;" and Mr. Gregson said he had had an interview with the Under Secretary of State, "who informed him that Lord John Russell had no objection to the appointment of a clergyman as governor, provided he was in all other respects properly qualified for the office; and that it had even occurred to his Lordship, before the communication from Mr. Gregson, that the appointment of a clergyman might in some respects be most desirable as a governor of the Penitentiary."

"Under these circumstances, the committee being of opinion that the Rev. Daniel Nihil, from the zeal and energy which he has shown in the performance of the duty of chaplain, and from the judgment and intelligence which he has displayed on the subject of prison discipline, is a most fit and competent person on this occasion to fill the situation of governor of the Penitentiary."

He was, therefore, duly appointed on the 29th April, 1837. But soon after this, Lord John Russell, having apparently reconsidered the question, called upon the committee to

* The pension granted him by the Treasury was £200 a year.

furnish him with their reasons, and the principles upon which
they had acted in filling up the vacancy.

They reported, accordingly, that from experience they had
found the great practical inconvenience of "having two
officers, each supreme in his own department: the governor
as the head of the penal, the chaplain of the religious part
of the system. In a penitentiary these two parts are so intimately blended that jars and jealousies between the governor
and the chaplain are inevitable when the authority is thus
divided. The governor being responsible for the maintenance
of the discipline of the establishment, and having the sole
direction and control of the inferior officers, is naturally satisfied with their conduct provided they maintain the discipline;
whereas the chaplain, if a conscientious man, is anxious that
together with the maintenance of discipline, the great re-
formative purposes of the institution should be promoted, or,
at least, not counteracted, by the inferior officers. The Rev.
W. Russell, late chaplain, in his evidence before Parliament,
complained that his ministerial labours were often thwarted
by the indifference to religion which was too generally manifested on the part of the inferior officers: and the present
chaplain concurs in the same complaint. Mr. Nihil was appointed because he seemed eminently qualified for the office
of governor, and it was in consideration of his personal fitness,
and without meaning to sanction the general principle that a
chaplain ought always to be the governor. But the supreme
authority over every part of the penitentiary system being now
exercised by the same individual, he will be enabled to select
and superintend the inferior officers, both with a view to the
maintenance of discipline, and also to the promotion of the
moral and religious objects of the institution. This will put
an end to the collision which has so frequently occurred between the rival departments, and will impart vigour and unity
to the whole system." There would be no larger salary given
to Mr. Nihil than Captain Chapman had, but it would be
necessary to appoint an assistant chaplain, by which arrangement the religious efficiency of the establishment would be
greatly increased, without any increase whatever of expense.

"The whole plan now recommended by the committee is

the result of a careful and anxious consideration of the various bearings of the subject. If one clergyman were to hold the office of governor only, and another that of chaplain, the latter, according to the Acts relating to the Penitentiary, would be the chief religious officer, and the clerical governor, if willing to take a portion of the spiritual labour, could only do so as an assistant or deputy to the chaplain, and such an arrangement would tend to revive those jealousies which have heretofore arisen from having two co-ordinate officers: whereas the plan now recommended obviates this difficulty by vesting in one individual the supreme authority both in the temporal and religious concerns of the institution, while it assimilates the relative positions of the two clergymen to those of a rector and curate of the same parish."

To this Lord John Russell replied, that being "unwilling to stand in the way of an arrangement which the superintending committee consider advisable, he is therefore prepared to sanction that which is now proposed of uniting the offices of governor and chaplain in the same person, and appointing an assistant chaplain. But his lordship desires that this arrangement may be considered only as an experiment, it appearing to him that the strict enforcement of discipline in a prison is a duty hardly to be reconciled with the consoling and charitable offices of a minister of religion, and that the governor and chaplain must lose by a combination of the two characters. The motives to which the governor must appeal, are the fear of punishments and the dread of privations,—the chaplain, on the contrary, uses means of persuasion, and rouses conscientious feelings. It will be a serious evil should the governor be deterred by his spiritual ministration from a fearless enforcement of the rules; or the chaplain find his instruction impaired by the association of punishment and severity with the exercise of his religious calling. Lord John Russell therefore hopes that in the selection of an assistant chaplain, the committee will endeavour to select a person who may be fully qualified for the duties heretofore performed by the chaplain."

I shall now proceed to give some account of the chaplain's reign in the Penitentiary. It will be seen at once that his mere

appointment as head of the establishment sufficiently shows the
influences that were in ascendant with the committee of the
Penitentiary. Not that this body were alone and peculiar in
their views. The general tone of public opinion at that time
turned towards entrusting the ministers of religion with full
powers to preach prisoners out of their evil courses into
honesty and the right path. Far be it from me to detract
from the efforts made in such a cause. The work of good and
earnest men, who seek to benefit their fellows, can never be
barren altogether of results. But it is greatly to be feared
that habitual criminals are not to be reformed by purely
moral and religious means. Those who from long experience
know the dangerous classes well have little hope of any such
permanent improvement. Mr. Elam Lynds, the well-known
governor of Sing-Sing prison, told M. de Tocqueville that he
did not believe in complete reform except in the case of young
offenders. "In my opinion," he says, "nothing is more rare
than to see a criminal of advanced age become a virtuous and
religious man. I put no faith in the holiness of those who
leave prison; and I do not believe that the chaplain's counsels
nor the prisoner's meditations will ever make of him a good
Christian." *

The fact is, that in seeking to reform the criminal we have
acted much as the surgeon does who would try to straighten
a withered limb—we have begun too late. The subject has
been allowed first to reach a stage beyond the action of our
healing process. To be efficacious, our treatment should have
been applied when the limb was susceptible; in other words,
if we would eliminate the dangerous classes, and stop recruiting for their ranks, we must act against them in the
earlier stages : as children, that is to say, through education,
reformatories, and industrial schools.

But the Millbank committee were sanguine still, in 1838,
when Mr. Nihil came into power under them. We shall see
now how far their agent, having *carte blanche*, and every
facility, prospered in this difficult mission.

His real earnestness of purpose, and the thoroughness of

* MM. Beaumont and De Tocqueville's Report on the Penitentiaries
of the United States.

his convictions, are incontestable. Immediately on assuming the reins he applies himself with all the energy of his evidently vigorous mind to the task before him, seeking at once to imbue his subordinates with something of his own spirit, and proclaiming in plain terms, to both officers and prisoners, his conception of the proper character of the institution he was called upon to rule. He considers it "a penal establishment, constituted with a view to the real reformation of convicts through the instrumentality of moral and religious means;" and I find in the official records the following entry, wherein he intimates his views, and appeals to those under him for co-operation and support.*

"Having, in my capacity of chaplain, observed the injurious effects arising from a habit which appears prevalent among the inferior officers, of regarding our religious rules as empty forms, got up for the sole purpose of prison discipline, and conceiving it right to let them understand the principles on which I propose to administer the prison, I drew up, and have since circulated, the following intimation :

"Having been appointed governor of this institution, I desire to express to the inferior officers my earnest and sincere hope that they will one and all bear in mind the objects of a penitentiary. The reformation of persons who have been engaged in criminal acts and habits is the most difficult work in the world. God alone, who rules the heart, can accomplish it; but God requires means to be used by man, and amongst the means used here, none are more important than the treatment of prisoners by the officers in charge of them. That treatment should always by regulated by religious principles. It should be mild, yet firm, just, impartial, and steady. In delivering orders to prisoners, care should be taken to avoid unnecessary offence and irritation, at the same time that those orders are marked by authority. Command of temper should be particularly cultivated. The rules require certain religious observance. It is of the greatest importance that the officers should always remember the reverence which belongs to sacred things, otherwise the prisoners will be apt to regard them not as religious services, but as matters of

* Governor's Journal, 1st May, 1837.

prison discipline. It should appear that officers have a concern
in religion themselves, and love and venerate it for its own
sake. I do not by any means wish them to put on an
appearance of religion which they do not feel—that would
be hypocrisy, but I wish them, as members of a religious
institution, to cultivate the feeling and demeanour of true
Christians—not only for the sake of the prisoners under
their charge, but for their own."

That the intention of this order was of the best no one
who reads it can deny; but its provisions were fraught with
mischievous consequences, as will soon appear. It struck at
the root of all discipline. The prisoners were insubordinate
and insolent, and needed peremptory measures to keep them
in check; they were already only too much disposed to give
themselves airs, and quite absurdly puffed up with an idea of
their own importance. In all this they were now to be
directly encouraged : for although the order in question was
not made known to them in so many words, they were quick-
witted enough, as they always are, to detect the altered
attitude of their masters. These masters were such, however,
only in name; and one of them within a month complains
rather bitterly that he is worse off than a prisoner. The
latter, if charged with an offence, need only deny it and it fell
to the ground, while a prisoner might say what he liked
against an officer and it could not be refuted. The governor
did not at first see how injudicious it was to weaken the
authority of his subordinates, and continued to inculcate
mildness of demeanour. In a serious case of disturbance,
where several prisoners were most turbulent and needed
summary repression, he takes a very old warder to task for his
unnecessary severity. One of these mutineers, whom they
had been obliged to remove by force, cried, "You have
almost killed me," though nothing of the kind had occurred.
This officer was injudicious enough to reply, "You deserve
killing." Upon this Mr. Nihil, as I find it recorded, states,
"I thought it necessary to reprove the warder for such
language. If the prisoners are to be properly managed, it is
by authority administered with firmness, and guided, not by
passion, but by reason and principle." No one could wish to

countenance anything like brutality or unnecessary harshness of demeanour; but when discipline is defied, and the peace and good order of the prison placed in jeopardy, there might surely be some excuse for this warder's words, and less so for such a severe reproof.

Later he issued the following order: "In consequence of what the governor has sometimes observed, he wishes to impress on the inferior officers the importance of coolness and command of temper in the management of prisoners. . . . Cases will, of course, arise when prisoners by their violence give much provocation. At such times it is particularly necessary that the officers should endeavour to maintain calmness and self-possession. The best way is to use as few words as possible, taking care at the same time to adopt the necessary means of securing a refractory prisoner; but to fall into a passion, or to enter into a war of words, only lowers the authority of the officer, and adds to the irritation it is intended to allay." Excellent advice, but not always easily followed. However much it is right to hold in check wrong-headed zeal, which is in danger of boiling over, the repression and the caution to the officials should be privately administered. No inkling of it should reach the prisoners themselves: for what weakens authority necessarily strengthens the hands of those in subjection. Strangely enough the governor did not himself realise the force of this reasoning, though he inadvertently admits it. He had not been two months in office before he comments on the relaxation of discipline observable in the prison. "The prisoners have no notion of their own position, and look upon every act of an officer by which regularity is enforced as a crying grievance which they are called upon to resent." *

Indeed, the condition of these officers was hardly to be envied. They were mostly men of the camp, soldiers who had served their time in the army, and fitted neither by previous training nor the habits of their mind for the task required of them now. Mr. Nihil, to be fully served and seconded in his conscientious efforts to effect reformation, should have been provided with a staff of missionaries; though these were

* Journal, January 31, 1838.

hardly to be got for the money, nor would they have been
found of much assistance in carrying out the discipline of the
prison.   As it was, the warders had to choose between
becoming hypocrites, or running the risk of daily charges of
irreligious impropriety, and of losing their situations altogether. Placed thus from the first in a false position, there
was some excuse for them in their shortcomings.   Not
strangely many went with the stream, and sought to obtain
credit with their chief by professing piety whether they felt it
or no, using Scripture phrases, and parading in the pentagons
and ward passages with Bibles carried ostentatiously under
their arms, though it could be proved, and was, that many of
the same men, when safe beyond the walls, were notorious for
debauchery and looseness of life.   It was in these days that a
curious epithet came to distinguish all who were known as the
chaplain's men.   They were called in the thieves' *argot*
" Pantilers," and the title sticks to them still. The "pantile,"
according to the slang dictionary, from which I must perforce
quote, was the broad-brimmed hat worn by the Puritans of old.
From this strange origin is derived a word which, with the
lower orders, is synonymous still with cant and a hypocritical
profession of religion to serve base ends.   Millbank was long
known as the head-quarters of the " Pantilers."

On the other hand, officers in whom the old mammon was
too strong to be stifled altogether, occasionally forgot themselves, and when accused or suspected of unorthodoxy or
unbelief they naturally went to the wall. Thus it was not
likely that one who was reported to be a confirmed infidel
would escape instant dismissal; though in this instance the
information was laid by a prisoner, and should at least have
been received with caution. The substance of the complaint
made by the prisoner was that the officer had asserted that the
nature of man was sinful, but that the worst man that ever
lived was no worse than God had made him, with other
remarks of a carping and irreverent character. Mr. Nihil
immediately sent for both officer and prisoner, and confronted
them together, questioning the former as follows:

"Mr. Mann, are you a member of the Church of
England?"

"No, sir."

"To what church, then, do you belong?"

"I was brought up a baptist, sir; but I am not a member of any society at present."

"Are you a believer in the Scriptures?"

"I would rather not enter into that subject."

"Did you not represent yourself a member of the Church of England when first employed?"

"I did not. I was never asked the question."

He was then asked if he had ever tried to controvert the religion of the Penitentiary, but he distinctly denied having done so.

Then came the prisoner's turn.

"I assure you, sir," he told Mr. Nihil, "that this officer on one occasion remarked to me that St. Paul took up several chapters in telling women what sort of ribbons they wore in their bonnets." And on this evidence Mr. Mann lost his situation; for, says the governor, "I considered his answers evasive throughout; while the prisoner being an exceedingly well-conducted man, I have no doubt, from the tenour of the whole proceedings, that he spoke the truth." Hard measure this, and scarcely calculated to maintain the discipline of the establishment.

Still harder, perhaps, was the dismissal of another officer, who was found using what was characterised as a species of low slang in speaking of prisoners. "It came out very artlessly," says Mr. Nihil, "as he was telling me of some boyish irregularity of a prisoner, whom he styled a 'rascal.' This, coupled with other appearances, determined me that the man may have meant no great harm, but that he was quite unfit for the moral charge here entrusted to him; and I thought it necessary, not only in regard to this offence, but that others might take a lesson from it, to mark my sense of the unfitness of one in the habit of familiarly using such language for the situation of warder." When a fate so severe overtook these two for the offences recorded, a third was not likely to escape who was proved to have occasionally sworn, and who admitted that he considered it was all humbug taking the prisoners to chapel. Although this culprit held the grade of taskmaster,

and had completed a service of many years, he too was forthwith sent about his business. But then it was brought home
to him that he had once been heard to say, "The governor
thinks himself a sharp fellow—I think him the——fool I ever
knew." It also appeared that this officer's familiar language
among other officers was very profane. He sometimes ridiculed
religion; and at one time scoffed at the miracle of the sun
standing still. On another he spoke of the chaplain's lectures
as humbug. "My own impressions of T.," goes on the governor,
"were that though he was an efficient officer, he was a conceited
self-sufficient man, and of his moral principles I had no good
opinion. Everything led to the conviction that he was a very
dangerous character in an institution of this kind; his general
bearing giving him influence over the inferior officers, and his
principles and habits being such as to turn that influence to
pernicious account." He was accordingly dismissed by the
committee "with the strongest reprobation of his abominable
hypocrisy."

Although thus studiously bent upon raising the moral
tone of his officers, in many other respects, hardly of
inferior importance, the utmost laxity prevailed. The rules
by which the Penitentiary was governed, and by which all
undue familiarity between officers and prisoners was
strictly prohibited; which forbade certain luxuries, such as
tobacco, ardent spirits, and the morning papers; and which
insisted upon certain principles to ensure the safe custody
of those confined—all these were often contravened or
neglected. Upon no one point are gaolers bound to be
more vigilant and circumspect than in the security of their
keys. In all well-ordered prisons now the most stringent
rules prevail on this head. To lose a key entails exemplary
punishment, heavy fines, or immediate dismissal. Yet in
these old Millbank days I find an officer coolly lending
his keys to a prisoner to let himself in and out of his
ward; and another who wakes up in the morning without
them, asserts at once that they have been stolen from him
in the night. In this latter case instant search was made,
and after a long delay one key was found in the ventilator
of a prisoner's cell, and below his window, outside, the

remaining three. This man was of course accused of the theft; and a circumstantial story at once invented, of his escaping after school, repairing to the tower, and possessing himself of the keys. He would infallibly have suffered for the offence, had it not been accidentally discovered that the officer who had lost them was drunk and incapable on the night in question, and had himself dropped them from his pocket. There were again escapes twice over, which though ingeniously conceived and carried out could never have succeeded but for a want of watchfulness and supervision on the part of the officer. Of the improper intimacy there could be little doubt, when it was proved that officers and old prisoners were seen in company at public-houses—the latter standing treat, and supplying bribes freely, to compass the conveyance to their friends, still inside, of the luxuries prohibited by the rules. All this came out one fine day, when it was discovered that, through the connivance of certain dishonest warders, several prisoners had been regularly supplied with magazines and morning newspapers. Wine, spirits, and eatables more toothsome than the prison fare, and the much-loved weed, found their way into the prison by the same reprehensible means. It is but fair to add here, that in this and in every other case, as soon as the irregularities referred to were brought to light, they were invariably visited with the condemnation they deserved.

Even a man of shrewd intelligence like Mr. Nihil could not fail to be occasionally taken in. On one or two points he was especially vulnerable. Signs of repentance, real or feigned, won from him at once an earnest sympathy which not seldom proved to be cruelly misplaced. There was also a certain simplicity about him, and want of experience, that sometimes made him the dupe of his subordinates when they tried to curry favour by exaggerating the sufferings of the prisoners. One day when he was *en route* to the dark cells, intending to pardon a culprit therein confined, the taskmaster who accompanied him voluntarily observed : "You are quite right to release him, sir. His legs would get affected, I am afraid, if he were left there any time, like all the rest."

"What do you mean by that?" asked the governor at once. "Explain."

"I mean, sir, that whenever a prisoner is kept any length of time in the dark, his loins are always affected. It may be seen in their walk. Take the case of Welsh. Welsh is quite crippled from being so much in the dark."

"Do they never recover it?"

"Never."

Mr. Nihil was naturally much struck with this observation, and gave it credence, "thinking the officer's opinion worth attention, as he is particularly shrewd and intelligent." But on consulting the medical man of the establishment, he found the statement quite without foundation. Nothing of the kind ever happened; there was nothing the matter with Welsh, and never had been. It was all pure nonsense.

Then there was the case of Stokes, a boy continually in mischief, an arrant young villain, who coolly tells the governor that it is no use sending him to the dark—the dark only makes him worse. "I reminded him that I had often tried kind and gentle methods with him in vain, and asked him what would make him better." Stokes replied that the only thing to cure him would be a good sound flogging—knowing full well that this was not possible to inflict except for certain offences, all of which he studiously avoided. Three days later when liberated from the dark, to which he had been sent in default of corporal punishment, he tried a fresh tack with Mr. Nihil. "This boy," he observes, "sent for me, and spoke as from the very abyss of conscious depravity. He complains of the hardness and wickedness of his heart. He thinks there is something wrong about him. He cried much. I urged him to pray, but he said his heart was too full—too full of wickedness to pray. I have promised to visit him in his cell, when I shall endeavour to soften and raise the tone of his mind, and pray with him." Of course his new attitude is all hypocritical deceit. Almost the next day he breaks out in conduct more disorderly than ever, and after smashing his window, spends his time in shouting to the prisoners below. The governor, now alive to his real character, declares "that the injury done to the discipline of the prison by the perpetual insubordination of this boy has become so serious, that I think he must be sent up to the committee as incorrigible." Again he wavers, and again he changes his mind. "John Stokes applied to me yesterday evening, and spoke so sensibly, with such an appearance of a sincere desire for reformation, that I must beg to suspend my recommendation for his removal to the hulks. The result of such removal would probably be to consign him to the destroying influences of the worst companions." Stokes did not remain long in this way of thinking, and continued still to be a thorn in the governor's side for many a month to come.

But we have in this an instance of the extreme pains Mr. Nihil was at to do his duty conscientiously by all. And if he had sometimes to deal with designing hypocrites, he was not always wrong—at least in cases like the following, the imposture, if any, was well concealed.

A woman comes forward of her own accord to confess that she had made a false charge against another prisoner.

"What led you to make the charge?" (She had accused the other of calling her names.)

"Spite."

"And what leads you now to confess?"

"I was so much impressed by the sermon I heard yesterday from the strange gentleman."

The governor admits that it was a most impressive discourse, well calculated to awaken the guilty conscience. "Being anxious," he says, "to foster every symptom of repentance, I did not punish this woman. She freely acknowledged she deserved to be punished, but I thought it might tend to repress good feeling were I, under the circumstances, to act with rigour."

Another woman, named Alice Bradley, sent for the governor, and told him that she had put down her name for the sacrament, but that she could not feel happy till she had told him all the truth.

"I encouraged her to make the communication, whereupon, with a subdued voice and many tears, she said:

"'I was guilty of what I was sent here for.'"

"This girl had invariably," goes on Mr. Nihil, "with much

appearance of a tender conscience, and a spirit wounded by
injustice, protested her innocence. This perseverance in her
protestations had now lasted six months, and it appeared that
the girl had imposed a persuasion of her innocence on her
nearest relations. I was much gratified with the contrition
that was now developed under the system of this place, so
consolatory amidst the numerous instances of a contrary
description which we daily ;witness; and I endeavoured to
trace the prisoner's impression to some distinct instrumentality, which might ;be improved to further usefulness.
She could only attribute her recent feelings to prayer—
doubtless the most genuine and satisfactory source from
which a contrite disposition can be derived, far beyond
sermons, or conversation, or any extraneous stimulus."

Again, there was the case of George Cubitt, who had been
extremely well-conducted since he came to the Penitentiary.
"He looks ill, and much altered within a short time, and
seems much distressed. He told me he had of late been
affected with the most dreadfully wicked thoughts, that he
had a strong temptation to sell himself to the devil, and
feared he had done so. That, on Friday week, when in bed,
he was much oppressed with these thoughts, which he long
resisted, but at last gave way, and made an oath to
himself to sell himself. He got up immediately, and felt a
chill all over him, as if his nature was quite changed. Ever
since he has been subject to the most shocking thoughts and
fears. He attributed the calamity to his having been alone,.
and seemed to dread the idea of returning to a cell by
himself. I see no signs of pretence about this boy, and
greatly pity him. His nerves have evidently been shaken by
confinement. I prayed with him, and said what I could to
dissipate his terrors, and bade him make the goodness of God
his protection. I could wish that in a case of this kind the
discipline of the prison admitted of a little labour in the
garden; but I see great practical difficulties in making
practical arrangements for the purpose."

Of course Mr. Nihil was in his element in dealing with a
case of this kind; just as the following claimed at once the
whole of his sympathy and attention.

A prisoner was seized suddenly with an attack of hydrophobia. The only cause known was that he had been badly bitten by a dog six or seven years before. "The poor patient was in a most distressing state, being a fine intelligent youth, and in an admirable spirit of Christian resignation. He observed to me repeatedly that he was a poor friendless boy, and that this was a wise and merciful providence, for if he lived to get his liberty he might get into trouble and come to a bad end. When I saw him next morning, most edifying was the whole tenour of his observations and his prayers. That night he grew to be in a state of high excitement, continually imploring me and every one for tea, while unable to taste a drop out of a basin which he held in his hand. About midnight he took a turn— no longer expressed any bodily want, but, as from a mind stored with Scriptural truths, poured out the most appropriate ideas and expressions, though in a raving and delirious manner. It was most gratifying to observe the just views he exhibited, and the expressions of his deep repentance and humility. But dreadful to our feelings was the succeeding phasis which his disorder assumed. He seemed to struggle with a deadly foe, beating about his arms, and striving with incessant violence, while he uttered the language of abhorrence towards his enemy. Then, after a while, he began to give utterance to the most senselessly obscene and filthy language and ideas, nor were we able to repress them; but with these were mixed pleasing expressions of a pious, confiding tendency. This mixed and incongruous exhibition continued till about 3 A.M., when he sunk into death."

Even if it could have been proved against Mr. Nihil that he was lacking in the resolute peremptoriness of persons bred to command, our chaplain-governor was, however, not wanting in many of the qualities of a good administrator. It must be recorded to his credit that he brought in many reforms, of which time has since proved the wisdom. There was for instance the change he instituted in the system of hearing and adjudicating upon charges of misconduct. It had been the custom for the governor to rush off post-haste to the scene of action, and then and there administer justice.

Now, Mr. Nihil resolved to take "the reports" the same hour every morning, "thereby economising time, and having the advantage of previous calm consideration. Besides," he says, "officers and prisoners are both much irritated when the offence is still fresh, and the frequent interruptions took the governor often away from other subjects which at the time had full possession of his mind." Again, after a daring and successful escape, he recommends that every prisoner at night should be obliged to put outside his cell gate all the tools, etc., with which he has been at work during the day. An obvious precaution, perhaps, which is the invariable rule now with all men, especially "prison breakers,"* but the necessity of it was not recognised till Mr. Nihil found it out. Although in his management of his officers he erred rather in being too anxious to obtain a standard of impossible morality, still he knew that more than mere admonition was needed to maintain order and obedience to the regulations. With this in view he instituted a system of fines, as the best method of ensuring punctuality and exact discharge of duties. It is really a marvel how the Penitentiary had been governed for so long without it. Nor did his tenderness and solicitude for the spiritual welfare of the prisoners prevent his entering a sound protest against over-much pampering them in food. "I have frequent occasion to observe," he remarks in one part of his Journal, "the extreme sauciness of prisoners with regard to their victuals. It appears from Mr. Chadwick's report, and the evidence that he collected, that the industrious labourers are the worst fed ; the next best are the poor-house paupers ; the next, convicts for petty thefts ; the best are felons, with the exception of transports, who are still more abundantly supplied abroad. The idle and the profligate act upon the knowledge of these facts, and we have in the Penitentiary several of that description. Their fastidiousness and im-pertinence strangely illustrate the fact that our diet is much too high for the purposes of a prison."

Certainly the calls upon his time were many and various. Now for the first time, in consequence of the great complaints made against the county gaols, " arising chiefly from the want

* Men who have attempted to escape.

of separate cells," the Penitentiary became the receptacle for soldiers sentenced to imprisonment by court-martial. And with the introduction of this new element he brought about his ears a crowd of new questions and new difficulties—a different dietary scale, different labour, and a great accession of misconduct of a new description ; above all, new officials to deal with, and plenty of punctilious red-tapeism, to which, as a civilian, he was altogether unaccustomed. Then, through strong representations made to Government of the scandalous manner in which female transports were shipped off to the penal colonies, it was decided that most of those who came from a distance should be lodged in Millbank to await embarkation. All these women were the scum of the earth, and added greatly to the governor's trials. They came to the Penitentiary in a miserable state of rags and wretchedness, shoeless, shiftless, and filthy.* They were often accompanied by their children of all ages, from infancy to fourteen or fifteen years; and in nearly every case the conduct of all was violent and outrageous beyond description. Knowing they had nothing to gain by a conformity to the rules of the establishment, and that by no possibility could they escape transportation, they gave vent to their evil passions and set all authority at defiance. In the next chapter but one, which I shall devote entirely to the female convicts, I shall be able to give more than one instance of the annoyance they occasioned to all, but especially to Mr. Nihil.

Another vexation, which pressed perhaps more sorely on him than any I have described, was the invasion of his

* The mode in which the female convicts were brought to embark was very objectionable. They arrived from the country in small parties at irregular intervals, travelling by stage coach, smack, or hoy, under charge of a turnkey; arriving and coming alongside in a wherry, way-worn and ill, a bundle of insufficient clothing their only provision for the voyage, and accompanied generally by destitute children. In one case the women arrived, not merely handcuffed, but with heavy irons on their legs, which had occasioned swelling, and even serious inflammation. Eleven came with iron hoops round their legs and arms, chained to each other. During their journey by coach, they were not allowed to get up or down unless the whole did so together. Some had children to carry, but they received no help or alleviation to their suffering.—*Memoir of Mrs. Fry.*

territory by a Roman Catholic clergyman, appointed under
a recent Act of Parliament to visit Roman Catholic prisoners.
I do not suppose that Mr. Nihil was more intolerant than were
others of his cloth in those days, when antagonism between
creeds ran unusually high, and there is much excuse for the
remarks he makes on the subject. By the Act provision was
made for the payment of the priest from the prison fund.
This Mr. Nihil characterises as tantamount to "establishment."
He does not see the necessity for anything of the kind,
especially as the scruples of all the Roman Catholic prisoners
have hitherto been most punctiliously respected.

Then Mr. Nihil went on to raise a number of points, few
of which happily came to an issue : How was the priest to be
appointed? by whom approved? When appointed, would not
his office be co-ordinate with that of the resident chaplain?
Where was the line to be drawn with respect to discipline?
Would not friction and difficulty arise from the Roman
Catholic prisoners placing themselves under the patronage of
the Roman Catholic priest in opposition to the governing
authority of the prison?

"If a Roman Catholic priest visits prisoners under the
permission at present accorded, he sees them at the taskmaster's tower, to which they are brought. If he becomes a
regular officer of the prison he will have free access to the
wards and infirmaries; and every one conversant with our
present system and the spirit of comparison excited by every
little distinction, must see that the presence of a rival chaplain
is likely to produce a controversial habit among the prisoners,
than which few things would be more baneful. I anticipate
nothing less than that many of them will be constantly
changing their religion according as it suits their caprice to see
one chaplain or the other, with the view to annoy the authorities.
The visitors are aware how apt prisoners are to indulge their
restlessness by applying to see those whom the rules entitle
them to see, when there is really nothing wanting. The
additional officer will enlarge this opportunity, and it is obvious
how much it will be in the power of a Roman Catholic
chaplain, under the circumstances, to foster a spirit of
proselytism, in which, indeed, he will have a pecuniary

interest—his appointment depending on number. The most popular chaplain in the prison—the man who will have most followers—will undoubtedly be the one who affords most encouragement to the prisoners, and does most to paralyse the authority of the officer in charge of them."

Happily, as I have said, these anticipations proved almost groundless, and, except in one or two trivial instances, which are hardly worth recording, no evil results followed the occasional admission of the priest to the Pentientiary.

HOWARD ESCAPING.

CHAPTER X.

ESCAPES.

THE most positive annoyance of all the anxieties that weighed upon Governor Nihil in these days, was the deportment of a certain Pickard Smith, who seemed more than a match for all the authority of the place. His case is interesting as an example of the length to which a prisoner can go, even in times when better influences were, it was hoped, at work with all.

On the day of his arrival at the Penitentiary in the name of Smith, it was discovered that he had been there before as Pickard, when he was known for notorious misconduct, though towards the end of his sentence "he had assumed the appearance of reformation." On his recommittal he was at first quiet and amenable to discipline, but he seemed to have conceived suddenly a desire to be sent abroad. From henceforth his conduct was detestable. At length he destroys everything in his cell: furniture, clothing, glass, books, including "Bishop Green's Discourses," and then he endeavours to brain the officer who comes to expostulate. "If I am to go to the dark, I may as well go for something," he says, and after he has been removed it was found that he had written the following lines on the back of his cell door:—

> "London is the place where I was bred and born,
> Newgate has been too often my situation,
> The Penitentiary has been too often my dwelling-place,
> And New South Wales is my expectation."

Not a very high poetical flight, to which the governor-chaplain remained insensible, and had the poet forthwith flogged.

The magistrate came as before from the nearest police office, for the express purpose of passing sentence. Seventy-five lashes out of three hundred ordered were inflicted, greatly to the benefit of other unruly prisoners, all of whom were brought out to witness the punishment. "They appeared much subdued in spirit," says Mr. Nihil, and for some days afterwards the prison exhibited quite an altered character. But upon the culprit himself the sentence had no effect whatever. He spends his time from that day forth in whistling, idleness, and impertinence, sometimes in his own cell, oftener in the dark. His insolence grows more and more insupportable; he tells the governor to hold his jaw, and his warder to go about his business. One fine morning it is found that he is gone. His cell is empty. He has disappeared.

"The mode of escape was most ingenious, daring, and masterly, though the prisoner is only eighteen years of age. There was a combination of sagacity, courage, and ready resource, indicating extraordinary powers, both mental and bodily."

He had got, unknown to his officer, an iron pin used for turning the handle of the ventilator of the stove. The stove not being in use the handle was not missed. The prisoner was let out of his cell by himself, being kept apart from other

prisoners "in consequence of frequent insubordination and the
mischievous tendency of his example." With this pin he had
made a hole in the brick arch which formed the roof of his
cell large enough to admit his body. The iron pin, stuck into
one of the slits for ventilation in the wall, served as a hook, to
which he had probably suspended a small ladder, ingeniously
constructed of shreds of cotton and coarse thread (which was
found in the roof); and with such assistance to his own
activity and strength he had got through the ceiling and into
the roof, along the interior of which he had proceeded some
distance, till he was able at length to break a hole in the
slates. But the battens to which the slates were fastened
were too narrow to let him through, so he travelled on till he
found others wider apart, and here, making a second hole, he
contrived to get out on to the roof. The descent was his next
difficulty, but he had provided for this by carrrying with him
a number of suitable articles to assist him in his purpose. It
must be mentioned that he had chosen his time well: not
only were the officers later coming in on Sunday mornings,
but on Saturday evenings the prisoners receive their clean
clothes (their dirty ones were not returned till next morning),
so that Smith had in his cell two sets of things—two shirts,
two pairs of long stockings, and two handkerchiefs. He had
washed his feet also on Saturday night, and had been given a
round towel to dry them. Having torn his blankets and rugs
into strips, he had sewn them together by lengths, making
each, like the round towel, a link in a chain to which his
neckerchiefs and pocket-handkerchiefs, similarly prepared,
added further lengths. With all of these, and attired in his
clean shirt, he had ascended as already described to the roof,
where he must have found his chain too short, for he had
added his shirt to the apparatus. This rope he fastened to one
of the rafters of the roof, and then slung himself down to
where he judged the attic window was to be found, and he
judged accurately. The sill of the window formed the first
stage, and to its bars he fastened part of his chain, thus
economising its length, instead of having one long rope from
the roof downwards. Descending in like manner to the
second window he repeated the process, and again to the third

(or first floor), after which he reached the ground in safety. His next difficulty was to scale the boundary wall. Much work happened to be going on, rebuilding the parts destroyed by fire, and a quantity of masons' and carpenters' materials were lying about. First he contrived to remove a long and prodigiously heavy ladder from against the scaffolding, which two men ordinarily could not carry, and this he dragged to the iron fence of the burial ground, against which he rested it, but he could not rear it the whole height of the boundary wall. Next he got two planks, and lashing them firmly together with a rope he picked up, he thus made an inclined plane long enough to allow of his walking up it to the top of the wall. Weighting one end with a heavy stone, he easily got the planking on to the wall and thus got over.

As soon as the escape was discovered immediate search was made in all adjoining lurking-places. Officers acquainted with Pickard's haunts were despatched to a far-off part of the town, information was lodged at Bow Street, and a reward of £50 offered by authority of the Secretary of State. He was eventually recaptured through the connivance of his relatives. Soon anonymous letters reached the governor, offering to give the fugitive up for the reward. A confidential officer was despatched to a concerted place of meeting, and by the assistance of the police—and his own friends—Pickard Smith was secured and brought back to the Penitentiary. Mr. Nihil was much exercised in spirit at his return. It appeared that he belonged to a family which had been all transported. He came to the Penitentiary himself as a boy, and grew up in it to manhood. Five months after his release he was again convicted, under a new name, and sent back to Millbank. "Had it been known that the benevolent system of the Penitentiary had been previously tried in vain upon him, he would not probably have been sent here a second time. It is plain that he was not a fit subject for it, and his previous experience within our walls, and probable acquaintance with their exterior localities, acquired during the interval of his freedom, rendered him a dangerous inmate. After his flogging continued misconduct rendered it necessary to keep him apart from other prisoners—a circumstance which

facilitated those operations by which he lately accomplished
his escape. It is now highly dangerous to keep him in the
same ward with other prisoners, our means of preventing
intercourse being extremely inadequate. On the other hand,
conversant as he is with the localities of the prison, aware of
the aid to be derived from the materials strewed about in
consequence of the extensive repairs after the late fire, and
flushed with his former success, it becomes no less objectionable to place him apart where he may be less liable to any
interruption in any attempt he may make. A man of his
capabilities ought not to be kept in a prison with so low a
boundary wall as ours. I do not fear his escape, watched as
he now will be, but I fear his attempts." *

Nevertheless, though repeated efforts were made to get
this prisoner removed to the hulks or to some other prison,
the Secretary of State would not give his consent. He said
it would be considered discreditable to the Penitentiary if
prisoners were transferred on account of its inability to
secure them. Why not chain him heavily? asks the Secretary of State. "Why not?" replies Mr. Nihil. "Because
if he is prosecuted and receives an additional sentence of
three years, we cannot keep him all his time in chains. The
peculiarity of our system," goes on the governor, "hardly
appears to be considered as an objection to his continuance
here. The principle of the Penitentiary was that it was
not merely a place of safe custody and punishment, but
a place of reformation; and, therefore, if it failed of this
latter object in any instance, a power was reserved of
sending away the prisoner as incorrigible, for fear of his
interfering with the progress of the system among other
prisoners." Next day he was told he would have to remain
three years extra in the Penitentiary, whereupon he promised,
of his own accord, to abstain from making any further
attempts at escape, provided he were allowed to go among
the other prisoners. He was so much more tractable and so
much improved in temper that his request was granted, and
he was brought once more under ordinary discipline.

Having remained quiet for a month or more, just to lull

* Journal, August 9th, 1837.

suspicion, he is again discovered—and just in the nick of time—to be on the verge of a second evasion. The window of his cell is found to have the screws taken out, with other suspicious symptoms. Smith declared that the state of his window was the result of accident. He was removed to another cell, and Mr. Nihil himself proceeded to examine the one he had left. His hammock when unlashed revealed the state of his rug and blankets. They had been torn up into convenient strips for scaling purposes. When the prisoner was himself searched, between his stockings and the soles of his feet were pieces of flannel, and in one of them was a small piece of metal, ingeniously formed into a kind of picklock. A piece of iron, for this purpose no doubt, was missed from one side of the cell window. He was placed in the infirmary "strong room" for safety; then apart in F gallery by day, sleeping at night in a small cell below. But soon he destroyed everything in F gallery, and then he was hand-cuffed. "His next method of disturbance was to make a violent noise by beating with his handcuffs against the door; upon which I ordered him to be removed to a dark cell, not for punishment, but to prevent disturbance." Presently a noise of loud hammering is heard in this same dark cell. The officers on duty rushed to the spot, and found that by some extraordinary contrivance Smith had possessed himself of one the staples by which the ironwork is made fast on the back of the door to the dark cell. By means of this instrument he had worked away an iron grating fixed for ventilation, and had been engaged making a hole in the wall by which he would have soon escaped. Smith was handcuffed and taken to another cell.

The governor is almost bewildered, and begs the com-mittee to get rid of this prisoner. It would be inexpedient to place him among other prisoners, and yet that can hardly be avoided soon, owing to the influx of military and other prisoners. "As to corporal punishment, he has already experienced it very severely without any beneficial effect. His knowledge of the localities, and the present unsafe con-dition of the prison, owing to the extensive repairs, will breed perpetual attempts, however unsuccessful, to escape."

Soon afterwards Smith asked to be relieved from his handcuffs. "What's the good of keeping them on me? I can always get 'em off with an hour's work." He was told they would be fastened behind his back. "I can slip them in front; you know that."

"I threatened, then," says Mr. Nihil, "to fetter his arms as well as his hands, and that seemed to baffle him. To-day I held a long conversation with him, and cannot but lament that the powerful qualities he possesses should have been so greatly perverted. He spoke with great candour of his former courses. He exhibited an affectation of religious impressions, though he acknowledged much the evil of his own character. By-and-by I asked him if he wished to have the handcuffs taken off. He did, much, because they made him feel so cold. 'Will you promise if I take them off not to attempt to escape?' 'I'll never make another promise as long as I am here. I have made one too many, and I am ashamed of myself for having broken it.' 'What am I to do with you? Where am I to send you?' 'It's no use sending me anywhere, sir. If you let me go among the other prisoners I am satisfied; from what I know of the place, there isn't a part from which I couldn't escape.'"

"Commiserating this unfortunate young man's condition, I subsequently ordered the handcuffs to be removed, but with a strict injunction frequently to examine his cell, particularly at night. While he is in the dark and closely watched I do not think the handcuffs indispensable." But Pickard Smith cannot remain for ever in the dark. Exercise in the open air becomes necessary, and the first time he is taken out is in a dense fog. Almost at once he eludes his officer's observation, and, slipping off his shoes, clambers up a low projecting wall that communicates with the boundary wall of the yard, mounts it, jumps over on the other side, and runs for the infirmary staircase where he hoped to hide. Fortunately the task-master, coming out of the tower, caught sight of his legs disappearing through the door, and running after him captured him on the stairs. The fellow was quite incorrigible. Again he goes to the dark, again and again is he released and recommitted, till at length his health breaks down. If in the

end he was tamed, it was of his own failure of strength, and
not of the discipline of the place. I believe he died in the
Penitentiary a year or two later, but I have been unable to
find any authentic record of the fact.

I have lingered thus long over his story, which is at best
but sad and disheartening, because it is a good illustration
of the methods of coercion tried in those days in the Penitentiary, and more because it opens up the whole question
of escapes from prison. Of course the convicted criminal
shares with all other captives an ever-present unsatisfied
longing to be free. Like a caged blackbird, or a rat in a
trap, the felon who has lost his liberty will certainly escape
whenever the opportunity is offered to him. To leave gates
ajar, or to withdraw a customary guard, supply temptation
as irresistible as a bone thrown to a hungry dog. And a
prisoner's faculties are so sharp set by his confinement,
that he sees chances which are invisible to his gaolers.
A resolute and skilful man will brave all dangers, will
exhibit untold patience and ingenuity, will endure pain and
lengthened hardship, if he sees but a loophole for escape
in the end. The fiction of Edmond Dantes and his famous
escape from the Chateau d'If, is but the embroidery of a
poetical imagination working upon a sober groundwork of
fact. The records of all ancient prisons could contribute
their quota of similar legends, showing how the fugitive
triumphed over difficulties seemingly insurmountable. Baron
Trenck's numerous escapes from Prussian fortresses, and
Casanova's from the *Piombi*, are familiar to us as household
words.

But in our modern days escapes are of rarer occurrence,
and for many reasons. It is not that prisons are really
more secure *per se*: so far as construction can be depended
upon, a gaol like Newgate seems as safe as stone and iron can
make it: but it is that the principles of security are better
realised and understood. Our forefathers trusted to physical
means, and thought enough was done. To-day our reliance
is placed on the moral aid of continuous supervision. An
escapade like that of Pickard Smith would be next to
impossible now. He would have been defeated with his own

weapons.   To compass his ends a prisoner must have privacy;
hours of quiet undisturbed by the intrusive visit of a lynx-
eyed official; and a cell all to himself.   He has now the cell
to himself—at least he has with him no companion felon—
but he is for ever tended by an "old man of the mountain,"
in the shape of his warder, who is always with him—"turning
him over," as the prison slang calls it; searching him, that is
to say, several times a day, both his person and the cell he
occupies.   To conceal implements, to carry on works like the
removal of bricks, of flooring, or of bars, is next to impossible,
or feasible only through a lack of vigilance for which the
official in fault would be called seriously to account.   How
nearly the methods of ensuring safe custody have been
reduced to a science may be seen any day now in our government prisons at places like Portland, Chatham, Portsmouth,
and Dartmoor, where the convicts seem held, so to speak,
only by a single thread.   They work *en plein air*, in the open,
miles beyond prison gates or boundary walls.   The staff of
officers in charge is less than ten per cent.; no ostensible
means of coercion are used; the prisoners, except in the case
of half-a-dozen of the most turbulent, wear no chains.   The
whole system depends on the close observance of certain
principles which have come to be regarded as axioms almost
with the officials.   No prisoner is allowed to be for one
moment out of the officer's sight; that officer starts in the
morning with a certain number of convicts in charge : he
must bring in the same number on his return to the prison.
Beyond the vigilant eye of these officers in charge of small
parties ranges a wide cordon of warder-sentries, who are raised
on high platforms and have an uninterrupted view around.   A
carefully prepared code of signals serves to give immediate
notice of escape.   A shrill note on the whistle, a single shot
from a sentry's breechloader sounds the alarm—"A man
gone!"   Next second, the whistles re-echo, shot answers shot;
the parties are assembled in the twinkling of an eye, and a
force of spare officers hasten at once to the point from whence
came the first note of distress.   It is next to impossible for
the fugitive to get away : if he runs for it he is chased; if he
goes to ground they dig him out; if he takes to the water

he is soon overhauled. The cases are few and far between of successful evasion. In every case the luck or the stratagem has been exceptional—as when at Chatham, a man was buried by his comrades brick by brick beneath a heap, and interment was complete before the man was missed; or when at Dartmoor, another broke into the chaplain's house, stole clothes, food, and a good horse, on which he rode triumphantly away.*

At Millbank from first to last the escapes, successful and unsuccessful, have been many and various. Pickard Smith's was not the first nor the last. The earliest on record occurred in April, 1831. One night about 10 P.M. it was reported to the governor that the rooms of three of the officers had been entered and a quantity of wearing apparel abstracted therefrom. Almost at the same moment the sergeant patrol came in from the garden to say that the patrol on duty in going his rounds had discovered two men in the act of getting over the garden wall by means of a white rope, made of a cut of cross-over.† Both men were on the rope, and when it was shaken by the patrol they fell off and back into the garden; but they attacked the officer, knocked him down, and then ran off in an opposite direction. The patrol, as soon as he could recover himself, gave the alarm, and presently the governor, chaplain, surgeon, steward, and a number of other officers arrived on the spot. They separated in parties to make search, while the governor took possession of the cross-over cut, which was fastened to the top of the wall by means of a large iron rake twisted into a hook. This rake was used in the ward for bringing out large cinders from the long stove. It was thought at first that, in the patrol's absence to give the alarm, the fugitives must have got over the wall; but the search was continued in the dark, in and

---

* The most amusing attempt was made at Millbank, by a convict, with the connivance of one of the maid-servants of a superior officer. Her master held also a place at Court, and wore at *levées* a handsome uniform of red and gold. The plot was to steal these clothes. Of course, thus arrayed, the convict could pass the gates without question; but I fancy that, once beyond them, his road would have led Whitechapel way rather than to Buckingham Palace.

† A piece of long yarn issued to be worked up in the looms.

out of the tongues between the pentagons, and through
all the gardens. Just by the external tower of Pentagon 4,
the governor and chaplain, who were together, came upon
two men crouching in close under the wall. These were
two prisoners, named Alexander Wallie, the wardsman, and
Robert Thompson, the instructor of C. Ward, Pentagon 5.
Thompson said at once, "You are gentlemen; we will surrender to you. We will make no resistance." But the
governor being immediately joined by the other officers, it
was as much as he could do to protect the prisoners from
attack and assault, as the former were greatly excited.
One of the prisoners was dressed in a fustian frock and
trowsers belonging to Warder Hay; the other had no coat,
but a waiscoat and trowsers belonging to some other officer.

At the top of the tower in C Ward, Pentagon 5, out of
one of the loopholes near the water cistern, another cut of
cross-over had been found hanging, by which the prisoners
had evidently descended. On going up to the place there
were found close by, a large hammer, a chisel, and a screw-
driver, articles used in repairing the looms, and the large
poker belonging to the airing stoves. Several bricks had
been removed from one side of the loophole, leaving a space
wide enough for one person to get through. To the iron
bar in the centre of the loophole one end of the cross-over
was made fast; the other reached the ground. The
prisoners' prison clothing was close by this cistern, and in
Wallie's pocket was a skeleton key made of pewter, which
opened many of the officers' bed-room doors. The prisoners
confessed they had let themselves out of their cells by means
of false keys made of pewter, and four of these were found
near the place where the prisoners had been caught crouching
down. The keys were partially buried into the ground.
There were two check-gate keys, one cell key, and a skeleton
key made of pewter.

Attempts at escape were not unknown in the interval
between this and the time when Pickard Smith bewildered
Mr. Nihil. But they were abortive and hardly worth recounting. It was not till years after the Reverend Governor
had resigned his command that serious efforts at evasion

became really frequent and successful. This was when Millbank had become changed in constitution, and from a Penitentiary had been made a depot for all convicts awaiting transportation beyond the seas. I shall have occasion to refer to this change in the next volume, but will so far anticipate as to include some of the escapes that happened then in the present chapter. The prison was filled to overflowing with desperate characters; every hole and corner was crammed; there had been no commensurate increase of official staff, and therefore those indispensable precautions by which only escapes could be prevented were greatly neglected. Weak points are soon detected by the watchful prisoner, and in these days every loophole of escape was quickly explored and turned to account. That some of these convicts were resolute in their determination to get free may be believed when it is stated that one, *en route* from Liverpool to Millbank, offered his escort a bribe of £600 to allow him to escape. There was no doubt that accomplices were close at hand ready to assist him, but happily the virtuous officers resisted temptation.

One of the first attempts of those days was made by a man named Cummings, who broke through the ceiling of his cell. He traversed the roof of his pentagon, but could get no further. Then he commenced to sing and to shout, and by this he was discovered. A ladder having been placed for him to descend by he was secured. The prisoner himself stated that he had got through the arch by means of a hole he made with a nail he had picked up in the ward. The man was evidently cowed when he found himself on the top of the Penitentiary, and declared while they were trying to secure him that he would throw himself down. He had made no provision for his own descent; his rug, blanket, towels, etc., were found in his cell all untorn. He had, however, traversed the roof along one side of the pentagon.

Soon afterwards seven prisoners made their escape in a body from the prison. They were lodged in a large room—now the officers' mess—the windows of which were without bars; and they were able therefore to climb through them on to the roof. They took their blankets with them, and making

a ladder, descended by it. The policeman on duty outside
roused the lodge-keeper, to say he had seen a man scale the
boundary wall between 1 and 2 A.M. A heavy ladder had been
reared against the wall. All officers were roused out and
stationed round the prison; while close search was made in
the numerous gardens, stone-yards, etc., about. At half-past
four, two officers came back with four prisoners in a cab.
They had been tracked almost from the walls of the prison
and captured at Chiswick. The other three were caught at
Watford by a recruiting-sergeant and an inspector of the
Hertfordshire police. They were on their way to Two
Waters.

Next day a conspiracy was detected among the prisoners
who brought in coke from the garden to escape while so
employed. Almost immediately afterwards four other prisoners
were caught in the very act of escaping through the top of
the cell they occupied. They had broken away the lath and
plaster ceiling of the cell, removed the slate slab above it,
and had taken off the roof slate to a sufficient extent to allow
of easy egress; their sheets had been torn up and were
knotted together, and everything was ready for their descent.

The next attempt, within a week or two, was made by a
prisoner who found that the mouth of the foul air shaft, to
which his cell was adjacent, was not protected by bars;
accordingly he broke through the wall of his cell, and having
thus gained access to the shaft, would have gained the roof
easily had his artifice not been discovered just in time. Two
others picked the lock leading to the garden, meaning to
escape in the evening; and just then by chance it fell out
that the prisoner bookbinders had been long maturing a plan
of escape. They had made a large aperture in the floor of
their cell, which hole had been concealed by pasteboard. The
whole of the party (three in number) were privy to the plot,
and each descended in turn to the vault below the cell,
which was on the ground floor, to work at the external wall
of the prison. This, when their plot was discovered, they had
cut three parts through. They had also prepared three
suits of clothing from their towels, and had hidden these
disguises beneath some rubbish in the vault, where were also

discovered a mason's hammer, the blade of a shears, and a cold chisel. A rope ladder had also been made for scaling the boundary wall, but it had been subsequently cut up as useless. The intending fugitives thought of making a better ladder from broom handles, to be supplied by a brush-maker in an adjoining cell, who was also in the plot. They had worked at night by candlelight. In this case it is not too much to say that the officials in charge of these prisoners were really much to blame. Had they exercised only ordinary vigilance the scheme could not have remained so long undiscovered. By the prisoners' own confession the hole had been in existence for more than three months, and therefore the cell could never have been searched.

But the most marvellous escape from Millbank was effected in the winter of 1847, by a prisoner named Howard, better known as Punch Howard. He had been equally successful before both at Newgate and Horsemonger Lane Gaol; but the ingenuity and determination he displayed in this last affair was quite beyond everything previously accomplished.

He was sentenced to transportation, and had only been received a few days when he was removed to a cell at the top of the infirmary, part of the room called now-a-days E Ward. The window in this cell is long and narrow, running parallel to the floor but at some length from it. The extreme length is about three feet, the width but six inches and a half. This may be measured at any time, and was by me before I wrote the last sentence. It was closed by a window that revolved on a central bar forming an axle. This bar was riveted into the stone at each end of the window.

In those days the prisoners used regular steel knives, which were given in for meal times, and then immediately removed. Howard at dinner-time converted his knife into a rough saw, by hammering the edge of the blade on the corner of his iron bedstead, and with this sawed through one rivet, leaving the window *in statu quo*. The whole thing was effected within the dinner hour: saw made, bar cut, and knife returned. No examination of the knife could have been made, and so far luck favoured the prisoner. As soon as the warders went off duty, and the pentagon was left to one single officer as patrol, Howard set to work. Hoisting himself again to the window, by hanging his blanket on a hammock hook in the wall just beneath, he removed the window bodily—one rivet having been sawn through, the other soon gave way. The way of egress, such as it was, was now open—a narrow slit three feet by six inches and a half. Howard was a stoutly built man, with by no means a small head, yet he managed to get this head through the opening. Having accomplished this, no doubt after tremendous pressure and much pain to himself, he turned so as to lie on his back, and worked his shoulders and arms out. He had previously put the window with its central iron bar half in half out of the orifice, meaning to use it as a platform to stand on, the weight of his body pressing down one end while the other caught against the roof of the opening, and so gave him a firm foothold. He had also torn up his blankets and sheets in strips, and tied them together, so as to form a long rope, one end of which was fastened to his legs. He was now half-way out of the window, lying in a horizontal position, with his arms free, his body nipped about the centre by the narrow opening, his legs still inside his cell. It was not difficult for him now to draw out the rest of his body, and as soon as he had length enough he threw himself up and caught the coping-stone of the roof above. All this took place on the top storey, at a height of some thirty-five feet from the ground. He was now outside the wall, and standing on the outer end of the window bar. To draw out the whole lengths of blanket and sheeting rope, throw them on to the roof, and clamber after, were his next exploits. His next job was to descend into the garden below, which encircles the whole of the buildings, and is itself surrounded by a low boundary wall. This garden was patrolled by six sentries, who divided the whole distance between them. He could see them as he stood on the roof between Pentagons 3 and 4. He took the descent by degrees, lowering himself from the roof to a third floor window, and from third floor to second, from second to first, and from first to the ground itself. The back of the nearest patrol just then was turned, and Howard's descent to *terra firma* was unobserved. Next moment he was seen standing in his white shirt, but otherwise naked, in among the tombstones of the Penitentiary graveyard, which is just at this point. Concluding he was a ghost, the sentry, as he afterwards admitted, turned tail and ran, leaving the coast quite clear. Howard was not slow to profit by the chance. Some planks lay close by, one of which he raised against the boundary wall, and walked up the incline thus formed. Next moment he dropped down on the far side, and was free. His friends lived close by the prison in Pye Street, Westminster, and within a minute or two he was in his mother's house, got food and clothing, and again made off for the country.

Naturally the excitement in the prison on the following morning was intense. Howard was gone, and he could be tracked by his means of exit from his cell to the roof, down the outer wall, across the garden, and over the boundary wall. Here the trail stopped; and though his home in Pye Street was immediately searched, no one would confess to having seen him. It was felt that recapture was almost hopeless. It occurred, however to Denis Power,* the warder of Howard's ward, that this man had come to prison with a "pal," a certain Jerry Simcox, who had been convicted at the same time and for the same offence. Mr. Power thereupon visited Simcox in his cell.

"So Punch has gone, sir ? "

"How did you know that ? "

"Why, sir, you couldn't keep him. We was in Newgate together, him and me, and in Horsemonger too; but we got out of both. There ain't no jail 'll hold Punch Howard."

"Oh, you got out together, did you ? " said the officer, growing interested.

"Yes, and could again out of any 'stir' in the three kingdoms, and they could not take us either. We got to too safe a crib for that."

"Yes ? " Power spoke unconcernedly. If he had appeared too anxious Simcox would have shut up.

"Punch has got an uncle down Uxbridge way—works at some brick-fields at West Drayton. Six or eight hundred of

* At this moment (1875) Mr. Power is the chief warder of Millbank.

them—Mr. Hearn's lot they is. That's where we went, and the police daren't follow us there. They don't allow no 'coppers' on the premises thereabouts, Mr. Power. That's the place to hide."

"No doubt," thinks Mr. Power; "and Howard's gone there now."

Within an hour he had obtained the governor's permission to go in pursuit, with a brace of pistols in his pocket, and unlimited credit.

At the inn of West Drayton he bought from the ostler a suit of navvy's clothes, and went thus disguised with a spade over his shoulder towards the brickworks. The field was full and busy. There was an alehouse close by, but, as it was early morning, no one about but a sort of serving wench, a middle-aged woman, one-eyed, and bearing on her face the marks of a life of dissipation and rough usage.

"Morrow, mistress. Any work going?"

"Ah! work enough," replied the woman, fixing him with her one eye, which was as good as four or five in any other head. "But you don't want no work."

"No?"

"No; I know you. You're not what you seem. That spade and them duds ain't no sort of good. You're after work, but not that sort of work."

Doubtful whether she meant to help or thwart him, Power could only trust himself to order a pot of ale.

"Have a drain, missus."

"And I'll help you too—no, not with the ale, but to cop young Punch."

"Punch?"

"Aye—Punch Howard. That's the work you're after; and you shall get it too, or my name's not Martha Jonas. This three-and-twenty years I've lived with his uncle, Dan Cockett, man and wife, though no parson blessed us. Three-and-twenty I slaved and bore with the mean white-faced hound, and now he leaves me for a younger woman, and I am brought to this. Help you!—by the great powers, I'd put a knife in Dan Cockett too."

"And how am I to take him?"

" Not by daylight. Bless you, if you went into that field they'd never let you out alive. Why, no bobby durst go there, nor yet a dozen together."

" Is Punch Howard in the field with them ? "

" There; look yonder. D'ye see that lad in the striped shirt and blue belcher tie, blue and big white spots? Can't you tell him a mile off ? "

Sure enough it was Punch Howard, standing by a brick "table," at which a number of others were at work, smoothing and finishing the bricks, or coming and going with the bearing-off barrows.

"Come to-night, master. They sleep mostly out there, on the top of the brick stacks—and heavy sleep, for the beer in this house isn't water. Come with a bobby or two, and look them all over. Punch'll be among them, and you'll be able to steal him away before the rest awake."

So Power went back to the village, interviewed the superintendent of police, kept quiet during the rest of the day, and that night came in force to draw his covert. Stealthily they searched it from end to end. Among all the villainous faces into which they peered there was not one that bore the least resemblance to Punch Howard. Had the woman played him false? Power could hardly make up his mind to distrust her, so earnest and embittered had been her language against Dan Cockett. No doubt another night he would have more success. Meanwhile time pressed, and he resolved to try a plan of his own.

" Have you a good horse and four-wheeled shay ? " he asked of the landlord next morning.

" The best in all England."

" Every man's goose is a swan," thought Power. " Let's see the nag."

He was a good one, and no mistake; but an out-and-out good one was wanted for the job in hand.

At one end of the brick-field—a spacious place covering 200 or 300 acres—was an office for the time-keeper and foreman of the works. He was an old police sergeant, long pensioned off, but who had his wits about him still. The office was approached by a narrow lane, with room for one

set of wheels only, a quarter of a mile in length, and
branching off from the high road to Uxbridge. Up this lane,
half hidden by the hedge, Mr. Power drove to the foreman's
shed. The ex-sergeant was alone, and readily fell in with
the plan proposed. "Here!" he cried to a young fellow
who went his errands and assisted in the office; "run up to
the field and ask Dan Cockett if he wants a job for that idle
young nephew. I see he's back in these parts. I need a lad
to screen coal dust, and I'll give him twelve shillings a week.
Look sharp!"

The messenger went off without.

"A job for my nephew?" said old Dan. "Ay—heartily
thank you too, master. You're a gentleman. Hi! Punch,
you're in luck. They say they'll take you on. Twelve
shillings a week. Run along with the master: they want to
'book you' at the office."

So unsuspecting Punch accompanied the other back to
where Power was waiting for his prey. It should be
mentioned here that this warder was an extremely powerful
man—tall, with tremendous shoulders, and just then in the
prime of life.

He stepped forward at once.

"What, Punch! What are you doing in these parts?"

"I'll swear I never saw you in all——" He never finished
those words. His captor was on him and had him fast.
In less time than it takes to describe, the handcuffs were
locked upon his wrists, and, taking him up in his arms, Power
fairly lifted him off the ground and carried him into the chaise.
Without losing his hold he took his seat too, gave reins to the
horse, and started off at a hand gallop down the lane. He had
the reins in one hand, the other arm tightly bound round
Howard's neck, and the hand used as far as it was possible as a
gag. But though it was possible to hold this captive tight, it
was not so easy to keep him silent. Before they had gone a
dozen yards Howard had managed to send off more than one
yell of distress, as a signal to his friends in the field. The
sight of the galloping horse, the burly figure of the driver,
and the lad crouching in close by its side—all three betrayed
the plot. Almost simultaneously several hundreds of men

dropped work and gave chase—some down the lane, others trying to head the trap at the junction with the high road. Power had his hands full: in one, a struggling criminal, desperate, ready to fling himself out of the chaise at any risk; in the other a bunch of reins and a whip. However, he had the start, and the heels of his pursuers. Once only was his escape in doubt: on reaching the road, the horse tried to turn sharp to the left, back to his stable at West Drayton, instead of to the right to Uxbridge. With a jerk that almost upset the trap, Power turned the horse in the right direction, and half-an-hour afterwards had left his pursuers miles behind, and was safe at the police station.

Within forty-eight hours of his escape Punch Howard was back in a Millbank cell, and Mr. Power was handsomely rewarded for the pluck and energy he had displayed.

A similar feat to Punch Howard's was accomplished by a man named Jack Robinson, at Dartmoor. This man had long pretended to be weak-minded, and had thus put his keepers off their guard. He was in the habit of exercising himself shoeless and bare-headed, and wearing an old hat without a brim. In his bosom he carried generally a few tame rats, which issued forth now and then to walk over his arms and shoulders, and to lick his hands and face. A frequent joke with Robinson was to tell the chaplain that he had put his feet too far through his trousers—which caused infinite amusement always to his convict audience. Jack, however, was fond of foretelling that he meant to make April fools of everyone—and so in effect he did. One morning he was flown, and with him two companions. He had cut through the bars of his cell by some artful contrivance; but what, remains a mystery to this day. Some think he used a watch-spring, others some chemical process. He was not recaptured, but later was reconvicted for stealing a railway rug.

No account of escapes from prison would be complete without some reference to George Hackett, who got out from Pentonville in a manner nearly marvellous. Through some neglect he had been allowed to take his sheets and bedrope into chapel with him. In those days the chapel was divided into a number of small compartments, one for each prisoner.

O

Hackett worked unobserved in his, till he had forced up the
flooring, and so gained the gallery; whence, by breaking a
zinc ventilator, he climbed through a window on to the parapet
leading to the governor's house. This he entered, and stealing
some good clothes, changed, and so got clean away. Soon
afterwards he wrote the following letter to the governor of
Pentonville:

" George Hackett presents his compliments to the Governor
of the Model Prison, and begs to apprise him of his happy
escape from the goal. He is in excellent spirits, and assures
the governor it would be useless to pursue him. He is quite
safe, and intends in a few days to proceed to the continent to
recruit his health."

Hackett was a very desperate man. He had already
escaped from a police cell at Marlborough Street, when
confined on a charge of burglary. The cell was secured by
two bolts and a patent Chubb lock. After his escape from
Pentonville he remained at large till the following Derby
day. He was then recognised going "down the road," by
a police officer, who proceeded to arrest him, but met with
violent resistance. Hackett knocked down the policeman
with a life preserver and made off, but was intercepted by
a labouring man, who, though badly mauled, succeeded in
capturing him. Hackett on all the charges was sentenced
to fifteen years' transportation.*

A later escape from Millbank was in 1860, when three
prisoners escaped, one Sunday, by working a hole in the
floor. They were located on the ground floor, and, having
removed the ventilating plate which communicated with a
shaft, got thus down into a cellar and so to a party wall with
iron gratings. These removed, they issued out into the
garden, where, as it was summer time, the thick vegetation
concealed them. By-and-by a gentleman passing gave the
alarm at the gate that he had seen two men climbing over
the boundary wall. Some officers immediately gave chase,
but the fugitives took a hansom and drove off. Their
pursuers followed in another cab, and presently ran down
their men somewhere near St. Luke's. The third prisoner

* Annual Register.

was caught in among the bushes of the garden, which he had never left.

In this case the officers of the ward were very seriously to blame. They were indeed suspected of collusion, and without that it is difficult to understand how the prisoners could have effected their purpose. They must have been long engaged in preparing to make good their exit, and in the cellar were found great quantities of weapons, tools, cards, and so forth.

Three years afterwards, in 1863, fortune favoured a convict named Sheen in every particular; and partly by lucky accident, partly by the negligence of the warders in charge of him, he managed to get out of the prison. Sheen was a man of education; by profession a surgeon; sentenced to penal servitude for forgery. After his arrival at Millbank he was found to be in the possession of funds, with which he used to tamper with his officers. Hence he was placed under others supposed to be above suspicion. But the latter were as careless as the first had been dishonest. Had they done their duty as regards searching the prisoner and his cell and belongings, he could never have effected his escape. It happened in this wise. One evening, just before locking up, he brought out his water-bucket in which he was supposed to have washed. His clothes lay at the top.

As a prisoner under special observation he was obliged to give up his clothes at night; but inside this bundle he had folded a sheet instead of his trousers, as he wanted the latter to escape in. Inside the bucket instead of dirt was a mass of brick rubbish, the result of his operation at the aperture in the angle of his cell window. During the night he continued to work at this hole until it was large enough to let him through; then, with a rope of the cocoa-nut fibre given him to pick, he made good his descent to the roof of the "General Ward," a low building in the yard below. He got into this ward by a skylight, and there supplied himself with several yards of sash-line belonging to the skylight, as well as with a piece of stout wood. After that he climbed back to his cell; placed the piece of wood between the window-bar and window-sash, and thus obtained a firm foothold on which he stood and thus reached the roof. When on the roof he slung the coir-rope round the chimney-stack and let himself down into the garden outside, and clear of the pentagons, although still within the boundary walls. To surmount this last obstacle he threw the sash-line over the boundary wall, on which it caught tight by means of a grappling hook formed of wires bound tightly together, swarmed up the rope, unloosed it, let himself down the other, and so got away. He was never recaptured.

The last escape from Millbank up to date occurred in September, 1882, and is one of the most extraordinary on record. A convict, named Lovett, a notorious burglar, who had just commenced a sentence of fourteen years' penal servitude, managed, partly by his own marvellous ingenuity, partly by the slackness of supervision, to break prison during the night. He was lodged in the top floor of one of the pentagons. There was a crack in the crown of the arch of the cell he occupied, and the discovery of this, together with his cleverness in obtaining a long length of rope, led him to attempt the escape. Works were in progress in the interior of the prison, with the usual consequences that materials likely to facilitate escape could be secured and secreted. With a long nail picked up in this way, Lovett began to make an aperture in the roof of his cell. He got up to his work by building up a platform; on his cell table he placed his rolled up bed, on that again his bucket, and thus reached to within four feet of the crown of the arch. The bed lay just opposite the "inspection hole" in the cell door, and so completely obscured the view into the cell. Lovett, according to his own account, as related after his recapture, began work at nine P.M., and by half-past one had completed an opening big enough to allow of his passing through into the roof. Once there, he removed without difficulty a batten and some slates from the rafters, and attached his rope, or, more exactly, his cord to the latter. This cord he had manufactured out of the rope or "pink" given him to unravel or pick into oakum. He respun it and so obtained a sufficient length to allow him to lower himself from the roof to within ten feet of the ground in the prison garden on the far side of the pentagon. He dropped this, and the first part of his task was accomplished successfully. Nothing remained but for him to scale the boundary wall. Here again the building materials came in with effective help. He easily picked up two planks, lashed them together with scaffold rope which lay about, and so made an inclined plane up which he walked to the top of the wall. To pull up his planks and make a new inclined plane on the far side was not difficult, and thus he descended to freedom.

Lovett was a Londoner, and he could not abandon his old haunts. Possibly he felt himself more safe in the great city. But the police obtained information by which he was speedily tracked and his movements watched. On Sunday morning, three days after his escape, he was caught in Gower Street, and within an hour was lodged in the police station on his way· back to Millbank.

FEMALE PRISONERS AT EXERCISE.

CHAPTER XI.

THE WOMEN.

It is a well-established fact in prison logistics that the women are far worse than the men. When given to misconduct they are far more persistent in their evil ways, more outrageously violent, less amenable to reason or reproof. For this there is more than one explanation. No doubt when a woman is really bad, when all the safeguards, natural and artificial, with which they have been protected are removed, further deterioration is sure to be rapid when it once begins. Again, the means of coercion in the case of female prisoners are necessarily limited. While a prompt exhibition of force cannot fail sooner or later to bring an offending male convict to his senses, a woman continues her misconduct unchecked, because such methods cannot be put into practice against her. Although in some cases the men have made a temporarily

successful fight against discipline, in the long run they have
been compelled to succumb. On the other hand there are
instances known of women who have maintained for months.
nay years, an unbroken warfare with authority, and who have
won the day in the end. Never beaten, they continued till the
day of their release to set every one at defiance. That obstinacy which has passed into a proverb against the sex, supported them throughout; this, and a species of hysterical
mania, the natural outcome of their highly-strung nervous
system.

A curious example of their strength of physical endurance,
and their almost indefatigable persistence in wrong-doing,
deserves to be mentioned here, though it occurred some years
later on. A strange fancy all at once seized a number of
women occupying adjoining cells to drum on their doors with
the soles of their feet. There is no evidence to show when or
how this desire first showed itself; but in less than a week it
had become general almost throughout the female prison. To
accomplish her purpose the woman lay full length on her cell
floor, just the right distance from the door, and began. She
was immediately answered from the next cell, whence the
infection spread rapidly to the next, and so on till the whole
place was in an uproar. These cell doors being badly hung
were a little loose; they rattled, therefore, and shook, till
the whole noise became quite deafening and incredible. Some
women were able to keep up the game for hours together, day
after day; in several cases it was proved that they had
drummed in this way for several weeks. They soon worked
themselves into a state of uncontrollable excitement, amounting
almost to hysteria. Many after a time became quite prostrate
and ill, and had to be taken to the infirmary for treatment.
The physical exertion required in the operation was so great
that women so employed for barely an hour were found literally
soaked in perspiration from head to foot, and lying, without
exaggeration, in pools of moisture. In numbers the kicking
superinduced diseases of the feet, the whole skin of the sole
having been worn away; for it is almost needless to observe
that very early in the affray shoes and stockings were
altogether destroyed, and it came to be a question of bare

feet. Several methods were tried to put an end to this
unpleasant practice—strait waistcoats, dietary punishments,
and so forth—but all without avail. In that particular instance
the disturbances continued till the women had fairly worn
themselves out.

Since then later outbreaks of a similar character were met
and subdued in a different fashion. The introduction of
"ankle straps," which confine the feet as handcuffs do the
wrist, was found a highly efficacious treatment—this, and the
invention of the "dumb cell." From the latter no sound can
possibly proceed: however loud and boisterous the outcry
within, outside not a whisper is heard. When women feel that
they are shouting and wasting their breath all to no purpose,
they throw up the sponge. But even more has since then
been accomplished by purely moral methods than by these
physical restraints. It has been found that the simplest way
to tame women thus bent upon misconduct is to take no
notice of them at all. When a woman discovers that she ceases
to attract attention by her violence, she alters her line of
conduct, and seeks to attain her ends by other and more
agreeable means. The most potent temptation with them is
the desire to "show off" before their companions. A curious
sort of vanity urges them on. It is all bravado. Hence we
find that when these tremendous "breakings out," as they are
termed in prison parlance, occur, they originate almost entirely
among the women who are "associated," in other words, who
are free to come and go and communicate with one another.
Separate them, keep them as much as possible apart and alone,
and you remove at once the strong temptation to gain an
unenviable notoriety at the expense of the discipline of the
establishment. This is proved by the experience of late years.
Thus at Millbank in 1874 there were only three instances
of this sort of misconduct, and in the previous year only
four.

But to return to Mr. Nihil. It appears that during his
reign the condition of the female pentagon was always
unsatisfactory. We find in his Journal constant reference to
the want of discipline among the female prisoners. Thus:
"The behaviour of the female pentagon is frightfully dis-

orderly, calling for vigorous and exemplary punishment.
Women contract the most intimate friendship with each other,
or the most deadly hatred." The bickering, bad feeling,
and disputes are increasing. After inquiring into one case
the governor observes: "Before the afternoon was over the
combatants had the whole pentagon in an uproar. One
smashed her windows to bits, and so did the other. They had
to be taken to the dark; but Walters produced a knife,
and would have wounded the matron." Again, "I had to
reprove strongly the taskmistress and warders for the
laxity of discipline prevalent therein." Later on, when
the rules of greater seclusion came into force, he again
remarks: "On the female side there is great laxity, no
discipline, no attempt to enforce non-intercourse. Instead
of a rule by which each individual would be thrown on
her own reflections, and secluded altogether, the female
pentagon is in fact a criminal nunnery, where the sister-
hood are linked together by a chain of sympathies and by
familiar and frequent communications. . . . .Although, to
the ladies who visit them, the females repeat Scripture
and speak piously, the communications which many of them
carry on with each other are congenial with their former
vicious habits, their minds being thus kept in a state at once
the most depraved and hypocritical."

These "ladies" to whom the governor refers were members of the celebrated "Ladies' Association," headed by
Mrs. Fry, whose long ministrations among female convicts
have gained them a world-wide reputation. Having done
undoubtedly excellent work where crying evils called for
reform, they were eager for fresh fields of labour. In 1836
they had applied through the Home Secretary for admission to the Penitentiary, which after some demur they
obtained. The committee urged that "although they felt
the sincerest respect for the benevolent motives of Mrs. Fry
and her associates, they are bound, in justice to the Penitentiary, to observe that the admission of ladies as visitors
into a prison like Newgate furnishes no legitimate reason
for admitting them on similar terms into the Penitentiary,
where the system in operation is exempt from those evils

which the ladies have been so laudably employed in correcting at Newgate." Upon this Lord John Russell remarks that he thinks it is manifest that an impression may be made by the ladies which the best instructions of the chaplain might not effect; and he is disposed to recommend that "the chaplain should confer with those ladies, and that he should endeavour to arrange with them certain periods at which they should be allowed to communicate with the female prisoners, but that it should be clearly understood by them that his report would be sufficient to deprive them of admission."

Accordingly they came and tried their best. It would be hardly fair to deny them all credit, or to assert that, because the women continued ill-conditioned throughout, the counsels and admonitions of these ladies had altogether failed of effect. It is obvious, however, from Mr. Nihil's remarks, that their services tended to produce hypocrisy rather than real repentance. The fact was there was a marked distinction between the work they had done at Newgate and that to which they put their hands in the Penitentiary. In this latter place the women were really sedulously cared for; they had an abundance of good food, clean cells, comfortable beds; they bathed regularly; they had employment, books, and the unceasing ministrations of a zealous chaplain. Newgate, on the other hand, when first visited by Mrs. Fry, was a perfect sink of abomination, rivalling quite the worst pictures painted by Howard. The women's side went by the name of "Hell above ground." Here, in four rooms, containing altogether some 190 superficial yards, were crowded 300 females of every category—tried, untried; felons, misdemeanants—with their numerous children. Many of these women were half naked, the rest in rags. They had no beds, and upon this floor whereon they slept they washed also, and cooked their food. On all sides the ear was assailed by awful imprecations, begging, swearing, singing, fighting, dancing, dressing up in men's clothes. "The scenes are too bad to be described," says Mrs. Fry in her evidence before the House of Commons. All visitors were clamorously attacked for alms, the wretched prisoners struggling wildly to get foremost and nearer the bars that parted them from the public, or stretching forth their wooden spoons, tied to the end of long staves, to collect the money. So great was the lawlessness that invariably prevailed that the governor of Newgate accompanied Mrs. Fry with reluctance, and by his advice the visitors left their watches and valuables behind in his house. "On that first occasion the sorrowful and neglected condition of these depraved women and their miserable children," says her biographer, "dwelling in such a vortex of corruption, deeply sank into her heart."

All that Mrs. Fry and her companions accomplished is a matter of history now. The object they had in view was "to provide for the clothing, instruction, and employment of the women; to introduce them to a knowledge of the Holy Scriptures; and to form in them as much as possible those habits of order, sobriety, and industry, which may render them docile and peaceable in prison, and respectable when they leave it." All this, and more, these ladies to their infinite credit performed, and in an incredibly short period of time. It was no slight feat to replace within a few months drunkenness, ferocity, and abandoned licentiousness by sober decency of demeanour; loud ribaldry and oaths by silence or edifying talk; squalor and semi-nudity by cleanliness and sufficiency in attire; to convert a den of wild beasts, where only filth, disgusting odours, and all abominations reigned, into a happy home of quiet and decorum. These were the changes they actually effected. And yet, valuable and remarkable as were these results, it must be confessed that they owed to contrast not a little of their importance. Compared with the first foul blackness, the new order of things seemed whiter than snow. It was because this Newgate gaol and its wretched inmates were fallen to the very depths of degradation, that the improvement worked in their condition appeared so tremendous and surprising. But it is easier to turn the positively bad into something comparatively better, than to make the latter superlatively and permanently good. Without presuming to detract from the efforts and success of the "Ladies' Association," there is too much reason to suppose that the results they obtained were evanescent and temporary. The reformation of Newgate was what in modern language would be styled a "revival," and the known tendency of such movements is to collapse when the first fire of frenzied enthusiasm is exhausted. We have, unfortunately, evidence that among the female convicts who were brought to bless the name of Mrs. Fry, many again fell away; partly, doubtless, from the shocking mismanagement of affairs at the antipodes,* whither most of them proceeded, and in a measure also because their conversion was transitory and did not rest on the sure foundation of really altered habits and thorough reform of character.

But the condition of Millbank under Mr. Nihil was not that of Newgate and other prisons in 1816. It could not be said the Penitentiary prisoners were neglected. No fault could be found with their treatment generally, or the measures taken to provide for their spiritual needs. Long before the arrival of the "Ladies' Association" the religious instruction of the female prisoners may be said to have reached a point of saturation: the preaching and praying, if I may say so, had been already a little overdone. Hence it was that their advent deepened only their outward hypocrisy and lip service, without changing one whit their evil natures, which still rankled like hidden sores beneath.

And so it is to-day. These lady visitors are "amateurs," and, like all other unprofessional people, the work they do is imperfect and incomplete. Their tendency is to waste their energy in the wrong direction. If they alone suffered we might pity them and pass on, but serious injury to discipline is another inevitable consequence, and this ought not to be ignored. From benevolent motives, no doubt, but by mistake, the worse "cases" are those which by preference the ladies take up: these they pet, encourage, and make much of; while a good peaceable prisoner, to whom a word or two of comfort would really be a boon, is neglected and left to herself. Seeing how much the visits of the ladies are appreciated, this plan of action is really placing a premium on misconduct. The regular official staff of the prison would

* See pp. 281, 282.

avoid an error like this. With trained professional eye they would sift the wheat from the chaff, and discriminate between impostors and the really deserving. Indeed the permanent officers of an establishment like Millbank are so amply sufficient for all needs that the necessity for outside extraneous assistance is not at once apparent—more especially when it is to be feared that evil rather than good is the consequence of these amateur ministrations.

There was, however, in Mr. Nihil's time, plenty of rough materials to work upon in the female pentagon. Some of the cases of misconduct recorded in the governor's Journals are far worse than anything we can even nowadays imagine. The women maintained the fight longer and with greater recklessness than would really be possible with our modern management in a modern prison. No doubt this was because the right methods of treatment were as yet hardly known, or, if known, were practised but imperfectly. I shall proceed now to detail one or two of the most flagrant instances of the protracted misconduct of those days, leaving it to the reader to decide whether the absence of similar outrageous behaviour now does not at least prove a certain superiority in our modern system of prison administration.

I have referred already to the additional annoyance entailed upon the governor by the consignment to his charge of the female transports awaiting transportation. None of these were worse than a certain Julia Newman, who was a Penitentiary prisoner, and whose case I shall describe directly at length, taking it as a type of the whole. But there were many others among the female convicts who were also very desperate characters indeed; such as the woman from Liverpool, concerning whom the governor of the gaol wrote to say that she was so desperate that he thought it would be necessary to send her tied up in a sack. Mary McCarthy was another, who was brought in handcuffs from Newgate, with a note to the effect that she required the greatest attention. She had several times attempted to strangle herself, and had therefore been handcuffed day and night and constantly watched. "She is a

most artful, designing woman, and will succeed, if not well
looked after, in her attempts to destroy herself."

Mr. Nihil found McCarthy submissive and tractable, but
after the above caution he thought it advisable to continue
the handcuffing, intending to withdraw the restraint as
soon as she abandoned her intention to commit suicide.   At
the end of two days she managed to rid herself of her handcuffs, having very small wrists; but as she evinced no signs
of violence or intractability they were not replaced, the
governor thinking from his experience with Newman, that
effectual and complete restraint was impossible if the
prisoner was determined.   McCarthy was, however, constantly watched, and for ten days she remained quite quiet.
On the 21st of October, a fortnight after her admission, she
begged her warder, Mrs. West, to come into her cell and
teach her to stitch.   Mrs. West did so readily, and all was
calm and peaceable for a while.   Suddenly, without giving
Mrs. West a moment's warning, McCarthy stabbed her from
behind, inflicting one severe wound on the forehead and the
other under the ear.   She appears to have used the utmost
violence.   Mrs. West got up, streaming with blood, and made
for the cell door, which she bolted behind her, thus securing
the prisoner inside.   Assistance was called at once, but on
going back to the cell McCarthy was found on the floor
insensible, with a big bruise on her forehead.   She continued
in this kind of trance for twenty-four hours.   It was a marvel
to everyone how she had got the weapon, for in consequence
of her known suicidal tendencies she had been furnished
with neither knife or scissors.   However, on returning from
exercise, as it was afterwards ascertained, she had seen a knife
lying on the floor in the passage, and stooping, as if to pull
up her shoe, had managed to secrete the knife in her sleeve.
So unprovoked and murderous an attack, coupled with the
previous attempts at suicide, indicated a maniacal ferocity.
The succeeding trance corroborated the suspicions; and
although the prisoner had exhibited great art in concealing
her weapon, such cunning was not inconsistent with mania.
She had also attempted to effect her escape by making a large
hole in the ceiling of her cell.   Therefore, a well-known

THE WOMEN.

physician, Dr. Monro, was now sent for, and at once, on
hearing the whole story, certified the prisoner to be insane.
She was now in the infirmary, "bound with several ligatures
by her feet and arms to the bed." The surgeon removed
those on her arms, on which the governor thought it prudent
to put her into handcuffs. In the night she was caught in
the act of getting her feet loose, and was evidently bent on
some further mischief. Thus baffled, she remained sullen for
some time, then sent for the governor and made a clean breast
of it, having been moved thereto by a passage in Psalm cxix.,
which another prisoner who watched her had been reading
aloud. The expression she noticed was about "going away
like lost sheep." She told the governor that while she was
in the trance she knew some gentlemen had come to see her,
and that one of them was a mad doctor. "I don't think
doctors know much about madness," she added, "or they'd
a understood me better." Mr. Nihil is now pretty sure that
McCarthy is no lunatic, but Dr. Monro and Dr. Wade adhere
to their former opinion, so she is removed to Bethlehem.

Another woman, Ann Williams, who was received from
Bath, proved a very desperate character. The governor of
Bath Gaol, who brought her up to London, declared he had
never had so much trouble with any prisoner before. She
also was determined to make away with herself, and the first
time left alone she had jumped out of a window an immense
height from the ground. This country gaoler, on seeing the
cell to which she was destined in the Penitentiary, protested
that it would be highly dangerous to allow her to have
pewter pint, or spoon, or cell stool. The moment her hands
were loosened she would be sure to thrust the spoon down
her throat, or attack some one with the stool. Even the
sheets should be removed, for she was capable of tearing
them into slips to make herself a halter. Directly she arrived
at Millbank she tried to dash her brains out by striking her
head violently against the wall—emulating in this respect
another prisoner for whom, some years later, a special head-
dress was provided, a sort of Turkish cap padded at the top,
merely to save her skull. Williams' language was dreadful,
and she refused all food. The governor now suspects her

strongly of artifice, and the doctor recommends that she should be punished with bread and water diet. That night she grows extremely turbulent. She is now tied down to her bedstead, and a sort of gag, brought from Bath for McCarthy, is used and has a great effect in curbing her rage. This gag was a wide piece of strong leather, having perforated holes to admit of breathing, but which completely silenced her horrible and violent expressions. After starving herself for four days she has still strength enough left to get out of her handcuffs, and would have done much mischief had not the other prisoners who were watching her held her down by the hair. After greasing her wrists it was found possible to replace the handcuffs. This was another case in which it was thought advisable to give the prisoner the benefit of the doubt, and she was also removed to Bedlam.

It was quite within possibility that in these two cases madness was proved. But it is often difficult to draw the line between madness and outrageous misconduct; and the latter is sometimes persisted in in order to make good a pretence of deranged intellect. Among the female prisoners there are numerous instances of this—and for the matter of that among the males also. Cases of "trying it on," or "doing the barmy," which are cant terms for feigning lunacy, used at one time to be more frequent than they are now, when longer experience protects prison medical men from deception.

The case of Julia St. Clair Newman—or Miss Newman, as she was commonly called in the prison and out—attracted considerable attention in its time, becoming indeed the subject of frequent discussion in Parliament, and being referred at length to a Select Committee of the House of Lords. Inside the walls Julia Newman was for many months the centre of all interest; she was a thorn in the side of all officials, visitors, governor, doctor, matrons, and even of her fellow-prisoners. Apparently of Creole origin—at least it was certain that she had been born in one of the West India Islands—she came home while still a child, and was educated at a French boarding-school. When sixteen she returned to Trinidad with her mother, remained there a year or two, and again came to England to live on an allowance made them by Julia's guardian. But whether this allowance was too small, or their natural proclivities would not be repressed, they soon got into bad ways. Repeatedly shifting houses, moving from one lodging to another, always in debt, and not seldom under suspicion of swindling and fraud. Three months in the King's Bench was followed by a lengthened sojourn in Whitecross Street Gaol; then came more shady transactions, mistakes like pledging their landlady's plate for their own, making away with wearing apparel and furniture, or absconding without payment of rent. At length, having left the apartments of a certain Mrs. Dobbs in a hurry, they packed up—quite by accident—in one of their trunks a silver spoon, some glasses, and a decanter, the property of the aforesaid Mrs. Dobbs. For this they were arrested, and as soon as they were in custody a second charge was laid against them for stealing a ring from a woman in the King's Bench, which Julia indignantly denied, declaring that she had picked it up in the pump-yard—where of course there were plenty of rings to be had simply for the trouble of stooping. Unfortunately the jury disbelieved the Newmans' explanation of both counts, and mother and daughter were found guilty and sentenced to transportation.

They were evidently a pair of ordinary commonplace habitual swindlers, deserving no special notice. But their rumoured gentility gained for them a species of misplaced sympathy; and they were excused transportation, to be sent instead, for reformation, to the Penitentiary, where they arrived on the 11th March, 1837. Of the mother it will be sufficient to say at once that she was an inoffensive, tractable old woman, who bore her punishment with patience, and eventually died in prison. But Julia was cast in a different mould. Under thirty—according to her own statement she was only nineteen—full in figure, and florid of complexion, possessed, as was afterwards proved, of extraordinary physical strength, she displayed, from the first moment almost, an incorrigible perversity which made her in the end a perfect nuisance to the whole establishment. There was something ladylike about

her when she was in a peaceable mood. Inexperienced people
would have called her a gentlewoman. Not handsome or even
good-looking, but decidedly "interesting," the matrons said
when questioned before the Select Committee. She was
accomplished: could draw and paint, and was very musical;
sang quite beautifully—and certainly during her stay at Millbank she gave plenty of proof of the strength and compass of
her voice; and with all this she was clever, designing, and of
course thoroughly unprincipled.

The day after her reception she endeavoured to tamper
with the wardswoman; seeking to obtain paper and pencil
"to write a letter to her mother." When taxed with this
breach of rules, she declared the wardswoman wanted to
force the things upon her. Then she was found to have
cut a page out of "The Prisoner's Companion," a book
supplied to all. "Questioned privately, Newman with many
expressions of grief confessed her guilt." Mr. Nihil, who was
still quite in the dark as to her real character, pardoned this
offence. She was next charged with an attempt to induce a
fellow-prisoner to pass on a message to her (Newman's) mother
—the substance of which was that the elder Newman was to
impose upon the chaplain by a hypocritical confession, to
obtain thus the daughter's release, Julia promising when free
to contrive means by which the mother should also be discharged. The "dark" became her lot for this, and to it she
again returned the following week, for refusing to clean out
her cell. When the governor reasoned with her, she merely
said she would be happy to pay some other prisoner to do it
for her. This second visit to the dark brought her under the
doctor's notice, who ordered her to the infirmary, as she
declared she was too weak to walk downstairs. Her face
having grown quite pale and ghastly, help was sent for, when it
was discovered that she had whitened it with chalk. She
again visited the dark, and when released began again to
communicate with her mother. Several "stiffs" * were
intercepted, in which she tried to persuade her to smuggle a
letter out to their solicitors. This discovery led to a strict

* "Stiffs" are letters written clandestinely by prisoners to one
another on any scrap of paper they can find.

search of Julia's cell and person, when large quantities of writing paper were found upon her, though "how she procured the paper, or the pen, or how she manufactured the ink, continued a mystery implying great laxity of supervision." Her anxiety to write thus checked in one direction found vent in another : with the point of her scissors she had scratched upon the whitewash of her cell wall four verses of poetry. The words were harmless, and as she asserted that she felt it a severe restriction being kept apart, the governor admonished her well for this offence.   This leniency was quite thrown away. A fresh attempt at clandestine correspondence comes to light within a week or two.   Newman passes a letter at chapel to Mary Ann Stickley, which is found in the other's bosom, the substance of it being that Newman professed a great regard for Stickley, and begged of her to excite the hatred of all the other prisoners against Ware for her recent betrayal of Newman.   A second letter was picked up by Alice Bradley in front of Newman's cell, addressed to a prisoner named Weedon, whom she abused in round terms for making a false charge against the governor to the effect that he had called her (Newman) by some horrid epithet—"which she could *never* believe of that good man."   Newman's cell was again searched, when an ink bottle was found in the hopper, and some substitutes for pens.   Her letters were found "replete with artifices respecting modes of communication."   Her next form of amusement was to manufacture a big rag doll for herself, out of a breadth of her petticoat. When this was discovered Newman was at exercise walking in the yard, and she heard that her cell was about to be thoroughly searched.   Whereupon she ran as fast as she could, back to her ward, and endeavoured to prevent the matrons from entering her cell.   When searched herself she resisted violently, but with the assistance of the wardswoman some written papers were taken from her, also some leaves from the blank part of her Prayer-Book, also written over.

"I understand," says the governor, "a most extraordinary scene took place when the prisoner apprehended a search. She rushed to the stove and thrust certain papers into it,

which but for the promptitude of the wardswoman, who
behaved admirably, would soon have succeeding in putting
them beyond investigation.   They were however rescued,
upon which she threw her arms around the warder's neck,
kissed her vehemently, went on her knees, supplicated concealment, tore her hair, and by such passionate demonstrations
evinced the great importance she attached to the papers.   The
warder wept, the taskmistress contributed her tears, the
wardswoman was overcome, but all stood faithful.   In the
midst of the screaming and confusion came the schoolmaster,
who was also assailed with all the tender importunities of the
fair prisoner, but all in vain."*

By this time the governor arrived upon the scene, the
officers partially recovered from their consternation, and Newman, much less excited, was disposed to make light of the
document recently esteemed so precious.   She said it was
only a copy, the original had been torn up.   "What is it
then?"   "A paper from which my mother and I expect to
gain our liberty.   It relates to a person who was the cause of
all our misfortunes."   On inspection it proved to be a statement, or dying confession, of one Mary Hewett, tending to
exculpate the Newmans at her own expense—probably a draft
of what Julia Newman wished Hewett to say.

Three days later Julia is reported to be in a state of fury
about 9.30 p.m.   Loud screaming proceeded from her cell.
"I found her in a most violent paroxysm of rage.   It was
most painful to see it.   Not genuine madness did she evince,
but that species of temporary frenzy to which an actress by
force of imagination and violent effort could attain.   Towards
me she expressed the utmost abhorrence, and slammed the
door in my face.   I sent for the surgeon and some male officers,
for her screams and yells, her violence in tearing her hair, and
knocking her head against the wall, made it probable that
forcible restraint would be necessary."

The surgeon did not wish to have her placed in a dark cell,
nor even in a strait-waistcoat, and at his recommendation
she was taken to the infirmary and put in a room by herself;
but she was not removed without a continuance of violent.

* Journal, vol. xi.

screaming, to the disturbance of the whole place. Papers were found in her cell, on one of which was written " a lampoon, composed in doggrel verses, in which she vented the bitterness of her revenge. I (Mr. Nihil) was the principal object of her ridicule. It is melancholy to see a young girl of talent and some attainments so bent upon deception, and when foiled in her artifice abandoning herself alternately to studied malice and furious rage." She remained in the infirmary for three days at the special wish of the surgeon, though the governor wanted to have her back in her cell. All the time she continued to feign insanity—a clear imposture, of which the doctors, the governor, and the assistant chaplain were all convinced. The governor visited her "to endeavour to convince her of the folly and hopelessness of this course; but the moment she saw me she addressed me with the most insulting expressions, and seizing a can full of gruel threw it at my head." She was restrained from further violence, but continued to use the most outrageous exclamations, to the disturbance of the whole prison. The surgeon now consented to have her removed to a dark cell; and the governor remarks, "I can account for her personal hostility to myself thus. She had been defeated in several attempts to carry on clandestine communications. Until Monday last she cherished a hope of getting back among the other prisoners, where she might still prosecute her schemes; but on that day I again refused her, and my refusal was such as it was hopeless for her to try to alter it." She continued in the dark, amusing herself by singing songs of her own composition, " too regular and too much studied for the productions of a genuine madwoman." She slept well and ate all the bread they gave her. The visitor, Mr. Crawford, saw her, and recommended another medical opinion. Accordingly Mr. White, the former surgeon to the establishment, was . called in, and stated that her madness was assumed, but he recommended she still should be treated as a patient.

Goaded at length by the continued annoyance, the governor writes to the committee as follows: " I submit that the case of Julia Newman calls for some decisive proceeding. There has been time enough—eleven days—to put to the test whether she is mad in reality or only in pretence. She has contrived

to set all discipline at defiance, continually singing so as to be
heard in every part of the establishment. Her conduct excites
universal attention, and furnishes an example of the grossest
insubordination. If the prisoner is mad, she ought forthwith
to be sent to a madhouse; if not, she ought to be sent abroad
as incorrigible. Yesterday she showed a disposition to return
to her senses, as if tired of the effort of simulation, but did not
know how to get out of her assumed character. To-day she is
as bad as ever. No doubt in time she would come all right, but
in the meantime what is to be done with her? I cannot venture
to place her among other prisoners. If she is to be kept apart
the whole time of her imprisonment (of which three and a half
years are unexpired), there is every reason to expect a constant
recurrence of violence and other modes of annoyance; for she
has no respect for authority, and after assaulting the governor
and counterfeiting madness with impunity, she will be em-
boldened to act as she likes. If put into a dark cell doubts as
to her sanity will arise, and perhaps her own self-abandonment
to violence may superinduce real madness, and then it will be
said that our system at the Penitentiary had driven her out of
her mind. She is far too dangerous a prisoner to be sent into a
ward with other prisoners. She has already tampered with
eight or ten prisoners, perhaps more."

There is no end to her deception. In one of the
papers taken from her she asserted that certain property
was secreted in a flower-pot, and buried in a garden
in Goswell Street, at the house of one Elderton. The
governor applied to Sir F. Roe, at Bow Street, who said,
"Newman has been before me already. She was charged
in an anonymous letter with infanticide; but on investigation,
I found the letter was a malicious composition of this Mr.
Elderton. The letter contained many revolting particulars,
and charged Newman with the utmost barbarity." The letter
was sent for and examined by Mr. Nihil, who at once recognised the writing as Newman's own; and she had evidently
written it with the object of ruining Elderton's character, and
to appear herself as the victim of a conspiracy. "So wily,
ingenious, clever, and unprincipled a deceiver as this prisoner
cannot, I submit, after all that has passed, be placed amongst

others without endangering the subordination and discipline of the whole ward; and unless the committee are prepared to direct that she be kept altogether apart, I hope they will bring the matter to a crisis and send her abroad."

For a month this violence of demeanour continued. She was found "uniformly ungovernable." In her cell, when searched at regular intervals, clandestine writings are always discovered; in one of which was a long and critical examination of the character of the young Queen, who had just come to the throne. Mr. Nihil begins to despair. "Julia Newman having continued her pretended madness up to the present time, to the frequent disturbance of the prison, and having committed innumerable breaches of order, it became my duty to put a stop to her proceedings."

There was no chance of getting rid of her by transportation, as the last shipload of female convicts for that season had sailed, and there would be no other till the spring. "This being the case, I thought it necessary to converse with the prisoner, with a view of convincing her of the folly of carrying on her attempts, and warning her of the consequence of any further disturbance. I found her with her head fantastically dressed, and other ridiculous accompaniments. She would not hear me—darted out of her cell—stopped her ears, and uttered several violent exclamations. I made several attempts at expostulation, but in vain, and therefore I sent her to the dark." The surgeon thought her madness all deception. Again: "As my visits to Julia Newman are only signals for violence, I have abstained from visiting her in the dark, but inquired into her demeanour from the surgeon. He said that in his presence she affected to beat herself violently, and passionately to wish for death. Afterwards, in a manner very unlike a madwoman, she said she had been put into a dark cell, but it was a matter of perfect indifference to her whether she was in a dark or light cell. As the surgeon turned away she swore at him violently." Next day she hammers out her drinking-cup quite flat; and when being locked up for the night, asserts loudly that she is quite well, sings and shouts violently. "There was an obvious effort of bravado in her madness." Still the same report comes from the surgeon

"J. N. continues her affected madness." The governor sends
word he will let her out of the dark as soon as she promises to
behave herself; and then Miss Neave, one of the lady visitors,
goes to her by the governor's request, "in the hope that the
conversation of a lady, against whom she could have no preju-
dice, might have a salutary effect." It proved ineffectual.
The prisoner said she did not want to be preached to; would
not listen to a word from Miss Neave, threw water at her,
singing also, and shouting in a most powerful voice, so as to
baffle all her attempts. Miss Neave was quite convinced the
prisoner's insanity was feigned, and that she was only acting
a part. At length she is removed to a sleeping cell in the
infirmary for treatment, and here, after a first paroxysm of
rage, in which she smashes a basin into atoms, she assumes a
timid aspect, and when spoken to by the taskmistress, weeps
like a child. "In the hope she might be a little softened,"
says Mr. Nihil, "I spoke to Miss Frazer, another of the visiting ladies, who agreed to go to Newman, saying that Julia
had always received her with gentleness and apparent pleasure.
On this occasion, however, Newman behaved with frightful
violence, refusing to have any visit, dashing her can upon the
table, and seeming as if she would strike Miss Frazer if she
could. She had already blackened her own eyes, and she
appeared so possessed by despair, that Miss Frazer thought
she might do herself some serious injury, and that her hands
should be secured."

Two days later we read: "Julia Newman is worse than
ever. The doctors say she is not mad, at least Dr. Monro
did. Mr. Wade is doubtful." The governor himself being
of opinion that she is only carrying on a deep scheme, "I
suggested," he says, "to Mr. Wade, a day or two ago, that if
any circumstance had arisen to make it probable that she was
really deranged, we had better have another opinion, and
send her to Bedlam; but there does not seem any ground for
this step. But is the prisoner to defy all authority, now that
the doctor has removed her from the dark to the infirmary?
Certainly not. I therefore called upon the doctor to report
whether there was any danger in subjecting her to fresh
punishment for fresh offences?" The surgeon thinks there

would be considerable risk in sending her to the dark cell on
bread and water at present. "Had I received a different
answer, I should have proceeded forthwith to act upon the
reports against her; but the committee will see how I am
situated. She is too ill for punishment, and gets more violent
and refractory than ever. Her acts of misconduct are: refusing to take her dinner, tearing up her Prayer-Book, singing
loudly all the fore part of the evening, and refusing her breakfast; grazing her nose, so that her face presents the most
frightful appearance; asking for a can of water, and then
throwing it all over the taskmistress." No further steps are
taken at the moment, beyond providing a special strait waistcoat to be used in case of emergency. But she still continues
to be in the dark. About 7 P.M. that evening she is heard
screaming loudly. After some time the governor sends to ask
the surgeon if he was aware of it. Answer comes to say
doctor was ill in bed. Second message (oh, cunning Governor-
General): "Would it be objectionable to her health to remove
her to the dark?" Surgeon, asking only to be left in peace,
replies, "Nothing to prevent her being placed anywhere."
This is all the governor wants. Off she goes to the dark,
where she remains till she is reported to be singing as loudly
as ever in her cell, and won't give up her rug. Next she is
found lying on her back, with a handkerchief knotted tightly
around her neck. As soon as she was better, she uttered the
following impromptu :

> "What a pity hell's gates are not kept by dame King,
> So surly a cur would let nobody in "—

Mrs. King being the infirmary warder. Then the assistant
chaplain visited her, and was treated with the utmost
insolence. She attacked Mrs. Dyett, another matron, and
knocked the candlestick out of her hand, "triumphing at the
same time at her exploit. Upon this I ordered her to be confined in the strait-waistcoat made expressly for her under
the directions of the surgeon." Some time after this the
doctor visits her, and finds she has not only rid herself of the
restraint, but she has also torn the waistcoat and most of her
own clothes to atoms. Nevertheless, he thinks her so unwell

that he removes her again to the infirmary. From this, in the course of a few days she returns to her ward. The cell, however, could not hold her, and she soon forced her way out into the passage. Another new, and much stronger strait-waistcoat, specially constructed, was now put on her by a couple of male officers. Within an hour or two it was found slashed to ribbons, and on a close search a pair of scissors were discovered under her arm, accounting no doubt for the destruction.

Her next offence is to slap a matron in the face. Again the strait-waistcoat is tried, this time a newer and a still stronger one; but it is found too large to be of any use, so she is sent to the dark instead.

For a time she appears tamed, and for quite a month she remains quiet, though still "uncomfortable." She is, however, next reported for making three baskets from the straw of her mattress and part of the leaves of her Bible. She has written a long incoherent statement, probably with a stocking needle for pen, and some blood and water for ink. The warders when questioned showed great lack of desire to perform their duties. "The truth is, the prisoner is very difficult to deal with, and they are all more or less afraid of her. It is no wonder that a person of her strength, violence, and mental superiority, combined with reckless determination and obstinacy, should inspire these terrors; and I really cannot blame these officers. Without perpetually searching her person, as well as her bedding, it would be impossible to guard against the practices just reported, but this would occasion perpetual disturbance, leading to no good end, but doing much mischief in the Penitentiary." Convinced that Millbank means of punishment are totally inadequate to attain the end of reforming her, or compelling her to obey the rules, the governor, to avoid constant worry, is content to leave her quite to herself, keeping her apart—in itself a heavy punishment—and restricting her to bread and water when she broke the rules.

Newman, however, would not consent to be forgotten. Her next offence was to refuse to give out her cell stool, and when the door was opened she flung it with great violence at her warder's head, but the latter fortunately evaded the blow. The governor and the male officers together repaired to the spot in order "to remove this most rebellious and dangerous prisoner to the dark. Her subsequent conduct has been of the same stamp. None but the most prominent features admit of being reported, her life here being in fact one continued system of insult and contempt. In the dark cell she levelled her tin can at the surgeon, and the contents fell upon the task-mistress; had either of them been struck by the vessel it might have been of serious consequence. Her cell has since been examined, and several figures and other articles have been discovered. They exhibit extraordinary resource and ingenuity, unhappily directed to the flagitious purpose of destroying property and manifesting contempt of authority."

As soon as she went to the dark, the surgeon recommended that she should be removed to the infirmary, as she appeared much exhausted. "I thought it necessary to remonstrate against this, as it appeared ill-timed lenity. I am very reluctant to liberate the prisoner from punishment for several reasons. Every fresh victory which, under the plea of ill-health, she has achieved has been productive of increased insolence; and I have often lamented to see her indulged with arrowroot and similar niceties at the very time she has been defying all authority. The female officers entertain just apprehensions in waiting on her in the usual manner when restored to a sleeping cell, and with regard to the mode of punishing her on fresh offences I am quite perplexed. I might again send her to the dark, again to be restored in an unsubdued state to a sleeping cell, and so on continually, but I am obliged to resort to male assistance, and this I find by experience has a very injurious effect upon the other female prisoners, many of whom take it into their heads to brave all female authority, and require the men to be sent for before they will submit." The governor thinks, "All prisoners whose insubordinate spirit does not yield to the ordinary method of treatment, should be reported as incorrigible, and removed. . . . The moral injury they do to the residue by long continued examples of rebellion is incalculable."

The assistant chaplain reports on 12th December, that he found Julia Newman exceedingly exhausted, and that the news of a letter from Trinidad to her mother failed to rouse

her. She had only eaten a little of the crust of her bread, and
he was alarmed as to the consequences which might follow if
she were allowed to remain longer in the dark cell. Mr. Nihil
is still firm. " I remarked that her exhaustion was owing not
to confinement in a dark cell, but to an obstinate refusal to
eat her bread; and that I could not compel her to eat; and
that if she would not eat unless humoured in this instance, she
might as well refuse to eat unless I let her out of the prison,
and that I should not be justified in complying from apprehension of danger to her health thus wilfully incurred. In
like manner it seemed now as if she chose to starve herself
because she was not allowed to throw stools at the heads of
officers. But of course I have no desire to keep her under
punishment a moment after she shows a disposition to conform
to the regulations, and maintain that quietness I am here to
enforce."

The surgeon was now sent for, and asked what he thought.
He was afraid it would be necessary to remove her on the
ground of safety, being persuaded she would sacrifice her life
sooner than yield.

" If you think she cannot be kept under punishment with
safety, I must submit to your opinion," says the governor.
" It is for you to determine that, otherwise I must distinctly
object; for the duties of my office will not permit me to give
in to her while she continues insubordinate."

" It's not the dark cell," replied the doctor, " that constitutes her danger, but her persistent refusal to eat so long as
she is kept there."

" Very well, then," said the governor; " you may remove
her. I cannot stand in the way and prevent you from acting
on your own judgment."

The surgeon went, and in five minutes returned.

"Well?"

"There's not much the matter with her yet. Directly she
saw me she began to sing and scream, with a voice as loud as
if she had lived always on solid meat. She pelted me with
bread—refused to come and have her pulse felt—abused,
insulted me in every way, and finally said she was just as well
in the dark as anywhere else."

Under these circumstances it was decided to leave her where she was for the present, especially as a forcible removal might have created a general disturbance in the prison.

The next step in the case was her removal to Bethlehem Hospital as mad. But even this was misconstrued; for when, in the February following (1838), a discussion arose in the House of Lords as to alleged ill-treatment of prisoners in the Penitentiary, Newman's case was mentioned as one in which, on the other hand, culpable leniency had been shown. Those who found fault declared that she had been sent to an asylum, not because she was mad, but because by birth a lady. The same people declared that it was well known she was not mad, and that she never had been. The matrons at Bethlehem knew this well, and had told her to her face that she was only feigning; whereupon she ceased to feign. Then as it was clear she was not mad, it was equally clear that Bethlehem was not the place for her. Accordingly, she was returned to the Penitentiary; and back she came, exhibiting throughout the most sullen contempt, and persistently refusing to open her lips. Directly she returned she again began her tricks. Deliberately insolent refusal to execute the orders she received, and open contempt of punishment, were the leading points on which she differed with the authorities. Again the governor urges on the committee that she may be removed " by transportation," she being, under existing circumstances, both intractable and incorrigible. "If I am to maintain discipline where she is, it must be by entering perpetually into fresh and perplexing contests, the outcome of which may be very awful as respects the prisoner and exceedingly embarrassing as respects the Institution." She next pretends to wish to lay hands upon herself, and her rug is found torn up and converted into a noose. It was hanging to a peg in her cell, like a halter ready for use. The authorities thence considered it advisable therefore to place her in restraint, in a new straitwaistcoat which fitted close. In an hour or two she had torn it all to pieces. The next proceeding was to confine her hands in a very small pair of handcuffs, and to pinion her arms with strong tape. The waistcoat appearing to have been cut, she and her cell was searched, but no knife or scissors could be found, but only a piece of broken glass which she must have used for the purpose. She soon afterwards loosened the tape, and was then bound with strong webbing to the bedstead. Next morning she was found to have got rid of the handcuffs, had cut the webbing to pieces, broken her windows, and destroyed her bedding. One of the female warders was therefore sent to a surgical instrument maker's to purchase some effectual instrument of restraint, and returned with a muff-belt and handcuffs, all united, and ingeniously contrived to defeat the struggles of lunatics— quite a new invention. Before long she completely destroyed the muff and got rid of the handcuffs attached to it. She was next secured to the wall by a stout chain.

An officer, Mrs. Drago, who visited her just now, asked her why she could make such a figure of herself, pretending to be mad too, when she wasn't. " I've been advised to do it by my solicitor. If I can only get out, I'll soon manage to get my mother out. I'm a person of large fortune, and can make it worth any one's while to do me a good turn. Mrs. Bryant used to, but she's gone. That used to be my larder, over there "—pointing to the window blind. Her evident object was to tamper with Mrs. Drago, and this of itself gave evidence that she could not be very mad.

The chain by which she is now confined was put round her waist, passed through a ring in the wall and padlocked. " This security was of short duration: before morning she had slipped through the chain. It was again placed on her in a more effectual manner, under, instead of outside her clothes. . . . As she had destroyed so much of her bedding I ordered her to have no more bed-clothes. In the evening she made the most violent demand for a blanket, and said she was dying of cramp and cold. . . . As a matter of discipline I thought it my duty to refuse the blanket unless ordered by the surgeon. When she heard this she quite frightened the female officer with the frightful and horrible imprecations she uttered."

In consequence of her getting out of her chain the manufacturer of restraints for the insane came to devise some fresh expedient for confining her. He made a pair of leather sleeves of extra strength, and fitted them himself. They came up to her shoulders, were strapped across, then also strapped round her waist, and again below, fastening her hands close to her side.

Next morning the taskmistress took the sleeves to the governor. In the night Julia had extricated herself from them, and then cut them into ribbons, using a piece of glass she had secreted. A new strait-waistcoat was now made for her, and she was specially measured by the manufacturer already mentioned; but it could not be ready before the morning, so she was left without restraint that night. Many of the officials were afraid she would commit suicide, but not Mr. Nihil. However, next morning she was found with her clothes torn to rags, and part tied tightly round her neck. As a measure of precaution the new strait-waistcoat was then put on, after she had been first carefully searched. A strong collar was also put round her neck to prevent her biting at the waistcoat with her teeth. "I lament exceedingly," says Mr. Nihil, "the necessity of resorting to such measures; but what is to be done with this violent and obstinate girl?" Next morning she was found to have got at the waistcoat with her teeth in spite of the collar, then one hand loose, after which she relieved herself of the apparatus altogether.

She was now left free, while fresh devices were sought to restrain her, but in the midst of it all came an order for her removal to Van Diemen's Land, whither she was in a day or two conveyed in the *Nautilus* convict ship. And here the curtain falls upon her.

ENTRANCE TO PENTAGON.

CHAPTER XII.

THE CASE AGAINST THE PENITENTIARY.

IN the midst of all this, while Mr. Nihil, backed up by his committee, was working thus indefatigably and with the best intentions, the credit of the establishment over which they reigned was suddenly impugned in no measured terms. It was doubtful indeed whether the ship could weather the storm of invective that broke upon it. Had the managers of Millbank been ogres instead of painstaking philanthropists working for the public good, they could not have been more rancorously assailed. But here was a case where people suffered because their rulers squabbled. It was a period when party warfare ran high, and the Opposition hailed eagerly any opportunity of bringing discredit upon the Ministry. The attack made upon the Penitentiary was really directed against the Government.

On the 26th of February, 1838, a noble lord rose in his

place to call the attention of the House of Lords to a grave failure in the administration of criminal justice. "All London, the whole country was ringing with it," said another noble lord. "It had been a topic of universal reprobation co-extensive with the hourly increasing sphere in which it has been known. All Westminster had talked of it, all Middlesex has pointed its eyes to the quarter in which the abuse occurred. I will venture to say," continued his lord-ship, "that it has been more talked of, more discussed, more indignantly commented upon in every corner of this great town and of this populous country, than any one subject either in or out of Parliament, or in any one of the courts of justice, civil or criminal." * It appeared that in Millbank, a prison exempt from the general jurisdiction of the county magistrates, and governed only by the Home Secretary, there had occurred five cases of unwarranted harshness and cruelty. Three little girls and two fine young men had been completely broken down by the system of solitary confinement therein practised. The children were mere infants: one, as it was alleged, was little more than seven years old; the other two were eight and ten respectively. Yet at this tender age they had been cut off entirely from the consoling influences of home and the kindly intercourse of relatives and companions, to be immured in solitary wretchedness for nearly thirteen consecutive months. So bitterly did these little ones lament the loneliment of their lengthened seclusion, that one asked piteously for a doll to keep her company, and all three were found at different times sleeping with their bed-clothes twisted to simulate a baby, so earnestly did they yearn for something like ideal society in their dreary confinement. More than this: the punishment of continued solitude had produced in them a marked infirmity of mind, manifested by great impediment of speech, and general difficulty in the expression of ideas. A gentleman, one of the Middlesex magistrates, who had visited the Peni-tentiary, described the effect upon their speech such as to render their voices "feeble, low, and inarticulate—to produce a kind of inward speaking, visible too, and palpable to every one who heard them." So much for the children. As to the

* Hansard's Parliamentary Debates, xli. p. 82 sqq.

Q

young men, one of them who had previously been remarkable
for great activity and intelligence, came out in a state of
idiotcy, and was afterwards retained as an idiot in St. Marylebone workhouse, reduced to such a state of utter and helpless
imbecility as to be incapable of being employed even in
breaking stones. The other was similarly affected. And yet
all this was contrary to law. Here were prisoners subjected
to uninterrupted solitary confinement for twelve or thirteen
months, when by a recent Act it was expressly ordered that no
such punishment should last for more than one month at a
time, and never for more than three months in the year.
Circumstances very disgraceful beyond doubt, if the charge
were only proved, and entailing a weight of awful responsibility
on those who were accountable to the public.

As the attack was made without a word of warning, Lord
Melbourne, at that time the head of the Government, was
unable to defend himself. All he could urge was that the
House should reserve its opinion until upon a close investigation the grievances and evils alleged should be proved to
exist. He deprecated the broaching of such a serious topic
without due notice. Had such notice been given, some one
would have been prepared with details to answer the charges
made, and to show how far they were correct, how far exaggerated or far-fetched; now, any explanation, however
satisfactory, must come a little too late. The first word was
of the utmost importance in all controversy. The effect of
a calm artful statement was not easily removed. Supported
by such powerful advocacy the impeachment of the Penitentiary must have sunk deep into the mind of every listener.
Yet he felt certain that the whole statement was exaggerated
and over-coloured; of this he had, indeed, no doubt, but he
must claim a little time before he made a specific reply.

Next night he stated that full inquiry had been made.
In the first place the ages of the children had been under-
stated. Each of them was at least ten years old. But
this was not a point of any very material importance. They
were all three very profligate children. One of the worst
signs of the day was the great increase of crimes committed
by children of tender age. The principal cause of this was,

no doubt, the wickedness of parents, who made their children
the instruments for carrying out their own evil designs. In
the present instance the three girls had been guilty of theft
and sentenced to transportation, but they were recommended
for the Penitentiary solely to remove them for a lengthened
period from the influence of their parents, and to give the
Government an opportunity of effecting a reform in their
character and conduct. The only place suitable for such an
attempt was the Millbank Penitentiary, and to this they were
removed. This establishment was governed by rules laid
down by the Lords' Committee of 1835, and, therefore, if
undue severity had been practised, it must have been done in
defiance of those rules. But it was quite untrue that any of
these prisoners had been subjected to protracted solitary confinement. There was no such thing in the Penitentiary
except for prison offences, and then only for short periods.
"Separate confinement there certainly was, but solitary confinement—complete seclusion, that is to say, without being
seen, without going out to public worship—as a general
practice is, I believe, unknown in the establishment.

"These children took exercise regularly twice a day, for
half an hour at a time, in company with other prisoners of
their ward; they had school also together twice a week; went
to chapel on Sunday; and were regularly visited by benevolent
Christian ladies (Mrs. Fry and her associates), who spent long
hours in their cells. Surely their condition was not one of
great hardship!

"The young men, Welsh and Ray, were notorious rogues,
who had also been sent to the Penitentiary to effect, if possible, some reformation in their ill-conducted and irregular
lives. Their behaviour had been very rebellious and disorderly, but though they had been frequently punished they
had left the Penitentiary at the expiration of their terms of
imprisonment in perfect health and full possession of all their
faculties."

The Opposition laughed at the explanation. Not solitary
confinement? what was it then? The children went out to
exercise. Yes; but they were not allowed to communicate or
talk to one another. They went to church, and to school, but

only for a few hours together in the week, and for the rest of
the time they were shut up in their cells alone, utterly alone.
Was not this solitary confinement? The distinction Lord
Melbourne has drawn between separate and solitary was
flimsy, shadowy, and unsubstantial. When applied to children
there was absolutely no difference whatever between the two.
And were these accusations all unfounded then? Had they
been disproved? Not yet. Let the Government wait till then
to assert that they were unfounded. Accordingly, a committee
of the House was appointed to inquire and report upon the
whole case.

Of course it will be readily understood that the secret of
all this coil was simply an effort to make political capital, and
to blame Government for mismanagement of its public affairs.
The excitement had owed its origin to "sensational" articles
in the morning papers, following a first sensational announce-
ment at a public meeting of magistrates, of the awful doings
that were perpetrated within the walls of the Millbank Penitentiary. In the House of Commons, when questioned, Lord
John Russell had simply denied the allegations, which he
characterised as totally false. And Mr. Nihil, who was behind
the scenes, enters in his Journal that it was evident that the
agitators had been made victims of the grossest delusion.
Nevertheless, the committee met, took evidence, and at the
end of a month sent in their report. It was quite conclusive. The whole of the charges necessarily fell at once
to the ground. "On the whole," they stated, summing up,
"the committee think it due to the officers of the Penitentiary
to state, that all the convicts have been treated with all the
leniency, and, in the case of the female children particularly,
with all the attention to their moral improvement that was
consistent with the rules laid down for the government of the
Penitentiary." The children had come in dirty, ignorant, and
in ill health; they were now cleanly, had learnt to read, could
make shirts, and were all quite well and strong. Nothing was
wrong with their voices: one could shout as loud as any girl of
her age, but she was shy before strangers; the second led the
singing of the hymns in her ward, though her voice was only
of ordinary power, and had been even husky from the time of

her reception; the third usually spoke from choice in a low tone, but she had been heard to shout often enough to other prisoners. It was quite evident, then, that in these three cases, not only had the cruelty been distinctly disproved, but it was equally clear that their imprisonment in the Penitentiary had been a positive benefit to the children in question. Nor was the charge a bit better substantiated in the case of the two "fine young men." Both of them had been cast for death at the Old Bailey, which was commuted afterwards to one year in the Penitentiary. One, Welsh, was a good-for-nothing vagrant, who had spent most of the seventeen years he had lived inside the Marylebone workhouse, and to this he had returned on his release from Millbank. He was a clever but unruly prisoner; he could read and write well, and his faculties had been sharpened rather than impaired by his residence in prison. The master of the Marylebone workhouse was decidedly of opinion that he had improved much: he was more civil now than before, and he was greatly grown. Welsh said himself he had no fault to find with the Penitentiary; in fact, he was quite ready to go back to it, if they would only take him in. But this Welsh was in the habit of counterfeiting idiotcy, either to procure some extra indulgences, or to amuse himself and others, and he played the part so well that many who saw him were deceived.

William Ray, the other "victim," was older, having reached his twenty-fifth year. He also had passed the greater part of his life in the Marylebone workhouse; but he had enlisted twice into the army, and had gone with Sir de Lacy Evans to Spain. He had been discharged for incompetence, and it was perfectly clear from the evidence taken, that he was a person of very weak intellect long before he became an inmate of the prison: he had a vacant countenance, a silly laugh, and a habit of blinking his eyes and tossing his head about. Still he perfectly understood what he was ordered to do. He had become a good tailor, and had improved in reading.

Thus all the charges were disposed of; the character of the Penitentiary was triumphantly vindicated, and Mr. Nihil was in a position to continue his onward progress undisturbed.

Naturally, the system in force having been held blameless, it
might fairly be continued without change. The system at
that time was simply this: The prisoners slept in separate cells
which opened into a common passage, and at the centre of the
passage was the warder's bedroom. The cells were ten feet by
seven, and had a partition wall between them fourteen inches
thick. The entrance to each cell had two doors—one of open
ironwork, the other of wood. At the first bell, every morning
about daylight, the prisoners were let out to wash, about six or
eight at a time; and they then returned to their cells for the rest
of the day, except during their two hours' exercise, and twice a
week when they attended chapel and school. Their meals were
brought to them in their cells by other prisoners let out for
the purpose. The chaplain, assistant chaplain, and schoolmaster were for ever visiting them. All day long the wooden
door of the cell remained wide open, and there were plenty of
opportunities of talking to their neighbours through the gate
of iron grating, where even a whisper could be heard. They
were always talking—at washing time, at exercise, even when
in their cells, with both doors locked and bolted. Now this
was manifestly not solitary confinement. Nay, more, it was
not even separate confinement. But yet, without the latter,
without perfect isolation and the prevention of all intercourse
and intercommunication, it was felt by Mr. Nihil that his
efforts to reform his prisoners were vain. Whatever good his
counsels might accomplish was immediately counteracted by
the vicious converse that still went on in spite of all attempts
to check it. It was found that extensive communications were
carried on; that prisoners learned each other's histories, formed
friendships and enmities, and contrived in many ways to do
each other harm. Unless this were ended all hope of permanent cure was out of the question. The governor and
chaplain must have their material to themselves; their process
must not be interfered with while on its trial. It was not
enough to turn over the new leaf: the page must be kept
quite white and clean, it must not be sullied by the baneful
talk of the old evil associates from which now the prisoner like
a new man was weaned. Mr. Nihil says, in 1838, that he is in
great hopes that by the thorough separation of the prisoners,

important advantages in respect to the efficiency of imprisonment and the reformation of the convicts would ensue. "The
more perfect isolation of the prisoner by non-intercourse with
fellow-criminals, not only renders the punishment more effective,
but places him in a condition more susceptible of the good
influences with which we seek to visit him—now constantly
frustrated by communication through the wards." This
sufficiently indicates Mr. Nihil's views, and from now henceforth it is his earnest aim and object to carry them out. He
endeavours to make the separation daily more and more
absolute, but not at first with success. Towards the end of
the same year he reports as follows : "I feel it impossible to
overrate the importance of using every effort to prevent communication between the prisoners. This is the most prominent
regulation in our scheme of discipline ; but the fact is, that it
is only superficially observed. Under an external exhibition
of silence, there is an effectual enjoyment of extensive intercourse among the prisoners. This proves to anyone conversant
with the working of our details that the rule is but a mockery,
and that this great object of our system is not attained." Not
alone in the iniquities that come to light, showing the positive
wickedness of the communications, the governor has forced
upon his observation "an unsubdued and audacious spirit and
a fraudulent state of mind, clearly traceable to the combination
and mutual impulse of everything wrong to which the intercourse of the prisoners gives rise."

"Possibly for this gigantic evil corrections may be applied.
The intercourse occurs at washing, going to and from exercise
and chapel, at the machine, when walking, in chapel itself,
at school, in the wards when unbolted, during the absence of
the officers, in the infirmary, and lastly in their cells when alone
at night. Chapel is the great occasion," goes on Mr. Nihil.
"Their intercourse is developed into a trade. The going to
and fro keeps the prisoners in a restless state, and the familiar
lectures, at which they are questioned in company, super-
induces vanity. The most forward and impudent are the
most ready to answer, and they pride themselves on the
display. . . . The chief result of chapel lectures is some
current familiarity with the leading doctrines of scripture

unaccompanied by humility or genuine pious feeling." In the same way little benefit resulted from the teaching at the night-schools. These schools were conducted by prisoner-monitors, who taught very indifferently; the warders exercised no supervision, and "this dry routine," Mr. Nihil observes, "of bandying sacred terms is apt to harden the mind."

Again, the governor is of opinion there should be cellular accommodation in the infirmaries; separation would diminish the instances of feigned indisposition. In the large wards they lounge away their time, enjoying plenty of good eating and drinking, with no lack of idle and corrupting talk. Their memories quite compensated for the deprivation of the style of literature they preferred, and it was proved that the substance of, or long quotations from many books of an improper character, were frequently heard, and that on one occasion a prisoner was known to repeat "Don Juan," aloud, from end to end.

So eager were the authorities to restrict the means of inter-course, that they were not above taking the advice of a prisoner on the subject. "His suggestions are such as a prisoner is qualified to give, being the fruits of experience, and an intimate acquaintance with the various devices that are practised." If talking was to be prevented, he said, several new arrangements must be made; thus the officer, when prisoners were at exercise, instead of standing motionless should walk on an inner circle, in an opposite direction to the prisoners, so as to see their faces. The prisoners always talked directly the officer's back was turned. Nor should they be allowed to eat while in the yard: under the pretence of chewing they really were engaged in conversation. Again, to put an end to clandestine letters, all the blank pages of library books should be numbered and frequently examined, so that none might be abstracted and used as writing paper. Nor should any whiting be issued to clean the pewters: the prisoners only used it to lay a thick white coat upon any damped paper, thus making a surface to write upon. By scraping off the whiting the same paper could be used over and over again. To make a pencil they scraped their pewter pints, then with the heat from the tailor's iron, with which many were supplied, they ran these scrapings into a mould. Lastly, all searching of cells and prisoners should be more frequent and complete ; care should be taken in the latter case to examine the cuff and collar of the jacket, the waistband and the lower part of the legs of the trousers, and the cap. In the cells, the bedding, all cracks in floor or shop-board, and the battens or little pieces below the tables should be thoroughly overhauled. With such precautions as these much might be effected ; nevertheless, said the informer, mis-conduct must always continue, for prisoners often incurred reports solely to gain the character of heroes.

And so with the new year many further changes were introduced. All the governor's recommendations were adopted, and not a few of the suggestions last quoted, in spite of the source from which they came. Within a week or two—rather soon, perhaps—the governor considers that the new discipline works extremely well. "Reports diminish, and the control of officers is more complete. Ill-tempered prisoners evinced great annoyance at the change; but by meeting this spirit by firmness and good temper it has, I trust, been repressed." Three months later he notices a distinct improvement in behaviour, traceable beyond question to the new rules. Prisoners formerly constantly reported now quite quiet, and in a very good state of mind—tractable, submissive, and grateful. "Several had learned to read; and many evinced a softened and subdued tone of feelings, and thanked God they had been brought to the Penitentiary. Some expressed a grateful sense of the value of the late regulations. One youth told me that previously they might almost as well have been in the same room with a crowd. . . . In Thomas Langdale, a desperate housebreaker and a very depraved man, the most hopeful change has taken place. He has written a most artless and interesting letter to his wife. . . . Some prisoners have acquired a great mastery over their violent tempers, and look quite cheerful and happy. . . . A few only stil manifest great discontent."

All that year the principle has ample trial. In April, 1840, the governor asserts that in his opinion the state of the prison is highly satisfactory. The prisoners, as testified by their letters (which were meant for him to see), were as happy as the

day was long. They had good food, good clothing, and spoke
with gratitude of the provision made for their religious instruction. Moreover, now the reins are as tight as they can
be drawn. "Separation has within the last two years been
much more carried out than formerly, and the effect has been
very materially to reduce offences and punishments, and to
promote reformation." His great difficulty now is that he
cannot ventilate the cell without opening the door to
communication. In fact he might seem to wish to seal up his
prisoners hermetically; but he says, "I do not mean to
advocate long separation from all social communication. I
should prefer a system of regulated intercourse upon a plan of
classification and superintendence and mutual education,
guarded by occasional separation. What I object to is nominal
separation accompanied with secret fraudulent vicious communication. Health is certainly a great consideration, but
are morals less? Ought health to be sought by the rash
demolition of an important moral fence? If health is alone to
be looked to it would be very easy to suggest very simple
means for keeping the prisoners in general good health;
but then the objects of imprisonment would be altogether
frustrated. Considering these objects indispensable, and that
one of them is the moral reformation of the prisoners, I
conceive it would be much better to leave them to the remedy
of opening their cell windows for fresh air."

Mr. Nihil's notions were certainly clearly developed. He
was not for half measures. But in his extreme eagerness
to push his theory as far as it could go, he actually courted
failure. He was apparently blinded by a misconception of
phrases. So long as he steered clear of what was called
solitary confinement he thought he was safe. But he forgot
that the more separation was insisted upon, the more nearly
solitude was approached. In point of fact there was absolutely
no distinction between the separate confinement practised at
Millbank, and that solitary confinement which had already
been universally condemned, and which by law was not to be
inflicted except for very limited periods of time. Naturally
the same fatal consequences, the inevitable results that follow
such imprisonment protracted beyond the extreme limit, began

to be plainly visible.   Cases of insanity or weakened intellect came to light, first in solitary instances, then more and more frequently.   The committee were compelled to run counter to Mr. Nihil, and relax the rigorous separation from which he hoped to effect so much.   I find in their report for 1841 that they consider it necessary to make great alterations in the discipline of the institution.   "In consequence of a distressing increase in the number of insane prisoners, the committee, under sanction of the medical superintendent, came to the resolution that it would be unsafe to continue a system of strict separation for the long periods to which the ordinary sentences of the prisoners extend.   They therefore propose that the system should be relaxed with regard to all classes of prisoners except two; viz., military prisoners whose sentences were extremely short, and persons convicted of unnatural offences; and that to all other prisoners the prohibition of intercourse should be limited to the first three months after their admission, and that upon the expiration of that period they should be placed upon a system of modified intercourse."   But they surrendered their views evidently with the utmost reluctance, and remarked further in this report that "they are, however, inclined to believe that no scheme of discipline in which intercourse between prisoners, however modified, forms an essential part, is ever likely to be made instrumental either to the prevention of crime or to the personal reformation of convicts to the same degree as a system of separation.   Whether the latter system can be rendered compatible with the maintenance of the mental sanity of the prisoners is a subject of much controversy, and can only be determined by actual experiment, accompanied by such advantages as are proposed in the Model Prison."

This model prison was that built at Pentonville, under the active supervision of Colonel Jebb, R.E., and a board of commissioners specially appointed by the Secretary of State. The first stone was laid in April, 1840, and it was occupied by prisoners in December, 1842.

But it now becomes plainly evident that the waters are beginning to close over the Penitentiary.   There are people outside its walls who are clearly not its friends, if not exactly open enemies. Thus dissatisfaction finds voice in the House of Commons, where, on the 15th March, 1841, Mr. Alderman Copeland asks for certain information which the prison authorities must have found it awkward to supply. This return called for was to show (1) the numbers sent to the Penitentiary during the past five years; (2) the numbers removed during that period for insanity, (3) for bad health, (4) pardoned, (5) died; and last of all it was to be stated how often the several members of the committee attended during the year. Here were evident symptoms that the public were not well pleased either with the results obtained at Millbank or with the services of its amateur managers. More plain-spoken still is the report issued by the inspector of prisons in 1842, in which the system of discipline enforced throughout the prison is characterised as "most unsatisfactory." "It is neither calculated to deter from crime, nor contribute to the personal reformation of the prisoner." About this time, too, was unearthed the great bugbear of the unhealthiness of the site—a fatal and unfair imputation from which Millbank to this day is unable to shake itself quite free. Still there was some foundation for the objection at the particular time of which I am writing. A formidable epidemic of dysentery had run through the prison in 1841, and in the following year Dr. Baly, the medical superintendent, gave it as his opinion that "the diarrhœa and dysentery prevalent in the prison are due to the malarious influence arising from the low, damp, and undrained ground immediately surrounding the Penitentiary;" and he finds that "other institutions in similar localities have been peculiarly subject to the same disease." His remedy was that "all unoccupied ground round about should be carefully drained, that the filling in of the moat should be completed, and that the deposit of decaying filth and vegetable matter upon the surrounding surfaces should be carefully removed and not allowed again to accumulate."

These and other necessary improvements in the immediate neighbourhood have long since been carried out, and with their completion the whole of the objections necessarily fell to the ground. But it is not so easy to silence the tongue of

false report, or to rehabilitate people or things whose reputation has once been impugned. Down to this day (1875) there
are rumours afloat condemning the site as unhealthy; and
even in the face of positive evidence to the contrary, the charge
is still maintained. But those who are most concerned know
that Millbank is as salubrious as any part of London. To prove
this I may advance such an unanswerable argument as that
there has been no epidemic known in the place since 1854.
Since that date also there have been two, and only two cases of
typhoid fever, both of which were imported. Again, although
London has been visited by the scourge of cholera more than
once, not one single attack occurred in Millbank in all those
years. Besides this, Millbank for the last twenty years has
exhibited an entire freedom from zymotic diseases; and
although this may be sufficient to retrieve its character as a
generally healthy site, more remains to show that for its own
special functions it is eminently suitable. Pulmonary consumption, which may be characterised as the true prison
scourge, is in this prison conspicuous by its absence. Over and
above all that I have advanced, I may add that Millbank may
stand low, but Buckingham Palace is really lower; and that
the health of all who dwell within the walls, or in its immediate
neighbourhood, appears from the returns of the Registrar
General to compare advantageously with that of any district
in London.

But that which can be triumphantly refuted at this late
date could not be authoritatively denied in 1842. Perhaps,
too, the charges rested on a certain foundation of fact; though
it is more than possible that the continual use of Thames water
for drinking purposes was really more to blame than the
actual unhealthiness of the site. This is a point which Dr.
Baly missed, but it came out afterwards.

But one way and another, from one cause added to the
other, the Penitentiary was drawing nearer and nearer to its
doom. At length its deathblow came, accelerated doubtless
by the sweeping alterations contemplated in our whole system
of secondary punishments. These changes, by which also the
whole constitution of the Penitentiary was changed, will be
detailed at length in my second volume, and the closing

chapter of this shall be devoted to winding up the affairs of
old Millbank.

It was on the 5th May, 1843, that Sir James Graham,
then Home Secretary, introduced a Bill for the better regulation of the Penitentiary. The House must be fully aware, he
said, of the Report (the Eighth Report of the Inspector of
Prisons) in which it was stated that as a *Penitentiary*, "Millbank Prison had been an entire failure." Its functions, therefore,
in that respect were now to cease. But the next thing was to
consider what use might be made of it, for it was a large
building and had many conveniences for a prison. Just at
this moment, however, the Government had determined to
carry out a certain new classification of all convicts sentenced
to transportation. In other words, felons were to suffer this
punishment in different degrees, according to their condition
and character. But to ascertain in which category offenders
should be placed a time of probation and proof was needed,
and this period should be passed at some general depôt, where
for nine or ten months the character of each convict might be
tested. Millbank was admirably suited for the purpose. From
thence, after the necessary interval, the juveniles were to be
sent on to the new prison at Parkhurst, the best and most
promising convicts to Pentonville, the rest to the hulks, but
one and all only *in transitu* to the Antipodes.

Nothing now remained but for the Penitentiary Committee
to go through the ceremony of the "Happy Despatch;" for
by the new arrangements the control of the prison was to be
vested in a body of Government Inspectors, and of a governor
acting under them. In a letter to the Secretary of State the
committee, while acknowledging that their time has come, are
clearly anxious to justify themselves in the eyes of the public.
The system of modified intercourse which they had introduced,
and for which they were to a certain extent blamed, was forced
upon them, they said, by the prevalence of insanity under their
former rules. They were, however, prepared to admit that the
plan substituted had been most unsatisfactory in its results
on morals and discipline, and they fully approved of the
new and improved arrangements which were now to come

into force; at the same time they expressed a fear "that
the effect of adopting the plan will be to divest the institution in a great measure of its character as a Penitentiary."
Under the new system "there will be a rapid succession of
transports continually passing through the prison; and the
shortness of their confinement, though very desirable on
the score of health, will necessarily militate against the
possibility of any great mental or moral improvement.
Nothing is intimated as to the nature of the discipline to
which the transports are to be subjected during their
detention here. The committee, however, are satisfied that
a vigorous system will be found necessary for the maintenance of order among criminals of so depraved and
desperate a character as the male transports are evidently
expected to be. In short, it is obvious that an entirely new
state of things is at hand, one never contemplated by any
members of the committee when they originally consented to
act; one moreover which will require, in their opinion, an
active and unremitting superintendence such as their other
avocations render them incapable of undertaking." Therefore
one and all of them were glad to resign their functions into
other hands. But they "cannot conclude without remarking
that the new system contemplated would never be properly
administered by a clerical governor, even if he considered it
consistent with his sacred functions to undertake such a
charge. They are assured, however, by Mr. Nihil that he
should deem it wholly incompatible with his character as a
clergyman to consent to hold the office of governor under the
new system; they fully concur in his views and feelings on
the subject, and they cannot permit themselves to doubt that
you (the Home Secretary) will also concur in them."

I find in the minutes of the committee on the 9th June,
1843, that all members are requested to attend at their next
meeting, "which would probably be their last." On the 16th
June, therefore, there were present—the Right Hon. Earl
Devon; the Right Hon. Lord Colborne; the Hon. F. S.
Calthorpe; the Right Hon. W. E. Gladstone, M.P.; Charles
Ross, Esq.; Thomas Greene, Esq.; William Gregson, Esq.;

the Rev. John Jennings; Benjamin Harrison, Esq.; Lieut.-
Col. G. E. Nugent; Thomas R. Wheatley, Esq.; Edward
Vansittart Neale, Esq.

This is their last minute:—

"As the Bill now pending in Parliament for effecting an entire change
in this establishment will very shortly pass into law, and the committee
may not have another opportunity of meeting, they are unwilling to separate to-day without placing the following resolution on record:—

"Resolved that the thanks of the committee be presented to the Rev.
D. Nihil, governor and chaplain, for the zeal, ability, and humanity with
which he has discharged his onerous duties, and especially for the earnestness with which he has uniformly endeavoured to render the administration of the discipline subservient to the great moral and religious ends of
the Penitentiary.

At the same time they passed votes of thanks also to the
assistant-chaplain, the medical superintendent, the matron,
manufacturers, steward, and officers generally. And from
that time forth Millbank, as a Penitentiary, ceased to exist.

IN THE PRISON GARDEN.

CHAPTER XIII.

So the Millbank Penitentiary, the great reformatory and moral hospital, the costly machine in which had been sunk half a million of money, was nothing but a failure after all. Such was the opinion of official inspectors, and this opinion was endorsed by the Secretary of State. Its great hopes and ambitious aims were therefore at an end : it was all a mistake, a mockery, a sham. After seven-and-twenty years of trial, unwearied efforts, and unlimited expense, there was nothing whatever to show. Even Mr. Nihil had admitted this much a year or two before. When examined by the Lords' Committee he had confessed that "as a means of reformation it had not been productive of as much good as might be anticipated." But at that time the Chaplain-Governor thought that his system had not had a fair and sufficient trial. There must be more separation, and there was—more and yet more in spite of dark forebodings—and still it was a failure. All at once, as we have seen, it collapsed and came to an end.

But though the system might fail the buildings remained, and these, as we have also said, were still to be utilised, but in another form. Millbank was destined now to become the starting-point of the new method of carrying out transportation. Brought thus into intimate connection with another branch of secondary punishment—one indeed with which it had hitherto competed with varying success, till at length it became distinctly subordinate to it—something more than a passing reference to that other system seems

R

called for in these pages. I propose therefore to recount, as briefly as the subject will permit, our plan of transportation beyond the seas, and all that has come of it. And although I shall be compelled at first to retrace my steps to a date much earlier than that at which my narrative has arrived, I shall by taking up the subject thus late be enabled to test the actual value of transportation as compared with other methods of secondary punishment.

I have already adverted to the rivalry that existed towards the end of last century between penal colonies and home penitentiaries; and I endeavoured to show how the latter, notwithstanding Howard's pleadings, had been eclipsed in the somewhat sentimental halo that surrounded transportation. No doubt, though based on theory rather than practice, though all its advantages were problematical if not entirely illusory, the principle of transportation was most attractive to statesmen and thinkers. For a long time after their inauguration public opinion ran high in favour of penal establishments beyond the seas. "There was general confidence," says Merivale, "in the favourite theory that the best mode of punishing offenders was that which removed them from the scene of offence and temptation, cut them off by a great gulf of space from all their former connections, and gave them the opportunity of redeeming past crimes by becoming useful members of society." Through whatever mire and discomfort it may have waded, beyond doubt Australia has risen to a rank and importance which entitles it to remember unabashed the origin from which the colony sprang. "It has long since outgrown the taint of its original impurity."* Another writer asserts that "on the whole, as a real system of punishment it (transportation) has failed; as a real system of reform it has failed, as perhaps would every other plan: but as a means of making men outwardly honest; of converting vagabonds most useless in one country, into active citizens in another, and thus giving birth to a new and splendid country, a grand centre of civilisation, it has succeeded to a degree perhaps unparalleled in history."† All this is of course indubitable.

---

* Merivale on Colonisation.
† Darwin's Voyage of the *Beagle*.

But in the process of manufacture, the mother country in fifty years expended eight millions of hard cash, and was more full of criminals than ever.

The early history of New South Wales as told in the pages of Collins reads like a romance. Captain Arthur Phillip, R.N., the first governor, started from Portsmouth in the month of March, 1787, with nine transports and two men-of-war—the "first fleet" of Australian annals. Unlike the *Mayflower*, bearing its Pilgrim Fathers, men of austere piety and worth, to the shores of New England, this first fleet carried convicts, criminals only, and their guards. Some vessels were laden deeply with stores, others with agricultural implements. Before the fleet was out of the Channel a plot was discovered among some of these desperate characters to seize the ship they were on board, and escape from the fleet. Nearing the Cape of Good Hope a second similar conspiracy came to light, and all through the voyage offences, such as thefts, assaults, abscondings, attempts to pass counterfeit coin, were numerous, and needed exemplary punishment. After a dreary eight months at sea, broken only by short stays at Teneriffe, Rio, and the Cape of Good Hope, the fleet reached Botany Bay in January, 1788. Never had name been more evidently misapplied. The luxuriant vegetation was all a myth, and on closer inspection the Botanists' Bay proved to be mere barren swamps and sterile sands. The anchorage though extensive was exposed, and in easterly gales torn by a tremendous surf. Before disembarking, therefore, Captain Phillip determined to seek along the coast some site more suitable for the settlement. Starting with a select party in a small boat for Broken Bay, he passed *en route* an opening marked upon the chart as Port Jackson, named thus from the look-out man in Cook's ship, who had made it out from the mast-head. This is known now as one of the finest and most secure harbours in the world. Here in a cove, where there was deep water for ships of the heaviest burthen close in shore,* the foundations of the new town were to be laid. It was christened Sydney, after the peer of that name who was at that time Secretary of State for the Colonies; and

* White: Journal of Voyage to New South Wales.

thither a party of convict artificers, guarded by marines, was
at once removed to clear land for the intended settlement.
When this was accomplished, the remainder of the colonists,
1030 souls in all, were put on shore.

There was plenty of work to be done, and but few hands
available. Enlarged clearings were needed; barracks, store-
houses, hospitals, dwellings for the superior and other officers,
huts for the convicts. Although at the time when the "first
fleet" sailed, many thousands of convicts awaiting deportation
crowded the various gaols of England, no attempt had been
made to select for the new colony those who from their
previous condition and training would have been most useful
to the young community. Of the six hundred male convicts
actually embarked, hardly any were skilled as artisans and
mechanics. Nay more, though it was meant that the colony
should be if possible self-supporting, and that every effort
should be made to raise crops and other produce without
delay, few, if any, of either the convicts or their keepers had
had the least experience in agricultural pursuits. Yet with
ordinary care the whole number might have been made up of
persons specially qualified, accustomed to work either at trades
or in the fields. Nor were there among the sailors of the men-
of-war many that could be turned to useful account on shore.

Again, it had been forgotten that if the convicts were to
be compelled to work, overseers were indispensable; for
laziness is ingrained in the criminal class, and more than
change of sky is needed to bring about any lasting change in
character and habits. To these retarding causes was soon
added wide-spread sickness, the result of long confinement on
ship-board, and an unvarying diet of salt provisions. Scurvy,
which during the voyage all had escaped, broke out now in
epidemic form. Indigenous anti-scorbutics there were next to
none, and the disease grew soon to alarming proportions.
Many convicts died, and others in great numbers sank under
an almost entire prostration of life and energy. On the voyage
out there had been forty deaths; now within five months of
disembarkation there had been twenty-eight more, while sixty-
six were in hospital, and two hundred others were declared by
the medical officers to be unfit for duty or work of any kind.

Another difficulty of paramount importance soon stared the whole settlement in the face. So far "the king's store" found all in food; but the supply was not inexhaustible, and might in the long run, by a concurrence of adverse circumstances, be almost emptied, as indeed happened at no remote date. Famine was therefore both possible and probable, unless in the interval the colony were made capable of catering for its own needs. To accomplish this most desirable end it was necessary to bring ground at once into cultivation, breed stock, and raise crops for home consumption. The first farm was established at Paramatta, fourteen miles from Sydney, and at the same time a detachment under Lieut. King, R.N., of the *Sirius*, was sent to colonise Norfolk Island, a place highly commended by Captain Cook for its genial climate and fertile soil. Here, "notwithstanding the various discouragements arising from droughts, and blighting winds, the depredations of birds, rats, grubs, and thieves to which the settlement was at first exposed, a large extent of ground was gradually cleared and cultivated, and the prospect of raising subsistence for a considerable proportion appeared in every respect more favourable than at Port Jackson." *

At the Head-Quarter Settlement in these earlier years prospects were poor enough. The land being less fertile needed more skill, and this was altogether absent. The convicts knew nothing of farming—how could they?—and there was no one to teach them. One or two instructors expressly sent out were found quite useless. The only person in the colony competent to manage convicts, or give them a practical knowledge of agriculture, was the governor's valet, and he died in 1791. To add to these troubles a lengthened drought afflicted the country during the first year of the settlement, under which the soil, ungenerous before, grew absolutely barren and unproductive. A man less resolute and able than Captain Phillip might well have recoiled at the task before him. The dangers ahead threatened the very existence of his colony. Hostile natives surrounded him, and within the limits of his settlement he had to face imminent starvation, and to cope with the innate lawlessness of a population for the most

* Laing's History of New South Wales.

part idle, ignorant, and vicious. For it soon became plain that to look for the growth of a virtuous community, except at some remote period, from the strange elements gathered together in New South Wales, was but a visionary's dream. England's social sewage was not to be shot down in Botany Bay, to be deodorised or made pure just because the authorities willed it. It was vain to count upon the reformation of these people in the present, or to build up hopes of it in the future. We have seen how their natural propensities displayed themselves on the voyage out. Directly the convicts were landed, these were developed with rapid growth, so that crimes and offences of a serious nature were soon extremely rife. The day on which the governor's commission was read, he had addressed the convicts, exhorting them to behave with propriety, promising to reward the good while he punished heavily all evil doers. Next morning nine of the people absconded. Within a week it was found necessary to try three others for thefts, all of whom were flogged. Before the month was out four more were arraigned charged with a plot to rob the public stores, for which one suffered death, and the others were banished from the settlement.* Yet at that time there was no possible excuse for such a crime. When goaded by hunger and privation in the coming years of scarcity, it was at least intelligible that desperate men should be found ready to dare all risks to win one plenteous meal, though even then each convict shared to the full as well as the governor himself.† But in the first year the rations were ample, and inherent depravity could alone have tempted these convicts to rob the common store. About this time another convict offender was pardoned on condition that he became the public executioner. Both "cat" and gallows were now kept busy, yet without effect. "Exemplary punishments," says Collins, "seemed about this period to be growing more necessary: stock was often killed, huts and tents broken open, and provisions constantly stolen about the latter end of the week; for among the convicts there were many who knew not how to husband

---

* Whither? On this point I can find no information.

† Each man's weekly allowance consisted of 7 lbs. biscuit, 3 lbs. peas, and 6 ozs. butter; 7 lbs. salt beef, or 4 lbs. salt pork.

their provisions through the seven days they were intended to
serve them, but were known to have consumed the whole at
the end of the third or fourth days. One of this description
made his week's allowance of flour (8 lbs.) into 18 cakes, which
he devoured at one meal. He was soon after taken speechless
and senseless, and died the following day at the hospital, a
loathsome putrid object." * Here again was felt the want of
overseers and superintendents of a class superior to that of the
convicts, through whom discipline and interior economy might
be maintained and regulated. Naturally those selected felt a
tenderness for the shortcomings of their fellows, and it was
more than difficult to detect or bring home offences to the
guilty. A common crime was absence. Many, undeterred by
fear of starvation, or savage natives, went off to the woods.
One remained there nineteen days, returning to the settlement
at night to lay his hands on food. In some cases the absentees
were murdered by natives, and their bodies found sometimes
with their heads pounded to jelly, but always mutilated, speared
or cut in pieces. There were other crimes quite new, as were
the punishments meted out to them. One impostor pretended
to have discovered a gold mine; but it was proved that he had
fabricated the gold dust he produced from a guinea and a brass
buckle, and he was condemned to be flogged and to wear a
canvas dress decorated with the letter R, "to distinguish him
more particularly from others as a rogue." This same offender
being afterwards caught housebreaking, he suffered death, but
not before he had betrayed his accomplices—two women who
had received the stolen property. One of these was also
executed, while of the other a public example was made. In
the presence of the assembled convicts the executioner shaved
her head, and clothed her in a canvas frock, on which were
painted the capitals R.S.G., "receiver of stolen goods." "This
was done," says Collins, "with the hope that shame might
operate, at least with the female part of the prisoners, to the
prevention of crime; but a great number of both sexes had
been too long acquainted with each other in scenes of disgrace
for this kind of punishment to work much reformation among
them." Thieving continued on all sides, and the hangman

* Collins, i. p. 32.

was always busy. Repeated depredations brought one man to
the halter, while another for stabbing a woman received seven
hundred lashes. Scarcely any of the convicts could be relied
upon, yet many, in the scarcity of honest freemen, were
appointed to posts of responsibility and trust. Generally they
abused the confidence reposed in them. The case is mentioned
of one Bryant, a seafaring west-country man, who was employed
to fish for the settlement. Every encouragement was held out to
this man to secure his honesty: a hut was built for him and
his family, and he was allowed to retain for his own use a
portion of every taking. Nevertheless he was detected in a
long-continued practice of purloining quantities of fish which
he sold for his own gain. But he was too useful to be deprived
of his employment, and he was still retained as official fisher-
man, only under a stricter supervision. Even this he eluded,
managing a year or two later to make good his escape from the
colony, together with his wife, two children, and seven other
convicts. Having for some time laid by a store of provisions,
and obtaining from a Dutch ship, in the port of Sydney, a compass, quadrant, and chart, together with information to help
him in reaching Timor and Batavia, he stole one of the
Government boats and made off. Bryant and his two
convict companions being well trained in the management
of a boat, and having luck upon their side, reached in due
course the ports for which they steered. Others were less
fortunate in their attempts to escape ; like those who tried to
walk to China northward through the Australian continent.
Nor did much success wait upon the scheme laid at Norfolk
Island to overpower their guards, seize the person of the
governor, and decamp en masse. But though too wild and
preposterous a plot to raise serious alarm, the very existence
of this serves to prove the treacherous, untrustworthy character of these felon exiles. Some years later, indeed, in the
reign of Governor King, an outbreak somewhat similar, but
planned with secrecy and judgment, came actually to a head,
and for the moment assumed rather serious proportions. In
this several hundred convicts combined "to strike for their
liberty." They had pikes, pistols, and several stands of arms.
The insurrection broke out suddenly. Two large bodies

marched upon Paramatta, but were closely followed by an officer, Major Johnson, with forty men of the New South Wales Corps, who brought them to an action at Vinegar Hill, and in fifteen minutes dispersed them with great loss.

It is abundantly evident from these and other instances, that the convict population could only be ruled by an iron hand. But I think Governor Phillip would have forgiven them much if they had but been more industrious. Everything hung upon their labour. The colony must continue to be dependent on the mother country for the commonest necessaries of life, until by the work of these felon hands sufficient food was raised to supply subsistence, and so make the colony to be independent of the public stores. Yet "the convicts by no means exerted themselves to the utmost ; they foolishly conceived that they had no interest in the success of their labours." * Task work had been adopted as the most convenient method of employing them; a certain quantity of ground was allotted to be cleared by a certain number of persons in a given time. The surplus gained was conceded to them to bring in materials and build huts for themselves. But few cared to take advantage of the privilege, preferring to be idle, or to straggle through the woods, or to visit surreptitiously the French war-ships lying in Botany Bay. Indeed, the sum total of their efforts was to do just enough to avoid immediate punishment for idleness. Moreover, as time passed, the numbers available for work dwindled down, till at the end of the first year, in January, 1789, that is to say, only two hundred and fifty were employed in the cultivation of land. Many were engaged at the wharves and storehouses, but by far the greater portion were utterly incapacitated by age or infirmity for field labour of any description. The evil days that were in store did not long delay their coming. Throughout the latter part of 1789, and the early months of 1790, the colony saw itself reduced to terrible straits for want of food. Relief was daily expected from England, but daily unaccountably delayed. Emptier and more empty grew the king's store. In the month of February, 1790, there remained not more than four months' provisions for all hands, and this

* Collins.

at half rations. To prepare for the worst, the allowance issued was diminished from time to time, till in April, that year, it consisted only of 2 lbs. of pork, 2 lbs. of rice, and 2½ lbs. of flour per head, for seven days. Robberies were more than ever prevalent in the general scarcity. Capital punishment became more and more frequent, without exercising any appreciable effect. Garden thefts were the most common. As severe floggings of hundreds of lashes were ineffectual to check this crime, a new penalty was tried, and these garden robbers were chained together in threes, and compelled to work thus ironed. "Any man," said, years and years afterwards, one of these first fleet convicts who had reached affluence and comfort at last—"any man would have committed murder for a month's provisions; I would have committed three for a week's. I was chained seven weeks on my back for being out getting greens and wild herbs." No doubt in those days of dire privation and famine the sufferings of all were grievous; but the statements of these people must be accepted with the utmost caution, even when divested of half their horrors. The same old convict told Mrs. Chisholm, that he had often dined off pounded grass, or made soup out of a native dog. Another old convict declared he had seen six men executed for stealing twenty-one pounds of flour. "For nine months," says a third, "I was on five ounces of flour a day, which when weighed barely came to four. The men were weak," he goes on, "dreadfully weak, for want of food. One man, named 'Gibraltar,' was hanged for stealing a loaf out of the governor's kitchen. He got down the chimney, stole the loaf, had a trial, and was hanged next day at sunrise."

Food, food, all for food! In its imperious needs hunger drove the unprincipled to brave every danger, and the foolish to excess not less terrible. Collins tells a story of a woman who devoured her whole week's allowance in one night, making up a strange compound of cabbage and flour, of which she ate heartily during the day, "but not being satisfied, she rose again in the night and finished the mess," and died. Throughout these trying times, Governor Phillip maintained a firm front. It is told of him, that seeing a dog run by he ordered it to be killed at once—as a mouth that was useless it could not in these days be entitled to food. Then, to ease the mother settlement, a large number of persons were drafted to Norfolk Island, where, thanks to the plentiful supply of wild birds, supplies were more plentiful. In transit, H.M.S. *Sirius*—the only ship left in the colony—was wrecked in full view of the settlement.

Relief came at length, but in driblets. At the time of greatest need, more mouths arrived instead of more barrels of pork and flour. In February, as I have said, there were but four months' provisions in the stores; yet on the 3rd of June, two hundred and twenty-two women arrived—"a cargo," says the chronicler, "unnecessary and unprofitable;" while H.M.S. *Guardian*, which came as convoy and carried all the stores, was lost at sea.

Another store ship, the *Justinian*, happily turned up about the 20th of June, and later in this month, eleven sail, composing the "second fleet," came into port. In this second fleet the arrangements made were about as good as in slave ships from the Guinea Coast. The mortality on the voyage out had been absolutely frightful. One thousand six hundred and ninety-five male convicts and sixty-eight females were the numbers embarked, and of these one hundred and ninety-four males and four females had died at sea; while "such was the state of debility in which the survivors landed in the colony, that one hundred and sixteen of their number died in the Colonial Hospital before the 5th December, 1791." * It seemed that the masters of transports were paid head-money for each convict embarked—a lump sum of £17 9s. 6d. each. The more therefore that died, and the sooner, the less food was consumed, and the greater the consequent profit. Even to the living, the rations were so much reduced below the allowance stipulated for by the governor, that many convicts were actually starved to death. In most of the ships very few were allowed to be on deck at the same time. Crowded thus together continually in a fetid atmosphere below, many peculiar diseases were rapidly engendered among them. Numbers died in irons; and "what added to the horror of

* Laing.

such a circumstance was that their deaths were concealed, for the purpose of sharing their allowance of provisions, until chance and the offensiveness of a corpse directed the surgeon, or some one who had authority in the ship, to the spot where it lay." In one of the ships a malignant fever had prevailed during the latter part of the voyage, under which the captain, with his first and second officers, had succumbed; while in another, the usual plot to take the ship was discovered, and had to be checked with severe repressive measures, which increased the tribulation of these hapless wretches. Colonel Collins gives but a sorry picture of the condition in which these ill-fated exiles of the second fleet arrived at New South Wales.

"By noon," he says, "the following day the two hundred sick had been landed from the different transports. The west side afforded a scene truly distressing and miserable; upwards of thirty tents were pitched in front of the hospital, the portable one not yet being put up, all of which, as well as the hospital and the adjoining huts, were filled with people, many of whom were labouring under the complicated diseases of scurvy and dysentery, and others in the last stages of either of those terrible disorders, or yielding to the attacks of an infectious fever. The appearance of those who did not require medical assistance was lean and emaciated. Several of these people died in the boats as they were rowing on shore, or on the wharf as they were lifted out of the boats; both the living and the dead exhibiting more horrid spectacles than had ever been witnessed in this country. All this was to be attributed to confinement of the worst species, confinement in a small space and in irons—not put on singly, but many of them chained together." *

The years immediately subsequent to these chronicled but a repetition of what had already occurred. The colony saw itself again and again brought to the lowest ebb; when in the last stage starvation stared it in the face, there came more convicts and more salt meat. All through, the health of the inhabitants continued indifferent, in spite of the natural salubrity of the climate. This was partly due to the voyage

* Collins: Account of New South Wales.

out; also to the diet, insufficient and always salt; and not a little to the gloomy out-look for all concerned in this far-off miserable settlement. Yet, through all vicissitudes, the governors who in turn assumed the reins bore up bravely, and governed with admirable energy and pluck. They were all—at least for the first twenty years—captains of the Royal Navy, trained in a rough school, but eminently practical men. Their policy was always much the same. They had to bring land into cultivation, develop the resources of the colony, coerce the ill-conditioned, and lend a helping hand to any that gave earnest of a reform in character.

It will be seen that so far the colony of New South Wales consisted entirely of two classes, the convicts and their masters. In other words, it was a slave settlement—officials on the one hand as taskmasters; on the other, criminals as bondsmen who had forfeited their independence, and were bound to labour without wages for the State. The work to be done in these early days was essentially of a public character. It was for the common good that food should be raised, storehouses erected; the whole body of the population benefited too by the hospitals, while the building of barracks to house the guardians of order was an advantage to all. But such preliminary and pioneer works fairly started, the next step towards a healthy and vigorous life for the colony was the establishment therein of a respectable middle class—a body of virtuous and industrious settlers to stand between the supreme power and the serfs it ruled. People of this kind were wanted to give strength and stability to the settlement, to set an example of decorum, and by their enterprising industry to assist in the development of the country. But they must come from England; they were not to be looked for "among discharged soldiers, shipwrecked seamen, and quondam convicts." Governor Phillip at once admitted this, and from the first strongly urged the home Government to encourage free emigration by every means. The distance from England was, however, too great to entice many across the seas, and the passages out would have swallowed up half the capital of most intending settlers. Several free families were therefore sent out in 1796 at the public expense, receiving

each of them a grant of land on arrival and free rations for
the first ensuing eighteen months.

But this assisted emigration was carried out in a very
half-hearted, incomplete fashion, so much so that for a
long time—till years after the peace of 1815—" a large
proportion of the free settlers are described as of a low
character, not very superior to that of the convicts."* Their
numbers were very small, being recruited indeed from the three
sources above mentioned—the soldiers, the sailors, and the
convicts themselves. Naturally, as time passed and sentences
lapsed, the last mentioned supplied a very numerous class.
Every effort was made to give them a fair start on the new
road they were expected to follow. They received grants of
land, varying from ten to sixty acres, with additional slices for
children or wife. Pigs, too, seed-corn, implements, rations,
and clothing were served out to each from the king's store;
and, thus provided for, straightforward industry would soon
have earned for them an honest competence. But in comparatively few instances did these convict settlers thrive. They
formed a body of small proprietors of the worst class, ruining
their land by bad farming, and making those still convicts far
worse by the example they set of dissoluteness and dissipation.

Society now, and for years to come, presented a curious
spectacle. Its most prominent features were its drunkenness
and its immorality. The whole community might be classed
into those who sold spirits and those who drank them. Everything went in drink. "The crops," says Collins, "were no
sooner gathered in than they were instantly disposed of for
spirits." Any hope of raising the general tone of society was
out of the question so long as this unbounded intemperance
prevailed. Besides this, there was neither marrying nor giving
in marriage. In Governor Bligh's time two-thirds of the births
were illegitimate. Bands of robbers, the first bushrangers,
infested the country, levying black mail, and entering the
homes of the defenceless settlers in open day, committed the
most fearful atrocities.

This general recklessness and immorality was fostered by
the monopoly of sale possessed by the officers of the New

* Heath: Paper on Secondary Punishments.

South Wales Corps. These gentlemen, who came out in 1792 as officers of this local regiment, were for very many years a thorn in the side of the constituted authorities. Bound together by *esprit de corps* and unity of interests, they were constantly at war with the governor, and generally successful. Everything was made subservient to them. They had become by degrees engaged in commercial operations, and in time they alone had permission to purchase all cargoes of merchandise that came into port. These goods they retailed at an enormous profit, so that the small farmers were nearly ruined by the prices they had to pay for such necessaries as they required. "Hence," as Laing says, "they (these small farmers) lost all hope of bettering their circumstances by honest industry, and were led into unbounded dissipation." The figure cut by officers who wore the king's uniform in thus descending to traffic and peddle is not over dignified. Nor were they always over scrupulous in their dealings. As my narrative is concerned rather with the convict element and the vicissitudes of transportation than with the general history of the colony, it would be beyond my scope to enlarge upon the well-known "rebellion," in which this New South Wales Corps played the prominent part. In a few words, this amounted to the forcible ejectment from office of the king's representative, Governor Bligh, by those who were themselves the guardians of the king's peace. It would be tedious to argue here the two sides of the question; but, even allowing that both sides were to blame, it seems clear that the rebellious troops were most in the wrong. Eventually this New South Wales Corps ceased to exist as such, and becoming a numbered regiment, the 102nd of the line, was removed from the colony.

Meanwhile the convicts continued to pour in. Between 1795 and 1801, 2833 arrived; from 1801 to 1811, 2398. In the years that had elapsed since the first and second fleets, attempts had been made to improve the arrangements for sending them out. As soon as the hulks at home were full, and the convicts began to accumulate, vessels were chartered for New South Wales. Each carried 200 with a guard of 30 soldiers. The men selected for transportation were always under fifty, and were taken from those sentenced to "life" or fourteen years. When these were found insufficient to provide the necessary draft, the numbers were made up from the seven years' men, and of these the most unruly were chosen, or those convicted of the most atrocious crimes. The females were sent indiscriminately, the only provision being that they were under fifty years of age. Lists accompanied them out in all cases. These lists were deficient in all useful information—without particulars of crimes, trades, or previous characters; points on which information had to be obtained from the convicts themselves. The transport ships were supposed to be well found in all respects; clothes, medicines, and provisions for the voyage and for nine months afterwards were put on board at the public expense. The owner supplied a surgeon, and the Admiralty laid down precise instructions for his guidance. The master, too, was bound over to be careful of his living cargo. On arrival his logbook was submitted for inspection, and the Governor of New South Wales was empowered to reward him with a special gratuity on the one hand, or on the other to mulct and prosecute him, according to his behaviour on the voyage out.* On arrival at Sydney the convicts were disposed of, either as servants to settlers or retained in Government hands. We have here the system of assignment, though still quite in embryo as yet. While settlers of any wealth were few there was little demand for convict labourers, except as simple servants; though in the case of some of the leading officials, who had already considerable grants of land under cultivation, as many as forty were, even in these early days, assigned to the same master.

The great mass of the convicts were therefore retained by the Government. They were fed, clothed, and lodged by Government, and organised in gangs. Each gang was under an overseer—an old convict—who was certain to err either on the side of culpable leniency towards his charge, or of brutal cruelty. Stories are told of an overseer who killed three men at the saw-mill in a fortnight from overwork. "We used to be taken in large parties," says the

* See chapter xxi., where these arrangements are more fully detailed.

same old hand that I mentioned before, "to raise a tree. When the body of the tree was raised, old ——— (the overseer) would call some of the men away, then more. The men were bent double, they could not bear the weight— they fell, and on them the tree, killing one or two on the spot. 'Take them away : put them in the ground.' There was no more about it." Another overseer was described as "the biggest villain that ever lived. He delighted in torment, and used to walk up and down rubbing his hands when the blood ran. When he walked out the flogger walked behind him. He died a miserable death : maggots ate him up. Not a man could be found to bury him." A third overseer was sent to bury a man who, though weak and almost insensible, was not dead. "For God's sake," cried the poor wretch, "don't cover me up. I'm not dead." "You will be before the night," replied the overseer. "Cover him up " (with an oath), "or we shall have to come back again to do the work a second time." On the other hand, it was known that overseers connived at irregularities of every description. The men were allowed to work as little as they pleased; many altogether left their parties to rob, and returned at nightfall to share their plunder with the overseers. Naturally the work accomplished for the public service did not amount to much. The hours of labour were from 6 A.M. to 3 P.M., after which the rest of the day belonged to the convict to be spent in amusement or labour profitable to himself. Even in these days the punishment of transportation fell most unequally on different men. While the commoner classes of offenders were consigned to the gangs or drafted off to be the slaves of the low-bred settler, persons who had held a higher station in life, or who had been transported for what came to be called " genteel crimes," forgery, that is to say, embezzlement, and the like, were granted tickets-of-leave at once, which exempted them from all compulsory labour and allowed them to provide for themselves. To them the only hardship entailed on them by their crimes was the enforced exile. These were the first of a class afterwards styled " specials," or gentlemen convicts, who were a fruitful source of annoyance to all Australian officials.

I have endeavoured to sketch thus briefly the manner in which the settlement of this, the first purely penal colony, was carried out, and to describe how it prospered in its early years. So far we have had to deal only with the difficulties encountered by the young colony and the steps taken to combat them. It is too soon yet to speak of the consequences that were entailed by forming a new settlement thus from the dregs of society. I will only state in general terms what was the actual state of affairs. A governor at the top of all, with full powers nominally, but not nearly autocratic; next to him, as the aristocracy, a band of officials not always obedient, sometimes openly insubordinate, consistent only in pushing forward their own fortunes. Between these and the general body of the colonists a great gulf; the nearest placed next to the aristocracy being the settlers—passing through several gradations—from the better class, few in number, to the pensioner or convict newly set free; at the very bottom, the slave or serf population—the convicts still in bondage.

This was the first stage in the colony's existence. With the breaking up of the power of the New South Wales Corps and the appointment of Governor Macquarie a new era opened, and to this I shall devote the next chapter.

NORTH AND SOUTH HEADS IN PORT JACKSON.

CHAPTER XIV.

TRANSPORTATION (*Continued*).

THE peculiar condition of the colony now was the presence therein of a quantity of convict labour, growing larger also from day to day as vessels with their cargoes arrived, for which there was no natural demand. When General Macquarie assumed the government the influx of male convicts had been so great in the five years preceding 1809, that the free settlers were unable to find employment for more than an eighth of the total number, though the labour was to be had for the asking, and cost nothing but the price of raising the food the convicts consumed. In point of fact, the free settlers were still too few and their operations too limited. Seven-eighths of the whole supply remaining on hand, it became necessary for the governor to devise artificial outlets. He was anxious, as he tells Earl Bathurst, "to employ this large surplus of

men in some useful manner, so that their labour might in some
degree cover the expense of their feeding and clothing." The
measures by which he endeavoured to compass this end I shall
proceed immediately to describe.

There is a stage in the youthful life of every colony when
the possession of an abundant and cheap supply of labour is
of vital importance to its progress. Settlers in these early
days are neither numerous enough nor wealthy enough to
undertake for themselves the works for reclaiming land,
for establishing harbours and internal communications on
a scale sufficiently wide to ensure the due development of
the young country. At such an epoch a plentiful supply of
convict labour poured in at the cost of the Home Government is certain to be highly valuable. Merivale points out
how some such timely assistance to British Columbia in
recent years would have given an enormous impetus to the
development of those provinces. It would be premature to
discuss, at this period of my narrative, the question whether
the advantages gained would outweigh the positive evils of
a recurrence to transportation on any grand scale. Some
of these evils might disappear if the system were carried
out with all the safeguards and precautions that our
lengthened experience would supply. But the main objection—the excessive costliness of the scheme—would remain,
and it is, I think, extremely doubtful whether the temper of
the nation is such as to encourage its statesmen to saddle the
exchequer with an immediate heavy outlay in order that in
the remote future another jewel might be added to her colonial
crown.

This stage had New South Wales now reached, and the
governor, finding himself amply supplied with the labour so
urgently needed, bent all his energies to bringing forward
the latent resources of the colony. His reign began at a
period of great scarcity. Repeated inundations on the
Hawkesbury had entailed disastrous losses on the whole
community. He decided, therefore, to form new townships
at points beyond the reach of the floods, and to open up
to them and throughout the province those means of communication which are so essential to the progress of a new

country. Upon the construction of these roads he concentrated all his energies and all the means at his disposal. Not much skilled labour was needed, yet the work was punitive and was also beneficial to the whole public. No better employment could have been devised for the convicts. Under his directions, towns before disconnected were joined by means of excellent highways, while other good roads were driven through wild regions hitherto unsettled if not altogether unexplored. The greatest exploit of that period was the construction of the road across the Blue Mountains to Bathurst, the whole length of which was 276 miles; and there were, besides, good wooden bridges at all necessary points. Beyond doubt, to these facilities of intercommunication is to be attributed the early advance of the colony in wealth and prosperity.

But Governor Macquarie's other undertakings, though well intentioned, were not equally well designed either for the improvement of the colony or the amelioration of its people. No doubt his was a difficult task, his course hard to steer. He had means almost unlimited, a glut of labour, and behind him were the open purse-strings of the mother-country. How was he to make the most of his advantages? This labour of which his hands were full, came from a mass of convicts, each one of whom represented already a considerable charge on the imperial funds. It had been expensive to transport him; now he was costly to keep. Could he not be made in some measure to recoup the Treasury for the outlay he occasioned? It was obvious that he should, if possible, contribute to his own support. Yet Governor Macquarie, in spite of his promises, aimed at nothing of the kind. His chief object—next after making roads—was to embellish the principal towns of the colony with important public works—works for the most part unnecessary, and hardly in keeping with the status of the young settlement. Roads were urgently needed; but not guildhalls, vast hospitals, spacious quays, churches, schools, houses and public offices. In these earlier years, buildings of more modest dimensions might well have sufficed for all needs. But under the Macquarie *régime* Sydney sprang from a mere shanty town

into a magnificent city. It was almost entirely reconstructed
on a new plan, the lines of which are retained to this day.
The convict huts gave place to prisoners' barracks, the mean
dwellings of the settlers to streets of imposing houses. The
whole external aspect of Sydney and Paramatta was changed.
In all the new public buildings numbered more than 250, and
the list of them fills ten closely printed pages of a parliamentary report.

Yet all this expenditure was not only wasteful and at the
time unnecessary, but its direct tendency was to demoralise
the population. The labourers required for works of such
importance were of course collected together upon the scene
of operations. In other words, crowds of convict artisans
were congregated in the towns, and countenanced each other
in vice. Many of the works were carried out by contract, the contractors employing convict hands, bond or free, still serving or
emancipated; and in both cases they paid wages half in cash, and
half in property, which consisted of groceries and ardent spirits.
This was the truck system neither more nor less, which the contractors made still more profitable to themselves by establishing
public-houses close to their works, at which the cash half of
the wages soon returned to them in exchange for the drink
supplied. Naturally vice and immorality grew apace. The
condition of the towns was awful, and the low pleasures in
which they abounded attracted to them many people who
might have otherwise been contented to live quietly upon
their grants of land. But the choice between congenial
society and plenty of drink, and the far-off clearing with
honest labour for its only joy, was soon made in favour of the
former, and every one who could, flocked into the towns. The
governor had indeed tried hard to form an agricultural population. With this object he had conceded larger grants than
his predecessors, in the hopes that convicts emancipated would
settle upon them and reform. It was thought that "the hope
of possessing property, and of improving their condition and
that of their families, afforded the strongest stimulus to their
industry, and the best security for their good conduct." But
these advantages were remote, and gave way at once before the
present certainty of being able to barter away the land they

got for nothing, in exchange for ten or fifteen gallons of rum.
If this plan of manufacturing industrious small proprietors out
of the recently emancipated convicts was meant to answer, the
grant of land should have been made conditional on actual
residence thereon, and accompanied by tangible results gained
by actual labour done, which must be shown before the acres
were finally conveyed. Now it was proved that many of
Governor Macquarie's grantees never took possession of their
land at all : the order for thirty acres was changed at once for
the much-coveted means of dissipation. Hence, though towns
grew fast in beauty and importance, the forest lands or wild
tracts in the interior remained unsettled; and the crowds of
ex-criminals which might, by judicious treatment, have turned
into virtuous bucolics, rapidly degenerated into a mass of
drunken dissipated idlers.

These were indeed fine times for the convicts. There was
labour for all, remunerative, and not too severe; liquor was
cheap, and above all the governor was their friend. It would
be, however, more than unfair to charge General Macquarie
with any but the best motives in his tenderness for the convict class. He conceived that the unfortunate people who
composed it were the especial objects for his solicitude. To
promote their reform, and to bring them to that prosperity
which should make this reform something more than mere
idle profession—these, as he thought, were among the first
of his duties as the governor of a penal colony. In his
prosecution of these views he did not halt half-way. The
manner in which he favoured and encouraged the emancipists came to be a by-word. It was said in the colony
that the surest claim on Governor Macquarie's confidence
and favour was that of having once worn the badge of a
convicted felon.* Very early in his reign he made it clear that
his policy would be this. The year after his arrival he
advanced one ex-convict to the dignity of a justice of the
peace; another was made his private medical adviser; and
both, with many others, were admitted to his table at Government House. Nor were the recipients of these favours always
the most deserving among their fellows for the honours

* Bigge's Report.

showered upon them. It was taken for granted that the possession of considerable wealth was proof positive of respectability regained; yet in the case of Governor Macquarie's emancipist magistrate, it was notorious that he had become rich by methods of which honest men would hardly be proud. Transported as a lad for rick-burning, after serving his time in the colony he had been a shopkeeper, a constable, and last a publican; in which line, by means of liberal credit, he had soon amassed a fortune. His case was only one of many in which ex-convicts had grown rich, chiefly by preying on their still more unfortunate comrades, taking mortgages on grants as payment for long arrears of accounts for groceries and drink, and by-and-by seizing all the land.*

Then, in many instances, members of the convict class were by far the shrewdest and best educated in the whole community. Settlers of the better class were few in number, so the sharp rogues had it all their own way. They had capital moreover. Several brought money with them to the colony, the fruit of their villanies, or their wives followed them with considerable sums acquired in similar fashion. For these men, especially if they had held fairly good positions at home, transportation was almost a farce. It merely meant removal at the public expense to a land, remote certainly, but in which they were little less comfortable than at home, and where they had moreover exceptional facilities for making money fast, and they had it all to themselves. Governor Macquarie discouraged free emigration. He did not want to see settlers. He looked upon them as out of place, nay more, as a positive encumbrance to the colony. New South Wales was a settlement, he said, made by convicts for convicts—"meant for their reformation; and free people had no right to come to it." So he continued to pat his favourites on the back: gave them land, and more land; as many assigned servants—their former partners possibly in many a guilty scheme—as they wished; and last not least, provided a market for the very crops he had assisted them (by convict labour) to raise. It was not strange then that with a yearly

* No more emancipists were made magistrates after 1824. Parl. Com. 1837: evidence of Sir F. Forbes.

influx of thousands of new hands, and the rapid upward
advance of all who were ordinarily steady and industrious, the
emancipists should come as a class to gain strength far in
excess of their deserts, and sufficient from their numbers to
swamp all other classes in the community.

There was frequent heartburning in New South Wales
during the reign of Governor Macquarie on account of his
overstrained partiality. The discontent was heightened by
his plainly spoken desire to force his own views down the
throats of those nearest him in the social scale : not satisfied with openly countenancing them himself, he insisted that
the officers of regiments should receive them as guests at mess.
Bigge says on this point : " The influence of the governor's
example should be limited to those occasions alone when his
notice of the emancipated convicts cannot give offence to the
feelings of others, or to persons whose objections to associate
with them are known. The introduction of them on public
occasions should, in my opinion, be discontinued. And when
it is known that they have been so far noticed by the
Governor of New South Wales as to be admitted to his
private table and society, the benefit of the governor's example
may be expected to operate; and it will also be exempt from
the fatal suspicion of any exercise of his authority." * Again,
when Mr. Bent, Judge of the Supreme Court, refused to allow
certain attorneys, ex-convicts but now free, to practise as
solicitors, the governor complained to the Home Government
that this judge was "interfering unwarrantably with a salutary
principle which he (the governor) had been endeavouring to
establish for the reformation of the convicts." Now at this
very time an Act was in force which deprived all persons
convicted of perjury or forgery from ever again practising in
the courts at home, and Judge Bent in refusing to administer
the oaths to these emancipist attorneys was but carrying out
the law; yet on the governor's representation he was removed
from the bench.

There were other cases not less plainly marked. As a
natural consequence, the antagonism was deepened between
the two classes which were so widely distinct—the virtuous

* Commission to inquire into the state of New South Wales.

266

pharisees, that is to say, and the thriving publicans. The
former despised all who had come out "at their country's
expense;" and the latter hated the settlers, as people of a
lower class not seldom hate social superiors to whose "platform" they are forbidden to hope to rise. Eventually, as we
shall see, after a long-protracted warfare and varying successes,
the free population gained the day; but not till the lapse of
years had strengthened their numbers out of all proportion to
their antagonists, and given them the preponderance they at
first lacked.

The struggles between the two classes fill up the whole
of the annals of the next years of the colony.

All said, however, it cannot be denied that under the
administration of General Macquarie the colony prospered.
The population was nearly trebled between 1809 and 1821,
and there was a corresponding increase in trade and in the
public revenue. Just before this governor left the colony it
contained 38,788 souls; there were 102,929 horned cattle,
290,158 sheep, 33,000 hogs, and 4,500 horses; and 32,267
acres had been brought under cultivation. The moral tone of
the community, too, was slightly raised; marriage had been
encouraged in place of an indifferent and disreputable mode of
life which till then had been largely prevalent. "In externals,
at least," says Laing, "the colony itself assumed quite a
different aspect under his energetic and vigorous management
from what it had previously worn."

Speaking of his own administration and his efforts to
elevate the convict population in the scale of society, Governor
Macquarie said for himself, as against his detractors,
"Even my work of charity, as it appeared to me sound
policy, in endeavouring to restore emancipated and reformed
convicts to a level with their fellow-subjects—a work which,
considered in a religious or a political point of view, I
shall ever value as the most meritorious part of my administration—has not escaped their animadversions."

And yet, however praiseworthy his efforts, they were
misdirected; and beyond doubt in his desire to discourage
the influx of free people he committed a fatal error. It was
his wish, of course, to further the development of the colony;

but he could not do this half so satisfactorily by the establishment of penal agricultural settlements, as could substantial emigrants working with capital behind them for their own profit. Moreover, these agricultural settlements started by Governor Macquarie cost a great deal of money. Again, the free classes of the community would not have found themselves for a long time outnumbered had not immigration been systematically discouraged. The formation of an independent respectable society, armed with weight and influence, was, as I have said, much needed in the colony. In this respect General Macquarie had departed from the policy of his predecessors. Captain Phillip was eager enough, as we have seen, to attract settlers, and had his recommendations been persistently followed the colony would have found itself the sooner able to raise grain enough for its own consumption.

Sir Thomas Brisbane, on the other hand, who came after Governor Macquarie, recognised the full importance of the principle, and his reign is memorable as marking the period when settlers first flocked in any considerable numbers to the colony. But it was no longer the humbler classes who came. None of these did the governor want, but persons who were well-to-do, who could take up larger grants and find plenty of employment for the rapidly increasing convict population. Sir Thomas Brisbane held out every inducement to attract such persons. At this period, thanks to the unceasing arrival of new drafts, the number of felon exiles on charge continued to form a serious item in the colonial expenditure. To get quit of all or any the governor was only too glad to offer almost any terms. The grants of land were raised from 500 to 2000 acres, which any one of moderate respectability might secure, provided only he would promise to employ twenty convicts; rations also were to be given from the king's store for self and servants for the first six months, and a loan of cattle from the Government herds. The new comers therefore were mostly gentlemen farmers, younger sons of land-owners, or commercial men who had saved something from a general crash in business. Most of these people were sufficiently alive to their own advantage to realise the advantages now

held out to them. Land for nothing, food and stock till the
first difficulties of settlement were overcome—these were baits
that many were ready enough to swallow. Labour, convict
labour, was provided also by the same kind hands that gave
the land.

For some years this more than parental encouragement
continued, till at length the influx of settlers came to be
thoroughly felt. The labour that was so lately a drug,
was now so eagerly sought that the demand grew greater
than the supply. The governor was unable to comply
with all the requisitions for servants made by the land
grantees. This at once brought about the abandonment of
the agricultural penal settlements established by General
Macquarie. Their success had always been doubtful:
although land to a considerable extent had been cleared,
timber felled, buildings erected, and farming attempted, no
great results had ever been obtained. Indeed now, when the
land which had thus been occupied was again resumed, it was
found to have been little benefited. One by one they were
broken up. They were costly and unproductive. On the
other hand, the settlers, old and newly arrived, were clamorous
for the hands thus wastefully employed. "So steadily," says
Laing, "did the demand for convict labour increase on the
part of the free settlers that, during the government of
Lieutenant-General Darling, there were at one time applications for no fewer than 2000 convicts lying unsatisfied in the
office of the principal superintendent of convicts."

We have now really arrived at the second stage in the
history of transportation. Although from the first origin of
the settlement convict servants were readily provided for any
master who might ask for them, the applications, as I have
said, were few and far between, amounting in 1809 to an
eighth only of the total numbers available, and requiring, as
late as 1821, to be accompanied by the bait of distinct and
tangible bribes. But now had dawned the days of "assignment" proper, the days of wholesale slavery, where private
persons relieved the State of the charge of its criminals, and
pretended to act, for the time being, as gaolers, taskmasters,.
and chaplains, in return for the labour supplied at so cheap a

rate. How far the persons thus called upon to exercise such peculiar functions were entitled to the confidence reposed in them was never in question till the last few years. Emancipists got their convicts too, and of course among the settlers many were quite unsuited for so serious a charge.

The failure of assignment as a method of penal discipline will be seen later on, when its great inherent evils had had time to display themselves. At first the chief fault was over-leniency—so much so that General Darling came out as governor charged with orders to subject the convicts to more rigorous treatment. Dr. Laing, in his "History of New South Wales," is of opinion that, about this date, much unnecessary severity was noticeable in the carrying out of the sentence of transportation. He states that convicts were now treated by the subordinate agents, who saw that severity was the order of the day, "with a reckless indifference to their feelings as men which their situation as criminals could never have warranted."

Nevertheless it must be confessed that the condition of convicts could not be irksome when soldiers envied it, and committed crimes on purpose to become felons too. This was proved in the case of certain soldiers who had turned thieves in Sydney simply that they might be sentenced to transportation. They were caught, convicted, and sentenced to seven years at Moreton Bay or Norfolk Island. Had their story ended here the bare record of it might suffice, but it so happened that very serious consequences ensued, and these I cannot refrain from recounting. As it came out quite clearly upon their trial what had been the object and design of their theft, Governor Darling resolved that they should be treated with extra rigour, "it being an intolerable and dangerous idea that the situation of a soldier was worse than that of a convict or transported felon." The seven years at a penal settlement was therefore commuted to seven years' hard labour in chains on the roads of the colony. The intention of this change was doubtless that their old comrades should sometimes see them as they were marched to and fro; but besides this, it was ordered that at the end of their sentence they should return to their regiments. Therefore, after the proceedings of the trial had been promulgated, the prisoners were publicly stripped of their

uniforms, iron collars with spikes projecting were placed
around their necks, from which iron chains hung and were
fastened to basils on their legs.   Thus arrayed they were
drummed out of their regiment (the 57th) to the tune of the
Rogues' March.   Under the horrors of this punishment one
man, Sudds, immediately sank, and died the following day.
The survivor then made a statement to the effect that Sudds
complained bitterly of his chains.   The projections on the
collar prevented the prisoners from stretching at full length
when lying on their backs.   They could not lie at full length
without contracting their legs, nor could they stand upright.
The collar was too tight for Sudds' neck, and the basils too
tight for the other's legs.

In reporting this whole case to the Secretary of State,
Governor Darling says: "However much the event is to be
regretted, it cannot be imputed to severity; none was practised
or intended. . . . With respect to the chains which are
designated instruments of torture, it will be sufficient to state
that they weigh only 13 lbs. 12 ozs.; and though made with a
view of producing an effect on those who were to witness the
ceremony, the extreme lightness of their construction prevented
them from being injurious in any respect to the individual."
On the other hand, Laing says the irons usually made for the
road gangs in the colony did not weigh more than from 6 to
9 lbs.; while those brought out for convicts on board prison
ships from England weighed only from 3½ to 4 lbs.

Following all this came vituperative attacks in the press.
Papers inspired by the Government defended General Darling,
and the fight was long and bitter.   One result was the passing
of several Acts known as " Gagging Acts," intended to check
the virulent abuse perpetually aimed at the Government, but
they failed to have the desired effect.   Governor Darling grew
more and more unpopular, and on leaving the colony he was
threatened with impeachment.   A Parliamentary commission
did, eventually, inquire into his administration, and completely
exonerated him from all charges.

Speaking of the trial and sentence of these soldiers, Laing
observes : "It would be unjust to consider Sir Ralph Darling's
sentence by the light of public opinion in England.   He was

governor of a colony in which more than half the community were slaves and criminals; he had to arrest and punish the progress of a dangerous crime; but he fell into the error of exercising by *ex post facto* decree, as the representative of the sovereign, powers which no sovereign has exercised since the time of Henry VIII., and violated one of the cardinal principles of the British Constitution by rejudging and aggravating the punishment of men who had been already judged. At the present day it is only as an historical land-mark that attention can be called to this transaction, which can never be repeated in British dominions." * It is more than probable that, as a military officer of rank, he was doubly disposed to reprobate the offence recorded. All his soldierly instincts were doubtless hurt to the quick by the notion that the private men of an honourable profession preferred an ignominious sentence to service with the colours of their corps. From this came his uncompromising attitude, and the seemingly unjustifiable violence of his measures.

But except in this one instance, Sir Ralph Darling proved himself an efficient administrator. His sympathies were certainly with the "exclusionists" as against the "eman-cipists;" and therefore by the latter and their organs he was persistently misrepresented and abused. But he was distinctly useful in his generation. A most industrious public officer, he spared himself neither time nor trouble. Every matter, how-ever unimportant, received his closest personal consideration. He may have made mistakes, but never through omission or neglect; besides which, he introduced order and regularity in the working of the State machine. Method followed dis-organisation; ease and freedom, where before had been friction and clogging interference between its several parts. One of his earliest acts had been to regulate the system of granting land, which under the previous administration had fallen into some confusion. It was he who established a Land Board, and who ruled that grants were to be made to people only according to their means of improving the acres they got, and not as heretofore, simply in answer to mere application.

In these and other useful labours the lead he gave was

* Laing: History of New South Wales, vol. ii. p. 82.

consistently followed by his immediate successor, Sir Richard
Bourke, who came to the colony in December, 1831. Although
by the extension of the colony the personal character of the
governor was no longer of such paramount importance as in
earlier days, the arrival of an efficient administrator was a
distinct benefit to the whole settlement. Sir Richard Bourke
was unquestionably a man of character and vigour. The
measures he introduced were all salutary. Not only did he
encourage free immigration, but he made fresh laws for the
distribution and coercion of the convict population. His
regulations for assignment—to which I shall refer directly—
were wisely planned; and the reforms he introduced in the
constitution of the courts of justice were as sensible as they
were necessary. He had found that the decisions of local
magistrates in the cases of the misconduct of convict
servants were extremely unequal: some were ludicrously
lenient, others out of all proportion severe. He thought it
advisable to establish some uniform system by which magistrates should be guided in the infliction of summary punishments; and he passed, therefore, an Act known henceforth as
the "Fifty Lashes Act." This substituted fifty lashes for the
first offence cognisable in a summary way, in lieu of one hundred
and fifty; and made the powers of a single magistrate somewhat
less than those of a bench of two or more. At the same it was
ruled that a "cat" of uniform pattern should be used in
every district. "Each bench had before superintended, or
left to its inferior officers, the construction of its own
scourges, which varied according to accident or caprice;
nor could it ever be ascertained by the mere number of
lashes ordered what degree of pain the culprit was likely
to have suffered." This restriction of their power was not
palatable to all the magistrates, and petitions were presented to His Excellency, protesting against his new Act.
They urged that now their authority was utterly derided.
"Such a feeling," says Sir Richard, commenting on their
petition, " is not to be considered extraordinary, as it requires
much judgment and moderation to overcome the instinctive
love of power. . . . The magistrates who felt the diminution
of their power as a grievance may perhaps have been excited

to expressions of complaint by the annoyance to which, in their character of settlers, they are exposed from the misconduct of their assigned servants. They do not perhaps consider that the natural dislike to compulsory labour, which is part of human nature, and has existed and ever will exist under every form or mode of government, must offer great difficulties to those who seek to carry on their business by such means. Severity carried beyond a certain point, especially towards men of violent and turbulent feelings, will only tend to inflame this indisposition to labour with more dangerous acts of desperation and revenge." However, to give the petitioners no just cause for complaint, he instituted a formal inquiry into "those circumstances connected with the discipline of the prison population which formed the subject of the petitions." Reports were called for from the police of the several districts. From them it was clearly apparent that fifty lashes with the new cat were quite enough for any one, provided they were properly administered. "The sufficiency of the law and of the instrument of corporal punishment, in all cases where proper superintendence is exercised, being thus established on unex- ceptionable evidence," His Excellency considered it would be inexpedient, nay, dangerous, to add to the severity of either, "merely because, in some instances, the wholesome vigour of the existing law has been impeded by a negligent or corrupt execution. In reading the reports which have been presented, the governor could not fail to observe that where punishments have been duly inflicted, the power of the magistrates has been anything but derided. While perusing these painful details, His Excellency has indeed had abundant reason to lament that the use of the whip should of necessity form so prominent a part of convict discipline in New South Wales; but believing it to be unavoidable, the governor must rely on the activity and discretion of the magistracy for ensuring its wholesome and sufficient application."

The clear-sighted policy adopted by Sir Richard Bourke in carrying out the last-mentioned reform was no less observable in his treatment of the question of assignment. The system by which servants were assigned to settlers was undoubtedly not altogether free from abuses. It was

alleged that successive governments worked it quite as a
source of patronage to themselves. Governor Darling had
however established an assignment board, which to some
extent equalised the distribution of the convicts among the
settlers. But it remained for Sir Richard Bourke to put
the whole question on a thoroughly satisfactory footing.
The rules he promulgated did not make their appearance till
he had been four years in the colony; after he had gained
experience, that is to say, and time to consider the subject
in all its practical bearings. Excellent though they were,
they were rather late in the field. From the date of their
appearance to that of the final suspension of transportation there were but five years to run. The pains taken by
Sir Richard Bourke are evident from his despatch to the
Secretary of State for the Colonies, dated June, 1835. He
observes: "My chief object in this measure has been to
substitute for the invidious distinction hitherto more or less
vested in the officers entrusted with the duty of assigning
convicts to private service, strict rules of qualification,
intelligible alike to the dispenser and receiver of penal labour,
and from which no deviation shall be permitted. It is not
until after much delay, and after maturely weighing the
suggestions of the various parties, that I have ventured to
deal with this important and difficult subject."

The main principle of the new regulations was that
servants were to be assigned solely in proportion to the
land the masters occupied. A carefully prepared scale was
drawn up fixing this proportion, which, speaking roughly,
was at the rate of one servant per 160 acres of ordinary land,
and one per 20 acres under plough or hoe culture. At the
same time it was ruled that, as all mechanics were more
valuable than mere labourers, each of the former should
be equal to two and sometimes three of the latter. Thus one
blacksmith, bricklayer, carpenter, or cooper, counted as three
labourers; while a plasterer, a tailor, shoemaker, or wool-
sorter, counted only as two. An entirely new process of
application for these servants was also laid down. A special
sessions was to be held in every district in September, for the
purpose of receiving and reporting on all such applications.

It was the duty of the magistrates in sessions to "inquire into the correctness of the facts stated in each, requiring such evidence thereof as to them shall seem proper; and they shall in no case recommend the claim of any applicant unless perfectly satisfied of the truth of the statement on which the application is founded."

Over and above this they were also required to look into the moral qualifications of the assignee. They were not to recommend any person "who is not free, of good character, capable of maintaining the servants applied for, and to whose care and management they may not be safely entrusted." Had this regulation been enforced at an earlier date the system of "assignment" might have been worked with greater success. The applications having been duly passed at sessions were then forwarded to the assignment board at Sydney. Throughout, the greatest care was taken to prevent underhand dealing: when eventually the time for actual assignment arrived, it was done by drawing lots, or rather numbers from a box in the office of the assignment board, and it was impossible for the officials to show favour or affection had they been so inclined. The whole spirit of these regulations was thoroughly equitable and straightforward. The only object was to be fair to everyone. Thus the land qualification was not insisted upon in the case of tradesmen who wanted assistance in their own calling; and respectable householders were also allowed to obtain indoor servants, though without an acre of land in the colony. With these rules were included others requiring masters to remove their servants without delay, and establishing certain pains and penalties against contravention of the new law.

These arrangements were indeed admirable, all of them, but they should have been earlier enforced. Not that Sir Richard Bourke was to blame for this. The change he instituted should have been carried out by his predecessors. But he was probably superior as an administrator to most who had gone before. At least he was clear-sighted enough to perceive that New South Wales had already outgrown the conditions of a mere penal settlement. He was of

opinion that convict labour was no longer required, and that
the abolition of transportation would be really a benefit to the
colonial community. He was perhaps in this ahead of his
time, but within a year or two of the close of his reign the
same views began to be widely entertained both at home and
abroad. In fact the period was now approaching when the
idea of the possible abandonment of transportation was to
take a tangible, substantial form.

SYDNEY IN 1835.*

CHAPTER XV.

CONVICT LIFE.

TRANSPORTATION divides itself naturally into three periods. The first comprises the early history of the penal colonies; the second treats of the days when "assignment" flourished, then fell into disrepute; the third saw the substitution of the "probation" system, its collapse, and finally the abandonment of transportation beyond the seas.† Having sketched this early history in the two preceding chapters, I propose to draw now a picture of convict life, and the state of the colonies generally during the second of these periods. I

---

* From a sketch by C. Martens.

† Transportation was really continued for some years after the collapse of the probation system in Van Diemen's Land, but only to the extent of sending a few hundreds annually to Western Australia.

shall, in this, confine myself chiefly to New South Wales, the
details of management and the results having been much the
same in Van Diemen's Land, or Tasmania as it is now called.
But I shall refer more especially to that island in a later
page.

To the voyage out and the internal management of convict
ships I intend to devote a special chapter. Let us imagine
that the anchor is dropped in Sydney harbour, and that the
surgeon superintendent has gone on shore to make his bow to
His Excellency the Governor of New South Wales and its
dependencies. There is already plenty of excitement in the
town. The ship had been signalled in the offing, and there
are numbers of good people on the look-out for useful hands
from among its cargo. The days when convict labour was
a drug in the market are past and gone; the rush for
"assigned" servants is now so great that requisitions far
in excess of the number available crowd the office of the
assignment board. All sorts of tricks have been put in
practice to get early information as to the qualifications of
those on board: although the indent bearing the names of
the new convicts goes first to the governor and thence to
the assignment officers, cunning old stagers—not a few of
them themselves emancipists—have found out privately from
the surgeon or the master of the vessel whether there are upon
the list any men likely to be useful to them. Thus a watchmaker seeks to obtain a watchmaker; an engraver, an engraver;
printers, compositors; merchants want clerks, as doctors do
assistants, or the genteel folk—"ancients" as they love to
style themselves—do cooks, butlers, and ladies'-maids. Many
got convicts assigned to them who were distinctly unfit and
unworthy of the charge. Cases were indeed known of settlers,
outwardly honest men, whose only object in asking for
servants was to get assistants in thieving, cattle stealing, and
other nefarious transactions. All who lived inland came off
second best in the general rush: unless they had some friend
on the spot to watch their interests they had to take their
chance later on. But these too are in want of skilled labourers:
one requires a carpenter to complete a new shed or roof to his
house; another a blacksmith for the farm forge; and all

would be glad of men with any agricultural training or skill. If the newly-arrived ship carries female convicts, there is similar anxiety. At one time governesses were frequently got from among these outcasts; but the practice of confiding the education of innocent children to such teachers appeared so monstrous that it was soon altogether discontinued. But nursemaids and other household servants were in eager request, and it must be confessed that the moral condition of the colony was such that many of the better-looking female convicts were obtained without disguise for distinctly immoral purposes.

But one and all were compelled to lodge their applications for assigned servants with the assignment board, where practically the decision rested. This board was governed latterly by the clear and explicit rules laid down by Sir Richard Bourke, to which I have referred in the last chapter, but before these regulations were framed many malcontents among the settlers were ready to declare that assignment all depended upon favour and affection. "If you had no friend on the board," says one, " you might get a chimney-sweep when you wanted a cabinet-maker." In the same way complaints were made that the members of this board, and other officials in high place, were given as many assigned servants as they asked for. Thus the Chief Justice of the colony had forty, the Colonial Secretary fifty or sixty, the Brigade-Major eight or ten. The principal landowners, too, were liberally supplied. One, a salt manufacturer, had sixty or seventy; another, with a farm of 40,000 acres, employed a couple of hundred servants. Laing declares that the assignment of useful hands depended often on petty services rendered to Government, and that many of the settlers succeeded in getting on the weak side of the governor and his advisers.

But to return to the ship, which meanwhile lay out in the stream. No one was allowed to communicate with her, except the Colonial Secretary or his assistant. One of these officials having gone on board to muster all hands, inspect them, and investigate any complaints, as soon as these preliminaries were concluded the disembarkation took place at the dockyard. Male convicts were at once marched to

the Hyde Park Barracks, where they paraded for the inspection
of His Excellency the Governor. Then the assignees, having
been first informed of the numbers they were to receive, waited
in person or sent for them, paying on receipt one pound per
head for bedding and the convict clothes. Assignees failing
to appear, or to remove the lots assigned to them, forfeited
the grant. With the women the system was much the same.
They were first mustered, then they landed, decked out in their
finest feathers. There was no attempt to enforce a plain
uniformity of attire; each woman wore silks and satins if she
had them, with gay bonnets, bright ribbons, and showy
parasols. Persons who had applied for female servants were
present at the dockyard to receive them. After that all who
remained on Government charge—and their numbers were
large, for female convicts were not in great demand—passed
on next to the great central depôt or factory at Paramatta.

As the Hyde Park Barracks and the Paramatta Factory
were to a certain extent depôt prisons for males and females
respectively, a word about both will not be out of place here.

Until later years the men's barracks had been very
negligently supervised. There was no attempt to enforce
discipline within the walls. The convicts were not even kept
under lock and key. Half at least were absent as a general
rule all night, which they spent in prowling about, stealing
anything they could lay hands upon. The officers at the
barracks were tampered with, and winked for substantial
reasons at the nightly evasions of the prisoners in their charge.
Even in the day-time, and inside the walls, drunkenness was
very rife, and with it perpetual pilfering from one another,
and much general misconduct. Naturally in this universal
slackness of control the lower officials battened and grew rich
at the public expense. Gross peculation and embezzlement
were continually practised. The storekeeper was known to
have abstracted supplies from Government stock ;* and others
on small salaries were found to have amassed considerable
fortunes, building themselves fine villas in the best part of the
town, and living on the fat of the land. Having thus full
scope for license and depravity, it will be conceded that there

* Parliamentary Commission of 1837 : evidence of Mr. E. A. Slade.

was no attempt at punishment and restraint in this the first halting-place of the transport in the land of exile.

The condition of the Paramatta factory was even more disgraceful. The building, not unlike an English poor-house, was large and stood amidst spacious courtyards and gardens. The accommodation provided was of the best. There was plenty of food and comfortable raiment. The women were not confined always within the walls, they had money in plenty, and there was little or no work to be done, even by those in the lower stages or classes. A few were made to wheel sand or gravel for gardening purposes, but the barrows used were of light construction, and the women laughed openly and made a joke of the labour imposed. The administration of the establishment was entrusted for years to a matron, whose character, to say the least of it, hardly entitled her to so responsible a charge. It was alleged that she misappropriated the labour of the convicts, keeping back the best prisoners to employ them for the benefit of herself and her daughters. It was openly said, also, that these daughters were not a bit better than they should have been. There was some attempt at classification among the female convicts according to conduct and character, but the lowest of these classes was filled with women who had been returned from service or who were sentenced to remain at Paramatta till further orders. This was just what they wished. All the women much preferred to be at the factory. It was far better, they said, than at service. If any servant misbehaved, and was taken by her master before a magistrate, she said at once, "Send me back to the factory. Send me back." These scenes in court supply curious evidence of the condition of affairs. The women constantly made use of the most desperate and disgusting language. One, after threatening her master, suddenly spat in his face. Another, when sentenced to ten days on bread and water, was so insolent that the punishment was increased to thirty. "Oh! thank you," she said coolly; "couldn't you make it thirty-one?"—knowing perfectly well that thirty days was the limit of the magistrate's power. No wonder that, with such material to choose from, decent people refused to receive convict maid-servants into their families. As a rule

their characters were so bad, they gave so much annoyance, and
disturbed to such an extent the peace and quiet of households,
that the settlers would rather be without their assistance
altogether. "They make execrable servants," says Mr. Mudie,*
speaking from long experience. In many years he had only
met one or two who were well-behaved. Some were exceedingly savage, and thought nothing of doing serious mischief
to any one. The most flagrant case of this was the assault on
Captain Waldron, a retired officer and settler. Having reason
to find fault with a woman for not cleaning his verandah, he
threatened to send her back to the factory. "If you send
her, you must send me too," cried another woman, coming
forward directly. High words followed; after which the two
women threw themselves without warning on their master, got
him down, and mauled him so seriously that he died of the
injuries he received. Other servants, convicts also, were
within earshot, but not one stirred a finger to help their
master.

Not a pleasant picture this of the actual consequences of
female transportation. Perhaps all the women were not
originally bad, but the voyage out was a terrible ordeal to
those who had still some faint glimmering left of the distinctions between right and wrong.† Another observer remarks
that the character and condition of these women were "as
bad as it was possible for human beings to be; they were
shockingly dissolute and depraved, steeped to the very
core in profligacy and vice." But I will now leave them
and return to the men, who formed really the bulk of the
convict population.

Let us take first the case of those assigned to settlers in
the interior. The assignee, as I have said, attended and
carried off his quota to dispose of them on his station, or
otherwise, according to his discretion. To get the men
home—often a long way off—was no easy matter. Sometimes the convict was given money and told to find his own
way; in other cases the master assumed charge, and marched

* Evidence before Commission of 1837.

† It is rather a melancholy reflection that many of these women
had been among Mrs. Fry's most promising pupils.

in company. Then it happened, either that those left to themselves made straight for the nearest public-house, or that those under escort gave their masters the slip and travelled in the same direction. The next the assignee heard of his new servants was a demand made upon him to take them " out of pawn." Joining with old pals, these new chums, fresh from the restraint of the convict ship, had soon launched out into drunkenness or worse. As often as not the master found them in the lock-up, with half their clothing gone, and charged with felony. Having cost money already, they now cost more; and the process might be repeated over and over again. Nevertheless, sooner or later, all or a part of the new labourers reached their destination. Here their position was quite that of slaves. The Transportation Act gave the governor of the colony a property in the services of every convict, and this property he made over to the assignee. The authority with which the settler became thereupon vested was not exactly absolute, but it was more than an ordinary master has over his apprentice. Nevertheless, the Australian master was bound to maintain and to protect his convict servant. He could not flog him, nor was he supposed to ill-treat him; besides, the law gave the convict the right of appeal and complaint against ill-usage. Their maintenance was likewise provided for by law. The regulation rations consisted weekly of seven pounds of fresh meat—beef or mutton—and eight pounds of flour, with salt, also soap and other necessaries; but this minimum allowance was often largely increased. The meat issue rose to eight or nine pounds; the flour to fourteen pounds; tea and sugar were added, and occasionally rum and tobacco. In spite of the danger of supplying such men with spirits, rum was openly given—as at time of sheep-shearing, and so forth, when it was supposed to be needed medicinally. The occasion of a harvest-home was often the excuse for a general jollification. Many masters found that it was to their interest to feed their convict servants well. This was bribing them to do good work, and not a few people had more confidence in the efficacy of such treatment than in purely strict and coercive measures.

Mr. Mudie, one of the settlers examined before the Parliamentary Committee of 1837, confessed to having provided one servant with a flute, just to keep him in good humour. A good master was anxious to make his servants forget, if possible, that they were convicts. Really profitable labour, they argued, could only be got out of them by making them comfortable. Here at once was a departure from the very first principles of penal discipline. It was hardly intended that the felons who were transported as a punishment beyond the seas should be pampered and made much of, simply to put money into the pockets of private individuals. As a matter of fact the average actual condition of the convict servant, as far as food and lodging were concerned, was far superior to that of the honest field labourer at home, and under a good master he was much better off than a soldier.* He might be under some personal restraint, and there was a chance of being flogged if he misbehaved, but he had a great many comforts. He was allowed to marry, could never starve, and if industrious, in no remote period of time might look forward to rise to a position of ease, if not of actual affluence.

At all the large stations the daily routine of life was somewhat as follows: The big bell on the farm rang out an hour before sunrise, a second bell half an hour later, and a third when the sun appeared. It was the night watchman's business to ring the bells. At the last summons all hands turned out. The mechanics went to their various works, the bullock drivers to their carts, the herdsmen to their horned cattle and pigs. As a general rule the heaviest labour to be performed was kept for the newest comers, so as to break them in. It was their business to clear the land, fell timber, and burn it. At eight came the breakfast bell, and with it an hour's rest. Dinner was at one, after which work was continued until sunset. At 8 or 9 P.M., according to the season, a night bell recalled every one, and after that no convict was supposed to leave his hut. On the surface, then, no great amount of rest appeared to be allowed, except at actual meal times or after sundown; but the whole character of the work performed was desultory and far from satisfactory. A convict servant's

* Parl. Com. 1839: Col. Breton's evidence.

value was estimated by people of experience at something much less than that of a free labourer; so much so that there were settlers who declared they would rather pay wages, as they lost rather than saved by this gratuitous labour. The convicts worked unwillingly almost always; sometimes they executed their tasks as badly as they could, on purpose to do injury. What leisure they had was not very profitably employed. One convict in twenty might read, and some few spent their time in plaiting straw hats for sale; but the greater number preferred to be altogether idle, unless they could get a pack of cards—forbidden fruit at every station, and yet generally attainable—in which case they were prepared to gamble and quarrel all the night through. There was little or no supervision over them in their huts. It was quite impossible to keep them inside. No kind of muster was feasible or even safe. The overseers were really afraid to visit much the men's huts after dark, fearing to be attacked or openly maltreated. It would have been far better if a strong stockade with high palisading had been in all cases substituted for the huts. The latter were open always, so that after the last bell at night, any—and they were not a few—who chose crept out and spent the whole of the dark hours on the prowl. Of course the convicts were incorrigible thieves, and the whole country side was laid under contributions by them while thus nightly at large. Sunday was another day which gave these idle hands abundant opportunities for mischief. Of course there was no regular work done on the farm on that day; but there was no attempt, either, to enforce religious observances in lieu thereof. The want of provision for public worship was at this time largely felt throughout the colony, and seldom were churches at hand for the convicts to attend, even if such attendance had been insisted upon. Some few superintendents of farms took their convicts to church, if there was one in the neighbourhood, but cases of this were few and far between. Even if there was a church, all that could sneaked out of the way on pretence of going to bathe, and so escaped the service.

Thus far I have described only the pleasant side of a convict's life up the country. On the whole it was far from

irksome. Nevertheless, as a set-off against the home comforts
and the comparative idleness, there was the total want of freedom of action, coupled with strictly enforced submissiveness
of demeanour. A convict was expected to be even cringingly
subservient in manner. For insolent words, nay looks, as
betraying an insubordinate and insurgent spirit, he might
incontinently be scourged. In this way he was subject to the
capricious temper, not only of his master, but of the whole of
that master's family. Then the local magistrates had great
powers. Singly a magistrate could sentence any man to be
flogged for drunkenness, disobedience, neglect of work, or
absconding; with others assembled in petty sessions, they had
power, however, to inflict heavier punishments for graver
offences. In "Byrne's Travels" I find mention made of
several convicts who had received in the aggregate many
thousand lashes. The same writer asserts that he once had an
assigned servant upon whom 2275 had been inflicted. This
man was said to have grown so callous that he was heard to
declare he would rather suffer a thousand lashes than the
shortest term of imprisonment. Life could not be very enjoy-
able to men liable to such treatment. And this code was for
the convicts and for them alone. Another law applied to the
masters, in whom, indeed, was vested a tremendous power for
good or evil. Some, as I have before remarked, were quite
unfit persons to have the charge of felon servants, being little
better themselves than convicts, and prepared at any time to
consort with them and make them their intimate friends.
Others of the better classes often delegated their authority to
overseers, being either non-resident on their farms, or not
caring to exercise personal control. In many cases these
overseers were ex-convicts, and although it might be considered advisable that the master should not make himself too
cheap, and that a middleman should be employed to come
into direct communion with the convict himself, still every
precaution should have been taken to prevent any abuse of
power. In point of fact every well-ordered establishment
should have been uniformly under the eye of its resident
owner.

But in reality the lot of the convict in assignment was

left altogether to chance. According to his luck in masters, he might be very miserable, or as happy as the day was long: one master might be lenient, giving good food and exacting but little labour in return ; another a perfect fiend. It was quite a lottery into which hands the convict fell, for until 1835 there was little or no inquiry into the character of applicants for servants, and except in the most flagrant cases requisitions were never refused.

This, indeed, comprises one of our chief objections to the system of assignment. It was altogether too much a matter of hap-hazard. No system of penal discipline ought to be left thus to chance. But assignment was objectionable in other ways: That it should be absolutely fruitless in reformatory results is not altogether strange, seeing that in every other case, even where no pains had been spared to secure this, one of the great objects of penal legislation, the failure was equally plain. As a punishment, however, for notorious offenders it was far too light and easy. There was, as we have seen, no supervision and little attempt to enforce hard labour or any strigent code of discipline. This neglect fostered evil courses, and tended to increase the temptations to crime. Nor was the style of labour provided that which was always most suited to the persons for whom it was intended. In some few cases it was proper enough. Men employed as shepherds were perforce compelled to drop into regular habits from being obliged to go out and return with their herds at fixed hours, and they lived much alone. But these were only a small proportion of the whole number, and the balance working in association had many opportunities for developing evil qualities by this corrupting intercourse. Especially was this the case with the mounted herdsmen, who were free to gallop about the country, collecting together in large numbers at the squatters' huts to drink and gamble and plot schemes of depredation.

These squatters, who about this period (1825–35) sprang up in rank growth round about the principal stations, did much to give annoyance, and to increase the difficulties of the settlers. They were mostly emancipists or ticket-of-leave men, who occupied crown pastures without paying for them,

or spent their energies in stealing horses and cattle. Sometimes they established themselves at the corners of the
settlers' own grants of land, getting as near to estates as they
could without detection. Their principal object in life seemed
to make themselves useful to the convicts employed near them,
and for whom they kept " sly grog-shops," where they sold or
bartered liquor for stolen goods. This ready market for stolen
property was a source of great loss to the settlers. One
calculated that it cost him £200 or £300 a-year. Pigs, sheep,
harness in bags, flour on its way to market—all these were
purloined in large quantities, and passed at once to· the
receivers, who gave rum in exchange, and sometimes tea,
sugar, and tobacco. The squatters were fined if caught at
these illicit practices, but to recover money from them was
like getting blood out of a stone. Another favourite *modus
operandi* was to knock up a sort of shanty close by some
halting-place on the main line of road, where there was water
handy and the drays could be made snug for the night. The
draymen naturally flocked to the grog-shop, and naturally
also obtained the sinews of war by making free with their
masters' property.

In the foregoing pages I have dwelt chiefly on assignment
to the country districts. But every convict did not of course
go to the interior. Many were assigned in the towns. Now,
whatever evils may have surrounded the system as carried
out inland, the practice of town assignment was infinitely
worse in every respect. In the first place, it led to the
congregation of large numbers in places where there were
many more temptations to profligacy and crime. And just
as these were increased, so were the supervision and control
that would check them diminished till they sank to almost
nothing at all. Country convicts, as we have seen, were
not much hampered by rules; but those in towns were free
to do just as they pleased. It was impossible for the
masters to enforce any regulations. In the hours of work,
such as they were, the convicts might perhaps be kept out of
harm's way more or less, according to the character and style
of their employment; but labour over, they had great license
and were practically free men. Household servants were

as well off as servants at home in England; they frequented
theatres and places of amusement, and the badge of their
disgrace was kept altogether in the background. Masters
were not compelled by law to enforce any particular discipline;
nor would the most strict among them dare to exercise
much surveillance over their servants. Such conduct
would have been rare and singular, and it would have
drawn down upon them the animosity, or worse, of the
whole convict class. Such was the state of affairs that this
body really possessed some power, and could not openly be
affronted. Convicts were required in the towns, as in the
country, to be within doors by 8 P.M.; but unhappily this
rule was quite a dead letter. The Sydney police was
miserably inefficient. Recruited from the convict ranks,
they were known on all occasions to favour openly their old
associates. If they gave information they were called
"noses," which they disliked; or worse, they were hooted,
sometimes attacked and half killed. They were known,
too, to take bribes, and to be generally most neglectful of
their duties. It was not to be expected, therefore, that from
them would come any zealous supervision of the convicts
still in assignment, even to the extent of sending all such to
their homes after 8 P.M., or of preventing the commission of
petty offences. But as a matter of fact, the police were never
certain whether half the men they met were convicts in
assigned service or people actually free. Sydney was by
this time so large, and the convicts so numerous, that it was
next to impossible for a constable to know every one he
met, by sight. None of the assigned servants in towns wore
any distinctive dress. Those in Government hands wore gray,
and the chain-gangs a parti-coloured suit of yellow and brown
cloth, but the assigned servants appeared in their masters'
liveries, or clothed just as it pleased them. Recognition was
not likely to be easy or frequent. Even in our day
in England, with admirable police machinery, the thorough
supervision of criminals at large is not always obtained.
In Sydney, forty years ago, it was lamentably below the
mark. Often enough men who had arrived in recent ships,
having been assigned in due course, were soon lost sight

of, to reappear presently under another name, as men
quite free. They had proved themselves so useful that
their masters wished to give them sole charge of a business,
which, if still convicts, they could not assume. In this
way it was discovered that an assigned convict servant had
charge of a tan-yard close under the eyes of the police, but
here it was proved that the police had connived at a grave
neglect of duty.

It followed, too, from the nature of their previous avocations, that the convicts assigned in towns were the sharpest
and most intelligent of their class. They were therefore the
more prone to dissipation, and the more difficult to restrain
within bounds. Knowing their value, they presumed on it,
and felt that they were too useful to be sent off as rough
farm hands into the interior. Here was another blot in the
system of assignment, and generally on the whole principle
of transportation. The punishment fell quite unequally on
offenders. The biggest villains and the most hardened
offenders fell naturally into the lightest "billets;" while
the half-educated country bumpkin, whose crime may have
been caused by ignorance or neglect, was made a hewer of
wood and drawer of water. Prominent among the first
category were the "specials," or gentlemen convicts, as they
were styled; men sentenced for "genteel" crimes, forgery only,
or embezzlement, but whose delicate fingers had never
handled the cracksman's jemmy, or tampered with fogle or
wipe. These genteel criminals were for ever, through all
the days of transportation, a thorn in the side of the
administration, and they were always treated with far more
consideration than they deserved. Some of these were well-
known men, like one who had been a captain in the royal
navy, and whose proclivities were so ineradicable that he
suffered a second sentence at Norfolk Island for forgery,
his favourite crime. From among this class the lawyers
selected their clerks, and the auctioneers their assistants.
If unusually well-educated they became teachers in schools,
and were admitted as such even into the public seminaries
of Sydney. A flagrant instance of the consequences of this
injudicious practice is quoted by Laing—a clergyman's son,

who had a convict tutor, coming himself under the influence
of such a man's teaching, to be also a convict sentenced to
transportation for life.

There was another very improper proceeding which for
a long time held among the convicts of this superior or more
wealthy class: their wives followed them out to the antipodes,
bringing with them often the bulk of their ill-gotten gains.
Having thus ample funds, they established themselves well
on arrival, and applied for a grant of convicts like the rest
of their neighbours. Naturally they took care to secure that
their own husbands should be among the number. There
was one man who had received a very heavy sentence for a
robbery on a custom house, who should have gone direct to
Norfolk Island. Through some bribery he was landed at
Sydney, and was made overseer at once of a gang working
in the street. Within a day or two he absconded. His wife
had joined him with the proceeds of the robbery, and they
went off together. Mr. Macarthur * gives another case of a
farrier who was assigned to him. This convict's wife followed
him, and asked permission to live with him on Mr. Macarthur's
farm. When this was refused the man managed to get
returned to Sydney, and was there reassigned to his wife.
To something of this kind some of the largest shops in
Sydney owed their origin.

Among the many lighter and more remunerative kinds of
employment into which the convict of the special class
readily fell, was employment on the public press. As time
passed there had grown up a strong antagonism between
bond and free, and both sides had their newspapers. The
organs which were emancipist in tone were not of the
highest class, but they were often conducted with considerable ability. Their staff was of course recruited from the
convict ships as they arrived, where compositors, leader
writers, and even sub-editors were occasionally to be found.
The most notorious instance of this description was the case
of W., who was originally assigned as a servant to the proprietor of the *Sydney Gazette*. This paper, which was then
only published three times a week, was an able and influential

* Evidence before Committee of 1837.

journal, and its editor and owner was a certain O'S., who had himself been assigned to a former proprietor, and by him employed as a reporter. To him came W., and these two, according to Dr. Laing,* bent all their energies to compass "the abolition of all the moral distinctions that the law of God has established in society; to persuade the public that the free emigrant was no better than the convict, that the whole community was equally corrupt, and those of the convict class were no worse than the best in the colony, their situation being the result of misfortune, as they pretended, and not of misconduct."

W. was a Scotchman, who had been outlawed for some misdemeanour in the office of a solicitor by whom he had been employed in Edinburgh; he then came to London, and was taken into a large mercantile house, Morrison's; from which, for embezzlement, he was transported for fourteen years. He came out in Governor Darling's time, and was sent to Wellington Valley, then a penal settlement for educated convicts. He stayed there but a short time, thanks to his interest with the superintendent, and returning to Sydney obtained a ticket-of-leave, being afterwards employed as a clerk in the corporation office, under the archdeacon of the colony. On the dissolution of the corporation he was no longer required there, but he found great demand for his services from editors of newspapers, having two sub-editorships offered to him at the same time. He went to the *Sydney Gazette*, and thenceforward had it under his entire control, the ostensible editor being a person of dissipated habits, who let him do as he pleased. This W. was a man of considerable talent. From that time forth he proved a source of prodigious demoralisation from the sentiments he disseminated, and the use he made of the powerful engine he had under his control, in endeavouring to exasperate the prison part of the population against the free emigrants. He was tried at length on a charge of having bribed a compositor to steal a printed slip from another newspaper office in the colony. The printed slip was a proof of a letter that had been sent for publication to the editor of the paper, and which contained libellous matter,

* History of New South Wales.

reflecting on the character of a certain emancipist. The letter was not very carefully examined by the editor until it had been set up in type, but on discovering the nature of its contents he considered that he ought not to publish it. Though actually printed, it never appeared in the paper. W. came to know that such a paper was in type, and he bribed a convict compositor in the office to which the letter had been sent to purloin a copy, or one of the proofs of the letter. He then sent the letter in an envelope through the post to the person libelled, in order that there might be proof of its publication. The person to whom the letter referred thereupon brought an action against the editor of the paper to which it had been sent, and endeavoured to establish the fact of publication from the circumstance of his having received the letter through the public post; but the action failed. On inquiry, W.'s complicity in the matter was discovered, and he was tried for being a party to the theft. Of this he was acquitted, as the property found was not of value sufficient to constitute grand larceny; but the judge considered that he should not be allowed to remain at Sydney, and the governor sent him to Port Macquarie, a station for gentlemen convicts. Though now two hundred and fifty miles from Sydney, he still continued to contribute articles to the *Sydney Gazette;* and soon afterwards the widow of the late proprietor of the paper, into whose good graces he had insinuated himself, went down to Port Macquarie and married him. Soon after this he got into trouble by stirring up a feud between the harbour master and a police magistrate. In the investigation which followed, both these officials were dismissed, and W.'s ticket-of-leave was cancelled. He was sentenced to be again classed with the convicts in Government hands, and on hearing this he absconded. Nothing more was heard of him.

I think it will be evident from what I have said that the actual condition of men who were in assigned service was not very disagreeable if they were skilful hands and useful to their masters. This much established, they found their lives were cast in pleasant places. They did not want for money: they were allowed openly a portion of their earnings, and these gains were often largely increased by illegal methods. Besides this, many masters gave their servants funds to provide for themselves. They went so far even as to allow their men to marry—saddling themselves with the responsibility of having perhaps to keep both convict and his family. These convict marriages, when permitted, took place generally in the convict class, though cases were known of free women who had married assigned servants, and *vice versâ*. Among the latter, Byrne, in his "Travels," speaks of a certain old lady, the mother of very respectable people, who had married when a convict, and who did not, to the day of her death, quite abandon the habits of her former condition. Her husband had been an officer of high rank, and her sons rose to wealth and prosperity in the colony; but no considerations for the feelings of those belonging to her were sufficient to wean her from her evil propensities. She was so passionately addicted to drink, that it was in vain her children sought to keep her with them : she always escaped, taking with her all on which she could lay hands, and returned to her favourite associates— the brickmakers in the suburbs of Sydney.

But such marriages as these were the exception. As a general rule the assigned servant, whether in town or country, paid a visit to Paramatta factory, and made his case known to the matron by whom it was governed. "Turn out the women of such and such a class," cries forthwith Mrs. G., and the marriageable ladies come trooping down, to be ranked up in a row like soldiers, or like cattle at a fair. Benedict walks down and inspects, then throws his handkerchief, and if the bride be willing, the two retire to a corner to talk a little together. If the conversation is not quite satisfactory to "Smith, *Aboukir*," or Jones, *Lady Dacre*,"* he makes a second selection ; and so on, perhaps, with three or four. Cases were known of fastidious men who had run through several hundreds, and had declared in the end that there was not a single woman to suit. Others were less particular. Men up country have been known to leave the choice to their masters, when the latter

* Convicts in Australia were always known by their name and the name of the ship in which they had come out.

next pay a visit to Sydney. There was of course no security against bigamy : often both parties to the colonial marriage had wife or husband alive at home, and just as inevitably the conduct of these factory brides was most questionable after the new knot was tied.

CONVICTS WITH DRAY.

CHAPTER XVI.

CONVICT LIFE AND THE STATE OF THE COLONIES.

IN the latter part of the preceding chapter I have dealt with convicts in assignment. These of course did not comprise the whole numbers in the colony. Putting on one side the ticket-of-leave men—who were still really convicts, though for the moment and during good behaviour masters of themselves—and not including emancipists, who though, to all intents and purposes, men free as air, still carried a class-brand which generations only could efface—there were, in addition to the servants assigned to private individuals, a large body of convicts retained in the hands of the Government of the colony. A certain proportion of these were men so chosen on arrival from fulfilling certain needs, and therefore kept back from ordinary assignment because the Government officials, so to speak, assigned them to themselves.

There were public works to be carried out, and the Government was clearly as much entitled to share in the supply of convict labour as the settler. It was said that the condition of these convicts in Government employ was always worse than those in private hands. About one-fourth of the whole available number were thus appropriated for the colonial works. But over and above these, the Government held also the whole of the refuse convictdom in the colonies. Every man who did not get on with his master; every man who committed himself, and was sentenced to undergo any correction greater than flogging or less than capital punishment, came back to Government, and was by it disposed of in one of three ways.

These three outlets were : (1) The road parties; (2) The chain-gangs; and (3) The penal settlements.

1. The road parties were employed either in Sydney itself and other towns, or along the many miles of roads wherever their services were required. Those at Sydney were lodged in the Hyde Park Barracks, whence they issued forth daily to their work, under the charge of overseers, at the rate of one to every thirty men. These overseers were themselves convicts; chosen for the post as being active, intelligent, and perhaps outwardly more respectable than their fellows. Naturally the control of such overseers was not very vigilant. They were paid no wages, and had no remuneration but certain increased indulgences, such as an allowance of tobacco and other minor luxuries. Hence they connived at the absence of any men who were disposed to forage in the town and run the risk of capture. If caught thieving or absent the culprits were to take the consequences; but if all went well, they shared whatever they met with during the day with their complaisant overseer. Parties in the country were under similar management, but they were dispersed over such a very wide area that efficient supervision was even more difficult. The Surveyor-General of the colony was the responsible head of the whole department; but under him the parties were actually worked by overseers and their deputies, both of whom were either convicts or ticket-of-leave men. These officials also connived at the absence of their men on all sorts

of false pretences. The convicts were free to come and go
almost as they pleased. Their dwellings were simple huts of
bark, which presented no obstacles to egress after hours at
night. In the day time they were equally unrestrained. They
did odd jobs, if they pleased, for the neighbouring settlers.*
Any artisan might earn money as blacksmith, carpenter, or
cooper. Many others were engaged in the straw hat trade, a
very favourite occupation for all the convicts. Great numbers,
less industriously disposed, spent their time in stealing. A
large proportion of the robberies which were so prevalent in
the colony were to be traced to the men of these parties on the
roads. They were highwaymen, neither more nor less; and
every settler far and near suffered from their depredations.
Sometimes they went off in gangs, and encamping by the
side of the road laid every passing team under contribution.
Increased facilities were given for the commission of these
crimes through the carelessness of the settlers themselves,
when they were permitted to employ men from the road parties
on Sundays or during leisure hours. Wages in cash were
paid in return, and the door was thus open to drunkenness
and the evils that follow in its train. Worse than this, at
harvest time, when the road parties were eagerly drawn upon
for the additional hands so urgently required, the settlers were
in the habit of giving the men they had thus employed passes
to rejoin the stations from which they had come. Of course
the convicts did not hurry home, and of course also they did
no little mischief *en route* while thus at large.

The work that was done by these parties was certainly
irksome in character. Breaking stones under a broiling sun
is not an agreeable pastime. But the amount of labour
performed was ludicrously small, and was described by an
eyewitness as a disgrace to those in charge.† On the whole,
therefore, the convicts of this class had no great cause of
complaint. They had plenty of congenial society, even outside their own gangs, for they were not prevented from

* Under Sir Richard Bourke's assignment rules, however, which
were promulgated in 1835, any settler who gave employment to convicts
from the road parties thereupon forfeited all his assigned servants.
† Mrs. Meredith.

associating with the assigned servants around; their food was ample; and they had abundant opportunities for self-aggrandisement in the manner most agreeable to themselves. It was not strange, then, that idle, worthless servants in assignment greatly preferred the parties on the road.

Nevertheless, there were not wanting among the free residents intelligent persons who saw how the labour of these road parties might have been made really productive of great benefit to the colony. There was still plenty of work to be done in developing colonial resources : over and above the construction and repair of roads, they could have been usefully employed in the clearance of township lands, the widening and deepening of river beds, in quarrying, fortifying, and building piers. But to have accomplished these results, a system more complete than any that was even dreamt of then must have been indispensable. Success only could have come from regular effective supervision by a thoroughly reliable staff, and by carefully constructed prison accommodation, such as was provided later in carrying out public works by convict labour in Western Australia.

2. In the chain-gangs there actually was greater restraint and some semblance of rigorous discipline. The convicts were relegated to this system of punishment as a general rule for colonial crimes, though at times new arrivals from England of a desperate character were also drafted into them at once. In these gangs the convicts were kept in close custody, and condemned to work which was really hard. There were some few chain-gangs in Sydney employed at the magazines on the island and in improving the streets ; * but as a general rule they were to be found chiefly at out stations, or in the interior. They were guarded always by a detachment of troops, and when most efficiently organised were governed by a military officer, who was also a magistrate. Under him there was also a superintendent in charge of each stockade or barrack, with a staff of constables in the proportion of one to seventy-five convicts. The duties of the constables were analogous to those of warders in permanent prisons at home. The stockades were substantial buildings, in appearance somewhat

* They lived on board a hulk.

similar to American log-huts, but of greater strength, sufficient to preclude all possibility of escape. These stockades
accommodated each one hundred or more men. They were
of simple construction: the walls formed of timber, split
into strong slabs, which rested in grooves at top and bottom;
the roof was of timber also, covered in with bark. In most
cases the materials were found close to the spot, timber
being everywhere plentiful; but it was possible to take down
the stockade and remove the pieces to another locality if
required. The prisoners were not badly fed—with flour,
maize meal, and beef. Their clothing was two suits a year.
They had medical attendance, and regular Divine worship.
Their beds were of plank, but there was no lack of bedding.
The great hardships were the unremitting labour—not less
than ten hours daily, and the chains—leg-irons weighing six
or seven pounds, which were never for a moment removed.
So important were these irons considered, that it was the
stockade superintendent's business to examine closely every
prisoner's chains daily before the stockade was emptied for
labour. In this way chiefly escapes were prevented, as the
convict carrying with him several pounds of metal, found
himself rather too heavily handicapped to run. One
other unpleasant feature at the stockade was the official
"scourger," as he was called—a convict specially appointed
to execute corporal punishment. He was not himself an
"iron-gang" man, but came from assigned service together
with the convicts' cooks and wardsmen required for the interior
economy of the stockade. What with work unremitting,
weighty chains that were never removed, isolation from the
dissipation of the towns, the convict in the iron-gang was
on no bed of roses. Nor could he, under the later *régime*,
escape easily as he had done heretofore. Sentries with
loaded muskets guarded every exit, and they gave him only
one chance to halt when summoned, before they fired. After
two years' trial Sir Richard Bourke reported that his new
system was eminently successful. By its assistance he
was at length enabled to dispense altogether with the road
parties without irons, which I have already described as
being so fruitful of evil to the community at large. Another

evil to which I have not referred, and which was attributable
to the slackness of control over these road parties and
chain-gangs, was the existence of a class of desperadoes
sufficiently well known to every reader—I mean the notorious
"bushrangers" of the Australian colonies. Certain numbers
of these were recruited from among the assigned servants,
who absconded when they and their masters could not
agree, but by far the greater proportion was furnished
by the Government gangs, escapes from which were for a
long time frequent and generally successful. Whenever a
man of courage and ability got clear away, he soon collected
around him a band of brigands like himself; and then, for
periods varying in length according to the nature of the
pursuit, these villains subjected the whole neighbourhood to
their depredations. They attacked chiefly the outlying huts
and houses, but seldom large establishments. One case
was known where some sixty men of a chain-gang had
plotted to break out simultaneously and make for the
bush. Thence they were to march on Macarthur's station,
bent on pillage. Nothing came of this plot, because precautions were taken to meet it. But at other times bloody
affrays were common enough between the bushrangers and the
mounted police. Indeed, it was well known that unless a
gang of these highwaymen was entirely exterminated there
was no peace for the district in which they were at large. If
one survivor escaped he soon became the nucleus of a new
gang. What between attacks on dwelling-houses, and the
daily stoppage on the highways of carts and waggons, the
country generally was most insecure. People went about in
fear of their lives.

3. The penal settlements, which were the ultimate penal
stronghold of the penal colonies, contained, as a matter of
course, the whole of the dregs of convictdom. These settlements were the superlative degree of infamy. The convicts in
the road parties and chain-gangs were bad enough, Heaven
knows, but they were angels compared to those in the penal
settlements. Offenders were not indeed transferred to these
terrible receptacles till all other treatment had failed. When
there, "it seemed," to quote Judge Burton's words, "that the

heart of a man was taken from him, and that he was given the heart of a beast." It will not beseem me to go fully into all the details of these cesspools of iniquity, but I shall have to refer at some length further on to Norfolk Island, the worst of them all. The settlements used as penal by New South Wales were Moreton Bay and Norfolk Island; that by Van Diemen's Land was Tasman's Peninsula. This place was cut off altogether from the settled districts, having only one communication—at Forestiers Peninsula—with the main island. On this neck of land, between Pirates' Bay and Norfolk Bay, stood an officer's guard; and besides his sentries, a chain of fierce dogs kept watch and ward from shore to shore. These dogs had been trained to give tongue at the slightest noise day or night. So successful was the guard they kept, that only two prisoners ever escaped from Port Arthur. One was recaptured, the other died in the woods. This station on Tasman's Peninsula had the great advantage that it was not, like Norfolk Island, distant several days' sail. Being but six hours from headquarters at Hobart, it was brought directly under the supervision of the governor and other officials.

I have now described the condition and style of life of all convicts, still such; of all, I mean, who were not yet nominally or actually free. The whole of these were comprised in the numbers at assigned service, in the road parties, chain-gangs, or penal settlements.

Next above them, on a sort of debatable land, free for the time being, but liable to degradation anew, stood the convict on ticket-of-leave. This expression and the practice to which it applies have been adopted into our home legislation and language, but the term itself was a colonial invention. The first tickets were granted by Governor Phillip with the intention of instituting some stage intermediate between complete freedom and actual restraint. As time passed new orders varied the details; but the meaning of the term remained practically the same. The holder of a ticket-of-leave was a convicted felon, who had permission to be at large before the whole term of his sentence had actually expired.

At the top of the convict ladder were the emancipists, whose term of transportation was at an end, who were free to return to the land from whence they came, and begin life afresh, but who were never actually whitewashed in the colonies, or permitted to rise in the social scale to an equality with the free settler who had never broken the laws. We have seen how successive governors sought to bring the emancipists forward, and the heartburnings it occasioned. Their efforts were doubtless supported by the wealth and importance of many of the emancipist class; but it was on this account that the antagonism exhibited by the free population was the more unvarying and bitter. Many of the respectable inhabitants had been outstripped in the race for fortune by men who had arrived in the colony bearing the felon's brand; and the free settlers felt that in fighting against the pretensions of these ex-convicts they were fighting for very life. The position of the latter was so strong, that with the slightest success they would have swamped the former altogether. No doubt the injudicious tone of the emancipist press, and the flagrant conduct of many of the principal emancipists, drove the free settlers into opposition more strenuous than was absolutely required. A man who had been a convict was not necessarily to be taken by the hand and made much of from pure sentimental philanthropy. But neither, on the other hand, should he have been kept perpetually at a distance, and treated as a native of the Southern States would at one time have treated any one of black blood or complexion. It was because the emancipists formed a body so powerful that their opponents were more or less afraid of them, and stood really at bay, fighting with their backs to the wall. Not a little of this bitter hostility has survived to the present day. Even now, in the towns where transportation took effect, the convict element stands in a class apart; there are caste distinctions stronger than any in the mother country, of which the barriers are rarely, if ever, overpassed.

But beyond question, many of the emancipists throve. The pictures drawn of their wealth and prosperity may be a little exaggerated, but in their main outlines they were undoubtedly true. There was one who had made a fortune worth five-and-forty thousand a year. Several others had incomes of £20,000. One or two of the largest shops in

Sydney were owned by them. They had public-houses, and farms, and ships, and newspapers, and all the outward signs of material wealth. They spared no pains or cost to get gorgeous furniture and costly plate. They had grand carriages and good horses, and were fond of lavish and ostentatious expenditure. But with all this, low taste prevailed. No one bought pictures or works of art: the only literature they valued was the "Newgate Calendar," and they preferred a prize-fight any day to an opera or a decent play. It was said, indeed, that the principal wealth of the colony was for a long time held in the hands of these emancipists. Honest people less successful in the race for money declared that these others made fortunes because they were quite unscrupulous. No doubt the accusation held. One case was proved in which a certain shop undersold all others, simply because its owner, an ex-convict, was a receiver of stolen goods, which he naturally was able to retail at remarkably cheap rates. A number made their fortunes by dealing only with their fellow-convicts, whom a sort of freemasonry attracted always to convict shops. The practice, at one time prevalent, and to which I have already referred, of giving small grants of land to ticket-of-leave men, was another opening to convict shopkeepers and general dealers. These farmers came into Sydney to sell their produce. As there were no markets, certain individuals bought all that came, paying for the same in "property"—in drink, that is to say, and other articles of consumption. The countrymen got drunk always, and stayed a day or two on the same spot: at last the landlord asked them if they knew how much they owed. "No." "Well, £50." "Why, how is that?" "You've been drunk all the time, and did not know what you were doing." Of course the victim was unable to pay, and had to sign a power of attorney, or paper binding himself to give up all his produce until the debt was cancelled. This scheme was repeated again and again, till all the poor man's property was pledged, and then he was sold up. One man had been known to drink away his farm of 100 acres in a single night. It was by carrying on this line of action that the emancipist already mentioned as worth £15,000 a-year became a large landed proprietor. But he was also a thrifty, careful man, from the time he had come out when almost as a boy with one of the first fleets. He was a sober man, moreover; and when spirits were issued to the convicts employed building at Paramatta, he saved his and sold it to his fellows. Then, putting by all the time he was a prisoner every shilling he could make, he was able when free to set up a public-house, and buy a horse and gig which he let for hire. One day when his trap was wanted he drove it himself, and had as "fare" an ex-convict woman who owned a little property—some two or three hundred pounds. This woman he married out of hand, and then little by little increased his connection.

On the whole it was not strange that there should be fierce warfare between the better classes and the emancipists as a body. Beyond doubt, it was plainly evident that the emancipists formed a very corrupting element in general society. They looked with leniency on men who had committed serious crimes, and welcomed those whom honest people naturally shunned. One of the sorest points of contention was the admission of these emancipists to serve on juries in criminal and other trials. It was not alone that they leant to the side of the accused, and could not, even in cases clearly proved, be persuaded to convict; but respectable people objected to be herded with them in the same panel. The question was warmly argued. Petitions were presented for and against; and this of itself showed the extent to which the convict element arrogated to itself power. One petition praying for the abolition of the practice was signed by the clergy, land-owners, merchants, and gentry generally; while the counter petition was prepared and signed mostly by men on ticket-of-leave. Irritated, undoubtedly, by the general state of affairs, a party among the settlers grew up, and daily gained strength, which was pledged to the abolition of transportation.

Truly the state of New South Wales was not at that time all that could be desired; crime was extraordinarily prevalent, a certain looseness of moral tone also, and abundant drunkenness; the latter indeed, at this time was the besetting sin of the colony. It affected all classes —drunken people were to be seen in all directions, men and women fighting in the streets, and riotous conduct everywhere. At the Rocks—the Seven Dials of Sydney—the scenes of debauchery were repeated and always disgraceful. In the upper classes, at the hotel bars, the same tastes prevailed; and the gentry fuddled themselves with wine, just as the lower orders did with rum. This *penchant* for drink was curiously contagious. Free emigrants who came out with sober habits were soon as bad as the old hands. Of course among the convict class the drunkenness knew no bounds. The favourite drink was rum—not fine old Jamaica, but East Indian, fiery and hot—which was handed round undiluted in a bucket at all regular "sprees." Often assigned servants were found downstairs hopelessly drunk while host and guests waited upstairs for dinner, the roasts being in the fire and the meat boiled to rags. Even good servants, fairly honest and capable, could not resist the bottle. The hardest drinkers were the "old hands," or convicts who had finished their terms and had become free. These fellows worked hard for a year or two till they had put by some £40 or £50, then posted off to Sydney to squander the whole in one big debauch. They stood treat to all around—rum flowed like water—and if the money did not go fast enough they called for champagne. "It is, in truth, impossible to conceive," continues the same writer, "the lengths to which drunkenness proceeds and the crime it leads to, not only to obtain the means of gratification, but as a consequence on indulgence." To purvey to the universal thirstiness there were dram-shops and publics by hundreds everywhere. Licenses were seldom if ever refused, even to persons of unknown character. For them it was quite sufficient to get the good word of the chief constable—himself an old convict. He was not above a bribe, and his recommendation always carried the day. "In no city of the world," says Byrne, "are there the same proportion of public-houses; every fifty yards in the streets brings you to one—paying high rent, and doing an excellent business. . . . From high to low—the merchant, mechanic, and labourer, all alike are a thirsty community. The bar-rooms of the hotels and inns are as much crowded as the taps of the dram-shops. Drink, drink, drink, seems to be the universal motto, and the quantity that is consumed is incredible; from early morning to night it is the same—Bacchus being constantly sacrificed to."

Of the extraordinary prevalence of crime there could be little doubt. One eminent judge spoke of the colony as composed of two classes, whose main business respectively was the commission of crime and the punishment of it. The whole colony, he said, seemed to be in motion towards the courts of justice. Beyond question the criminal statistics were rather startling. The number of convictions for highway robbery in New South Wales alone was equal to the whole number of convictions for all offences in England. Murders and criminal assaults were as common out there as petty larcenies at home. The rate was as one offender to every twenty-two of population; while in England about the same period it varied from one in seven hundred and forty to one in a thousand. It is but fair, however, to state that nearly the whole mass of crime proceeded from the convicts, or those who had been such. Among the reputable portion of the population the proportion was no greater in New South Wales than elsewhere. Sydney was a perfect den of thieves; and these, being indeed selected from the whole felonry of England, were quite masters of their business, and stood at the head of the profession. The report of the police magistrate of Sydney, printed in October, 1835, gives a nice picture of the state of the town. Of the whole population of twenty thousand a large proportion were prisoners, past or present, " whose passions are violent, and who have not been accustomed to control them, yet for the most part have no lawful means of gratifying them. It includes a great number of incorrigible bad characters, who on obtaining their freedom will not apply themselves to any honest mode of earning their living, but endeavour to support themselves in idleness and debauchery by plunder."

"There is more immorality in Sydney," he goes on, " than in any other English town of the same population in His Majesty's dominions." It contained two hundred and nineteen public-houses, and there were besides sly grog-shops innumerable. "There is no town which affords so much facility for eluding the vigilance of the police. The unoccupied bush

near and within the town itself will afford shelter to the
offender and hide him from pursuit; he may steal or hire a
boat, and in a few minutes place an arm of the sea between him
and his pursuers. . . . The drunkenness, idleness, and careless-
ness of a great portion of the inhabitants afford innumerable
opportunities and temptations by day and night to live by
plunder." Sir Francis Forbes, the Chief Justice of the colony,
endorses the foregoing statements. "That this is a true
description," he says, " of the actual state of Sydney cannot be
denied."

Another powerful voice was raised by another judge—
Judge Burton—whose charge to the grand jury of Sydney in
November, 1835, attracted universal attention. Not alone
were crimes constantly detected and punished, but others,
often the most flagrant, stalked undiscovered through the land.
And numerous executions exercised no effect in deterring
from crime. The example of repeated capital punishments
caused no alarm. There was no attempt by the masters to
raise the moral tone of their convicts; no religious worship on
Sundays, as we have seen; and instead of it, drunkenness and
debauchery. Masters, indeed, exercised hardly any control
over their men. To this Judge Burton traced nearly all the
crime. Many of the most daring robberies were to be
attributed to this, and this alone. Convict servants, as many
as five and six together, went about openly to plunder, masked
and armed with muskets—a weapon not capable of much
concealment. Even in broad daylight, and in the open highway, harmless folk had been stopped by these miscreants and
robbed.

In a word, Judge Burton intimated clearly that transportation must cease. The colonies could never rise to their proper
position; they could not obtain those free institutions for
which even then they were agitating; in a word, the whole
moral aspect of the colony suffered so terribly by the present
system, that the time must come when it must be abandoned
altogether.

The reader who has followed me through this and the
preceding chapter will probably admit that the method of
transportation, as it had been administered, was indeed a

failure. Looking at the actual tangible results, as they appeared at that date, at an early period of the colonial history, and before years of subsequent prosperity and cleanly life had purged the colony of its one constant cancerous bane, they were most unsatisfactory. Hardly any one could be said to have profited in all these years but the convicts for whom transportation had been instituted. But it had been instituted as a punishment, not as a boon; and although we cannot actually quarrel with a system which had the undoubted effect of turning large numbers of criminals into wealthy and therefore, to a certain extent, honest men, we may fairly condemn it on principle. Reformation and restraint from crime we are bound to accomplish; the only question is whether we should have been so liberal to the criminal class. Transporting them to the antipodes was about the kindest thing we could do for them. It was, indeed, removing them to a distance from their old haunts and ways of life, but they went to a land flowing with milk and honey. After the earlier years the vague terrors of that unknown country had disappeared. There was money to be made out there; a certainty of food, light work, and no great isolation from the company of their choice. Hardly a family of thieves but owned one or more relatives at the other end of "the pond." Those without relatives had numerous friends and pals who had gone before. Besides which there was this distinct anomaly, that convicts were now sent for their crimes to lands which were held out as a land of promise to the free emigrant. " It not unfrequently happens, that whilst a judge is expatiating on the miseries of exile, at the same time, and perhaps in the same place, some active agent of emigration may be found magnifying the advantages of the new country; lauding the fertility of its soil, and the beauties of its climate; telling of the high wages to be there obtained, the enormous fortunes that have been made; and offering to eager and willing listeners, as a boon and especial favour, the means of conveyance to that very place to which the convict in the dock has been sentenced for his crimes."

But all the arguments against transportation are now as clear as noonday. It failed to reform, except in a curiously

liberal, unintentional fashion; it was no punishment; it was
terribly costly; and as carried out was, at least for a time,
distinctly injurious to the best interests of the colonies in
which it took effect.*

* "In any of the leading requisites of any system of secondary
punishment transportation was defective. Thus, it was neither formidable—in other words, the apprehension of it did not operate as
much as possible to deter men from crime, and thus prevent the necessity
of its actual infliction—nor was it corrective, or at least not corrupting
—tending to produce in the criminal himself, if his life be spared, and
in others, either a moral improvement, or at least as little as possible of
moral debasement. Nor, lastly, was it cheap, so as to make the punishment of the criminal either absolutely profitable to the community, or at
least not excessively costly. In all these requisites transportation had
been found deficient, but chiefly in the most important, viz. in the power
of exercising a salutary terror in offenders."—Archbishop Whately:
"Thoughts on Secondary Punishment."

" PROBATION " STATION IN VAN DIEMEN'S LAND.

CHAPTER XVII.

SUBSTITUTION OF PROBATION FOR ASSIGNMENT.

WE have now arrived at a new stage in the history of penal legislation. The time had at length come when transportation was to be distinctly discountenanced and its approaching abolition openly discussed. Many concurrent causes contributed to this. Sir William Molesworth's committee, in 1837, had spoken against transportation, and in the plainest terms. The punishment was condemned because it was unequal and too often without terrors to the criminal classes; it was extravagantly expensive, and most corrupting to convict, colonist, and all concerned. The forcible oratory of Archbishop Whately and others had urged with incisive language the necessity for its discontinuance. Last, but not least, the protest of the colonists themselves, now for the first time formulated and put forward with all the insistence that accompanies the display of a virtuous determination, could not be entirely ignored. Important changes therefore were inevitable, nor could they be much longer delayed.

In point of fact, in the matter of secondary punishments it was a return to the position of fifty years before. Then we had no system at all; now the system, such as it was, was found to be entirely at fault. Transportation as conducted had quite broken down, the hulks at home were open to the severest criticism, and Millbank Penitentiary was a failure. The situation was full of difficulty. Lord John Russell, the then Home Secretary, may well have felt himself in the horns of a dilemma. At one and the same moment the three outlets through which the graver criminals had been disposed of were practically closed: the antipodes, by agitation and the strident voice of public opinion; the hulks, by the faultiness of their internal management; and the great reforming Penitentiary, by the absolute barrenness of results. If deportation beyond the seas were to come to an end, then the convicts must remain at home. But where? Not in the hulks; that was out of the question. Sir William Molesworth had recommended more penitentiaries, as the Nabob ordered more curricles. But the country grudged another half million: there had been little or no return for that spent years before on Millbank. Then it was suggested that large prisons should be constructed on the principle of Pentonville, for ordinary offenders, while the more desperate characters were to be drafted to Lundy Island and other rocks that might hold them. A third scheme was to construct convict barracks in the neighbourhood of our dockyards, to replace the hulks; but this, which contained in itself the germ of our own present prison system, was far too radical a change to be tolerated at that time or for many years to come. All action being thus impeded and beset with difficulty, the Government temporised and steered a middle course. It was thought that by grafting certain important so-called improvements upon the old system it might be retained. Doubtless, when judged by later experience, the plan appears shifty and incomplete; but in theory and as seen at the time it was excellent. It was deduced by sound logical arguments from given premisses, and had those premisses remained unchanged the system might perhaps have existed longer without collapse. But reasoning on paper is not the same as in real life: one small accident will upset the profoundest calculations. The plan of "probation" which I am about to describe was admirably devised; but it failed because the condition of the colonies varied, and because small obstacles, that were at the time of conception overlooked or ignored, grew in course of time sufficiently powerful to upset the whole scheme as originally devised.

Beyond question the task was not a light one. The Government did not shirk its duty, but it was fully alive to the difficulties that lay in the way. Speaking some years later, a member of that administration thus deprecates adverse criticism. "We could hardly hope," says Earl Grey,* "to succeed at once in devising a system of secondary punishments effectual for its purpose and free from objections, thereby solving a problem which has for many years engaged the attention of the legislators and statesmen of most civilised countries, and has hitherto proved most difficult for them all." But they met the question manfully, and this is what they devised.

Transportation was to continue in force, but it was to be governed by certain checks and safeguards which had been altogether absent before, through all the long years that convicts had been sent out to the antipodes. And now the whole stream was to be directed on Van Diemen's Land alone. This Van Diemen's Land, which was thenceforth to be only a colonial prison, had been settled some years later than Botany Bay, by a party under Colonel Collins from the parent settlement. It had struggled for life amid the same vicissitudes of famine and privation as New South Wales, and similarly some years elapsed before its home products were sufficient for its own support. Up to the year 1821 it was solely a penal settlement for the transportation of convicts from Sydney; but after that date a few free settlers flocked to it, and by-and-by ships landed their living cargoes at Hobart Town direct from England,

* Earl Grey: Colonial Policy, ii. 14.

just as they did at Sydney in New South Wales. The system
of assignment was practised precisely as in the senior
settlement, with this difference, that the discipline was more
perfect, and the machine worked with greater ease in Van
Diemen's Land. Two-thirds of the whole number there were
thus in assigned service, the balance being employed as in New
South Wales in chain-gangs, at penal settlements, or on the roads.

Colonel Arthur, who was for many years governor of the
colony, and who was well known as a strenuous supporter of
transportation, claimed, and with some show of right, that
the management and treatment of convicts had been attended
with a greater measure of success in Van Diemen's Land than
elsewhere. This may have had some weight with the Government; for the existence of a good system of administration was
essential to the execution of the new project : but it is probable
that Van Diemen's Land was chosen as the sole future receptacle of convicts because as yet it had had no thought of
refusing so to act. New South Wales had rebelled, but Van
Diemen's Land was still obedient ; and no time was lost in
turning its willingness to good account. Although for years
it had been more or less a penal settlement, as now constituted
it became essentially a colonial prison. Vast masses of convicts were to be congregated in its chief towns; its out-stations
were to be overrun with convicts in various stages of eman-
cipation; free convicts were to be the pioneers and settlers
of its back lands; in a word, the whole colony was to be
permeated, inundated, swamped with the criminal class. That
I am using no figure of speech, and to give some idea of the
amount of evil with which a small colony had now to deal,
I will mention here that in four years no less than sixteen
thousand convicts were sent out to Van Diemen's Land, and
that the average annual number in the colony of transported
convicts was nearly thirty thousand. Here at home, in the
year 1874, the total convict population in prison numbers
from seven to eight thousand : there are, roughly, fifty-four
thousand at large ; but our population is twenty-three millions,
while in Van Diemen's Land, at the time of which I am writing,
the number of persons who were free and without stain
amounted only to thirty-seven thousand.

The new method of carrying out transportation came into force on the 20th May, 1840. It was christened the "Probation" system, because the progressive improvement of the convicts was intended to depend on their progress through certain periods of "probation." Every convict was to be subjected to certain punishments and restrictions peculiar to the stage in which he found himself; but these rigours were to diminish, step by step, till he had passed by many gradations from actual imprisonment to the delights of unshackled, unconditional freedom. No doubt in theory the principle was excellent, and had those who were to be subjected to it been anything but living men, it might have succeeded. We can pass a piece of metal, or a quantity of yarn, through several stages of manufacture with a reasonable hope that the result, or product, will be something near that which we expected; but human beings, especially of the criminal class, will not "come out" like combinations of figures calculated exactly, or chemical processes duly set in motion. Our idea, now, was to pass our convicts through a species of crucible of discomfort, hoping that in the end, under this new treatment, they would turn out reformed. The attitude of the convict while undergoing the process was to be taken as the test of his amendment: good behaviour then was assumed to be an earnest of good behaviour in the future. Here was the fallacy. We were taking promise for performance; in other words, accepting a temporary amendment, put forward in most cases to gain certain ends, as real *bonâ fide* reform. There was this grave fault even in the theory of the new plan; in practice there were others, and greater, which soon became distinctly apparent.

The plan of procedure is fully detailed in a despatch addressed by Lord Stanley, on the 15th November, 1842, to Sir John Franklin, then Lieutenant Governor of Van Diemen's Land. All convicts, with certain exceptions, were to be subjected to the new process. By it, as I have said, the convict was compelled to pass through certain stages, five in number; and his progressive escape upwards was to be regulated altogether by his good conduct in each stage.*

* The rules were the same for boys and females, only their stations were of course different.

Stated briefly these five stages were: (1) Detention at a purely penal station in a state of real imprisonment; (2) Removal to gangs working in various parts of the colony for Government, but still under restraint; (3) The first step towards freedom, in which the convict was granted a pass to be at large under certain conditions, and to seek work for himself; (4) The second step to freedom, when the convict gained his ticket-of-leave, and was free to come and go much as he pleased; (5) And lastly, absolute pardon.

1. Only the worst criminals entered the first stage, and for them Norfolk Island (a) and Tasman's Peninsula (b) were set apart. These were the colonial convicts, and men sentenced at home to "life," or fifteen years for heinous offences. The term at Norfolk Island was to be not less than two years, and not more than four; but misconduct consigned an offender to an indefinite term within his sentence.

(a) And first as to Norfolk Island.

Situated in semi-tropical latitudes, richly gifted by nature, picturesque, fertile, of fairly equable climate, this small spot seemed to contain within itself all the elements of a terrestrial paradise. It was finely timbered, chiefly with the graceful tree known as the Norfolk Island Pine; limes, lemons, and guavas were indigenous; all manner of fruits—oranges, grapes, figs, loquots, bananas, peaches, pomegranates, pine-apples, and melons—grew there in rare profusion. Flowers, wild or cultivated, throve all around. Everywhere the eye rested on long fields of oats, or barley, or Indian maize. And yet the social condition of the island, as compared with its external aspect, was as the inner diseased core of an apple to its smooth and rosy skin. From the earliest days of the Australian colonies this bountifully gifted island had been made the receptacle—the sink, simply—of all the lees and dregs of mankind. Occupied in the first instance on account of its fertile aspect, it was soon afterwards abandoned for no sound or substantial reasons. By-and-by it was again reoccupied, but then only as a penal settlement. And as such it served New South Wales during all the years that transportation was in full swing. It was a prison, and nothing more; convicts and their keepers were its only population. The former at times

varied in numbers: one year there were five hundred, another
seven; but their lot and condition was always much the same.
The worst wore chains. All worked, but not excessively; and
the well-conducted were allowed, as their time dragged along,
certain immunities from labour and a modicum of tobacco.
Occasionally the gaol-gangs, the most depraved of this gathering of wickedness, broke loose, and attacked their guards with
brutal desperation. Numbers were always shot down then and
there, and of the balance when overpowered a fair proportion
were forthwith hanged. Stated broadly, life in Norfolk Island
was so bitter to the convict that many for choice sought a
shameful death.

Thus was Norfolk Island constituted, and such the condition of its residents, when the Home Government, in working
out its new penal scheme, resolved to increase the numbers on
the island, by drafting to it the most flagrant offenders from
home. We have come by this time to accept it as an axiom in
prison affairs, that it is unwise to concentrate in one spot the
pith and essence of rascality; preferring rather to subdivide
and distribute the most dangerous elements at several points.
But the statesmen who were then legislating on penal matters
ignored this principle; they forgot that they were about to
recruit the old gangs at Norfolk Island by the very men most
predisposed to become as bad as those they found there. If
the administration had been really anxious to perpetuate the
leaven of wickedness already existent in the penal settlement,
they could not have devised a plan more likely to attain the
result required.

Under the new rules Norfolk Island was intended to contain—and hereafter usually did—some 2000 convicts. Of
these about two-thirds came from England direct, the rest
were sentenced in the colonies. There were three stations:
the Head-Quarters Settlement or "King's Town," Longridge,
and Cascades. The first, situated on the south side of the
island and facing the sea, was the most important. Here was
the principal landing-place; but a coral reef prevented the near
approach of shipping, and the anchorage outside it was insecure.
Hence all loading and unloading was done by boats; and this,
in itself a tedious operation, was rendered more difficult and

dangerous by the heavy surf that rolled perpetually across the
bar. But except those that came on the public service no
vessels visited the island. There was another landing-place
at Cascade Station, on the north side of the island, which was
used when the state of the bar at King's Town rendered it
absolutely impracticable for boats. At King's Town the bulk
of the convicts were retained. Here were their barracks, in
which some 800 convicts slept; here the lumber-yard, where
the same numbers messed; here too the hospitals, and the
gaols for the retention of those again about to be tried for
fresh offences in the island. The barracks, built of substantial
limestone and surrounded by a high wall, stood some eighty
yards from the beach; the lumber-yard close at hand was
simply a high enclosure, two sides of which were roofed in and
provided with rough chairs and tables; the whole area within
about half an acre, no more. Next to the lumber-yard, through
which was the only entrance, stood the slaughter-houses and
cooks' houses, all filthy in the extreme. There was no supervision over the issue of rations: meat was sold openly at a
penny per pound, and the convicts went to and fro from this
and the bakehouse just as they pleased. The gaol stood close
to the landing-place, and close in front of its chief entrance,
the gallows—" so placed that you cannot pass the doorway
without coming almost in contact with this engine of death."*
The hospital accommodation for the whole settlement was
here at King's Town, and it amounted to twenty beds, with
a detached convalescent ward, cold and cheerless, and this
for a population of 2000, in an island where epidemic dysentery of a malignant type, especially during the summer, was
by no means uncommon. In matters of supply the settlement was equal to its own requirements, except after seasons
unusually bad. There was abundance of water in the neighbouring creeks, and, although this was rendered impure by
flowing past gardens and stock-yards, it was easily filtered:
and there were springs too in abundance. Stock was raised
and grain chiefly at Longridge, a mile and a half from Head-

* Report on Norfolk Island made to the Comptroller-General of
Convicts. 1846. (From which I have quoted largely.)

Quarters. The soil was fertile naturally, but light, and required good management.

The day's work began at the several settlements at daylight, when the men were roused out by a bell. Any, and they were not few, who felt idle and indisposed to work, remained behind in bed. But presently—let us stand and look on—some 600 or 700 men have collected in the barrack yard, and are to be seen walking leisurely about, waiting for the chaplain to say morning prayers, or if he failed to appear —and this was not unusual—waiting for the commencement of muster. Should the chaplain show himself, some ten or twenty prisoners go with him to the chapel which is close at hand; the rest remain outside, and no effort is made by the overseers to compel their attendance. The overseers are indeed powerless then, as at other times, and exercise no authority whatever.

Prayers over, muster follows; but the performance is as unlike the strict parade it should be as anything it is possible to conceive. There is no attempt at formation by classes, messes, or wards; no silence, no order. The convicts lounge to and fro, hands in pockets, and talking to one another while their names are read out by convict clerks from the superintendent's office—the assistant superintendent, whose duty this would be, being generally unable to read or write. As each convict hears his name he answers or not, as it suits him, and then saunters over to join the working gang for which he has been detailed. As soon as the muster is concluded the men disperse, leaving the yard in groups or one by one, and proceed to breakfast. Here the whole body breakfast on hominy—or paste made from maize meal—seated under cover or in the open areas, preserving no appearance of order, talking and laughing just as they please among themselves. Breakfast over, some go to work, but a great many do not. They have their bread to bake; and this each man does for himself, spending half the day in sifting meal, kneading dough, and loitering leisurely to the bakehouse and back. The only men told off to regular labour are the two gangs who work the crank-mill, and the labour there was so regulated that half in

turns were idle half the day; while those at work were riotous
and disorderly, shrieking, yelling, hooting, and assailing every
passer-by, whether subordinate official, magistrate, or the commandant himself, with the vilest personal abuse. The great
mass of the convicts were engaged in quarrying or in agricultural pursuits. They were superintended by convict sub-over-
seers, and not by free persons; and the work done was naturally
not large, more particularly as these convict overseers went in
daily terror of their lives. Indeed, at the time of which I am
writing—after the introduction of "probation," that is to
say, and probably before it too—there was practically little
or no discipline whatever maintained among the convicts.
But for the bayonets and bullets of the military guard by
which they were more or less awed—though even against
them they rose at times, to their own disadvantage—they
would have become the real masters of the island; and if they
were thus restrained by fear from overt rebellion, they did not
hesitate to display as much sullen disobedience and active
insubordination as they dared without bringing on themselves
retaliatory and coercive measures. They were, in fact, for
ever in a state of semi-mutiny which is always present among
a body of determined but badly governed men whose rulers
are weak, not to say cowardly. This ill-conditioned attitude
towards authority was displayed repeatedly. Day after day
for a week together the whole body stationed at one or other
of the settlements refused to turn out for labour, alleging
as cause some trivial unendorsed complaint about their food
and lodgment.

Flagrant outrages, like the seizure of boats which carried
stores, were not uncommon, on which occasions the men of the
military escort were usually thrown overboard. But perhaps
the following occurrence, which took place before the eyes of
a special commissioner sent from Hobart Town, will prove
most forcibly the anarchy and indiscipline that prevailed. I
cannot do better than use this gentleman's own words.*

"On the first of my morning visits to the lumber-yard,
accompanied by the superintendent of English convicts, I
observed, on our entry, a man very deliberately smoking,

* Report on Norfolk Island, by Mr. R. P. Stewart, dated June 20th, 1846.

standing among a crowd round the fire, inside the cook-house."
An officer advanced to make the man give up his pipe; but he
was received with a look of the most ineffable disdain, and the
smoker, getting up with his hands in his pockets, moved to a
part of the mess known as the "Ring," where all the worst
characters collected. On this an order was issued to have the
man taken to gaol; but no one stepped forward to execute it,
until at length the acting chief constable, "who had been
standing in the rear, advanced with admirable coolness and
determination to the spot. The whole yard was now like a
disturbed hive, and the superintendent expressed his conviction
that there would be a riot, as the men would never suffer the
culprit to be taken into custody. However, after a short time
had elapsed, the culprit was seen emerging from the dense
crowd by which he had been surrounded, with hands in pocket,
attended by, rather than in custody of, the chief constable of
the island. He (the convict) deliberately advanced to the
superintendent, who was standing by my side, and in a most
insolent manner said, 'What have you ordered me to gaol
for?' The superintendent very coolly expostulated with him
and advised him to go quietly, when he deliberately struck
him two blows in the face, and using some very opprobrious
expressions, fiercely rushed upon and nearly threw him upon
the ground." He was seized by a constable, who asked if he
should shoot him. But both convict and constable were borne
away to another part of the shed by a dense crowd. The men
got out their knives, and matters looked desperate, when the
acting chief constable again went forward and persuaded the
offender to give himself up. Had it not been for the presence
of Mr. Stewart, an officer accredited from His Excellency the
Governor of Van Diemen's Land, a very serious disturbance
might have been expected. As it was, the most foul and
abusive language was used by the convicts to all the officials
present.

This "Ring" which has just been mentioned was in itself
a power on the island. All the worst men were leagued
together in it, and exercised a species of terrorism over the
rest. This was especially noticeable on the arrival and debarka-
tion of a batch of new convicts from England, when every

effort for their protection made by the proper authorities
proved always ineffectual.   If the new hands were lodged
under lock and key, the men of the Ring contrived generally
to break into the ward and rifle them of all they possessed.
If they were marched under an escort of constables to
bathe, the old stagers attacked them *en route*, or while they
were in the water plundered them of their clothes.   Thus
banded together and utterly reckless the more depraved
exercised a power almost absolute over their fellows, so that of
these even the well-disposed were compelled to submit, in
mortal terror of the deadly threats of this vicious, tyrannical
confederacy.   A convict whose conduct was good could not be
protected from violence if there was even a suspicion, with or
without reason, that he had borne witness against any member
of the Ring, or was otherwise distasteful to it.   Speaking in
general terms of Norfolk Island, Mr. Stewart states that he
is satisfied, from his inquiry, that a confirmed insubordinate
spirit exists among the convicts, " constantly exhibiting itself
in threats of personal violence towards subordinate officers,
towards the constabulary if they resolutely do their duty, and
towards their fellow-prisoners if they should be suspected of
giving information or assistance to their officers; which threats
are rendered more serious and alarming from the general
practice of carrying knives, and from their having been
fulfilled in instances of stabbing, or assaulting by beating to a
cruel, nearly mortal extent, and of personal injury in attempted
disfiguration by biting off the nose, and in other overt acts of
such a character as to produce a most serious effect in deterring
all holding subordinate authority from the vigorous and prompt
performance of their duty."

I have lingered thus long over Norfolk Island because it
was the starting-point and centre of the new scheme of penal
legislation.   In actual truth the picture I have drawn is painted
in with colours far less sombre than the subject deserves.   I
have shown how beyond the absolute isolation and exile the
punishment was not severe, the work light, food plentiful, and
discipline a mere farce.   I have shown how the most criminal
were banded together to defy authority and exercise a species
of awful tyranny over the timid and weak; I have shown how

these malefactors who were supposed to be expiating their crimes swaggered about, armed, and with knives in their hands, insulting their keepers with vile abuse, lording over their weaker fellows, using violence whenever the spirit moved them to murder a constable, beat a comrade to death, or make a mouthful of his nose. I have said that when matters went too far firearms and the halter were called into play, and for a time worked a certain cure; but from this, the relapse was worse than the original disease. On other points I have not touched, because I do not care to sully my pages with reference to other atrocities perpetrated in that loathsome den—atrocities the existence of which was not and never could be denied, and for which those who inaugurated the system can hardly be held blameless. Regarding these, it must suffice that I refer to them thus vaguely and pass on.

(b) But Norfolk Island was not the only penal settlement: that at Port Arthur, on Tasman's Peninsula, was also included by the new scheme as one of the first-stage depôts. Being within easy reach of Hobart Town, and not, like Norfolk Island, hundreds of miles away, Port Arthur was under the more searching supervision of the supreme authority. The peninsula was separated from the mainland by a narrow isthmus, across which, as I have said, sentries and fierce dogs for ever kept watch and ward, and escape thence was next to impossible. At the southern extreme of the peninsula is Port Arthur, having an excellent harbour, of difficult entrance but wide within, and with plenty of deep water. To Port Arthur were sent all convicts in a category a little less criminal than those of Norfolk Island, their number being some 1200, their work chiefly what is called in the Western Hemisphere "lumbering." or procuring wood for the sawyers and shipbuilders, who were also convicts. Every now and then a ship of decent tonnage was launched, and much coal and timber were also exported. There was a tread-wheel and a corn-mill, and the settlement was to a certain extent self-supporting. The convicts were lodged in hut barracks, in association with each other, but not in great numbers. On the whole, the establishment at Port Arthur was as well managed and the discipline as good as could be expected with such insufficient prison buildings. The

conduct of the convicts was generally good, and punishments
few and far between.

2. And now for the second stage.

Norfolk Island and Port Arthur, the purely penal settlements, I have described. At one or other of them, subject to
such restraints as they found there, the nature of which I have
already detailed, the convict of the worst class remained till
he earned by good conduct his removal to the second stage,
or that of the probation gang. To this second stage those
convicts whose crimes were less serious had been inducted on
first arrival from England. They might therefore be supposed
to avoid a certain amount of contamination. But if they
escaped the island, they could not escape from those who had
been at it; and around these seemingly purified spirits hung
something of the reeking atmosphere of the foul den through
which they had passed. In this way the contagion spread; for
wherever there were convicts there were those who had been
at Norfolk Island, and their influence, if not in the ascendant,
was always more or less felt. But even without the presence
of this pernicious virus wherewith the whole mass might be
permeated, the probation gangs as constituted were bad
enough to originate wickedness of their own. Having, therefore, errors inherent, without counting the superadded vice that
came from the first-stage men, they served admirably to perpetuate the grand mistake of the whole new scheme. Soon
after the development of this new order of things there grew
to be sixteen of these stations. Four of them were on Tasman's
Peninsula, and of these, one was for invalids, and three solely
for those who had misconducted themselves in other gangs. The
men worked in coal mines, or raised agricultural produce. Then
there were five stations on the coast in the neighbourhood of
D'Entrecasteaux Channel, placed where the land was heavily
timbered, all of which, when cleared, was to be devoted to
crops; others, also, more inland, and three at which the convicts
laboured exclusively at making and repairing roads. In
principle, then, probation stations were intended to give
convicts, from the first, a certain habit of industry and
subordination, and if they had come from the penal settlements, to continue the process. The probation stations were

abundantly furnished with religious instructors, and a minute system of notation was introduced to record exactly the conduct of the prisoners from day to day. It was according to his attitude while thus in probation that the next step in the relaxation of his condition was to be regulated. No doubt in many places the work accomplished by these probation parties was not inconsiderable. Naturally the first aim was that they should raise crops enough to suffice for their own support; but after that, their labour was directed into many chaunels that brought direct advantage to the colony. So far, too, as there were means available, the administration was conducted intelligently. But the whole numbers poured into Van Diemen's Land were so far in excess of the resources of the colony that adequate lodgment could not be provided. From this, and the difficulty of obtaining respectable supervisors in anything like due proportion, there resulted such a state of things that in course of time the probation gangs were not less a reproach than the penal settlements.

3. The third stage was reached as soon as the convict had given, as it were, an earnest of his improvement. The Comptroller-General of convicts was constituted the judge, and it rested with that functionary whether the convict, after a certain period, should receive the boon of a "probation pass." The holder of this was privileged to hire himself out: to enter private service, and make his own terms with his future master. But there were certain distinctions among pass-holders. Those in the lowest class had to ask the governor's sanction to the employment they chose; they had to be contented with half their wages, while the other half was paid into a savings bank. Other classes could engage themselves without sanction, and got certain larger proportions—half, two-thirds, in the last class all their wages. These passes were liable to resumption for misconduct, and the holder was then sent back to the gangs. The chief distinction between these pass-holders and the men on ticket-of-leave, to whom I shall come directly, was, that the latter were free to roam where they pleased within certain districts, while the pass-holders were retained at hiring depôts till they had found employment for themselves; and even when in service they were under the

direct control of a local magistrate, by whom they were inspected every month. These hiring depôts were at the chief towns—Hobart Town, Launceston, and elsewhere. The numbers thus on pass came to be considerable; and, later on, when work was slack and labour scarce, they grew to be the most serious difficulty which colonial legislators were called upon to face. But in this I am anticipating.

The two last stages, of (4) Ticket-of-leave, and (5) Pardon, were not peculiar to the new system, and differed in no respect to the same named condition of existence under other rules, except that both were to be gained less easily now, and in no case as a matter of right.

I have given now an outline of the system introduced by Lord Stanley's despatch of 1842, and, advancing a year or two where it was necessary, have shown how it was practically carried out. Of the extraordinary results that followed from it I shall speak also at length, but in a future chapter. The evils with which it was to be beset were not at this time foreseen, although there were some—and to these I have referred—which should have inspired the theorist with a certain dread. But it did seem in itself so symmetrical and so immeasurably superior to the system of assignment, that its authors may be pardoned almost if they hoped that transportation thus carried out must undoubtedly prove an unmixed success.

INTERIOR OF CELL WITH LOOM.

CHAPTER XVIII.

CAPTAIN GROVES AT MILLBANK.

LET us return now to Millbank. We left it labelled a failure; and we take it up where it was, but with name, character, and constitution all alike changed. Penitentiary no longer, for it does not now deserve the high-sounding title, the lofty purposes with which it started remaining unfulfilled, and its future usefulness will be made to depend upon the wide area it embraces within its gloomy walls, rather than on the results

its reformatory system might be expected to achieve. But as
a plain prison, it may render more tangible service to the
State. And just as its destination is now to be more practically
useful than heretofore, so those who rule it are no longer
amateurs, but officials who have made of prison matters a
profession and a business. The superintending committee,
composed of well-disposed gentlemen of rank, have given
place to a board of three permanent inspectors, two of whom
are already well known to those who have read thus far. Mr.
Crawford, the senior member, had given much time to the
examination of the American prisons; and Mr. Whitworth
Russell, the second member, was for years chaplain of Millbank. Both also had been long employed as inspectors of all
prisons in England. The voluminous Blue-Books which
contain their annual reports will best prove their diligence
in discharging this duty. Under them was a new governor—
a person of a different stamp to mild Captain Chapman, or
pious painstaking Mr. Nihil. Captain John R. Groves, a
gentleman of position and well known in society, was also a
military officer of distinction. He did not seek the appointment, but as those in high place who knew his character
thought him eminently well suited for the post, he was told
that if he applied he could have it. A soldier, firm and
resolute of will, but clear-headed, practical, able, Captain
Groves had but one fault—he was of an irascible temper.
However, like many other passionate men, though quickly
aroused, he as speedily cooled. After an outburst of wrath he
was as bright and pleasant as a summer landscape when the
thunderstorm has passed. Added to this was a certain rough-
ness of demeanour, which, though native often to men of his
cloth, might easily be mistaken for overbearing, peremptory
harshness. But that Captain Groves was well suited for
the task that had devolved upon him there could be little
doubt. The Millbank he was called upon to rule differed
greatly to the old Penitentiary which had just been wiped
out by Act of Parliament. The population was no longer,
so to speak, permanent, but fluctuating: instead of two or
three hundred men and youths specially chosen to remain
within the walls for years, Captain Groves had to take in all

that came, *en route* for the colonies; so that in the twelve
months several thousands passed through his hands. Moreover, among these thousands were the choicest specimens of
criminality, male and female, ripe always for desperate deeds,
and at times almost unmanageable; yet these scoundrels he
had to discipline and keep under with such means only as Mr.
Nihil had left behind: for the most part the same staff of
warders and with no increase in their numbers. And with
all the difficulties of maintaining his repressive measures, were
the gigantic worries inseparable from a depôt prison, such as
Millbank had become. The constant change of numbers;
the daily influx of new prisoners, in batches varying from
twos and threes to forties and fifties, in all degrees of discipline — sometimes drunk, always dirty, men and women
occasionally chained together; the continuous outflow of
prisoners to the convict transport ships — a draft of one
hundred one day, three hundred the next, all of whom
must carefully be inspected, tended, and escorted as far
as the Nore—these were among the many duties of his charge.

But Captain Groves soon sat himself down in the saddle,
and as soon made himself felt as master. The promptitude
with which he grasped the position is proved by his early
orders. On the first day he found out that there were no
standing regulations in case of fire. No fixed system or plan
of action was established, but it was left to the governor, at
the moment of emergency, to issue such instructions as might
suggest themselves. There were no stations at which the
several officials should take post on the first alarm, no regular
practice with the fire-engine; the machine itself was quite
insufficient, and the hose out of repair. There had been one
or two fires already inside the prison, and the consequences
had been sufficiently disastrous; yet no attempt had been
made to reduce the chances by previous forethought and
arrangement. Captain Groves prayed therefore to be permitted
to frame regulations in advance and in cold blood, instead of
leaving the calamity to be coped with amid the excitement of
an actual conflagration. The fire question disposed of, the
governor turned his eyes upon the appearance of the men
under his charge; and, true soldier again, I find him com-

plaining seriously of the slouching gait and slovenly garb of
the warders trained under the late *régime*. "I think," he says,
"that the officers when together on parade, or at other times,
should present something of the appearance of a military
body." He wishes, therefore, to give them drill, and a waist-
belt, and smarter uniform. Again, he finds fault with the
armoury, and remarks that all the firearms in the prison
consist of one or two old blunderbusses, with brass barrels
exceedingly short, and he suggests a stand of fifty carbines
from the Tower. Next comes a raid upon the dishevelled locks
of the convicts. "The practice of cutting the prisoners' hair
appears to be much neglected. I observe the majority of the
prisoners' heads are dirty; the hair long, and the whiskers
growing under the chin." To remedy this, he introduces
forthwith the principles of the military barbers of that time:
hair to be short on top and sides of the head, and whiskers
trimmed on a level with the lower part of the ear—an innova-
tion which the prisoners resent, and resist the execution of the
order, one to the extent of saying that the next time he is
given a razor he will cut his throat with it. But the rules are
enforced, as are all other rules that issue from Captain Groves.
Not that the adjustment of such trifles satisfies his searching
spirit of reorganisation. He is much annoyed at the idleness
and determined laziness of all the prisoners. They don't do
half the work they might. The tailoring was a mere farce,
and little boys in Tothill Fields Prison picked twice as much
coir-junk as full-grown men in Millbank, and in a shorter
time. As for great coats, the average turned out was one per
week; while they should be able to complete three or four at
least. The governor attributes this chiefly to the "under-
current of opposition" to his orders from officers of the
manufacturing department.

Indeed, not only from this branch, but from all his subordinates, Captain Groves appears to have got but half-hearted
service. The double-faced backbitings, which had brought
many to preferment in the last *régime*, were thrown away on
the new governor. He preferred to see things with his
own eyes, and did not encourage officers to tell tales of
one another. When a senior officer reports a junior for

using bad language, Captain Groves remarks, "I must state my apprehensions that the practice which has prevailed of *watching* for bad or gross language uttered by warders off duty, and reported without their knowledge, accompanied by additions to the actual offence—such a system I consider will introduce discussion and discord into the prison, and produce universal distrust and fear. No warder can feel himself safe when he knows that an unguarded word may be brought against him at some future day." The practical common sense of these remarks no one can deny; but those who knew Captain Groves will smile as they remember that his own language at times savoured "of the camp," and he possibly felt that under such a system of espionage he himself might be caught tripping. But in setting his face against the old practices he was clearly right, although it might bring him into disfavour with those hypocritical subordinates who felt that their day of favour was over. Of most of the Penitentiary officers, indeed, Captain Groves had formed but a low estimate. In more ways than one he had found them lax, just as he found that the routine of duties was but carelessly arranged. There was no system: the night patrols, two in number to every two pentagons, slept as they pleased half the night or more, and were seldom subject to the visits of "rounds" or other impertinences from over-zealous officials; no one was responsible for the prison during the night; strangers came and went through the inner gates and passed on to the innermost part of the prison, ostensibly to buy shoes and other articles made by the prisoners, but really to see their friends among the latter; coal porters, irresponsible persons, often from the lowest classes (one was afterwards a convict), were admitted with their sacks into the heart of the wards, male and female, and could converse and traffic with the prisoners all day long. There was no notice board at the gates or elsewhere to warn visitors of the penalties of wrong-doing.

In all these matters the reform that was so urgently needed Captain Groves introduced, and that with no faltering hand. Naturally in the process he trod on many toes, rubbed up many old prejudices, and made himself generally unpopular. Nor was the bad feeling lessened when it became known that

he looked on the bulk of the old officers as inefficient, and
recommended their dismissal *en masse*. Discontent grew and
rankled among the majority; but although nearly all chafed
under the tightened bit, few for a long time went beyond a
certain insolent restiveness, though some were brave enough
to complain against the governor's tyranny and to talk of
active resistance. It was not, however, till Captain Groves
had been in office nearly three years that all these muttered
grumblings took shape in an actual combination against him.
Of this he had notice, for a paper was put into his hand giving
full disclosures and a list of the conspirators, many of whom he
had thought trustworthy men; but he disdained to act on the
information. The malcontents were not however to be disarmed
by his magnanimity. Feeling certain that their case was
strong, and that they could substantiate their charges against
him, one of their number, in the name of all, presented a
petition to the House of Commons, praying for an inquiry
into the condition of Millbank Prison. This petition was
signed by Edward Baker, ex-warder, and it was laid upon the
table of the House by Mr. Duncombe, M.P.

Baker's petition set forth that he had filled the office of
warder for more than three years, but that he had at length
been compelled to resign "in consequence of the oppressive
and tyrannical conduct on the part of Captain Groves, the
governor of the prison, towards the prisoners and officers
themselves. He also impugned the character of the governor,
charging him with drunkenness and the habitual use of foul
language; and indirectly reflecting on the three inspectors,
who in permitting such malpractices had culpably neglected
their duties.

1. The first allegation was that on one occasion a prisoner,
Chinnery, had a fit in the airing-yard, just before the governor
entered it. "What's the matter here?" asked Captain
Groves. "A prisoner in a fit." "A fit—he's not in a fit!"
(He was standing on his feet.) "No, he's reviving." "Nonsense," said the governor, "he never had a fit. If this
man has any more of his tricks report him to me." Further,
the governor had sent the supervisor to bring up the prisoner
for this same feigning of a fit, and had sentenced him, without

medical testimony, to three days' bread and water. Yet this very Chinnery had been in the prison under a previous sentence, and had been lodged always next door to a warder, so that assistance might always be at hand when he had a fit.

2. The next charge was that the governor had sentenced three boys, for opening their Bibles in church, to seven days' bread and water, censuring them for such conduct, " which he considered irreverent." (The words are Baker's.)

3. The third, that a prisoner who had assaulted and wounded a warder with a pair of scissors, had not only been flogged, but the governor had specially sentenced him to be deprived henceforward of all instruction, religious or moral.

4. The fourth charge referred to a prisoner, Bourne, whom it was alleged the doctor had neglected, refusing to see him, although he was actually in a dying state. At length the officer of his ward sent specially to the doctor, who came and had Bourne removed to the infirmary, where he died two days afterwards. "It was the governor's plain duty to have prevented such a catastrophe," said Baker.

5. A prisoner, Harris Nash, died of dysentery after three months of the ordinary discipline. "The body was what may be termed a perfect skeleton."

6. Another prisoner, a boy Richmond from Edinburgh, died after four months, having been confined in a dungeon on one pound of bread and two pints of water per diem, for an unlimited number of days. At night he lay upon the boards and had only a rug and a blanket to cover him.

7. That several prisoners who had been present at the infliction of corporal punishment had immediately after hanged themselves, shocked by the sight they had seen.

8. Many instances were quoted of the governor's harshness and partiality: fines inflicted unequally, old officers punished through his misrepresentation, others deprived of their situations as inefficient, though for years they had been considered efficient; while several had resigned sooner than submit to such tyranny.

9. Edward Baker further asserted that the reply furnished to the House to his first petition was garbled and untrue. It had been prepared secretly in the prison; it was altogether

false ; facts had been suppressed or distorted ; and that besides, the "cats" used were not those sanctioned by law.

10. That the governor had exceeded his powers of punishment, and that in some cases prisoners had undergone as many as eighteen days' bread and water in one month.

Finally, to quote the words of the petition, Baker urged that—"During the last three years the cruel conduct of the governor is known to have induced twenty prisoners to attempt suicide, and that four have actually succeeded in destroying themselves, and that others are constantly threatening self-destruction; forming a melancholy contrast with the system pursued during the twenty-three preceding years at the Millbank Penitentiary, that system being free from any such stain during that period." *

"That the severity of punishments for alleged offences has led to the removal of many prisoners in a dying state to the invalid hulk at Woolwich, where every seventh man has since died, although when they came into the prison they were in good health. This cruel removal takes place to prevent the necessity for coroner's inquests within the walls and exposure of the discipline of the prison."

The petitioner therefore prays for an immediate inquiry into the manner in which Millbank is conducted, the deaths that have occurred, the cruelties that are practised, the dying prisoners that have been removed; also into the numerous reports and irregular hours and conduct of the governor, and how far the inspectors have done their duty by allowing such irregularities to pass unnoticed; "such facts being notorious to all the prison."

In consequence of this petition an inquiry was instituted by the House of Commons; and the Earl of Chichester, Lord Seymour, and Mr. Bickham Escott were appointed commissioners.

A very searching and patient investigation followed, the full report of which fills an enormous Blue-Book of hundreds of pages. It would be tedious to the reader if I were to go through the evidence, in anything like detail, of the many

* Mr. Baker was a little misinformed on this point, as will be evident to all who have read chapters vi. and vii.

witnesses examined; the commissioners may be trusted to have done this conscientiously, and their summing up in deciding on the allegations against Captain Groves I shall quote directly. The evident animus of the subordinates against their governor is very clearly shown in every page : nothing he did was right, and the complaints when not actually false, as in the case of prisoner Chinnery, were childish and almost beneath consideration. One officer declared that Captain Groves did not like the old prison officers; that he had said openly "he would get them all out." They could never please him ; they got no credit however much they might exert themselves. Another told the governor he was breaking his (the officer's) spirit and his heart. "He (Captain Groves), after making his rounds, would send for supervisors and warders in a body and reprimand them in his office. Once when an officer expostulated with him, Captain Groves struck him to the ground with his stick, and swore he'd have none of his d——d Penitentiary tricks." Another officer, who had been on duty to Pentonville and came back without an important document, complained that he had been sent again all the way to the Caledonian Road to fetch it. Mr. Gray (the victim) considered this was a great hardship, although he admitted that he was none the worse for his walk. All the officers were positive they had much more to do now than ever before. Mr. Gray, above-mentioned, complained also that he had been deprived of his lawful leave ; yet he admitted that when all the paint work of the prison was filthily dirty and had to be scrubbed, it was badly done; and that the governor had only insisted on officers remaining on duty till the whole was properly cleaned.

It was indeed quite evident from cross-examination and from the evidence of Captain Groves, that the bulk of his officers were slovenly, slack in execution of their duties, and litigious. Captain Groves, on the other hand, was doing his best to improve the tone of discipline. No doubt he was stern and peremptory in his dealings. We can quite understand that his reprimands were not couched in milk-and-water language; that he more than once said, "By this, or that," and swore he would not suffer such doings to pass unpunished, and that those who opposed him should forthwith be dismissed.

But it is also clear that he was not well served. Those who held under him important posts were not always reliable and fitted for the charge. On one occasion, for instance, an officer was so negligent of the prisoners in his charge, that the governor, as he came by, was able to remove one unobserved. This prisoner he takes back to his cell, and then returns to the spot to ask the officer how many he has in charge. "So many." "Are you sure? Count them." "No; I am one short!" "Ah!" said the governor, and added something more in rather stronger language. Again, in the case of two barefaced escapes the governor expresses himself in these terms:

"Prisoner Howard escaped under the very nose of No. 2 sentry. The night was clear and fine, and the governor cannot acquit the sentry of No. 2 beat of great negligence. It is quite impossible, on such a night as the night of last Friday, for any individual to have performed such work in the garden as raising planks, etc., against the boundary wall without detection had common care been taken." *

"In regard to the escape of Timothy Tobin, the operations he had recourse to, to break through the cell, made great noise, and attracted the attention of several of the night guard; and the governor is concerned to find that the principal warder in charge of the prison as orderly officer made no effort to detect the cause of the constant knocking in Pentagon 5, but contented himself with the reports of inferior officers, without rising from his bed or anticipating his intended time of going his rounds. The qualifications which entitle an officer to promotion in this and every other establishment, are intelligence, activity, and a sense of individual responsibility; and no person is fit for the situation of supervisor or principal warder who is not prepared to exercise them on all occasions."

This was our friend Mr. Gray again; and it was he who, with others equally negligent, were so sensitive, that they felt aggrieved at Captain Groves' seemingly merited reprimands. But in actual investigation all charges of this kind melted into thin air as soon as the commissioners looked

---

* This escape has been described in chap. x.

into them. The charges of tyranny were not substantiated, because they were far-fetched and exaggerated. Such stories must have been difficult to find when one of the charges trumped up against the governor was that he had kept the chaplain's clerk one day without his dinner. We should even assert that the whole inquiry was another monument of mis-directed zeal, were it not that the original petition opened up serious topics which demanded attention. Whether or not the mere details of administrative bickering might not have been better settled by officials within the department than by parliamentary interference, I will not presume to decide; but when it is alleged in an indictment that unfor-tunate prisoners, without a friend in the world, are done to death by ill-treatment, it is clearly necessary that the said charges should be sifted without delay. In this way the inquiry was distinctly useful, and I shall now give the decision at which the commissioners arrived.

"These petitions seriously impugned the character and conduct of the Governor of Millbank Prison; and consequently imputed to the inspectors, under whose superintendence the government of this prison is placed, a culpable neglect of their duty in having permitted such maladministration to continue.

"1. The allegation respecting the treatment of Chinnery is the only charge on which the petitioner could prove anything from his own knowledge; and, since it occurred after he had sent in his resignation, could not be one of the instances of cruelty in consequence of which he resigned. The fault or innocence of the governor on this occasion depends entirely upon the validity of reasons alleged by him for concluding that the prisoner was only feigning a fit. There being no other witness but himself and Baker, we cannot pronounce a decided opinion upon so very doubtful a question. Reviewing, how-ever, all the circumstances which were brought under our notice in connection with this case, we think the governor should, before awarding the punishment, have made a closer investi-gation into all the facts, and have consulted the medical officer for the purpose of testing the probable accuracy of his impres-sions. In this case, therefore, we are of opinion that the punishment, whether merited or not merited by the prisoner, was injudiciously inflicted by the governor.

"2. The commissioners think the governor rather over-strained their powers in punishing the boys for reading their Bibles in chapel.

"3. The prisoner Bunyan was sentenced and punished by flogging, as described, for an aggravated and malicious assault. The second allegation, that he was ordered to receive 'no instruction, either religious or moral,' is untrue. He was visited by the chaplain, and had the usual access to religious books.

"4. No evidence to support charge against the governor in case of H. Bourne; but the latter was certainly not well treated by the resident medical officer.

"5. Harris Nash died of a severe attack of dysentery. He was an ill-conditioned, mutinous prisoner, who frequently attacked his officers; but, though he was often punished, his death was attributable to the dysentery and nothing else.

"6. No responsibility rests with the governor as to Richmond's death. No symptom of disease on him when first he arrived at Millbank, and he was never punished when the disease showed itself.

"7. There does not appear to be the slightest foundation for the suggestion insinuated in this charge; neither of the three prisoners named having witnessed any punishments calculated to produce a bad effect on their minds.

"8. The charges of partiality were distinctly disproved; as were also the allegations contained in 9 and 10, which were found to be quite 'unfounded, in fact.'

"Upon the general charge of irregularity, and especially upon a charge of intoxication preferred by some of the witnesses, after a minute consideration of all the circumstances detailed in the evidence, we feel bound to acquit the governor, and to express our strong disapprobation of the manner in which the charge was attempted to be proved.

"Having thoroughly sifted the complaint against the governor, and made some allowance for exaggeration on the part of witnesses, whose accusations were seldom warranted by the facts which they attempted to prove, we have no hesitation in pronouncing our opinion that he has endeavoured to perform his duties with zeal and intelligence, and has done nothing to discredit the very high testimonials which he possesses from the officers in the army under whom he formerly served. His treatment of the prisoners, except in the two cases above mentioned, appears to have been judicious and considerate. Cases were indeed brought under our notice in which the prisoners complained of excessive severity; but the responsibility for these cases rests upon the subordinate officers, as it does not appear that the governor was made acquainted with these complaints. The substitution of the punishment of reduced diet in lieu of a dark cell appears to have been made by the governor from motives of leniency and with a view to preserving the health of prisoners.

"The only faults with which he appears justly chargeable are :—

"1. A too hasty method of dealing with his officers when reported to him by others, or detected by himself in some neglect of duty; not always giving them a sufficient opportunity for explanation or defence.

"2. The occasional use of improper or offensive expressions, of which we should express our condemnation more strongly were it not that the instances adduced by all the witnesses amounted only to three.

"3. An insufficient attention to the rules of the prison; it appearing from his own evidence that he was entirely ignorant of the legal force of the old penitentiary rules, and that in two important instances the rules actually stuck up in the prison were not strictly attended to by him.

"The want of a complete code of rules suited to the present government of the prison has apparently given rise to many of the charges and to much of the ill-feeling which have come under our observation during this inquiry.

"No doubt there existed a very extended feeling of discontent among the officers. It is probable that this may partly have originated in the changes which took place at the organisation of the present establishment, by which the duties of the prison were necessarily rendered more irksome and severe.

"The old prison possessed more of a reformatory character : the prisoners were confined there for much longer periods, were under the influence of stronger motives to good conduct, and by habits longer exercised became more accustomed to the regular routine of prison life. In the prison, as now constituted, few of the adult convicts remain for more than two, or most, three months ; and of those who remain for a longer period, the most part are criminals of the worst description, who are awaiting embarkation for their final destination, Norfolk Island.

"The effective government of these convicts can only be carried on by a very strict and vigilant attention on the part of the officers. We must add that these important changes had to be commenced and carried out by a new governor with an old set of officers, and, in our opinion, with an inadequate addition of strength. It was but natural that the old officers, receiving little or no increase of pay, while their duties were generally augmented, should have felt some dissatisfaction, and that a portion of it should have vented itself in personal feelings towards the governor, who appears to be both a zealous and energetic officer, giving his orders in a peremptory manner as a man accustomed to military life, and expecting them to be obeyed with soldierlike precision. We regret however to observe that, whilst these officers omitted to make a single complaint or suggestion of grievance to their legitimate superiors, they formed a kind of combination amongst themselves for the discussion of their supposed wrongs and for collecting matter for complaint against the governor."

On the whole, then, Captain Groves came triumphantly out of the inquiry into his conduct. Beyond doubt his task was a difficult one. He had within the walls of his prison a large body of criminals who were not to be managed easily. Their offences were more deliberate, and their violence more systematic than anything which I have described in the Penitentiary days. When they assaulted officers, which they did frequently, from Captain Groves himself downwards, it was with the intention of murdering them ; and when they wished to escape, as often as not they managed to get away. They stabbed their officers with shoemakers' knives, or dug scissors into their arms; while one, when searched, was found with a heavy cell stone slung to a cord, supplying thus a murderous weapon, of which he coolly promised to make use against the first who approached. Another ruffian, named Long, a powerful, athletic man, dashes at his officer's throat and demands the instant surrender of his keys. Edward King, another, meeting the governor on his rounds, assails him with abuse, then strikes him on the mouth; whereupon Captain Groves promptly knocks him down. And of all the annoyances, none equalled those that came from the "juvenile ward," as it was termed.

In this Captain Groves had raised a sort of Frankenstein to irritate and annoy him, which he found difficult to lay. Early in his reign he had felt the necessity for some special treatment of boy prisoners. There were nearly 200 of these; and though styled boys, they were many of them youths of ages varying from seventeen to twenty years. After much anxious consideration he constructed from his own plans a large general ward to accommodate the whole number. This building still exists, although it has since been converted into a Roman Catholic chapel. It is built of brick, only one storey high, with a light roof supported by slender iron rods. Around the wall were bays, holding each three hammocks by night, but in which these juveniles worked during the day. And they could work well if they pleased. For general intelligence and astuteness these boys were not to be matched in all the world. They were the *élite* of the London *gamins*, the most noted "wires," the cleverest thieves, and the most unmitigated young vagabonds of the whole metropolis. It was a similar gathering, but on a larger scale, to that with which we are familiar in the pages of "Oliver Twist." Properly directed they had talent enough for anything. They were soon taught to be expert tradesmen; could stitch with the best tailors, and turn out an upper or a half-sole without a flaw. It was part of Captain Groves' scheme to drill them; and these active lads soon constituted an uncommonly smart battalion.

So far we see only the bright side of the picture; the reverse is not so exhilarating. The mere fact of bringing

together in this way a mass of juvenile rascality, without
adequate means of restraint, was to open the door to mutinous
combinations and defiant conduct. Over and above the
buoyancy of spirits natural to youth, which tempts every
school-boy to mischief, there was present among the inmates
of this juvenile ward an amount of innate depravity, due to
early training and general recklessness of life, which soon led
them to the most violent excesses. Within a week or two of
the opening of the ward under the brightest auspices, the
governor records that already they exhibit strong tendencies
to run riot. They use threatening language to their officers,
are continually at loggerheads with each other, and their
quarrels soon end in blows. Presently one makes a violent
attack on his warder, and kicks his shins; but for this he is
incontinently flogged, and for a time the lightheartedness of
the ward is checked. But only for a time: within a week the
bickering recommences, and there are half a dozen fights in
less than half a dozen days. Appeal is now made to the birch-
rod, also for a time effectual. But the temptation to misconduct
in marching to and fro from drill, exercise, or chapel is too
strong for these young ragamuffins, and their next feat is to
put out the gas as they go, then lark along the passages. The
governor prays for more powers to punish them. "By their
refractory and insolent conduct," he says, "they wear out the
patience of every officer set over them, and turn him into an
object of ridicule and contempt."

It occurs to them now that they can cause some considerable inconvenience by breaking out at night; so night after
night, when the watch is set and the prison is quiet, they
burst out into yells and general uproar, till the night guards are
compelled to ring the alarm bells to call assistance. This
continues to such an extent that Captain Groves fears it will
be impossible to persuade officers to remain in the general
ward after dark. Of course they are all experienced thieves.
On one occasion an officer on duty has his pocket picked of a
snuff-box. "I know where it is," volunteers a boy; but after
a long search it could not be found in the place he indicated:
then they search the boy himself, and find the box secreted
on his person. Another lad, with infinite cunning, nearly

succeeds in effecting his escape. One night after midnight he left his bed, and crawling under the other hammocks, he got to a wide stone which covered the entrance to the ventilating flues. This stone he removed, and then descended into the flue, meaning to follow it till he reached the airing-yard; thence he meant to climb to the roof and descend again. In view of this he carried with him a long cord, made of sundry skeins of thread, which from time to time he had stolen and secreted. As it happened, a warder going his rounds set his foot on the mat which the boy had placed over the hole into the flue, tripped, and nearly tumbled in; then the prisoner, who was in the flue, fearing he was discovered, came out. But for this accident he might have got clean away. After this the uproarious behaviour of the boys waxed worse. The governor begins to have serious apprehensions that discipline will greatly suffer. Stronger measures of repression are tried, but without effect. They continue still fighting, refusing to work, yelling in concert after dark, assaulting and maltreating their officers by throwing brooms at their heads and kicking their shins. Throughout, too, their conduct in chapel was most disgraceful, and it became a serious question "whether they ought not to be kept away altogether from divine service, as their example would certainly attract followers among the general body of the prisoners."

At length it comes to this, that the ward must be broken up, and the boys distributed among the various pentagons. It is felt to be dangerous to keep so many elements of discord concentrated together in one room. This was accordingly done; but by-and-by, for reasons that are not given—probably on account of want of space in the crowded condition of the prison—the general ward is again occupied with these precocious juveniles. Yet, as I find it recorded, within a few days a scene took place in the room at a late hour of the night, which called for immediate decisive action.

About 11 P.M. the governor was sent for. The ward was described to be in a state of mutiny. On his arrival the prisoners appeared much excited, but comparatively quiet. At his order they assembled quietly enough and fell in by word of command. He then asked what it all meant, and heard that from 10 to 10.30 there had been periodic shoutings, and this chiefly from one particular boy. As it rose at last to something serious, the alarm bell was rung, and on the arrival of the reserve guard the ringleader was pointed out, by name Sullivan, who had shouted the loudest. Ordered first to get out of his hammock, he obstinately refused to move, and when at last dislodged by force, he broke away from the officers, jumped on to the hammock rails, and thence to the iron girders of the roof. An officer promptly followed him, and "a scene ensued which it is impossible to describe." He was at length captured, however; but upon the whole incident the governor remarks as follows: "These circumstances afford matter for grave consideration. Hitherto, owing to strict discipline and energy on the part of the officers, the system of the juvenile ward has been successful, with occasional exceptions in regard to misbehaviour on the part of a few turbulent characters. Of late, generally speaking, their conduct has been insubordinate and disorderly, and the fact is that the officers in charge of them are under serious apprehensions for their own personal safety. Besides, as I have before noticed, owing to the paucity of their number, their rest is broken night after night by being obliged to rise from their beds to quell disturbances; whilst the night guards, who ought to be taking their rest in the day time, are obliged to attend at the prison for the purpose of substantiating their reports of the previous night.

"It is quite evident that an *émeute* among so many prisoners (180) assembled together would be difficult to quell; and in my opinion their age is a very dangerous one, ranging as it does from seventeen to twenty years. Many of them are athletic, and formidable in point of temper likewise."

The governor decided to place additional patrols in the juvenile ward taken from the garden, although he was loth to denude the garden of guards, seeing that the prison was full to overflowing of convicts.

I have dealt in the last few pages with the misconduct of the boys as it showed itself in a comparatively short period of time. I might continue the narration, but it would be simply to repeat what has gone before. The contumacy of these lads continued for more than a year: again and again they broke out, insulted, bearded, browbeat their officers till the latter stood almost in awe of their charge; night after night the pentagon was made hideous with their outcries and uproar. The governor was pressed to abolish the ward altogether; but the project was a pet one, and he hesitated to abandon it. He never got quite the better of the boys; but in the end firmness and a resolute exhibition of authority had its effect, and the ward, if not for ever quelled, was at least brought to something like subordination and order.

THE FEMALE PENTAGON.

CHAPTER XIX.

THE MILLBANK CALENDAR.

It is of course clear to the reader that the convicts who were now and hereafter contained within the Millbank walls comprised the cream of the criminal class. There is this difference between the calendars at Newgate and at Millbank, that at the former place the worst criminals pass without delay beyond the ken of man, while at the large depôt prison they at least continue alive.

The calendar of such a county gaol is but a record of executions, and its experiences are chiefly with the condemned cell, the shrift of the Ordinary, dying confessions, and the last awful act. At Millbank there was no infliction of the extreme

penalty of the law: the prison received only those who just
escaped hanging, as the saying is, by the skin of their teeth.
In previous years, under a more barbarous code, Tyburn would
have been their inevitable fate; but now the punishment to
which they were doomed was secondary, not capital. These,
then, without exception came to Millbank, at least for a time.
A few among them there were who might be styled unfortunate, perhaps—men who had been drawn into misdeeds by
accident, by weakness, or a long chain of misfortunes; but the
larger proportion were undoubtedly men who would to-day
be styled "habituals," and who stood quite at the head of their
infamous profession. The registers of Millbank prison therefore contain many notorious names, and its records bear
witness to many curious circumstances connected with these
desperate characters. I shall devote a couple of chapters now
to some reference to the most remarkable cases.

Foremost on the Millbank calendar stand those of the
upper classes, who would have been styled in Australia,
"specials," or "gentlemen convicts." It was said, that of
these there were at one and the same time in Millbank two
captains, a baronet, four clergymen, a solicitor, and one or two
doctors of medicine. The tradition is *ben trovato*, if not
exactly true. Of course in such a prison there would be
representatives of every class, and although the percentage of
gentlemen who commit crimes is in the long run far below
that of the middle or lower classes, there is no special natural
law by which the blue blood is exempted from the ordinary
weakness and imperfections of humanity. Most of these
genteel people who found themselves in Millbank owed their
fate to forgery or fraud. There was the old gentleman of
seventy years of age, who had been a mayor in a north-
country manufacturing town, and who had forged and
defrauded his nieces out of some £360,000. The officers
speak of him as "a fine old fellow," who took to his new task
of tailoring like a man, and who could soon turn out a soldier's
great-coat as well as anyone in the prison. Another convict
of this stamp was Mr. T., a Liverpool merchant in a large way
of business, who was a forger on quite a colossal scale. It was
proved at his trial that he had forged in all thirty bills of

exchange, amounting in all to £32,811, and that he had a
guilty knowledge of one hundred and fifteen other bills, which
were valued in all at £133,000. In his defence it was urged
that he had taken up many bills before they were due, and
would undoubtedly have taken up all had not the discovery of
one forgery exposed his frauds and put an end suddenly to
his business. Still, said his counsel, his estate could have
paid from twelve to fifteen shillings in the pound, and it could
hardly be maintained against him that he had any moral
intention of defrauding. Judge Talfourd appears to have
commented strongly, in summing up, upon such an idea of
morality as this; and then and there sentenced Mr. T. to
transportation for life. Unfortunately for the criminal himself, his sentence came a little too late: had he gone out to
New South Wales twenty years earlier, with his commercial
aptitude and generally unscrupulous plan of action, he would
have run well to the front in the race for wealth amidst his
felon competitors.

More contemptible, but not less atrocious, was the conduct
of B., who had taken his diploma as surgeon, and had practised
as such in many parts of the country. His offence was bigamy
on a large scale: he was guilty of a series of heartless
deceptions, so that it was said the scene in court when this
Blue Beard was finally arraigned, and all his victims appeared
against him, was painful in the extreme. He was brought to
book by the friend of a young lady to whom he was trying to
pay his attentions. This gentleman, being somewhat suspicious,
made inquiries, and discovered enough to have B. arrested.
Four different certificates of marriage were put in evidence.
It seemed that, although already married in Cornwall, he
moved thence and took a practice in another county, where he
became acquainted with a lady residing in the neighbourhood,
who had a little money of her own. He made her an offer,
married her, and then found that by marriage she forfeited the
annuity she previously enjoyed. After a short time he
deserted her, having first obtained possession of all her clothes,
furniture, trinkets, and so forth, which he sold. His next
affair was on board an East Indiaman bound to Calcutta, in
which he sailed as surgeon—wishing doubtless to keep out of

the way for a while. Among the passengers was a Miss B., only fifteen years of age, who was going out to the East with her mother and sisters. He succeeded in gaining her affections, and obtained the mother's consent to the marriage on arrival at Calcutta. He made out, by means of fraudulent documents prepared on purpose, that he had inherited £5000 from his father, and offered to settle £3000 on his bride. The marriage came off in due course at Calcutta, and then the happy pair returned to England. Soon after their arrival, B. deserted his new wife in a hotel in Liverpool. Before long he began the affair which led to his detection.

B. is remembered in Millbank as a man of considerable attainments. He was well educated, and spoke several languages. One of his favourite feats was to write the Lord's Prayer on a scrap of paper not larger than a sixpence, in five different languages. In his appearance there was nothing to justify his success with the female sex. If anything he was plain, thereby supporting Wilkes, who asserted that he was only five minutes behind the best-looking man in a room. In complexion B. was dark, almost swarthy; in figure, stout. He could not be called even gentlemanlike in his bearing. But he had a good address; spoke well and readily; and he was extremely shrewd and clever. As a prisoner his conduct was all that could be desired. He passed on like the rest eventually to Australia, where he again married.

The clergymen whose crimes brought them to Millbank were rather commonplace characters; weak men, mostly, who could not resist their evil propensities. Of course they were not always what they pretended to be. One of the most noteworthy was the Honourable and Reverend Mr. ———, who was really an ordained minister of the Church of England, and had held a good living in Ireland, worth £1400 a year. But he was passionately addicted to the turf, and attended every meeting. His luck varied considerably—sometimes up and sometimes down. He came at length to lose every shilling he had in the world at Manchester races. The inveterate spirit of gambling was so strong within him that he was determined to try his luck again. He had been staying at a friend's house—a careless

man, of good means, who left his cheque-book too accessible
to others. The Honourable and Reverend Mr. ———— went
straight from the course to his friend's study, filled in a
cheque, forged the signature, took the bank *en route* to the
races, and recommenced operations forthwith. Meanwhile
his friend went also, quite by accident, to the bank for cash.
They told him a large cheque had only just been paid to his
order. " I drew no cheque ! " " Why, here it is ! " " But
that is not my signature." Whereupon the honourable and
reverend gentleman was incontinently arrested in the middle
of the grand stand. His sentence was transportation for life,
and from Millbank he passed on in due course to the antipodes. He was a poor creature at the best times, and under
prison discipline became almost imbecile and useless. After a
long interval he gained a ticket-of-leave, and was last heard of
performing divine worship at an out-station at the rate of a
shilling a service.

Of a very different kidney was the Rev. A. B., a man of
parts, clever and dexterous, who succeeded in everything he
tried. He spoke seven languages, all well ; and when in prison
learnt with ease to tailor with the best.

Somewhat similar to him in character was the Rev. Dr. B.,
a doctor of divinity according to his own statement, whose
career of villainy is not closed even yet. This man has done
several long sentences, and he is again, while I write, in
durance. He also was a man of superior education, who could
read off Hebrew, so the warders said, as easily as the chaplain
gave the morning prayers. Dr. B. was discovered one day
writing the Hebrew character in his copybook at school time,
just when a party of distinguished visitors were inspecting the
prison. One of them, surprised, said, " What, do you know
Hebrew ? "

" Yes," was the impudent reply, " I expect a great deal
better than you do."

A better story still is told of this man later, when set at
large on ticket-of-leave. Through barefaced misrepresentation he had been permitted to take the duty of a beneficed
clergyman during his absence from the parish. In due course
came an invitation to dine with the local magnate, whose place

was some distance from the rectory. Our ex-convict clergyman ordered a carriage and pair from the neighbouring town, and drove to the hall in state. As he alighted from the carriage, his footman, hired also for the occasion, recognised his face in the blaze of light from the open door. "Blow me, if that ain't Slimy B., the chaplain's man, who did his 'bit' along with us at the 'Steel.'" Both coachman and lacquey were ex-convicts too, and after that the secret soon leaked out. The reverend doctor found his country parish rather too hot to hold him. His later misdeeds, as brought to light in the last year or two, have been decoying and plundering governesses in search of situations; he has also established himself in various neighbourhoods as a schoolmaster, and more than once has again succeeded in obtaining Church duty.

Of the military men the most prominent was a certain Captain C., who belonged to an excellent family, but who had fallen very low, going by degrees from bad to worse. He was long known as a notorious gambler and loose liver. At length, unable to earn enough money to gratify his vices by fair means, he sought to obtain it by foul, and became allied to a mob of ruffians who style themselves "Men of the World." In other words, he took to obtaining goods under false pretences. Captain C. was principally useful as a respectable reference to whom his accomplices could apply when they entered a strange shop and ordered goods. "Apply to my friend Captain So-and-so, of such-and-such a square; he has known me for years." Reference is made to a house gorgeously furnished, an establishment in every way *bien monté*, the master thereof a perfect gentleman. "Do I know Mr. ———? Oh, dear, yes; I have known him for a long time. He is one of my most intimate friends. You may trust him to any amount." Unhappily the pitcher goes often to the well, but it is broken at last. And at this game of fraud the circle of operations grows naturally more and more narrow. At length the whole conspiracy became known to the police, and Captain C. found himself ere long in Millbank. He seems to have been treated there rather too well. An idle, good-for-nothing rascal, who would do no work, and who expected— so said the officers—to be always waited upon. Undoubtedly he was pampered, had his books from the deputy-governor's own library, and extra food. More than this, his wife—a lady once, also of good family, but fallen with her husband to an abyss of infamy and depravity which made her notorious for wickedness even in this wicked city—was frequently admitted to visit him, coming always in silks and satins and flaunting attire, which was sadly out of keeping with her husband's temporary abode.

Another ex-military officer was Mr. P., whose offence at the time created wide-spread indignation. This was the gentleman who, for some occult reason of his own, committed the atrocity of striking our young Queen in the face just as she was leaving the palace. The weapon he used was a thin cane, but the blow fell lightly, as the lady-in-waiting interposed. No explanation was offered, except that the culprit was out of his mind. This was the defence set up by his friends, and several curious facts were adduced in proof of insanity. One on which great stress was laid, was that he was in the habit of chartering a hansom to Wimbledon Common daily, where he amused himself by getting out and walking as fast as he could through the furze. But this line of defence broke down, and the jury found the prisoner guilty. He himself, when he came to Millbank, declared that he had been actuated only by a desire to bring disgrace on his family and belongings. In some way or other he had seriously disagreed with his father, and he took this curious means to obtain revenge. The wantonness of the outrage called for severe punishment, and Mr. P. was sentenced to seven years' transportation; but the special punishment of whipping was omitted, on the grounds of the prisoner's position in life. Whether it was that the mere passing of this sentence was considered sufficient, or that the Queen herself interposed with gracious clemency, this Mr. P. at Millbank was treated with exceptional leniency and consideration. By order of the Secretary of State he was exempted from most of the restrictions by which other prisoners were ruled. He was not lodged in a cell, but in two rooms adjoining the infirmary, which he used as sitting and bedroom respectively; he did not wear the prison dress, and he had, practically, what food he liked. He seems to have awakened a sort of sympathy on the part of the warders who attended him; probably because he was a fine, tall fellow, of handsome presence and engaging manners, and because also they thought his offence was one of hot-headed rashness rather than premeditated wickedness. Eventually Mr. P. went to Australia.

A good deal of attention was attracted in 1844 to certain frauds connected with wills. The chief offender was a solicitor belonging to a respectable firm, but he had accomplices, and they came all of them to Millbank. The details of the fraud show considerable ingenuity on one side and not a little foolishness on the other. A certain lady, Miss Ann Slack, had a sum of money in the three per cents., the dividends on which were paid to her as she required money, by her guardian, who had been her father's agent. The whole stock was £6000, and it was kept at the Bank of England in two sums in her name. Presently the guardian dies, and Miss Slack goes to live with a married sister, continuing to receive her dividends, but only on one sum. Apparently she was quite in the dark as to the value or extent of her own property. Year followed year, and still she failed to claim the dividends due to her on the second sum, which was altogether forgotten. At length, after ten years had elapsed and the sum was still unclaimed, it was transferred in due course to the Commissioners for the reduction of the national debt.

Now commenced the fraud. By some means or other the solicitor came to know of this transfer. He concluded, shrewdly enough, that the real owners of the stock so transferred had forgotten all about it, and he proposed, therefore, to appropriate it to himself. To accomplish this he made it appear that Miss Slack was dead, and that she had willed the sum in question to Miss Emma Slack—in other words to himself. It was necessary that he should have the testator's signature, and this he obtained by calling on her at her brother-in-law's and pretending that money had been bequeathed to her, but that her signature was required before it could be handed over. Her name thus obtained, the other will was soon manufactured. A person to personate Miss Emma Slack was next procured, who wrote through her solicitor, claiming the money, and

begging it might be transferred to her name. The same
person attended also at the Bank of England, was identified—
by her own solicitor—and from that time forth received the
dividends. This was the principal offence, as far as amount
was concerned; but in another, the guilty parties had continued for no less than ten years to enjoy their ill-gotten gains.
Another lady had been discovered who had left money behind
her which no one claimed. For her, also, a false will was
manufactured, by which she bequeathed her fortune in the
three per cents. to her nephew Thomas Hunt. Fletcher, one
of the culprits, appeared to personate Thomas Hunt, and as
such received the dividends for nearly ten years. The fraud
was discovered by an error in dates. The forgers made it out
that Mrs. Hunt died in 1829, whereas she had died really three-
and-twenty years previously.

These are a few of the most prominent of the criminals
who belonged to the upper or professional classes. Others
there were, and are to this day; but as a rule such cases
are not numerous. Speaking in general terms of the
"gentleman convict," as viewed from the gaoler's side, he is
an ill-conditioned, ill-conducted prisoner. When a man of
energy and determination, he wields a baleful influence around
and among other prisoners if proper precautions are not taken
against inter-communications. His comrades look up to him,
especially if he is disposed to take the place of a ringleader,
and to put himself forward as the champion of insolence and
insubordination. They render him too, a sort of homage in
their way, scrupulously retaining the titles which have been
really forfeited, if indeed they were ever earned. Mr. So-and-
so, Major This and Captain That, are the forms of address
used by Bill Sykes when speaking of or to a gentleman convict.
For the rest, if not openly mutinous, these "superior" felons
are chiefly remarkable for their indifference to prison rules,
especially those which insist on cleanliness and neatness in
their cells. Naturally, by habits and early education they are
unskilled in sweeping and washing, and keeping bright their
brass-work and their pewter utensils. In these respects the
London thief or hardened habitual criminal, who knows the
interior of half the prisons in the country, has quite the best of it.

Somewhat lower in the social scale, but superior also to the common burglar or thief, are those who occupy positions of trust in banks or city offices, and for whom the temptation of an open till or slack administration are too strong to be resisted. A good instance of this class was B., who was employed as a clerk in the Bank of England. With the assistance of a confederate who personated a Mr. Oxenford—there was no special reason for selecting this gentleman, more than there might be to take Mr. Smith or Jones—he made over to himself stock standing in Mr. Oxenford's name to the tune of £8000. His accomplice was a horse jobber. The stock in question was paid by a cheque on Lubbock's for the whole sum, whither they proceeded, asking to have it cashed—all in gold. There were not eight thousand sovereigns available at the moment, but they received instead eight Bank of England notes for £1000 each, which they promptly changed at the bank for specie, taking with them a carpet-bag to hold the money. The bag when filled was found to be too heavy to lift, but with the assistance of the bank porters it was got into a cab. They now drove to Ben Caunt's public in St. Martin's Lane, and there secured a room for the night; the money was transferred to their portmanteaus, several in number, and next morning they took an early train to Liverpool *en route* for New York. The steamer *Britannia*, in which they took passage, started almost immediately, and they soon got clear out of the country. But the detectives were on their track: within a day or two, officers followed them across the Atlantic, and landing at Halifax found the fugitives had gone on to Boston and New York. They were followed thither, and on, also, to Buffalo and to Canada. Thence back again to Boston. Here the culprits had taken up their residence—one on a farm, the other in a public-house, both of which had been purchased with the proceeds of the fraud; £7000 had been lodged also in the bank to their credit. One of them was immediately arrested, and hanged himself. The other escaped in a boat, and lay hid in the neighbouring marshes; but the reward that was offered led to his capture, and he was brought home to England, where he was tried, found guilty, and sentenced to transportation for life.

Within this category come also ship captains who betray their trust, like Captain T., who was sent by his owners to the Gold Coast for a cargo of gold dust. On the voyage home he carried with him a box containing gold dust to the value of £700. This, on arrival at Portsmouth, he declared he had thrown overboard when in a fit of delirium. Several of the crew were called upon to testify that he had been suffering from illness—real or feigned—and had kept his cabin several days, till one morning he rushed on deck apparently delirious, carrying a box which he then and there cast into the sea, shouting, " Ah! you may kill me now—but you shan't have it —there ! " Unfortunately his owners were not well satisfied with the explanation, and on making inquiry they found that Captain T. had sold a quantity of gold dust to a jeweller on Portsmouth Hard soon after his arrival in port. He was accordingly arrested, when 116 lbs. of gold were found upon him, and a bundle of bank notes; also a belt filled with gold dust, which he had used apparently for smuggling his stolen property on shore. Captain T. was found guilty, and came to Millbank in due course.

I must insert here the story of one, V. P., who was in 1853 taken up as a convict returned before his sentence of trans-portation had expired. P. made out a long statement in his defence, which may be worth giving, as it is a sort of *résumé*, from a convict's point of view, of the strange vicissitudes of a felon's life. It will be found in the " Sessions Papers," vol. 1852-3, p. 428, as follows : " At the period of the offence for which I was convicted I was suffering from the most acute pecuniary distress, with a wife and large family of children. A series of misfortunes—the most heavy was the death of my second wife, by which I lost an annuity of £150, with a great falling off, notwithstanding all my exertions, in my occupation as reporter to the public press—brought about mainly the distress in question. Previous to the commission of the offence I had through life borne an irreproachable character. In early life, from 1818 to 1822, I held some most responsible appoint-ments in Jamaica and other West India Islands; from 1829 to 1834 I held the appointment of Magistrate's Clerk and Postmaster at Bong Bong in New South Wales; afterwards

was superintendent of large farms in Bathurst, over the Blue
Mountains, in the same colony. At the later period I had a
wife and family of young children; the former, a most amiable
partner, I had the misfortune to lose in 1838, leaving me
with seven young children. My connections are most respectable. My late father was an officer of rank, and of very
meritorious services. My eldest brother is at present a major
in the Royal Marine Corps. I was convicted in October, 1846;
was three months in Millbank Penitentiary, at which period
fears were entertained that my intellect would become impaired
in solitary confinement; subsequently I was three years and
two months in the *Warrior* convict ship at Woolwich, during
which period I was employed on the Government works in the
dockyard; and was sent abroad in March, 1850. At Millbank
and the hulks I had the best possible character, as also on my
arrival at Hobart Town, Van Diemen's Land, after a passage
of four months. On my arrival I received a ticket-of-leave,
which I retained until I left the colony, never having forfeited
the same for a day by any kind of insubordinate conduct. My
motive in leaving Van Diemen's Land was to proceed to the
gold-diggings, in the hope that I might be successful and
better the condition of my family at home, who were in very
impoverished circumstances; but although my exertions were
very great in California, Victoria, and New South Wales, I
was unsuccessful. It is true I made, occasionally, some money;
but I was robbed of it on the road by armed bushrangers, and
frequently ill-used and robbed at Melbourne and Geelong by
the worst of characters. I was shipwrecked twice, and once
burnt out at sea: the first time in Torres Straits, between
New Holland and New Guinea, on a reef of coral rocks. Upon
this occasion I lost between £70 and £80 in cash, and all
my luggage. Eleven of us only got ashore, out of a ship's
company of twenty-seven, chiefly Lascars, Malays, and China-
men. After thirty days' great suffering and privation we
were picked up by an American whaler, and ultimately reached
Sydney, New South Wales. I was subsequently wrecked in a
brigantine called the *Triton*, going from Melbourne to Adelaide,
and lost all I possessed in the world, having another very
narrow escape of my life. In returning from San Francisco

to Melbourne in a vessel called the *White Squall*, she caught
fire about three hundred and fifty miles from Tahiti (formerly
called Otaheite). We were obliged to abandon her and take
to the boats; but a great number of the crew and passengers
perished by fire and water. The survivors in the boats
reached Tahiti in about eight days, in a state of great
exhaustion, many of whom died from the effects of the same.
I had the misfortune to lose nearly all I possessed upon this
occasion. On reaching Melbourne I was very ill and went
into the hospital. I left in about five weeks, intending to go
again to Mount Alexander diggings; but, owing to ill-health,
bad state of the roads from the floods, and limited means, I
abandoned such intention. I had a twelvemonth before been
to Ballarat, Mount Alexander, Forest Creek, Bendigo, and
many other diggings: but at this time no police was organised
or gold escort troopers, consequently nearly all the unfortunate
diggers were robbed of what they got by hordes of bushrangers, well mounted, and armed with revolvers and other
weapons to the teeth. In returning to Melbourne from Forest
Creek the last time, I was beat, stripped, and robbed of all I
had, in the Black Forest, about halfway between Melbourne
and Mount Alexander. I left Melbourne in the brig *Kestrel*
for Sydney, New South Wales, at which place I was acquainted
with many respectable parties, some of whom I had known as
far back as 1829, when I first went to Sydney with my wife
and children. The *Kestrel* put in at some of the settlements
of New Zealand, at one of which (Auckland) was lying a
barque, bound for England, in want of hands. The temptation was great to reach my dear family, for which I had
mourned ever since I met with my misfortune. I shipped
myself as ordinary seaman and assistant steward. We left
the settlement in July, with a miserably crippled ship's
company, and made a very severe passage round Cape Horn,
in the winter season, which carried away masts, sails, rigging,
boats, bulwarks, stanchions, etc., etc. Some of the crew were
lost with the yards, and most of us were frostbitten. We put
into Rio de Janeiro, Brazil, South America, to refit and provision. We proceeded on our passage, crossed the equator,
touched at Funchal—one of the Azores—for two days, and

reached England in September, after a severe passage of four months and twenty-six days from New Zealand. Under all the circumstances of my present unhappy condition, I humbly hope the legislature will humanely consider the long, severe, and various descriptions of punishment I have undergone since my conviction. I would also most respectfully call the attention of the authorities to the fact, that the offence for which I have so severely suffered was the first deviation from strict rectitude during my life; and that I have never since, upon any occasion whatever, received a second sentence even of the most minor description. It was only required of me by the then regulation of the service, that I should serve five years upon the public works at Woolwich. On my embarkation for Van Diemen's Land I had done three years and four months: if I had completed the remainder twenty months I should have been discharged from the dockyard a free man. I also humbly beg to state, at the time I left Van Diemen's Land, six years after my conviction, I was entitled by the regulations of the service to a conditional pardon, which would have left me at liberty to leave the colony without further restraint. I beg to state that during the period of three years and four months I was at the hulks I worked in all the gangs in the dockyard. Upon several occasions I received severe injuries, some of which requiring me to be sent to the hospital ship. I was ruptured by carrying heavy weights, the effect of which I have frequently felt since, and do to the present day. During the two periods when the cholera raged in the hulks, I attended upon the sick at the hospital ships. I humbly implore the Government will have compassion upon me for the sake of my numerous and respectable family, for my great mental and bodily sufferings since my conviction, and for my present weakly, worn-out, debilitated state of health, and award me a mild sentence. During my captivity and absence my unfortunate wife has suffered from great destitution, and buried two of her children. She is again bereaved of me in a distressed condition with her only surviving child, a little girl of ten years of age."

This man was set at large without punishment.

The case of the Frenchman, Dalmas, should not be omitted

here, not only because he was above the degree of a common
criminal, but because it was an early instance of how nearly
the ends of justice may be defeated when doctors differ as to
soundness or unsoundness of mind. Dalmas was a Frenchman,
long resident in England, a clever, intelligent man, a linguist,
and an excellent chemical operative. He was employed at
some chemical works near Battersea; but, on one occasion,
through family dissensions, he ran away from home. His
daughters, thus deserted, found a friend in a Mrs. Macfarlane.
By-and-by Dalmas reappeared, and his wife having died in
the interval, he showed his gratitude by offering marriage
to Mrs. Macfarlane. Her friends, however, dissuaded her
strongly from the match, and Dalmas was much annoyed,
although he continued on the surface to retain amicable
relations with her. One evening the two, Dalmas and Mrs.
Macfarlane, went with one of Dalmas' daughters to "a
place" which had been obtained for her through the kindness of the latter. The two elders left the girl at the house
about half-past eight at night, and they were afterwards
seen together at Battersea Bridge. Mrs. Macfarlane was
heard protesting that she could not remain out all night.
Nothing more was positively known till Mr. Perkins, a silver-
smith, crossing the bridge, was followed by a woman, reeling
and staggering in her walk, who asked him to conduct her to
the toll-house. This was Mrs. Macfarlane. Presently she
fell to the ground, and it was found that her throat was cut—
a terrible gash, extending from the *trachea* to the right side
of the spinal chord, which must have been done with some
very sharp instrument. Dalmas surrendered, and was found
guilty, but respited on the ground of insanity. Here began
the conflict of medical testimony. However, it was decided
to remove him to Millbank for an extended observation, and
this ended in a second report corroborating the madness.
From Millbank he passed on to Bethlehem Hospital ("Bedlam"), but in the eight months following he showed no symptoms of madness at all. Accordingly he was again sent to
Millbank by order of the Secretary of State, and eventually
went to the antipodes.

There were many other criminals who came in these days

to Millbank who belonged at least to the aristocracy of crime, if not to the great world. Some of them, to use their own language, were quite top sawyers in the trade. None in this way was more remarkable than old Cauty, who was called the "father of all the robbers." Few men were better known in his time and in his own line than Cauty. He was to be seen on every race course, and he was on friendly terms with all the swells on the turf. He had a large acquaintance also among such of the "best" people in town as were addicted to gambling on a large scale. He was in early life a croupier or marker at several West-end hells; but as he advanced in years he extended his operations beyond the Atlantic, and often made voyages by the West Indian packets. He liked to meet Mexicans and rich Americans; they were always ready to gamble, and as Cauty travelled with confederates, whose expenses he paid, he seldom lost money on the cards.

These, however, were his open avocations. Under the rose for many years he devoted all his abilities and his experience to planning extensive bank robberies, which were devised generally with so much ingenuity, and carried out with so much daring, that a long time elapsed before the culprits could be brought to justice. He had many dexterous associates. Their commonest plan of action was to hang about a bank till they saw some one enter whom they thought likely to answer their purpose. They followed and waited till the victim, having opened his pocket-book, or produced his cheque, was paid his money over the counter. At that moment a button dropped, or a slight push, which was followed by immediate apology, took off attention, and in that one instant the money or a part of it was gone—passed from hand to hand, and removed at once from the building.

Cauty came to grief at last. Of course he was known to the police, but the difficulty was to take him red-handed. The opportunity arrived when, with an accomplice, he made an attempt to rob the cashier of the London and Westminster Bank of his box. They were both watched in and out of the bank in St. James's Square day after day. The police kept them constantly in sight, and the cashier himself was put on his guard. The latter admitted that the

cash-box was at times left unavoidably within the reach of
dishonest people, and that it contained property sometimes
worth £100,000 'or more. But if the police were patient in
the watch they set, the thieves were equally patient in waiting
for a chance. Once at the moment of fruition they were just
" sold " by the appearance of a police-sergeant, who came in
to change a cheque. But at length, almost like a conjurer does
a trick, they accomplished their purpose. Cauty went in the
bank first, carrying a rather suspicious-looking black bag.
Three minutes afterwards he came out without it, and raised
his hat three times, which was the signal "all right " to his
accomplice. The latter, Tyler, a returned convict, thereupon
entered the bank in his turn, and almost immediately brought
away the bag. The two worthies were allowed to go without
let or hindrance as far as the Haymarket, and then secured.
The black bag was opened—inside was the cash-box.

This brought Cauty's career to an end. He got twenty
years, and then it came out how extensive was the business he
had done. Through his hands had passed not a little of the
"swag"* in all the principal robberies of the day—all the
gold from the gold-dust robberies, all the notes and bills
stolen from big banking houses. It was said that in this way
he had touched about half-a-million of money.

Some years afterwards another leader and prince in the
world of crime was unearthed in the person of a Jew—Moses
Moses—whose head-quarters were in Gravel Lane, Hounds-
ditch, and who was discovered to be a gigantic receiver of
stolen goods. He was only detected by accident. A quantity
of wool was traced to his premises, and these were thereupon
rigorously examined. In lofts and so forth, and other hiding-
places, were found vast heaps of missing property. Much was
identified as the product of recent burglaries. There was
leather in large quantities, plush also, cloth and jewellery. A
waggon-load of goods was, it was said, taken away, and in it
pieces of scarlet damask, black and crimson cloth, doeskin,
silver articles, and upwards of fifty rings. An attempt was
made to prove that Moses was new to the business, and had

* "Swag" is the proceeds, in cash or otherwise, of any felonious
transaction.

been led astray by the wicked advice and example of another man. But the Recorder would not believe that operations of this kind could be carried on by a novice or a dupe, and he sentenced Mr. Moses to transportation for fourteen years.

For unblushing effrontery and insolence, so to speak, in criminal daring, the case of King, the police-officer and detective, is almost without parallel. Although supposed to be a thief-taker by profession, he was really an instigator and supporter of crime. He formed by degrees a small gang of pickpockets, and employed them to steal for him, giving them full instruction and ample advice. He took them to the best hunting-grounds, and not only covered them while at work, but gave them timely warning in case of danger, or if the neighbourhood became too hot to hold them. His pupils were few in number, but they were industrious and seemingly highly successful. One boy stated his earnings at from £90 to £100 a week. King was a kind and liberal master to his boys. They lived on the fat of the land. Reeves, who gave information of the system pursued by King, said he had a pony to ride in the park, and that they all went to theatres and places of amusement whenever they pleased. The rascally ingenuity of King in turning to his own advantage his opportunities as an officer of the law savours somewhat of Vidocq and the *escrocs* of Paris. King got fourteen years.

But the most notorious prisoners in Millbank were not always to be found on the "male side." Equally famous in their own way were some of the female convicts—women like Alice Grey, whose career of imposture at the time attracted great attention, and was deservedly closed by committal to Millbank on a long sentence of transportation. Alice Grey was a young lady of artless appearance and engaging manners. Her favourite form of misconduct was to bring false charges against unfortunate people who had never seen her in their lives. Thus, she accused two boys of snatching a purse from her hand in the street, and when a number were paraded for her inspection she readily picked out the offenders. "Her evidence was so ingenuous," says the report, "that her story was implicitly believed, and the boys were remanded for trial." As a sort of compensation to Miss Grey (her real name

was "Brazil," but she had several—among others, Anastasia
Haggard, Felicia Macarthy, Jane Tureau, Agnes Hemans, etc.)
she was given a good round sum from the poor-box. But she
was not always so successful. She was sentenced to three
months in Dublin for making a false charge, and eighteen
months soon afterwards at Greenock. At Stafford she accused
a poor working-man of stealing her trunk, value £8; but
when put into the box she was taxed with former mistakes
of this kind, whereupon she showed herself at once in her true
colours and reviled every one present in a long tirade of abuse.
Her cleverness was, however, sufficient to have made her
fortune if she had turned her talents to honest account.

There was more dash about women like Louisa M. or
Emily L. The former drove up to Hunt and Roskell's in her
own carriage to look at some bracelets. They were for Lady
Campbell, and she was Miss Constance Browne. Her bankers
were Messrs. Cocks and Biddulph. Finally she selected
bracelets and head ornaments to the value of £2500. These
were to be brought to her house that evening by two assistants
from the shop, who accordingly called at the hour named.
The door was opened by a page. "Pray walk upstairs."
Miss Browne walks in. "The bracelets? Ah, I will take
them up to Lady Campbell, who is confined to her room.
The head assistant demurred a little, but Miss Browne said,
"Surely you know my bankers? I mentioned them to-day.
Messrs. Hunt and Roskell have surely satisfied themselves?"
With that the jewels were taken upstairs. Half an hour
passes. One assistant looks at the other. Another half-hour.
What does it mean? One rings the bell. No answer. The
other tries the door. It is locked. Then, all at once discovering the trap, they both throw up the window and call in
the police. They are released, but the house is empty.
Pursuit, however, is set on foot, and Miss Constance Browne
is captured the same night in a second class carriage upon the
Great Western Railway, and when searched she was found to
have on her a quantity of diamonds, a £100 note, rings and
jewellery of all sorts, including the missing bracelets. She
had laid her plans well. The house—which was Lady Campbell's—she had hired furnished, that day, paying down the

first instalment of £42. The page she had engaged and fitted with livery also that very day, and the moment he had shown up the jeweller's men she had sent him to the Strand with a note. Here was cleverness superior to that of Alice Grey.

Probably Emily L. carried off the palm from both. As an adroit and daring thief she has had few equals.* She is described as a most affable, ladylike, fascinating woman, well educated, handsome, and of pleasing address. She could win almost any one over. The shopmen fell at her feet, so to speak, when she alighted from her brougham and condescended to enter and give her orders. She generally assumed the title of Countess L., but her chief associate and ally was a certain James P., who was a lapidary by trade, an excellent judge of jewels, and a good looking respectable young fellow—to all appearance—besides. They were long engaged in a series of jewel robberies on a large scale, but escaped detection. Fate overtook them at last, and they were both arrested at the same time. One charge was for stealing a diamond locket, value £2000, from Mr. Emanuel, and a diamond bracelet worth £600 from Hunt and Roskell. At the same moment there cropped up another charge of stealing loose diamonds in Paris to the tune of £10,000. Emily was sentenced to four years, and from the moment she entered prison she resolved to give all the trouble she could. Her conduct at Millbank and at prison, to which she passed, was atrocious; and had the discipline been less severe she would probably have rivalled some of the ill-conducted women to whom I referred in a previous chapter. But at the expiration of her sentence she returned to her evil ways, outside. Brighton was the scene of her next misfortune. She there entered a jeweller's shop, and having put him quite off his guard by her insinuating manners, stole £1000 worth from under his nose, and while he was actually in conversation with her. The theft was not discovered till she was just leaving Brighton. Apprehended at the station, she indignantly denied the charge, asserting that she was a lady of high rank, and offering bail to any amount. But she was detained, and a London detective

* She was seen in 1875 in her carriage, in a crowded thoroughfare, by one of the Millbank female officers.

having been called in, she was at once identified. For this she got seven years, and was sent to Millbank once more. This extraordinary woman, notwithstanding the vigorous examination to which all incoming prisoners are subjected, succeeded in bringing in with her a number of valuable diamonds. But they were subsequently discovered in spite of the strange steps she took to secrete them.

Some of the names with which I shall close this chapter are so well known that it is useless to attempt disguise. Agar, " Jim the Penman," " Velvet Ned," Poole, Pullinger, Redpath, Robson—the particular felonies of which these criminals were guilty are still fresh, no doubt, in the minds of many. But I cannot omit them from the Millbank calendar, as they were certainly not the least notorious of those who passed through the prison.

"Velvet Ned " was one of the greatest and most successful cracksmen in England. 'It was he, with Scottie Brown and Caisley, who broke open the iron safe at the shop of Mr. Walker the watchmaker. This was a case that created some excitement at the time, because Mr. Walker brought an action against the patentees of the safe. They had certified that it must take at least eleven hours and a half to break it open : a statement altogether ridiculed by "Velvet Ned," who when in custody declared he had opened it—and could any other— in less than a couple of hours. Caisley was the "approver," who turned Queen's evidence and gave the judge full information how the job was done. As it needed much hammering and wedging, and there was a policeman on the beat close by, it was necessary to watch for his approach to knock off work. Caisley was on the roof, and as he heard the footsteps of the policeman he rang a bell which communicated with the room in which the safe was. These prisoners when at Millbank were supposed to have several thousands to their credit in various banks, but in other names. In their days a felon's property was confiscated, and to preserve it the greatest caution was required.

Never, perhaps, was such unrivalled patience and ingenuity devoted to a base end as in the robbery of bullion upon the South Eastern Railway in 1855. All attempts to unravel the

mystery were quite unsuccessful. It was known that the gold
had been abstracted between Boulogne and Paris, and that was
all. The boxes from which it had been stolen were iron-
bound, locked and deposited in iron safes, also locked with
patent Chubbs. The keys of both box and safe had been
throughout in the hands of confidential officials, and the boxes
themselves had been conveyed in the guard's van. Probably
the secret would have remained hidden for ever, but for the
meanness of one of the accomplices.

In 1855 a man named Agar was tried and sentenced to
"life" for forgery—after a certain term at Millbank, he went
thence to Pentonville, and on to Portland. While at Portland
he heard by letter that his wife and child were in distress,
although at the time of his conviction one Pierce, an ally in
various undertakings, had promised to provide for them.
Enraged against Pierce, Agar came forward and confessed
voluntarily that he and Pierce, with two others, were the men
who had stolen the bullion two years before. Agar's evidence
was most circumstantial and graphic. Pierce, who was ticket-
porter, had originally proposed the robbery, but Agar would
not agree, thinking it impracticable. He said, however, if
impressions of the keys could be obtained he would carry out
the job. Some time elapsed; the matter was dropped, then
reopened. At length Pierce and Agar went down to Folkestone, took lodgings, and devoted themselves to watching the
trains in and out. They did this so constantly that they themselves were at length watched by the police, and they had to
leave the town. But Agar had noticed the arrival and departure of the bullion, and on one occasion had seen the chest
opened. A clerk came with the keys, which he afterwards
deposited in the cash till. Agar therefore returned a little
later to Folkestone, and tried to make friends with this clerk;
but all to no purpose. He was "a very sedate young man,"
who would not be seduced from his allegiance. At length
Agar and Pierce managed to get into the railway office one
day, while the clerks were absent, and took impressions in wax
of the keys.

Two others were in the "swim." Burgess, one of the
guards, and Tester, who was station-master at Dover. It was

arranged that Agar should go down several times with bullion
in the van with Burgess, so as to try the false keys.   He did
go—seven or eight times before he could get them to work.
But at length, when all was ready, they prepared a number of
bags of shot, and went to the station more than once when
Burgess was guard.   At length one night he gave the signal,
wiping his face as they passed.   Bullion was to go down that
night.   Tester and Pierce took tickets.   Agar waited on the
platform till the train was in motion, then jumped into the
guard's van, and Burgess covered him with his apron.   Agar
soon set to work.   Opening one safe, he extracted a wooden
box, sealed, and fastened with iron bands and nails.   This he
broke into and took from it four bars of gold, replacing by
shot the precious metal.   The gold itself was put into a bag
and handed out to Tester at Reigate, who returned with it to
London.   The next box Agar opened contained American
gold coins; the third, small bars of gold.   Just as much of
each was removed as they had shot to make up weight with.
The safes were taken out at Folkestone, but Agar and Pierce
went on to Dover.   Here they had supper, and then went back
to London by the 2 A.M. train, carrying with them two carpet
bags "that appeared to be particularly heavy."   The gold,
which was in value about £12,000, was all melted down at
Agar's house in Shepherd's Bush, and part of the ingots
disposed of.   Pierce, Tester, and Agar got each £600, Burgess
£700.   Tester and Burgess were sentenced to fourteen years'
transportation, and Pierce to two years' imprisonment.   Agar
soon afterwards went to Australia.   The others did their
"time" between Millbank and Portland, and were eventually
released on ticket-of-leave at home.

A more serious robbery than this had occurred some years
previously on the Great Western Railway, also through the
connivance of the guard.   At that time the mail bags were
carried in the guard's van.   This was well known, and a plan
was accordingly concocted in London to rob the mail on its
journey.   One of the guards, P., was enticed to join; and a
first-class thief, one Nightingale, a shrewd active fellow, was
sent down from town by the swell mob to carry out the
robbery.   A third man, Warrup, a mere tool, was called in to

assist. Nightingale and Warrup having called tickets in the usual way, passed along the train while it was in motion till they got to the guard's van. There P. was waiting for them, and all three fell forthwith upon the mail bags, from which letters, containing money and other securities, were abstracted to the value it was said of nearly a million of money. As soon as the robbery was completed, P. had the train slackened to allow his accomplices to jump down and make off across country with their booty. All three were, however, eventually apprehended, and sentenced to long terms of transportation.

P. was removed later on from Millbank to Bermuda, where he distinguished himself greatly during an epidemic of yellow fever, during which the hulks were decimated and hundreds of both officers and convicts were swept away. P., at a time when others feared to go near the sick, had, singlehanded and alone, the charge of two whole shiploads. For his courage and devotion he was specially pardoned and returned to England. I believe he is now doing well somewhere in the west country.

I will close the chapter with a short account of Saward, or "Jem the Penman," who was long considered by the swell mob as one of the most useful men in London. He was the master mind of a gang of forgers who committed great depredations before they were discovered. He had been called to the bar and was an excellent scholar, besides which he was endowed with great intelligence and ingenuity of mind. Whenever blank cheques fell into the hands of burglars they were passed on into Saward's hands to be if possible made use of. It was Saward's business to ascertain who kept accounts at the various banks for which the cheques were valid, and the amounts which might safely be drawn. He had also to provide the necessary signatures. There were many methods of obtaining them; but a favourite one was to call on a solicitor and beg of him to recover a debt from Mr. So-and-so. By-and-by Mr. So-and-so paid his bill, and the solicitor passed the money on to his client by cheque. Clumsiness on

2 B

the part of one of his agents, who applied to three different
solicitors at the same time with the same story, led first to
suspicion and then to full discovery. Saward at Millbank
looked like a common drunken sot, but he conducted himself
fairly well in prison.

A "BIG" CRIMINAL.

CHAPTER XX.

THE MILLBANK CALENDAR (*Continued*).

OLD prison officers have often remarked to me that there is a great deterioration in the physique of convicts, taking them as a class. On this point doctors differ. Many prison medical men support the theory; on the other hand, Dr. Guy's exhaustive statistics are opposed to it.* Nevertheless, the fact remains that one type of criminal who was once constantly to be met with in our convict prisons is seldom seen now. I

---

* Results of the Censuses of Convict Prisons in England for 1862 and 1873, by Wm. A. Guy, M.B. In a preface to this pamphlet Colonel Du Cane, C.B., R.E., remarks: "It is curious to find that the opinion so generally expressed by medical officers of prisons and others, that the male convicts are less physically able-bodied than in former years, is not at all borne out by these statistics. Some difference, in fact, of the present condition in that respect is no doubt due to the retention in this country of able-bodied men who were at the time of the last census transported, but transportation had been very limited for some years previous to the last census."

2 B 2

allude to the burly, brawny scoundrel, well built, strong and
able, to whom crimes of atrocious violence were as child's play.
That ruffians of this class exist to the present day we have
evidence just now in the criminal records of some of the
northern counties; but as the law is at present administered,
these clog-kickers and wife-beaters are not generally consigned
to the Government prisons.* It may be that the new race is
not as the old was; or, more probably, under modern prison
management the criminal class do not thrive to the same
extent. But at Millbank, in the days of which I write, there
were many fine specimens of this now rarer criminal. One
ward was especially filled with them. These were half of them
murderers; some of them had even a second sentence of "life"
recorded against them. The discipline to which these men
were subjected was not of a kind to keep them in proper
subordination. They were petted, and persuaded, and made
much of. Anything that might annoy or irritate them by
word or deed was most scrupulously avoided. It was "please"
here, and "please" there, to which the only answer was a
curse, and often as not a distinct negative or refusal. Several
of these men were afterwards leaders in the revolt at Gibraltar,
when the deputy-governor was stabbed. A prominent figure
in this mob was Mark Jeffries, a tall Irishman, six feet and
more in height, who was the terror of nearly all the officers
who came near him. He was a most uncultivated, savage
scoundrel, who refused to obey orders or submit to any
discipline at all. If he was in his cell and wanted anything,
he simply kicked for half an hour at his door with the toe of
his hob-nailed boot, disdaining altogether the use of a signal
stick.† If it was necessary to take him before the governor
or to the board-room, half-a-dozen officers were hardly strong
enough for the task. They were all afraid of him; many
indeed carried knives to defend themselves against his brutal

* But I believe that quite lately several offenders of this class have
been sentenced to penal servitude. One of them died in Millbank, in
the early part of 1875, by his own hand.

† A narrow slit in the wall of a Millbank cell allows the passage of
a thin "signal stick," by which means the ward officer's attention is
called to the wants of any particular prisoner.

violence. Hardly inferior in coarse ferocity was George
Talmage, a Manchester man, who was famed for his skill in
" putting on the crook "—a practice older in criminal traditions
than that of garroting, but quite as effectual. The present
plan, I am told, is to put a thumb on each side of the victim's
head behind his ear, and press his jugular vein till he becomes
unconscious. "Putting on the crook" is performed by
throwing the left arm round the neck of some unsuspecting
person, bringing the left knee into the small of his back, and then
pulling back his head by the hair with the hand that is free.
While this treatment is in progress by one from behind, others
work in front and rifle the victim's pockets. If held too long
in this position, death of course ensues. Talmage was a great
professor in this line of business : he was a short, stout man,
of immense strength, with a large head and a thick neck like
a bull's, and his grip was not to be got away from easily.
Still he declared he had never murdered any one; that is to
say, he had never beaten out anybody's brains. But he had
choked four—by pure accident of course. He had held them
a little too long in the crook, but "that wasn't like murder, oh
dear no ! " Talmage had worked chiefly in the country, and
his victims were generally people returning from market with
the proceeds of their sales in their pockets.

In his way, Isaacs the Jew, who went at the time by the
alias of Fletcher, and who murdered warder Hall in Millbank,
November, 1849, was quite as great a ruffian as any to whom
I have referred. Isaacs was comparatively young. At the time of
the murder he was little more than twenty-five or twenty-six—a
stout-built, red-haired youth, who had been a thief from infancy,
and who had been already once or twice at the hulks. He
was always badly behaved, and was continually under punishment at Millbank. One day he said openly to an officer, " I'll
murder some one, and soon." " Well, why not me ? " replied
the officer. " No, no; you're too big, and I've known you
too long." Time passed, and Isaacs' threat was forgotten.
By-and-by he came to be under the control of warder Hall,
a mild, easy-going fellow, who had once been a publican,
but who had no idea of dealing with such desperate villains
as Isaacs. He treated the prisoner always with the utmost

leniency, but there was no such feeling as gratitude in the breast of Isaacs, and he resolved to do for Hall. He got his opportunity when out of his cell one morning emptying his basin. Hall was stooping down over a writing-desk, making an entry in one of the ward-books. Without a moment's warning Isaacs rushed on Hall and knocked him down with the basin. Hall was stunned by the fall, and while thus helpless, Isaacs battered out his brains, long before help could arrive.

It was of course taken for granted that Isaacs would be inevitably hanged. But he escaped on the plea of lunacy. Even before his trial came off, so say the traditions of the place, he seemed to know that he would escape capital punishment. Some one went to see him in his cell on the day of poor Hall's funeral. "Do you hear them tolling the bell for poor Hall? You'll be hanged for this, Isaacs. "I shan't —not I," said Isaacs. "The Rabbi was here last night. He'll get me off. There hasn't been a Jew hanged this hundred years." Rightly or wrongly, Isaacs did in effect escape the extreme penalty of the law. He was found guilty, but respited as insane, and removed to Bedlam, where they kept him, so it was said, in an iron cage for a couple of years. Within a month or two another and a similar attack was made upon an unsuspecting officer, but happily without fatal results. The warder showed fight and defended himself till help arrived, but he was none the less severely mauled.

Other men of this savage character were to be found in plenty in those days at Millbank. There was Elijah Bullick, who travelled to and fro between Millbank and Pentonville, Dartmoor, Portland, and the hulks, and was found incorrigible in all. On one occasion, at Millbank, he struck an officer in the face in the middle of divine service. Edward Grey was no better. He, too, was moved from one prison to another, but could be tamed in none. Eventually his career of violence was brought to an end by his death, of which he was himself the cause. Climbing up to look out of the window when in a refractory cell, he strained himself so badly that death ensued. Death had been recorded against Michael Henry, for attempting to

murder an officer in Exeter gaol; but he came to Millbank
with a commuted sentence of transportation for life. Here
his conduct continued throughout desperate in the extreme.
Soon after his arrival he made a second and nearly successful
attempt on the life of one of the prison officers. He then
passed on to Gibraltar, where he was the terror of all who
came near him. For a third attempt at murder he was tried
for his life, and sentenced a second time to the extreme
penalty of the law. But he again escaped, and was sent back
to Millbank, where he remained for many years. The case of
John Gough was nearly parallel. He went from prison to
prison, fighting, slashing, and trying to murder every one he
could. For an attempt to murder an officer at Dartmoor he
was sentenced to death at Exeter, but returned instead to
Millbank. This prisoner's conduct was so atrocious that it
would have been quite inexplicable except on the grounds of
madness. He was subject, it appeared, to fits of maniacal
rage, at which times it took several men to hold him and
prevent him from tearing the flesh off his hands with his
teeth. Gough left prison in 1874.

The gang known as the Uckfield burglars was also a
product of these times. This was an admirably planned
organisation for evil, and while it lasted it was strangely
powerful. The year 1851 was remarkable for the number and
atrocity of its burglaries. It was at this period that the
Frimley murder was perpetrated by burglars, who were,
however, captured; but those at Uckfield got off scot-free—
at least, if they were lodged at Millbank it was not for this
particular offence. Their operations were extensive. For a long
time they kept three counties—Surrey, Sussex, and Kent—in
constant dread. Their most daring act was breaking into a house
near Lewes, inhabited by certain maiden ladies. The night was
dark and tempestuous, and under cover of the storm they
broke into the dairy through a lattice window, thence to the
cellar, and so to the kitchen. After that the gang divided
into two parts. One half attacked the man-servant, the other
proceeded to rouse the old ladies. The butler showed fight,
but he was disarmed and forced to confess where the plate
was kept. In the same way the ladies were terrified into

giving up all their valuables. These ruffians were disguised
in masks of black crape, and they were all armed with either
staves or pistols. The ramifications of the confederacy were
wide. It embraced a number of stationary accomplices, who
worked as shoemakers, basketmakers, and so forth. The spies
trudged about in the guise of hawkers, or simply as tramps.
In all cases the will of the captain was supreme; mutiny was
punished by death, and so were cowardice and desertion from
the colours of the corps.

The transition seems complete from such stalwart ruffians
who made a capital of their strength, to cripples like Mason,
the man known as " the devil on two sticks," or " Crutchy "
Jones. But the latter, though maimed and halt, were not
disabled, and in their own way they did quite as much mischief in prison or out. Mason was an experienced thief, but
he was chiefly notorious for his persistent misconduct in
prison. He was so fluent of speech that he possessed extraordinary weight among his comrades, and could persuade
·them almost to anything. He was full of tricks and artful
dodges. At one time he had followed the calling of a sheriff's
officer; and he used to recount with pride his success in
serving writs. None of these was better executed than the
one in which he made friends with the debtor's dog, putting
at length the writ into its mouth. The little animal trotted
confidently into his master's house, and gave the writ into his
hands, as he had been taught to do with other things. Of
course the writ was actually served. Mason was paralysed
in his lower limbs, but still was dangerously active, and if
thwarted or out of temper he stopped at nothing. On one
occasion he sharpened the point of a pair of scissors, and took
post near the chapel door, meaning to stab the governor just
as he entered his pew. But he was detected before any ill
consequences ensued. Mason eventually died of poison. He
had been given some belladonna ointment for outward application; he took it internally, hoping thereby to make himself
ill enough to be taken into hospital. But he swallowed too
much, with fatal results.

" Crutchy " Jones first came to Millbank twenty-five years
ago, when quite a lad. He is there now, as I am writing these

lines, doing his fourth or fifth sentence, under the name of McQuinn, which is, I believe, his proper designation. Watches were the rock on which he split. He is said to be one of the best judges of a watch in England; and at his last affair, when taken red-handed with one which he had but just removed from a gentleman's fob, Crutchy declared that he only borrowed the watch for a moment to look at the works. All his convictions were for stealing watches: sometimes working alone, sometimes in company with others. His speed on his crutch was quite remarkable: though crippled he could run faster than most men using both their legs, and he could climb a pole against any acrobat or sailor in the world. He is really a genius in his way. While at Dartmoor, to which place he was sent from Millbank, he invented an apparatus for cutting turf, which had in it all the elements of success, had it had a fair trial. Another of his schemes was a patent for raising sunken ships. He was really without education. What he knows of reading and writing he has picked up in prison. Inside he is famous as a prison lawyer, and will argue by the hour—if allowed—the rights and wrongs of himself and his fellow-prisoners. One of his favourite amusements when in a punishment cell at Dartmoor, was to go through his trial at the Old Bailey from beginning to end. He could mimic the voice of the judge; would give the counsels' speeches and the cross-examination *in extenso*, and to the life.

A more painful phase of human nature is to be found in the insane criminals, with whom Millbank has at times had plenty to do. For years the prison has been the receptacle of all convicts who become insane during their imprisonment. A distinction must be drawn between these and offenders found on arraignment of unsound mind, together with those actually tried but acquitted on grounds of insanity, all of whom are then and there ordered to be kept in a criminal lunatic asylum during the Queen's pleasure. The Millbank lunatics are sane when sentenced; mental aberration has not shown itself till after they have been consigned to prison. But feigned insanity is no new wile with convicts, and to guard against imposture, all who betray symptoms of this kind are thereupon removed to Millbank for "further observation." A second medical

opinion is thus obtained upon the case of each—a matter
of no slight importance; and, by thus bringing the lunatics
together in a body under one system and one supervision,
increased facilities are gained for dealing with them singly or
in the aggregate.

But for these reasons there are at times a large proportion
of insane prisoners temporarily at Millbank. Taken in connection with the Millbank population, this proportion has
often appeared extraordinarily large, and certain theorists
have found therein a peg on which to hang an unfair comparison between lunacy and crime. As Millbank got all
lunatics from all Government prisons, the ratio should have
been struck—not against the 1100 that Millbank held, but
against the total prison population of seven or eight thousand
souls.

It may be taken for granted, of course, that all the
common cases, such as are seen at ordinary asylums, would
be found also among criminal lunatics. But the latter have
certain peculiarities of their own. I do not refer merely to
such curious vagaries as the consumption of pebbles, blankets,
and gutta-percha pint-pots, which these men have been
known to eat in great quantities,* but to certain special
phases of insanity to which criminals appear alone liable.
Although the whole subject is somewhat too painful to be
treated otherwise than in sober seriousness, some of the cases
seen at Millbank are too curious to be altogether omitted
from these pages. I propose, therefore, to enlarge upon
sundry of the groups into which criminal lunatics may be
divided. Among such may be mentioned strange forms of
delusion, of hallucinations, of religious mania, of exaggerated
destructive tendencies, of curious attempts at suicide, and last
of all, of persistent feigning, ending at length in real insanity.

Criminal lunatics probably suffer more than any from
delusions in various forms. Prominent among these are
mistaken notions of ill-usage. For instance, numbers are

* One prisoner swallowed pebble after pebble, as fast as a man eats
peas, till he got 4 lbs. of stones inside him. Another preferred blankets,
which he tore up into bits six inches square, to his regular diet. This
man made nothing of a pound of candles if he could get them.

possessed with an invincible suspicion that their food has been poisoned. To combat this they are allowed to choose their own from a group of a dozen or more tea-cans and dinner-tins; but even then they are hardly satisfied. Of course, the fact of their taking this supposed fatal food for weeks and months together, without the least harm to themselves, is not a sufficient argument to them as it would be to others. No matter what measures are taken to convince them, they return persistently to the charge. One says his food does him no good and barely keeps him alive—"no wonder, when there are flies put in it." He feels certain that the doctors have combined together to murder him, so he puts his finger down his throat to see what there is on his chest. If he could only muster up courage he would murder the doctor, and so save dozens of lives. They might take him to the gallows; but so much the better—the truth would come out. He declared at another time the doctor was only keeping him to make a living lantern of him—till he is so reduced in flesh that people can see through his side with the naked eye. The doctor will then publish what he sees for the instruction of students, and so gain a name like Dr. Jenner.

Another complains bitterly of the insults passed on him from day to day; they will send him grease in with his food— lamp oil it is, which is intended to injure him, to dry up his brain and make his eyes run over. He was drugged till his head was actually bursting. H. said that his broth was enchanted, and that he had a ring in his throat. P. refused his dinner because the tin was marked with a white cross:* that meant mischief, he said. One said he had mercury put into his barley-water merely to annoy him. F. L. gave a great deal of trouble in this respect. He declared that at another prison a man got his (L.'s) dinner by mistake, and was never heard of more. L. always refused his food if the cup or tin was in the least bent or disfigured. Another man, G., will not allow any one to see him eat or drink, but hides behind his bed at meal times, lest the officer should lay a spell

* In the prison kitchen, for convenience in issuing provisions, it is customary to mark each batch of tins with numbers, crosses, and so forth.

upon his food. Everything W. gets is adulterated, even the
water. The bread is poisoned, and he will drop a corpse
sooner than eat a morsel of food. L. declared isinglass and
laughing gas were given him in his cocoa, and swelling
powder which made him as big as a mountain. The laughing
gas was to keep him in good humour, but it tastes like candle
tallow, and only makes his pulse beat the faster. It is all
meant to turn him silly. But the officer will be clever who
persuades him to take it. Another cunningly refuses his
food because if "they" knew he took it they would put
something into it. R. was especially suspicious of his food ;
rejected the milk brought him because there was a crumb
floating in it. At another time he gets very angry because
there are three spots on the egg brought to him. "What are
they here for ?" he asks. "What is the meaning of this ? "
It was impossible to persuade him that nothing could well be
put inside the shell of an egg. As a rule this man insisted on
the officers eating a portion of every ration first.

These are but a few of the cases which indeed might be
multiplied without end. A second form of delusion as to ill-
usage, is the dread of the determined hostility of all or a
portion of the officials towards them. They fancy themselves
victims of conspiracies againt them; and assert that they
hear the officers concocting schemes to do them injury, sometimes outside their doors, or in the airing-yards, or wherever
they may be brought in contact. Thus A. T. asserts that the
whole of the prisoners and officers persist in telling lies about
him, and making false charges. They accuse him of being
(1) a Fenian ; (2) a haymaker ; (3) that he is acquainted with
men outside who have committed a robbery ; (4) that he is a
pickpocket ; (5) that he is in the habit of passing bad coin.
There are in all forty charges, he says ; but he stuffs his ears
with cotton wool, so that he may hear none of them.

A third common form is the influence of electrical machines.
In this respect many labour under most extraordinary delusions ; fancying, for instance, that they are still under the
influence of a governor of a far-off prison, who they think can
affect them still even at that distance. In this way one has
the magnesium light turned on him ; or they blow mercury

into his head, which makes it rotten; or attack his eyes, so
that he has to wear a handkerchief over them to keep the
electric flashes out. Another declares that the doctor is in
the tower working a machine which sends electric shocks up
through the flags, and under his bed and up into his legs,
which prick him like a needle. A third writes as follows, to
his friends: "One mode of torture in this modern inquisition
is the toothache, earache, tic-douloureux, and thrilling pains in
the gums, which I have had all together; and various pains
which they put on regular for complaining; they also give
me the toothache every meal time, and sometimes for twenty-
three hours every night." F. declares that he had the gas
turned on to him, after which he was made insensible and
drugged with opium. Then Madame Rachel was brought in
to take a plaster cast of his head; but the wax was put on so
hot that it has injured him for life.

More sad than any of the foregoing, are the delusions of
wealth and grandeur: symptoms of a grave description these,
because they usually end in the general paralysis of the insane.
They are extraordinarily prevalent among criminal lunatics,
and show themselves in many curious shapes. E. W. said he
was paid £1000 a day while he was kept in Millbank. This
was for looking after the prisoners. He is to be made king of
the moon; no one else has any right to it. He does not want
to go to Heaven, he has the moon for a dominion to all eternity.
Draws his crest on a slate—a circle topped with a crown, and
inside an orange blossom. Then tells off his servants, with
their wages opposite each. They are all to wear gilt buttons,
and to have £700 a year apiece. He styles himself "Your
Royalty," and says he means to come down on the national
debt to pay all expenses. Another, S. I., has power over the
sun; can make it shine when it is a wet day. He has power
also over the moon, and means to make the sun and moon
change places. In fact he can move the sun which way he
pleases; and he is for ever climbing up to the window to see
the moon rise. G. D. announces that he is the Prince of Wales
—prophet, priest, and king. This man says the Queen is his
god-mother, and that he means to get the doctor a good
Government appointment for restoring his eyesight. B. C.

states gravely that he is commander-in-chief, conqueror, and emperor of the world; he has besieged millions of castles, and carried off thousands of golden boats. But the officers have robbed him of all, and besides, of a number of field and pawnbrokers' chronometers. He says next that he is Baron Rothschild; that he owns steel mountains, and mountains of gold, banks also, and breweries, and pawnshops without number. He thinks nothing of spending £1000 a day; often goes to Paris for a fortnight, and gets through thousands of pounds. O. B.'s sister, again, is Queen of New York, and he has an army of several millions in Wales fighting to get him back to the throne. He has a number of half-crown tickets to give away, he says; he has got thousands of them, but the officers shall not have them, only the poor. He shall have an ox killed without delay, and so much given to each officer according to the number of his children. J. R. has had a long law suit, he says, but he has proved his legitimacy at last, and has won the estate. He is the owner now of R—— Park, but of course there is a steward to look after it while he is himself away. This man is so rich, that when he is given some cloth to do repairs with, he makes it up into two great pockets inside his coat, and said that they were an investment for his money. At another time he is king of Woking, and Colonel of the Madras Fusiliers; sends his compliments to the Governor of Millbank, and informs him that either the prison or the neighbouring gas-works must come down—they are too close together. J. R. then decides himself that the prison shall fall, and thereupon marks off the whole of the cells and corridors within his reach into lots, and labels them "for sale," with a bit of white chalk. After which he jumps on his bed to sell the whole place by auction, going through the whole performance most accurately. "Any advance? Who bids? Going, going, gone!" This man was so puffed up with his own importance that he could not bear the sight of the other prisoners, calling them common convicts, and treating them with the greatest contempt. Whatever they got was too good for them. Acorns and glue were the sort of stuff they should be fed upon.

Another group of delusions are those of great genius and

great inventive power. One man says he is wiser than
Solomon, that he has more knowledge in his finger nail than
all the Solons in Europe. He has invented a machine by
which thieves may be detected when they are breaking into
a house, but he will only show it to the governor, for fear
some one else should get out the patent first. Another, D. B.,
has invented a flying-machine, and he can make a pig fly—and
"that is a very unlikely bird." Now he only wants feathers
to make its wings. This he intended to have done with his
hair and whiskers, only they have been cut off. However, he
completes the machine and tries it, returning to inform his
friends that he had put his head through the first heaven, but
he could not breathe, and had to pull it back again. He only
met a raven in his flight, which seemed very much surprised
to see him. "It is a glorious treat to sail around the world in
a balloon." Next time he tries his wings he means to take
up a box of cigars, to hand to those officers he likes as he
passes the prison ; but for those whom he hates he shall take
up a bottle of vitriol, and drop it on their heads. To prove
the value of his machine, he is to walk feet uppermost, along
a rope stretched from the " doom " of St. Paul's to the top of
the Monument. Unfortunately at the last, he declared he was
no longer able to fly, as he had been steeped in salt and water
and was now too weak.

In the case of T. K. the "invention" delusion went much
further. He gave himself out as the sole inventor of the
" cork ship," which no one knew how to build but himself
and the Americans ; and if they were to bring out a vessel of
this kind it would sink the whole British fleet. He thinks it
right our Government should know what a tremendous
weapon they may have to contend against. However, he has
plenty of the cork ships on hand, and will part with them if
the Admiralty likes to speculate. He was continually harping
upon these ships : night and day he asked every one who
approached whether any answer had come from the Government on the subject. At last he got leave to write to the
authorities himself. This is his letter :

"Your excellency, considering the present state of the
policies of Europe and America, and seeing that the best

statesmen and politicians are hard at work trying to promote
their own ends—when wars and rumours of wars happen to
be one of the principal orders of the day, I think your
excellency will not consider me rude, seeing that I am an old
acquaintance, for troubling you with this document at a time
when it may be more than needed. My mean object in
addressing your excellency at present, is to call the Prussian
Government's serious attention to the very superior means
that are now afloat both by sea and land for to accomplish
warlike designs. The Prussian Government may or may not
have satisfactory information of corked ships, but the sooner
they shall have those ships the better for themselves. This
corked style is altogether a new style for constructing heavy
armour-clad war ships, far superior to the original style; they
carry plates that make them superior to land fortifications, and
I am told that nine or ten of them are sufficient to destroy all
the war ships at present in Europe: They are to be found in
the Mediterranean and the Baltic. Does the British and
Prussian Government know this? (There are a few particulars in Alsace and Lourain, and in Berlin, that the
Prussian Government would do well to know something
about.) If your excellency will please put yourself in communication with the Secretary of State, or the first Lord of
the Admiralty, you may hear of something to your advantage."

The letter was addressed to Count Bismarck, and poor
T. K. waited in vain for a reply. At first he hoped for a
large sum of money and his liberty as reward for the invention. But time passed, and he got neither the one nor the
other. Latterly he took to standing in one particular place
in the ward for two hours together without moving, and
without speaking to or noticing any one the whole time, intent
only on the door through which he expected the messenger
with an answer to his important letter.

Last among the delusions, I must mention those of wrong-
ful detention, mistaken identity, unjust sentence, and so forth.
These are naturally extremely common. Even sane prisoners
almost universally persist in proclaiming their innocence; these
of unsound mind therefore may be forgiven for falling into a
similar error. The delusion shows itself mostly in the same

way. Always asking to be set free, to be allowed to go home, to return to Newgate, to be sent back to their own town to be tried again on a new indictment, that they have been kept in prison over their time—these are the strings on which they harp for ever. Sometimes one more violent takes the law into his own hands, and tries to make his escape. Thus W. R. gets up one morning and says he is not in his right place. He has had enough of this crib. "What is the damage for my night's lodgings?—I'm off. I only enlisted for nine months." After that he was always trying to run away. If he saw a door open he made straight for it. At early "unlocking" of the cells he would often gather up his clothes, both bedding and wearing apparel, and make a run for the gate. At other times he climbed to the window and tried to force his way through the bars. He was fond of remarking, "Ah, I lost a fine chance to-day; I could have got away easily enough," and so on.

The next principal group are hallucinations or delusions of the senses, either as to seeing or hearing. In the former cases the sufferer sees visions that are absolutely without corporeal existence; in the latter, hears sounds altogether imaginary. The visions are very various. One man is visited at night by the whole of his family; the wife and child of another come to see him in his cell, but Tim Dooley always appears and drags them away, holding a knife to their throats. A third sees his father lying in front of him as plain as can be, with his throat cut. Others are worried by evil spirits. J. B. says they put bad words into his mouth when he is eating or saying his prayers. He sees them fly out of his mouth, and then back again right down his throat. Next they get into his hair, and he wants a small-tooth comb to get them out. J. L. jumps suddenly off his seat one day, and rushes along the side of the wall, crying, "I'll knock your ugly head off." When asked what it all meant, he replied an ugly devil with horns on its head was sitting at the edge of his bed. It had a two-edged axe ready to strike him. R. M. cries out, "Fire! fire! the devils are having a banquet in my head." Then he rubs his head against the brick wall, and lies down underneath the water-tap to let the stream play on his head. At another time R. M. sees a man in front of him at night, dressed in white, continually grinning at him. Next, evil spirits float through the air and spit nasty stuff at him as they pass; sees little men, dwarfs all about, and wants to be bricked up in a dungeon so that no one can come near him. J. W. spends the night creeping under the different beds in the ward, saying there is some one after him with a carving-knife. H. J. walks about the yard very much excited, saying some woman is following him wherever he goes; runs first to one side and then to the other, and motions her away, his eyes full of water, and every now and then he gives a loud shout. F. L. sees white pigeons continually flying about his cell. H. P. is troubled with musicians in his head, playing fifes, violins, bugles, and drums. "Play up, play up!" he constantly cries, "get up the steam, you black devils—play up." To R. S., invisibles come in the night and lift the corner of his bed and put animals underneath, and then screw him down through the back and head. But instances of this form of delusion might be multiplied indefinitely.

Religious mania is very prevalent among criminal lunatics. It is not easy to give any thoroughly satisfactory reason for this; but this fact is patent, that all prisoners are brought into closer and more continuous contact with religious matters than others of the same class who have kept always out of trouble. This is especially true of those sentenced to long terms of imprisonment. They hear the same expressions and witness the same ceremonies daily year after year. Good may —and undoubtedly does—at times result; but the inevitable consequence is that all are more or less saturated with the mere jargon of creeds, and can rattle off as glibly as you please all manner of formulas, scriptural names, expressions, texts, or tag-ends of hymns. Hence it is that any among them who are disposed to feign madness not unfrequently adopt this line; while it is not impossible that others—brooding continually over these awful subjects in the solitude of their cells, with but a limited library and no escape from, or variety for, their thoughts—may and do actually become mad on the subject of religion.

I will describe briefly some of the most interesting cases of religious mania.

A. F. had been a soldier, and spent three years in prison out of eight for various military crimes. He was afterwards sentenced to penal servitude for burglary. Signs of mental derangement soon became apparent. This man was always thirsty, and he would drink all the water he could lay hands upon. He said he drank water for the salvation of his soul. He does not know how soon he may be called upon to part from life. No one can hurt him: he has power over angels, and means to have all Government prisons destroyed. P. C. says there is something wrong between him and the church, and he would like to go out to make it all right. He has a mission to preach the gospel and salvation; and is always quoting scripture. He is persecuted, but he will bring out the church brighter than a rose. He has more power than the Bishop of Canterbury. Next he is king of Italy, but does not know yet whether he is to announce himself as such or turn priest. He has received a prerogative from Heaven to write what is revealed to him; has indeed supernatural power bestowed on him for the benefit of the human race. This man is a curious contradiction. In the midst of his sermons he is often violent and abusive; throws a spittoon at an officer's head, and calls him all the vile names he can recollect. Alternately he prays and uses the most frightful imprecations. In the middle of regular prayers in the ward, just as the scripture reader is about to commence, P. C. throws his boots into the middle of the room so that they make a great noise. "Why did I do it?" he replies when asked. "It answered for itself. Do you see that hook in the wall? What is it for? It answers for itself."

I. H. spends half the day on his knees at prayer, but the moment he gets up he challenges a man to fight. He says he is not half enough punished for the crimes he has committed. H. McK. in the same way is always praying. In the airing-yard he rushes off to a corner and remains there on his knees, beating himself on the breast and calling aloud on all the saints to save him. H. C. wishes to communicate his religious feelings to others: gives out prayers, and writes instructions for the other prisoners on every slate he can find, and when interfered with says he is only doing his

duty. Some of these religious lunatics are very quarrelsome.
They are always arguing, and the argument soon develops
into a fight. Most are gloomy, many supremely contemptuous,
as showing their great superiority over every one else. Others
continually use most blasphemous expressions, crying out,
" Eli! Eli!" and asserting they are the Supreme Being. One
man is sent as ambassador to the pope—is the pope's equal.
Another has been sent on earth to save sinners; a third has
the keys of the gates of hell; a fourth says his father studied
the Bible so much that it drove him mad.

A form of mania which is more often seen among criminal
lunatics than with others is the tendency to destructiveness.
There are some who, simply from irresistible impulse and quite
without motive, will destroy everything within reach, even to
their own manifest discomfort. One will break all the glass
in his cell windows. Another will tear up all his warm clothing
and body clothing specially issued to him. Even if fresh be
supplied, he will tear that too into ribbons. J. F. actually took
to tearing the nails off his toes, and when checked at this he
attacked his finger nails. This man would never allow a button
to remain on his jacket or waistcoat—tore them off as quickly
as they were sewn on. The only remedy for cases like this is
the use of a quilted canvas suit. W. M. when excited seemed
actually compelled to commit some damage, walking up
deliberately to the nearest chair, which he would smash to
atoms; doing the same with panes of glass, lamps, and
crockery; throwing tin plates, tables, everything he could
lay hands on, out of the window. T. J. violently resists all
attempts to cut his hair; then when it is done he destroys
his sheets and blankets, saying there is no more harm in that
than in their cutting his hair. This was on a par with another
who having torn up his clothes objected to be punished.
" Why should I be punished? Job wasn't when he rent his
clothes—I have Scripture proof of it: why should I?"

Suicidal mania is common enough among all lunatics, but
none go the length of criminal lunatics in refusing all food
and endeavouring to die by starvation.* The other attempts

* This must, however, be qualified a little. An eminent physician
mentions a patient who was so persistent that he had to be fed 8000

have nothing peculiar about them, and they are probably more easily checked so long as the lunatic remains in a prison, because prison officials are perhaps more keenly alive than ordinary asylum attendants to the necessity of strict searching to deprive dangerous men of anything that might possibly serve as a lethal weapon.

Feigned madness is naturally more likely to be seen among criminals than others. As a general rule ordinary people have little to gain by being considered mad; convicts, on the other hand, if they can succeed in imposing upon those in authority, are likely to obtain the benefit of release from severe labour, better diet, and a cheerful location at Broadmoor. Hence there are often cases of imposture sustained for periods almost beyond belief. With such men, only the lynx-eyed prison medical officer, backed by long experience, sooner or later detects the flaw. Unless, indeed, as has happened, the wretched impostor goes too far, and from pretending too much, lapses at length into real insanity. T. W. was an instance of this. He arrived at Millbank shrewd of intellect and in excellent health. But soon his conduct became so eccentric that he was taken to the infirmary "for observation." For months he kept up the deception. The doctors thought all the symptoms feigned, and yet such was the prisoner's pertinacity that they began to doubt. Through it all they maintained the closest watch, and under this the prisoner probably broke down. The extreme tension of his nervous system, persevered in night and day, was more than he could stand, so that finally he became undoubtedly mad, and was sent to a regular asylum. A similar case, so far as persistent imposture, was that of Richard Davis, who was tried at Maidstone, and sent to Millbank in 1854. This man acted the part so well that he was actually removed to Bethlehem Hospital, and thence to Fisherton Asylum. Sometimes he abstained from food and drink for as long as eight days together. However, he was returned to Millbank, and he

times with the stomach-pump. This is worse, I believe, than anything which has occurred in prison. The medical officer of Millbank informs me that he never knew any prisoner to refuse food for more than seven or eight days.

confessed that he had never been mad at all. "A good sound
flogging would have cured me," he admitted, frankly enough.
Between 1850–6 cases of feigned insanity and assumed
epileptic fits were extremely common in Millbank.

I have in the preceding pages touched upon the principal
groups into which criminal lunatics—as seen for only a
limited length of time—have generally grouped themselves.
My remarks have been based mostly on personal observation, and they are unsupported by any special professional
knowledge, therefore they must be taken simply for what they
are worth.

Over and above the several classes to which I have referred,
most of which amounted to distinct insanity, there are many
poor creatures among the criminals in prison, who are imbeciles
only, and no more. It is among these weak-minded men that
others more intelligent and more designing select their tools.
They get into prison, these imbeciles, really through no fault
of their own. They have been used as "cats' paws," and
they are only to be pitied. The blame of their misdeeds rests
more on their parents from whom they have inherited their
mental shortcomings, and, even in a greater degree, on the
vile tempters to whom these unsuspecting simpletons have
fallen an easy prey.

THE " FIRST FLEET."

CHAPTER XXI.

THE CONVICT SHIP.

No account of transportation beyond the seas would be complete without some reference to the passage out to the antipodes, which naturally was an integral part of the whole scheme. From first to last many hundreds of ships were employed on this service. Those that composed the "first fleet," under Captain Phillip, in 1788, head the list; last of all comes the steamer *London*, which went to Gibraltar in November, 1871. The *London* was the last prison ship that has left our shores. In the long interval between these dates, the conditions under which deportation was carried out have varied not a little. Abuses in the earliest days were many and flagrant. As time passed, came all that was possible in the way of reform, and those charged with the execution of

the system did their utmost to reduce the evils inseparable
from it. But even to the last they were hardly obviated
altogether; and this difficulty of carrying out under proper
restrictions the removal of convicts by sea-passage to a distant
land, is one—and by no means the weakest—of the many
arguments against transportation.

At the close of the last century, and during the early years
of this, when the whole system was still somewhat new and
untried, the arrangements were about as bad as it was possible
for them to be. I have already described* the horrors that
were perpetrated in one particular convoy: the neglect and
starvation, the sickness and the terrible mortality that ensued.
These shameful proceedings were due entirely to the rapacity
and dishonesty of the ship-captains, who sought to increase
their profits by improper means. But no sooner was their
misconduct brought to light, than any repetition of it was
prevented by the enforcement of certain new and salutary
regulations. The ships were no longer victualled by the contractors, but stores were put on board by the commissioners of
the navy, and certain checks and safeguards were introduced
to ensure the issue to every man of his proper allowance.
Nevertheless, the mortality continued at times to be dispro-
portionately large. Especially was this the case in the ships
General Hewitt, Surrey, and *Three Bees;* and, aroused thereby
to the necessity of further reform, Governor Macquarie instituted at Sydney, in 1814, a full inquiry into the conduct of
convict ships in general. Great alterations were recommended
by Dr. Redfern, at that time the assistant surgeon of the
colony. His suggestions embraced principally the points on
which he was specially competent to speak—the necessity,
that is to say, for the proper issue of clothing, for sufficient
diet and air space, with proper medical assistance if required.
Most of his recommendations were adopted, and they were all
amply justified by the diminished mortality in subsequent
voyages. Previous to this period the owners usually provided
a surgeon, who was paid by them, receiving only from Government, after the completion of his duty, a reward; but this
reward was dependent on the production by him of a certificate

* Chap. xiii., p. 251.

from the Governor of New South Wales, to the effect that the
latter was perfectly satisfied. The surgeon's letter of service
stated that, on the production of this certificate, he would be
recompensed for his "assiduity and humanity by a present at
the discretion of His Majesty's Secretary of State. On the
other hand, any neglect of essential duties will not fail to be
properly noticed."   Full instructions were issued for the
guidance of the surgeon.   He was to inspect the "people"—
this term seems to have been adopted from the earliest times
to describe the convict passengers—daily ; the sick twice a
day, those in health once. The former he was to treat according to his judgment ; the latter were to be examined closely for
signs of fever, flux, or scurvy, in order that "early and
effectual means may be taken to stop the progress of their
diseases." He was moreover to keep a diary for the entry of
everything connected with the sick, noting also the "daily
number of convicts admitted upon deck, the times when the
decks were scraped, the ship fumigated, the berths cleaned
and ventilated, and all other circumstances which may, immediately or remotely, affect the health of the crew or convicts."
How closely he performed his duties may be judged by the
fact that Mr. Commissioner Bigge advances* as one reason for
keeping the hospital in the fore part of the ship, that "any
arrangement by which the personal inspection of the surgeons
is frequently directed to the whole of the prison (which must
be the case if they have to traverse it on their visits to the
hospital), ought not to be exchanged for another, and more
commodious position of that apartment, unless the advantages
of such a change are clear and decisive."   This does not look
as if these surgeons were over zealous, at least in the duty of
frequently visiting and inspecting the prison decks.

Similarly, precise rules governed the conduct of the master
of the ship. He also was promised a reward if his conduct
gave satisfaction. He was especially desired to see to the
preservation of health, by keeping his ship constantly sweet
and clean, and by taking on board before departure all articles,
fumigating and others, necessary for the purpose.   The

* Mr. Bigge's Report on New South Wales, p. 6. Parliamentary
Reports, June, 1822.

master was especially charged with the care of provisions, and
in this respect his conduct was to be closely watched. The
fear was not so much lest the convicts should receive short
allowance, although this happened too, in spite of all precautions, but that there should be a substitution of inferior
stores for those of Government, which were always supposed to
be good of their kind. The former fraud was to some extent
guarded against, chiefly by publishing plainly, in several parts
of the prison, the scale of diet to which every convict was
entitled; but even this was sometimes upset by the captain
giving money compensation at the end of the voyage to
the convict for food not issued. Another precaution lay in
making every man of each convict " mess " attend in rotation
to receive the rations, instead of having one standing delegate
for the whole voyage as heretofore. It was found that
imposition and corruption were less frequently tried with
many than with few. As to the other kind of dishonesty,
it was provided for by requiring the surgeon's attendance at
the opening of each new cask of provision—a sufficient check,
no doubt, so long as the interests of captain and surgeon were
not identical. It was just possible, however, that they might
play into each other's hands.

But one of the wisest steps taken after 1814, was when
the Government itself appointed the medical officers, giving
the preference, as far as possible, to surgeons of the Royal
Navy. On this point Bigge says, "A great improvement has
undoubtedly arisen in the transportation of convicts from the
appointment of naval surgeons to the superintendence of the
ships taken up for this service. Much attention has been paid
by them to the instructions of the Navy Board, that enjoin an
attention to the performance of religious duties; and their
efforts in preserving health have been no less conspicuous and
successful. In promoting these it does not often happen
that they meet with direct opposition from the masters of
convict ships; but as there are points in their conduct,
respecting which no other individual than the surgeon can be
expected to hold a control or afford information, it is of no slight
importance to make the surgeons as independent as possible of
the favour of the master and the bounty of the owners."

There was every reason to expect that the Government would be better served by an officer of its own, than by some one taken indiscriminately from outside. But equally probable was it that there would be a conflict of authority between the master, who had been hitherto practically supreme, and the new style of official, who might be said to possess, to some extent, the confidence of the Crown. This came to pass; and the difficulty was not smoothed away by the tenor of the early acts regulating transportation. These had adopted the provisions of the 4 Geo. I., cap. 11, by which a property in the services of the convict was vested (or assigned) to the persons who contracted to transport them. The master of the ship, as representing the contractors, had this property with all its responsibilities; but he was bound also to obey all orders from the commissioners of the navy and attend all requisitions from the surgeon-superintendent. This apparent contradiction led to frequent altercations between these two modern Kings of Brentford. Where one looked only to the preservation of health, the other thought chiefly of safe custody. If the doctor wished to fumigate the prison, or send the "people" all on deck, the captain demurred, and talked of the danger he ran of losing his ship and his cargo, too, by one and the same blow. Being thus personally concerned in the security of all they had on board, the masters of convict ships for a long time maintained that they must be the fittest persons to hold the supreme power. On the other hand, many of the higher authorities leant towards entrusting the real command to the surgeon. This, which was clearly the proper plan, did in time become the rule. The reasons for it yearly became more apparent. In the first place, the naval surgeon, as a commissioned officer, was more under the control of the Crown; besides which, by degrees these surgeon-superintendents could fairly claim that they had gained experience, and had proved their aptitude for the service in which they were employed. As ship after ship was chartered the captains came and went. There was no certainty that the same vessel with the same master would be taken up twice over for the conveyance of convicts. But the surgeons remained, and sailed voyage after voyage to the penal colonies. Ere long, the power which had been at first contested rested altogether in their hands.

All trustworthy authorities give but a sorry account of the condition of the convicts during the passage. Even when everything that was possible had been done to reduce the death-rate, by ensuring a sufficient supply of food and proper medical attendance, the plain fact remained that here were a couple of hundred felons (or more) boxed up together for months, with no other employment or object in life than that of contaminating one another. As a rule the whole mass of the " people " remained idle throughout the voyage. A few might assist in the navigation of the ship so far as was possible without going aloft. Others who were mechanics found it to their interest to make themselves useful in their particular trades, gaining in return greater freedom as to coming up on deck, and perhaps some additional articles of food. " But the greater proportion of the convicts," says Bigge, " are sunk in indolence, to which the ordinary duties of washing and cleansing the prisons, though highly salutary in themselves and performed with great regularity, afford but slight interruption."

They spent their time in gambling, quarrelling, and thieving from one another. In these relaxations the crew generally joined, as it was impossible to prevent intercommunication between convicts and sailors. The latter were not always immaculate, and were not seldom charged with purloining the private property of the prisoners, which had been provided by friends when leaving England. The medium for gambling was chiefly the wine and lime juice issued as part of the daily rations. If the convicts had money—which was unusual, except in small quantities—then they played for cash, but this was prevented by taking all money from them, as far as possible, on embarkation, to be kept for them till the voyage was at an end. The other method of speculation was also checked to some extent by " strictly observing that the allowance of wine and lime juice is taken by every convict in the presence of an officer at the time of distribution." Another plan was to deprive the offenders of their allowance, but to compel them to attend at the " grog-tub," and administer that which they had thus forfeited to some other prisoner who had behaved well.

The only discipline enforced on board, was just so much as was necessary to ensure a moderate amount of repression. For this purpose the people were all for a time in irons; for the same reason, only certain fixed proportions of the whole number were allowed upon deck at one and the same time. As a final bulwark behind all, should an ultimate appeal to the strong arm be at any time needed, stood the military guard. Every ship carried a detachment of soldiers: recruits sometimes, going out as drafts to join their regiments in Australia; at others, part of a whole battalion, which embarked thus piecemeal, ship after ship, ending, according to one writer, with the commanding officer and the band. The guard, or the portion of it actually on duty, carried always loaded firearms; from it came sentries for ever on the watch, some at the doors of the prisons, others upon the poop. As a general rule, ships with poops were preferred for convict ships, because the soldiers stationed thereon were sufficiently elevated above the deck to be able to control the movements of the convicts at exercise, though altogether separated from them.

The dread of some outbreak among the "people" seems to have been an ever-present sensation with those in authority on board these ships. Nor was the alarm confined to those connected with the ship itself. Whenever a strange sail, in those days of profound peace, appeared above the horizon, she was set down always as a convict ship seized by its felon passengers, who were supposed to have turned pirates, and to have hoisted the black flag to range the high seas in search of plunder. I suppose there was not one among the hundred ships that left the Nore or the Mother Bank, through the long years that transportation lasted, in which rumours of conspiracy did not prevail at some time or other during the passage. Yet nine times out of ten these fears were absolutely groundless. Outbreaks did occur, of course; but few of them were serious in nature, and nearly all were forestalled by the timely perfidy of one of the conspirators. Colonel Breton, in his evidence before the Parliamentary Committee of 1837, said that he had heard of one ship with female convicts which had been captured by the crew and carried into Rio.* But I can find no corroboration of this statement elsewhere. The same authority talks vaguely of another plot in his own ship, which came to nothing, because another and a more desperate character turned informer.

More serious was the conspiracy which was discovered in a ship, of which Dr. Galloway, R.N., was the surgeon-superintendent. This was brought to light just after the ship had left Plymouth Sound—as a general rule all such attempts are made in the early part of the voyage—and it was discovered by a sentinel who overheard a fragment of a conversation by the hatchway during the morning watch. The plot was cleverly laid. The convicts had observed that the old guard discharged their firelocks always at sunrise, and that the new guard did not reload till eleven o'clock. They planned therefore to mutiny in the early morning, just after the guard had fired, resolving to seize these weapons, and then to overpower the captain, the rest of the soldiers, and the crew. The total strength of the military detachment was forty, and the convicts were two hundred and fifty. The plotters of this outbreak were promptly punished on proof of their guilt, twelve of them being obliged to carry double irons for seven or eight weeks.

In one of the earliest ships the opposing parties actually came to blows—so says Mr. Barrington,† at least, who went

---

* Convict ships with females on board were as a rule more easily managed than those with males. But the following extract from a letter from the matron on board the convict ship *Elizabeth and Henry*, in 1848, relates a curious incident :

"*Off Cape of Good Hope (April 30th).*—We were likely to have a mutiny on board a few weeks since. The prisoners laid a plan for strangling the doctor, but providentially it was made known by M. A. Stewart, a convict, just before it was executed. McNalty and Brennan were the ringleaders in the affair. When it was known, the officers of the ship went down in the prison with firearms. Fancy the scene! The doctor has now promised to forgive them if they conduct themselves well the rest of the voyage."

† The memoirs of this Barrington (a very different person to Sir Jonah Barrington) were widely successful, and soon ran through several editions. His career of crime was more than curious. His hunting-grounds were royal levées, court balls, Ranelagh, and the

as a convict in 1790 to Botany Bay. According to his account two Americans among the people persuaded the others to conspire to seize the ship. They declared that the capture effected, it would be easy to carry the prize into some American port, where all would receive a hearty welcome. Not only would all obtain their liberty as a matter of course, but Congress would give them also a tract of land, and a share of the money accruing from the sale of the ship and her cargo.

The plan of action was to seize the arm-chest while the officers were at dinner. This was kept upon the quarter-deck, under the charge of sentries. The latter were to be engaged in conversation till the supreme moment arrived, and then at a signal given, seized. This was to be followed by a general rush on deck of all the convicts from below. Barrington relates that he was standing with the man at the wheel when the mutiny actually broke out. Hearing a scuffle upon the main deck, he was on the point of going forward, when he was stopped by one of the Americans, who made a stroke at his head with a sword taken from a sentry. "Another snapped at me a pistol. I had a hand-spike, and felled the first to the ground." Meanwhile the man at the wheel ran down and gave the alarm. The captain was below, seeing to the stowage of some wine; but Barrington held the mutineers at bay, at the head of the companion ladder, till the captain came up with a blunderbuss in his hand and fired. This dispersed the enemy, and they thereupon retired. An immediate example was made of the ringleaders in this affair. Two were forthwith hanged at the yard-arm, and a number flogged. To Barrington, the captain and his officers were profuse in thanks, and at the end of the voyage they made him a substantial present. Told in Mr. Barrington's own words, the story of this mutiny tends rather to his own glorification. It is just possible that he may have exaggerated some of the details—his own valiant deeds with the rest.

opera-house. At the palace he found it easy in the crush to cut the diamonds out of orders and stars. At the opera he picked Prince Orloff's pocket of a snuff-box worth £30,000, but being collared by the owner he restored the booty. He was eventually transported for stealing a gold watch at Enfield races from Mr. H. H. Townshend.

But as a rule the efforts made by the convicts to rise against their rulers on shipboard were futile in the extreme. Even Mr. Commissioner Bigge, in 1822, laughs at all notion of the convicts combining to capture the ships. He is commenting on the different practice of different doctors and captains, as to allowing the people upon deck and removing their irons. Some, he says, who are inexperienced and timid dread the assemblage of even half on the upper deck, and they would not for worlds remove the irons till the voyage is half over. Others do not care if the whole body came up together, and they take off all irons before the ship is out of the Channel. But he considers the free access to the deck so important in preserving discipline, as well as health, during the voyage, that " no unwarrantable distrust of the convicts " ought to interfere with it, and " no apprehension of any combined attempt to obtain possession of the ship." He thus continues :

" The fear of combinations among the convicts to take the ship is proved by experience of later years to be groundless ; and it may be safely affirmed, that if the instructions of the Navy Board are carried into due effect by the surgeon-superintendent and the master, and if the convicts obtain the full allowance of provisions made to them by Government, as well as reasonable access to the deck, they possess neither fidelity to each other, nor courage sufficient to make any simultaneous effort that may not be disconcerted by timely information, and punished before an act of aggression is committed. A short acquaintance with the characters of the convicts, promises of recommendation to the governor on their arrival in New South Wales, and an ordinary degree of skill in the business of preventive police, will at all times afford means of obtaining information." *

The passage out of all these convict ships was upon the whole exceedingly prosperous. The voyage could be performed with perfect safety. Mr. Bigge says that up to his time no ships had arrived disabled; more than this, no disasters had occurred to any in Bass Straits, where serious mishaps so frequently happened. The chief and only difficulty really was the tendency to delay upon the road.

* Bigge's Report, p. 3. Parliamentary Reports, June, 1822.

There was a great temptation to both master and surgeon to
call at Rio. All sorts of excuses were made to compass
this—that the ship was running short of water, for instance,
or that the passengers absolutely required a change of diet.
Sugar was to be bought at Rio, and tobacco, and with a
freight of these the officials could make a profitable speculation on reaching Sydney. For the doctor the temptation
was especially strong, because he was for years allowed to
land his goods at New South Wales duty-free. But if the
superiors thus benefited themselves, it was at the cost of the
discipline of the convicts, such as it was. The ship was for
the time neglected utterly; the captain was busy and so was
the doctor with their commercial enterprises. The convicts
for security sake were relegated to irons; but means were
taken by them to obtain surreptitiously spirits from shore, and
wholesale intoxication and demoralisation naturally followed.
In view of all this the masters of convict ships were ordered
to make the run outwards direct. The requisite supplies
might be calculated with care in advance, so as to preclude
the chance of any scarcity before the end of the voyage. But
if it so happened that to touch at some port or other was
imperative, then the Cape of Good Hope was to be invariably
chosen instead of Rio.

These orders to bear up for the Cape in case of necessity
were clearly right and proper, but in one case they were
attended with very serious consequences. I allude to the
loss of the *Waterloo* convict ship in Table Bay, in the month
of September, 1842. In this case scurvy had appeared on
board, and therefore the surgeon-superintendent gave the
master a written order to change his course. It was necessary
to touch at the Cape to obtain supplies of vegetables and fresh
meat. To Table Bay they came in due course, and there
remained—ignorant, seemingly, of the danger they ran, of
which they would have been duly warned had the naval
authorities been aware of their arrival. But the surgeon-
superintendent failed to report it; and "in this omission,"
says Vice-Admiral Sir E. King when animadverting upon the
whole occurrence, "he has only followed the common and
very reprehensible neglect of duty in this respect of surgeon-

superintendents of convict ships." Ill-luck followed the
Waterloo. The master went on shore and left his ship to the
care of his chief mate, a young and inexperienced seaman,
who showed himself when the moment of emergency came
either utterly incompetent or culpably negligent—probably
both. One of those sudden gales which frequently ravage
Table Bay rose without warning, and the *Waterloo* went
straight on the rocks. Nothing was done to save her. The
masts were not cut away, and everybody on board seemed
helpless. Another ship, the transport *Abercrombie Robinson*,
which was lying in Table Bay at the time, was also driven
ashore; but her people were rescued, and she did not become
an entire wreck. But the moment the *Waterloo* struck she
broke up, and went to pieces. Terrible loss of life followed:
188 out of a total of 302 on board were drowned, and but for
the merest chance not a soul among the convict passengers
would have reached the land alive. The prisoners had been at
first set free, but they were then ordered below again by the
surgeon-superintendent, who feared they would rush violently
into the surf boats coming to the rescue, and so swamp them.
The poor creatures went below obediently enough, and then
followed one of those fatal but inexplicable mistakes which might
have led to the most terrible consequences. The doctor as a
matter of precaution had ordered the prisons to be bolted down,
but the bolts in the hatches could have been easily at any
moment withdrawn. However, the officious corporal in command
of the military guard *proprio motu* affixed a padlock to the bolt
to make it secure, and quite forgot to take it off again. The
excuse made for him was that he was " under the influence of
the panic incident to the unexpected and almost instantaneous
demolition of the ship." Thus several hundred men were in
momentary danger of being drowned like rats in a hole.
" Most providentially," says the report from which I quote,
" the awful consequences of the unaccountable conduct of the
corporal were averted by one of the prisoners striking off the
padlock with a hammer that had accidentally been left in the
prison early that morning, it having been used to remove the
irons from the only prisoners who wore them for some offence."
So the convicts reached the deck in time to avail themselves

of such means of escape as offered. But these were few.
Had the masts been cut down, when the long boat was lowered,
they might have formed a temporary bridge over which the
people might have passed in comparative safety to the surf boats.
As it was, nearly two-thirds of them were drowned.

This catastrophe attracted great attention at the time. At
Cape Town the sudden and apparently unaccountable destruction of the ship led to great excitement in the public mind. A
very searching inquiry was therefore set on foot. The *débris* of
the wreck having been carefully examined by Captain Sir John
Marshall, R.N., he reported unhesitatingly that the *Waterloo*
must have been unseaworthy when she left England. "General
decay and rottenness of the timbers appeared in every step
we took." She had been repeatedly repaired at considerable
outlay, but she had run so long that she was quite beyond cure.

As a further explanation of the disaster the mate and crew
were charged with being drunk at the time the ship struck.
But the only evidence in support of this was an intercepted
letter of one of the convicts who had been saved. He asserted
that the chief mate could not keep his legs; that in trying to
drive in a nail he staggered and fell. The rolling of the vessel
was deemed a more than sufficient explanation of this.
Another charge was made against one of the seamen who
swam back to the ship after he had once actually reached the
shore. No man in his sober senses, urged the convict witness,
would have risked his life in this way; whereas it was clearly
proved that no man otherwise than sober could possibly have
battled successfully with the surf.

It is but fair to add that the unseaworthy condition of the
Waterloo was distinctly denied at Lloyd's. They certified
that at the time of sailing she was "in an efficient state of
repair and equipment, and fully competent for the safe performance of any voyage to any part of the world." And as
the credit of the transport office had been more or less impugned, a return was about this time called for by the House,
of the number of convict-ships which had foundered at sea, or
not been heard of, between 1816 and 1842. It was satisfactorily
shown that in this way not one single ship had been lost
through all those years.

But there had been other shipwrecks, and among these none with more fatal results than that of the *Amphitrite*, which went ashore at Boulogne, in September, 1833. The story of this mishap is an instructive homily in more ways than one. The ship was proceeding gaily down channel, with a freight of one hundred and eight female convicts, when she was met by a violent and unexpected gale, accompanied by a very heavy sea. She was on a lee shore. The conduct of the master in presence of danger is described as seamanlike, judicious, and decisive. Seeing no help for it, and that he could not save his vessel from the land, he said openly to the mate that he must look for the best berth and run her straight on shore. They ran her up as high as possible, hoping the tide as it rose would drive her higher. Then with as much complacency as if they were safely lodged in a secure harbour, the crew went below, had supper and turned in. Before daybreak the ship was smashed to atoms, and only three lives were saved. The ship's fate was indeed sealed from the moment she went ashore. Nothing possibly could have saved her, and it was a matter of surprise to all who witnessed the catastrophe that she was not deserted while there was yet time. "All might have been saved, but for the deplorable error in judgment on the part of the crew."

More than this, the lives at least of the female convicts might have been preserved but for the strange obstinacy of the surgeon's wife. According to the evidence of one of the survivors, the doctor ordered the long boat to be lowered soon after the ship struck. He was not in the least afraid of losing his prisoners, and meant to put them all forthwith on shore. Here, however, his wife interposed. She would not go ashore in the boat. Nothing would induce her to sit in the same boat with the convicts. "Her pride," says the narrator, "revolted at the idea." Whether her husband expostulated does not appear; but in the end he gave way. No boat should leave the ship that night. Next morning it was too late. Complete destruction, as I have said, followed the rising of the tide.

But I fear I have lingered too long over these early days. Let us return now to Millbank.

It was not till the time of Captain Groves that the prison
was first brought into close and almost daily connection with
the "bay ships," as they were commonly called.   While
Mr. Nihil was governor, batches of transports awaiting passage were occasionally lodged in the Penitentiary, and plenty
of trouble they gave.* But after the new *régime* was introduced
by the Act of 1843, embarkation of drafts for Australia took
place every week or two from the stone steps on the river
bank, opposite the main entrance of the prison.   The dawn is
just breaking as they file silently across the deserted roadway,
and down unto the tug that is to convey them to the Nore.
Only the night previous were they made aware that the hour
of their departure had arrived.   Then had followed such
necessary preparations as a close medical inspection, to guard
against the propagation of infectious disease; shaving, bathing, and the issue of the necessary clothing and kit bags.
Every convict was furnished with a new suit, which was to
last him all the voyage; but they carried a second suit in
their bags, with underclothing, and, in some cases, an outfit
to serve on landing at their journey's end.   Substantial shoes,
and gray guernsey night-caps completed their attire.

Next morning the whole of the draft were roused out about
three o'clock, when they breakfasted.   They were then marched
to the reception ward, where their names were called over by
the chief warder.   Next came the "shackling," or chaining
them together in gangs of ten men upon one chain, which
chain passed through a bracelet on each man's arm.   The
same plan is pursued to this day in ordinary removals from
prison to prison, except that a D lock is now introduced
between every two prisoners.   This practically handcuffs the
men together two and two.   Under the old system, if one
link in the chain was cut, the whole ten were free ; now, when
a link goes five *couples* only are set loose.   .As soon as these
precautions were completed, the side door of the reception
ward was opened, and the prisoners passed on to the outer
gate, and so to the river side.

If the embarkation was to be at low tide, old Collins, a
well-known bargee, who had permission to make his boats fast

* Chap. xi.

opposite the Millbank steps, had brought them some hours before and run them aground, so as to form a passage or gangway to the steam-tug. This Collins was a well-known character in his time. His spare hours were devoted to gathering up the bodies of people drowned in the Thames. It was said that he had secured in this way no fewer than two hundred corpses. The parish authorities paid him at the rate of ten shillings per head. It was his invariable custom, so he assured the coroner, to wash the face of every corpse he picked up and kiss it. But he did other jobs, such as dredging for sand, which he sold to the builders, and anything else that he might pick up. It was all fish that came to his net. On one occasion he found a bag full of sovereigns, upon which, so the story runs, both he and his family lived gloriously till the money was all gone. This piece of ·luck proved fatal to his wife. Returning from one of her drinking bouts to her home on board a barge—for Collins occupied the oldest of his boats, roofed in—Mrs. Collins slipped off the plank into the Thames, and was picked up by her husband next day. He had lived all his life in this barge, rearing there a large family, most of whom, I believe, turned out ill. His daughters were, however, known as the best oarswomen on the river. Poor old Collins himself came to a bad end. He was caught in his old age, in the act of stealing coals from a neighbouring barge, and for this he was sentenced to six months' imprisonment. When he came out the barges were sold, and the place knew him no more.

But for many years he actively assisted in all embarkations from Millbank stairs. Of course there was a large staff of officials who were really responsible. In charge of all generally went the deputy-governor, and under him were sometimes as many as thirty warders. Their duties were principally to ensure safe custody, and to enforce silence and soberness of demeanour on the passage down stream. Occasionally the tug halted at Woolwich, to take in more passengers from the hulks; more often it made the run direct to Gravesend or the Nore. Here, with blue peter flying and anchor atrip, was the prison ship waiting for its living cargo. The surgeon-superintendent is on board, ready to sign receipts for the bodies of

all committed to his charge; the convicts go up the sides, are
unshackled, told off to messes, and sent below. Before midday the ship has got under weigh, and has taken her place
among the rest of the outward bound.

The interior fittings of all the old convict ships varied little.
The "prison" occupied the main deck. It was separated
forward and aft by strong bulkheads, sheeted with iron. In
the forepart the crew were lodged as usual; aft, the military
guard. The only access from the prison to the deck was by
the main hatchway. This was enclosed by barred gates at
the foot of the ladder, so that the prison within looked like
a huge cage. A substantial bulkhead ran across the upper
deck, so as to divide off the part used by the prisoners from
the poop. There were doors in this, at each of which a sentry
was always stationed. The hatches were also provided with
stout padlocks. Down below the prison was parted off into
"bunks" or "bays," as in a troop-ship, each of which had
a table for eight men, and at night eight hammocks. For
a long time prison ships sailed always without any special
staff for supervision. Later a small proportion of warders
embarked in each. During the day these officers took it in
turn to patrol the deck and keep a general look-out. But on
the whole, they preferred to interfere as little as possible with
the "people." At night five convict sentries kept watch on
deck, and were held responsible that no others came up; but
below, the whole of the prisoners were left always entirely to
themselves. This, of itself, was one of the chief blots in the
whole plan of deportation. To permit men of this class to
herd together just as they please, is the surest method to
encourage the spread of wickedness and vice. There may be
some who are good, but these are certain to go to the wall.
The tendency of any collection of human beings, it is to be
feared, is rather to sink to the level of the worst than to rise
to that of the best. In a ship-load of convicts, free to talk
and associate at all hours of the day and night, the deterioration is almost inevitable. For this reason, the elaborate
machinery for providing for the religious wants and teaching
of the ships sent out in later years was rendered nearly useless.
A slight veneer of propriety in diction and demeanour might

lie on top, but beneath the real stuff was as bad as ever.
This could not be denied even in after years, when every
possible precaution had been taken.* It was admitted
before the parliamentary commission on transportation in
1861, that "the horrors of convict ships were really past
description."

I cannot refrain, however, from paying a tribute here to
one who appears to have worked wonders in the various ships
he had in charge. I allude to Dr. Browning, who has himself
given us an interesting account of his labours, and the success
that attended them.† He was clearly a man of great piety,
gifted also with singular earnestness of character. The
influence of such a person cannot fail to be soon felt, especially
in a society of which he is himself the recognised head.
Wonderful as were the results obtained by Dr. Browning, they
are substantiated by the testimony of high colonial officials.
Writing on the subject, Sir George Arthur, the Lieutenant-
Governor of Van Diemen's Land, says, "The convicts brought
out in the *Arab*, in 1834, were put on board, I have every
reason to believe, as ignorant, as profane, and in every respect
as reckless as transported criminals usually are. But when
they were disembarked, it was evident the character of many
of them had undergone a most remarkable change. Their
tempers had been subdued : they had been induced to think
and reflect ; and they had been instructed, so as to know them
familiarly, in the principles of religion." It was said that in
after years the convicts whom Dr. Browning reformed, seldom
if ever fell away; but on this point I can find no reliable
evidence. That quoted above refers only to these men at the

---

* The arrangements for the conveyance of convicts by sea were never
really put on a satisfactory footing until 1870, when the steamship
London was especially fitted up for the purpose of taking convicts to
Gibraltar ; a portion of her fore hold being turned into a "prison,"
in every respect the same as a separate prison on shore. Here officers
patrolled on duty day and night. This, with the rapidity of the voyage,
reduced the chances of contamination to the lowest.

† The Convict Ship and England's Exiles. By C. A. Browning, M.D.,
R.N.

moment they landed on shore, when Dr. Browning's impressive periods were still ringing in their ears. An examination of the parliamentary returns, however, leads me to conclude that instances of after misconduct, as proved by the number of summary and other convictions on shore, were just as plentiful among the men of Dr. Browning's ships as in others.

But I should be loath to detract from Dr. Browning, who, besides a preacher of some power, was also a practical man with considerable talent for organisation. His ships must have been patterns of propriety and cleanliness. Yet he worked single-handed. The only officials under him were convicts chosen among the "people," according to character received with them, and "the impression," to use his own words, "formed on my own mind by the expression of their countenances, and general demeanour." At the doctor's right hand was the first captain, who was at the head of the whole establishment; next to him came a second captain; and below them the captains of divisions. Each had his duties prescribed according to a carefully prepared scale. There were also appointed cooks, barber, delegates, head of messes, a clerk, librarian, hospital steward, and, last not least, schoolmasters and inspectors of schools. The routine of work for every day of the week was also laid down, and was punctually carried out. As a rule, after the necessary cleaning operations, this resolved itself almost entirely into school instruction, and constant exhortation from the surgeon himself. Dr. Browning was apparently much beloved even by those criminals; and his orders are said to have been readily and implicitly obeyed. In return his confidence in them was so great that when he was attacked with serious illness he had his hammock hung inside on the prison deck, and gave himself up to be nursed altogether by the convicts.

In after years the example set by Dr. Browning was so far followed that every ship carried a religious instructor to teach, and perform the services—duties which every surgeon-superintendent could not be expected to perform, as did Dr. Browning. These instructors were selected from among the scripture readers and schoolmasters at Millbank or Pentonville, and no doubt they were conscientious men, fairly anxious to do their best. But this best fell far short of that which an enthusiast of superior education like Dr. Browning could accomplish; and in most of the ships, in spite of all the efforts of the instructors, wickedness continued to the last to reign supreme.

OUTER LODGE AT MILLBANK.

CHAPTER XXII.

THE CRASH OF "PROBATION."

WITHIN three years of the establishment of the new system, already described at length, by which transportation was to be robbed of all its evils, the most deplorable results showed themselves. The condition of Van Diemen's Land, according to a reliable authority, was most lamentable. It was filled to overflowing with convicts. There were in all 25,000, half of which were still in the hands of Government; and besides these numbers there were 3000 pass-holders waiting for hire, but unable to obtain employment. The latter would be reinforced by as many more in the year immediately following. The colony itself was on the verge of bankruptcy; its finances embarrassed, its trades and industries in every branch depressed; with all this was a wholesale exodus of all classes of free people—the better orders, to avoid the ruin that stared them in the face, and working men, because higher wages were offered elsewhere in the neighbouring colonies. Already, in fact, the new system of probation had broken down. It had given rise to evils greater than any which it had been expected to replace. Not only was Van Diemen's Land itself on the brink of ruin, but the consequences to the convicts were almost too terrible to be described. Mr. Pitcairn, a resident of Hobart Town, raised an indignant protest, in which he urges that "all that the free colonists suffer, even the total destruction of Van Diemen's Land as a free colony, is as nothing to what the wretched convicts are forced to submit to. It is not bodily suffering that I refer to: it is the pollution of their minds and hearts which is forced upon them, which they cannot escape from. Loathsome as are the details of their miserable state, it is impossible to see thousands of men debased and depraved without at least making an attempt to save others from the same fate." The congregation of criminals in large batches without due supervision, meant simply whole-sale, widespread pollution. Assignment, with all its faults, had at least the merit of dispersing the prisoners over a wide area.

But not only in its debasing effects upon the convicts themselves was the system quite a failure—half the scheme became a dead letter from the impoverished condition of the colony. Of what avail was it to prepare the prisoners gradually for honest labour when there was no labour upon which they could be employed? The whole gist and essence of the scheme was that after years of restraint the criminal, purged of his evil propensities, would gladly lend himself out for hire. But what if there were no hirers? Yet this was practically the state of the case. Following inevitably from the unnatural over-crowding of Van Diemen's Land, there came a great redundancy in the labour market. Had the colony been thoroughly prosperous, and as big as the neighbouring island-continent, it could hardly have found employment for the thousands of convicts poured in year by year. But being quite the reverse—small and almost stag-nant—a species of deadlock was the certain result of this tremendous influx. To make matters worse, goaded doubtless by the excessive costliness of the whole scheme, the Imperial Government insisted that all hirers should pay a tax over and above the regular wages for every convict engaged, and this whether the hirer was a private person or the public works department of the colony. Neither private nor public funds could stand this charge. In the general distress, employers of labour could hardly afford the moderate wages asked; while the local revenues were equally impecunious. Yet there were many works urgently needed in the colony, which the Colonial Government were quite disposed to execute—provided they got their labour for nothing. But to pay for it was impossible. In fact, this Imperial penuriousness defeated its own object. The Home Government would not let out its labour except at a price which no one would pay; so the thousands who might at least have stood at their own charges, remained at that of the Government. They were put to raise produce for their own support; but they earned nothing, and ate their heads off into the bargain. They had, moreover, a grievance. They were denied all fruition in the status to which, by their own conduct and according to prescribed rules, they arrived. They had been promised that after a certain probationary period they would pass into a stage of semi-freedom. Yet here, after all, were they in a condition little superior to the convicts in the gangs—in the very stage, that is to say, which the pass-holders had left behind them. The authorities had, in fact, broken faith with them. This was a fatal flaw in the scheme; a link out in the chain; a gap in the sequence of progressive probation enough to bring the whole to ruin.

But at any rate the pass-holders were better off than the conditional-pardon or ticket-of-leave men. The former had still a lien on the Government. They were certain of food, and a roof over their heads at the various hiring depôts. But those who were in a stage further ahead towards freedom were upon their own resources. These men were "thrown upon the world with nothing but their labour to support them." But no labour was in demand. What, then, was to become of them? They must steal, or starve; and as the

outcome of either alternative, the community might expect
to be weighted with a large and increasing population of
thieves and paupers.

Nor would any description of the main island only suffice
to place in a proper light the actual state of affairs. Norfolk
Island, the chief penal settlement, had deteriorated so rapidly,
that all which was bad before, had grown to be infinitely
and irremediably worse. A Mr. Naylor, a clergyman, writing
about this time, paints a terrible picture of the island.
Rules were utterly disregarded; convicts of every degree
mingled indiscriminately on the settlement. Some of the
prisoners had been convicted, and reconvicted, and had passed
through every grade of punishment in hulks, chain-gangs, or
penal settlements—among them were " flash men," who kept
the island in awe, and bearded the commandant himself;
bodies of from 70 to 100 often in open mutiny, refusing to
work, and submitting only when terms had been arranged to
their satisfaction; the island kept in perpetual alarm; houses
robbed in open day, yet no successful efforts were made to
bring the culprits to justice.* By one of these ruffians the
commandant was deliberately knocked down, and received
severe contusions. The state of the island might well awaken
alarm. No time, said Mr. Naylor, should be lost in taking
steps for the prevention of a catastrophe of the most frightful
kind.

In 1846 a special commissioner was despatched from head-
quarters at Hobart Town, to report from personal observation
on the state of the settlement. It is abundantly evident from
his report, which will be found *in extenso* in a Blue Book on
convict discipline, issued in February, 1847, that some terrific
explosion of the seething elements collected together at Norfolk
Island might be looked for at any early day. Mr. Stewart,
the commissioner, attributed the condition of the settlement

---

* As to the immunity of offenders, one of the officials long resident
on the island has told me that a favourite parrot with its cage was
stolen from his house. The thief was known, and he was seen with the
bird. More; he kept the bird in his barrack-room, and took it daily
with him to his work. Yet no one dared to interfere with him ! The
bird was left in his possession, and he altogether escaped punishment.

chiefly to the lax discipline maintained by its commandant.
This gentleman certainly appears to have been chosen un-
wisely. He was quite the wrong man for the place, utterly
unfitted for the arduous duties he was called upon to perform.
Of a weak and vacillating disposition, he seldom had the
courage to act upon his own judgment. It was openly alleged
that his decisions rested with his chief clerk. Most of his
subordinates were at loggerheads with one another, but he
never dared to settle their quarrels himself. Points the most
trivial were referred always to head-quarters. He was equally
wanting in resolute determination in dealing with the great
mass of convicts who constituted the bulk of his command.
With them he was for ever temporising and making allow-
ances ; so that rules, never too severe, came by degrees to be
sensibly relaxed, till leniency grew into culpable pampering
and childish considerateness. As might have been expected,
the objects of his tender solicitude were utterly ungrateful.
He interfered sometimes to soften the sentences of the sitting
magistrate, even when they were light enough ; but his kindness was only mistaken for weakness, and the men in his
charge became day by day more insolent and insubordinate.
Where firmness was required in almost every particular, in
order to maintain anything like a controlling supervision, it
was altogether wanting. This commandant was considered by
his supreme chief, "either from want of experience, or from
an absence in his own character of the qualifications necessary
to control criminals," to be "totally unfitted for the peculiar
situation in which he is placed."

Of a truth, Norfolk Island was not a government to be
entrusted to any but iron hands. That this commandant
was clearly the wrong man for the post cannot be questioned ; nevertheless, he was not altogether to blame for the
existing terrible state of affairs. No doubt by his wavering
incompetence the original condition of the island was greatly
aggravated, but all these evils which by-and-by broke out and
bore such noxious fruit, had been germinating long before
his time. It had been the custom for years back to treat the
convicts with ill-advised leniency. They had been allowed
practically too much indulgence, and were permitted to forget

that they owed their location on that island solely to their own grievous crimes and offences. They had been kept in order by concession, and not by stern force; persuaded to be good, rather than coerced when bad. As I have already had occasion to remark, such a method of procedure can but have one result with criminals. It is viewed by them as weakness of which they are bound to take every advantage. Here, at Norfolk Island, under a loose *régime*, the convicts had always been allowed their own way: half the officers placed over them trafficked with them, and were their free-and-easy familiar friends. On the introduction of the new system, no attempt was made to sweep the place clean before the arrival of greatly increased numbers. Old officers remained, and old convicts; enough of both to perpetuate the old evil ways, and to render them twice as harmful under the new aspect of the settlement. Gardens were still allowed; great freedom to come and go hither and thither, with no strict observance of bounds; any number of private shops, whereat the convicts bought and sold, or bartered with each other for pork and vegetables and other articles of general use. Worse than this, the " Ring " was left untouched, and grew daily more and more powerful, till a band of some forty or fifty cut-throat scoundrels ruled the whole convictdom of the settlement. The members of this " Ring " were in league with the cooks, from whom they obtained the best of food, abstracted from their fellow-prisoners' rations; but no one dared to complain. Such was the malignant terrorism inspired by these fifty ruffians, that they kept the whole body of the convicts in awe, and their wholesale plunderings and pilferings were in practice long before any attempt was made to put them down. Under such conditions as these, the management of the convicts in Norfolk Island certainly left much to be desired.

But following Mr. Stewart's visit, a more stringent system was attempted, if not entirely carried out. The commandant was informed that he must pamper his convicts no longer. One by one the highly prized privileges disappeared: trafficking was now for the first time openly discountenanced, and the prisoners at length saw themselves debarred from many little luxuries and indulgences. A strictly coercive labour-gang

THE CRASH OF "PROBATION." 417

was established; the gardens were shut; the limits of bounds rigorously enforced; and, last but not least, a firm attack was made upon the method of messing, to check, if possible, the unlawful misappropriation of food. In this measure was the beginning of serious trouble. It interfered directly with the vested interest of a small but powerful oligarchy, the members of which were not disposed to surrender lightly the rights they had so long arrogated to themselves. From the moment that the robberies in the cook-house had been discovered, a growing spirit of dissatisfaction and discontent was observable among the more influential prisoners.

A second authorised attack in the same direction brought matters to a crisis. Not the least of the evils attending the old plan of messing was, that the prisoners themselves, one by one, were allowed access to the kitchen, where they might cook anything they happened to have in possession, whether obtained by fair means or foul. To meet these culinary requirements, most of the "flash men" had collected pots and pans of various sorts, constructed chiefly from the regulation mess-tins and platters. It was decided as a bold stroke against illicit cookery, to seize every *batterie de cuisine* in the place. Accordingly, one evening, after the convicts had been locked up for the night, a careful search was made through the lumber-yard (the mess-room, so to speak), and everything of illegal shape was seized. The whole of these articles were then and there removed to the convicts' barrack store. It must be remarked here that several of the officials shrunk from executing this duty. One free overseer, named Smith, who was also superintendent of the cook-house, urged that he was all day among the prisoners, and felt his life hardly safe if it were known that he had taken part in the search. Others demurred also; but eventually the work was done.

Next morning, when the convicts went to breakfast, they missed their highly prized kitchen utensils. Quickly a storm gathered, and broke forth with ungovernable fury. A great mass of men, numbering several hundreds, streamed at once out of the lumber-yard, and hurried towards the barrack stores. Everything fell before them: fastenings, woodwork, doorposts. There within were the cans, the cause of all this coil. These they gathered up at once, and then turned back, still *en masse*, to the lumber-yard. They were in search now of victims. Their thirst was for blood, and nothing less would quench it. They sought first the officers they hated most; and chief among these was Smith, the overseer of the kitchen. A man named Westwood, commonly called Jacky-Jacky,* was ringleader, and marched at the head of the mutineers. All were armed—some with long poles, others with axes, most with knives. It was a case of *sauve qui peut* with the officers. There were not more than half-a-dozen constables on duty, and warning came to four of them too late. Smith, who had remained in the cook-house, was caught and murdered on the spot. Another officer, Morris, was also killed. Two others were struck down with mortal hurts. All the wounds inflicted were about the head and face. One man had his forehead cut open so that you might see into the cavity of the head. He had also a frightful gash from the eye down the cheek, through which the roof of the mouth was visible. Another had the whole of one side of his face completely smashed in, from the temple to the mouth. A third unfortunate man had his skull fractured. All this had happened in less time than it takes to tell. Then the mutineers cried out for more blood. Leaving the lumber-yard, they made for the police huts, driving the few remaining constables before them, and striking down all they overtook. At the police huts they smashed the windows and did what damage they could. They were then for proceeding onward. "Let's get that villain Barrow," was now the cry—Mr. Barrow being the stipendiary magistrate, and they hated him with especially keen hatred. They were determined, so it was afterwards said, to murder every official on the island, and then to take to the bush. But by this time active opposition was close at hand. First came a military guard, which formed across the road, and checked all further advance of the mutineers. Presently Mr. Barrow himself appeared upon the scene with a larger detachment of troops, and in the presence of this exhibition of force the convicts retired quietly enough to their barracks.

The strength of the storm therefore was now spent. The

---

* Jacky-Jacky was by birth a gentleman, and had received a superior education.

mutineers were either for the moment satisfied with their efforts, or—which is more probable—they were cowed by the troops, and felt that it was now the turn for authority to play its hand. Accompanied by a strong escort of soldiers, the stipendiary magistrate went in amongst the convicts, examined all carefully, and then and there arrested every one who bore a single spot or stain of blood. Seven were thus singled out at once, among them Jacky-Jacky and several members of the ring. Forty-five others, who were strongly suspected of complicity in the murders, were also arrested; and the whole, heavily ironed, were for immediate security chained together in a row to the iron runners of the boat-shed. But such was the alarm on the island, that the commandant was strenuously urged to remove these ringleaders at once to Van Diemen's Land.

Indeed it was felt on all sides that there was no longer any safety for either life or property. The convict population had reached the pitch of anarchy and insubordination. It was indeed thought that the storm would soon break out with renewed fury. The success which the mutineers had won, would doubtless tempt them to fresh efforts. They gave signs too that they were ready to recommence. When the corpses of the murdered men were carried past the barracks the convicts within yelled in derision, and cried that these victims should not be the last. The apprehension was so great that some officials maintained that the convicts ought to remain immured in their barracks until a reinforcement of troops arrived. There were some, too, who doubted the loyalty of the soldiers, saying that the troops would yet make common cause with the convicts. But this was never proved. What was really evident, was that the soldiers were harassed and overworn by the incessant duties they had been called upon recently to perform. They had been continually under arms, and were often on guard six nights out of the seven. Fortunately Sir Eardly Wilmot, Governor of Van Diemen's Land, had acted on Mr. Stewart's representations, and had despatched reinforcements long before this, which landed on the island a day or two after the actual outbreak. The most serious dangers were therefore at an end.

But the state of Norfolk Island called for some radical

reformatory measures. If anything further had been needed
to prove the incompetence of the commandant, it was to be
found in his latest proceedings. Sudden changes, passing
from laxity to strictness, had been made in the regulations ;
yet no precautionary measures were taken to meet that violent
resistance which the convicts had long openly threatened.
The last act of authority, the removal of the cooking utensils,
should at least have been backed by an imposing exhibition of
armed force. It was, indeed, time to substitute new men and
new measures. The Hobart Town executive council resolved
unanimously to suspend the commandant and to replace him
by Mr. Price, the police magistrate of Hobart Town, a gentleman of " knowledge, firmness, and long experience with the
convict population in this island." His instructions were
precise. He was to disarm the convicts and take from them
the knives they habitually carried ; to make all wear, without
distinction, the convict dress; to compel close observance to
Divine Service ; to institute messes, regulate the muster,
insist upon exact obedience to all rules, and above all, to
attend the due separation of the convicts at night. By close
attention to these regulations it was hoped that peace and
good order would soon be restored to the settlement.

At the same time condign punishment was meted out to
the mutineers. A judge went down post-haste to the island,
a court was formed immediately on his arrival, trials proceeded with, and fourteen were hanged the same day. This
salutary example, with the measures promptly introduced by
Mr. Price, soon restored order to the island. The new commandant was undoubtedly a man of great courage and decision
of character. He acted always for himself, and looked into
everything with his own eyes. Being perpetually on the
move about the settlement, nothing escaped him. Frequently
when he met convicts, though he might have with him only
one constable as orderly, he would halt them, and search them
from head to foot. If they had knives or other forbidden
articles, he impounded them forthwith ; saying as often as
not, " I'll have you to understand, my men, that in twelve
months you shall see a gold watch upon the road and yet not
pick it up." Under his able government the evils of Norfolk

Island were sensibly lessened; but nothing could wash the place clean. So convinced was the Imperial Government of this, that they had resolved, even before the news of the mutiny, to break up the settlement. But after that, positive instructions were sent out to carry this into effect, and by degrees the place was altogether abandoned.

Indeed, the results of "probation," as they had shown themselves, were far from ignored at home, and the members of successive administrations had sought anxiously to provide some remedy for evils so plainly apparent. Mr. Gladstone among others, when Under-Secretary of State for the Colonies, propounded an elaborate scheme for the establishment of a new settlement in North Australia. This new colony was to provide an outlet for the overplus in labour, which at that time in Van Diemen's Land choked up every avenue to employment. "It was founded"—I will use Mr. Gladstone's own words—"as a receptacle for convicts who, by pardon or lapse of time, have regained their freedom, but who may be unable to find elsewhere an effective demand for their services." It was to be a colony of emancipists. The earliest settlers would be exiles sent out from England, with whose assistance the governor of the new colony was to prepare for the arrival of the rest from Van Diemen's Land. The first points which would require attention, were the selection of the best sites for a town and harbour, the reservation of certain Crown lands, and the distribution of the rest to the various sorts of settlers. All these points were fully discussed and provided for minutely by Mr. Gladstone. Every other detail was equally well arranged. As economy was to be the soul of the new settlement, its officials were to rank lower than those of other colonies. The governor was to be styled only superintendent, and the judge, chairman of quarter sessions. The whole settlement was to be subordinate to New South Wales. And, as the word "convict" was somewhat unsavoury to the Australian colonists, Mr. Gladstone provided also for this. In anticipation of the possible objections of the people of New South Wales to the establishment of a new convict settlement on the continent of Australia, Mr. Gladstone put his foot down firmly, and declared he would admit no such protest. "It would be with sincere regret," he says, "that I should learn that so important a body of Her Majesty's subjects were inclined to oppose themselves to the measures I have thus attempted to explain. Any such opposition must be encountered by reminding those from whom it might proceed, in terms alike respectful and decided, that it is impossible that Her Majesty should be advised to surrender what appears to be one of the vital interests of the British Empire at large, and one of the chief benefits which the British Empire can at present derive from the dominion which we have acquired over the vast territories of the Crown in Australia. I think that by maintaining such a colony as a depôt of labour, available to meet the local wants of the older colony, or to find employment for the capital accumulated there, we may rather promote than impede the development of the resources of New South Wales. But even if that hope should be disappointed, I should not, therefore, be able to admit that the United Kingdom was making an unjust or unreasonable exercise of the right of sovereignty over those vast regions of the earth, in thus devoting a part of them to the relief of Van Diemen's Land, and consequently to render that island the receptacle for as many convicts as it may be hereafter necessary to transport there. Having practically relieved New South Wales, at no small inconvenience to ourselves, from the burden (as soon as it became a burden) of receiving convicts from this country, we are acquitted of any obligations in that respect which any colonist, the most jealous for the interests of his native or adopted country, could ascribe to us."

But it never came to this. No antagonism in this instance ever arose between the Colonial and Imperial Governments, for Mr. Gladstone and his colleagues just then went out of power, and the project of the new colony in North Australia was given up by the new ministry. Earl Grey, who succeeded Lord Stanley at the Colonial Office, wrote at once to the Governor of New South Wales to declare that the new cabinet dissented from the views of the late administration. They considered the formation of a settlement in North Australia impolitic and unnecessary, and they revoked, therefore, the letters patent under which it had been constituted. But they had also their own ideas. The great question remained unsolved, and they attacked it with more originality, perhaps, and greater determination than their predecessors. From their treatment of the subject resulted the third and last system of carrying out transportation.

They had to deal with the question in two phases : first, the evils actually in existence from the over-crowding of Van Diemen's Land must be mitigated, if they could not be removed; and secondly, some plan must be adopted to obviate their recurrence in the future. The first point was touched by suspending transportation altogether for two years. The stream thus checked, would have to be directed elsewhere ; but in the meantime, Van Diemen's Land would be relieved : in the course of two years the probation-gangs would be emptied, and the great labour pressure caused by the crowds of pass-holders would have disappeared. To deal still further with the actual difficulty, new and able men were appointed as administrators : Sir William Denison was to go out as governor, and Mr. Hampton comptroller-general of convicts. The former, an engineer officer of wide experience, accustomed to deal with large works and large bodies of men, would, it was hoped, find new outlets for the superabundant labour ; while the latter had been long connected with convicts as a surgeon-superintendent of convict ships, and his energy and knowledge were already well proved. The measures which these two working in concert were expected to carry out were indicated in a lengthy despatch. They consisted chiefly in a careful revision of the discipline of the probation-gangs and insisted on the construction without delay of prisons, wherein each man was provided with a separate cell for himself. This would supply work for many hands ; the surplus were to be employed in raising stock for the whole body, and in building villages for the occupation of labourers—mostly ticket-of-leave men—and their families. Lastly, all demands made by the local Government for labour to carry out colonial public works were to be complied with, and for this labour no charge was now to be made. On the whole, the plans devised for the management of the convict population already in the

colonies, were based on intelligent principles, and they were
in a measure successful.   So much for the first point.

The second embraced a wider field.   The Government was
bound, not only to provide for the thousands with which it
had saddled itself by the cessation of transportation to Van
Diemen's Land for a couple of years, but it had to look further
ahead and legislate for all the years to come.   To Sir George
Grey, the Home Secretary, the task was confided; and the
plan he proposed, with the arguments by which he arrived at
his decision, shall now be described.

Transportation, as it had hitherto been understood and
carried out, was now to come to an end.   Although two years
only had been the limit of its temporary suspension, Sir George
Grey admitted at once, that any expectation of recurring to
the old system at the end of that period, was "altogether
illusory."   He then proceeds to discuss the question.

So far, within the term transportation two distinct punishments had been comprised.   One was pure exile; the other
penal labour, whether under Government or an assigned
master.*   In the new arrangements these leading features
were retained.   Exile was of course a punishment felt as such
by many of those sentenced to it: a fact proved by the frequent
petitions from the friends of convicts that it might be remitted,
and by the anxiety shown by the exiles to obtain full pardon
—in other words, permission to return home.   Yet simple
exile of itself could be no sufficient punishment, seeing
that thousands of our fellow-countrymen—free emigrants, that
is to say—voluntarily submitted to it.   To sentence criminals
to nothing more would therefore be a simple absurdity.   Hence,
through all the systems of deportation, enforced labour and
restricted liberty had accompanied the actual removal beyond
the seas.   But penal labour, as such, could not be effectually
carried out at a great distance.   This had been proved already by
the failure, first of assignment, and latterly the collapse of the
plan of probation.   But what if this penal labour were carried
out at home?   In every way the resultant advantage was
plain.   Supervision could be near at hand, correction of abuses

* Earl Grey: Colonial Policy, vol. ii. p. 14, et seqq.; from which I
quote largely in the paragraphs that follow.

immediate, and the establishments would be governed by officials who from first to last might be drawn from a superior class. And here, at length, the authorities struck a key-note. They were at length approaching the proper solution of the question, though it was forced on them rather by the practical logic of circumstances, than obtained by exhaustive deduction. By adopting this principle, Lord John Russell's Government created in the germ our present penal system.

The new system, stated briefly, was to consist of a limited period of separate imprisonment, succeeded by employment on public works, either abroad at Bermuda or Gibraltar, or in this country; and ultimately followed in ordinary cases by exile or banishment for the remaining term of the original sentence. Lord Grey thus describes what would now be the convict's career:

1. A term of separate confinement, continuing from six to eighteen months, according to sentence and the manner prisoners bore the punishment.

2. Forced labour at home penal establishments, or at Gibraltar or Bermuda; this term to depend also on sentence, but the time by arrangement of tasks might be shortened by industry.

3. Ticket-of-leave in the colonies.

This, the new system, was certainly symmetrical, nor was any portion of it too high-flown for execution. The difficulty at first lay in the insufficiency of means for carrying out the first two stages. Pentonville prison, which had been in existence now since 1842, contained only a limited number of cells; however, there was Millbank to relieve the pressure for separate confinement. But places for penal labour did not exist, nor could they be improvised in a day. Eventually Portland came to be built, and advantage was taken of the old French prisons on the wilds of Dartmoor. But these two establishments, of which I shall speak more at length in the next chapter, could not in themselves absorb the thousands that multiplied on Government hands. Then Bermuda was pressed into the scheme, Gibraltar also; and provision was made for the accommodation in these two imperial colonies of numbers varying from two thousand to two thousand five hundred. It must be remarked that the very objections to penal establishment beyond the seas were repeated here at Gibraltar and Bermuda. Both these stations were too distant from home for effective supervision; and in 1862 Bermuda ceased to be a penal station, while now as I write the Gibraltar convict prison is on its last legs.* But they served their purpose for a time. Any convenient outlet was readily accepted in those two years when transportation to Van Diemen's Land was suspended. As many as 6000 convicts accumulated even in that short space of time, and those numbers were greatly augmented by the increased convictions due to the Irish famine. But, as I have said, the provisions made, whether at Portland or Dartmoor, at Gibraltar or Bermuda, were a makeshift only and far from complete. It has taken five-and-twenty years to provide sufficient accommodation, and put the home penal establishments on a thoroughly satisfactory footing.

The third stage was, however, the most distinctive part of Sir George Grey's new scheme, and in it we see the last vestige of transportation—all that remained, as piece by piece, inch by inch, the old system was hacked away by trenchant necessary reforms. "In considering the question of transportation," says Sir George Grey, "one important point has been overlooked, viz., the distinction between the fitness of the Australian colonies as places for the reception of criminals after having undergone their punishment, and as places in which transportation is itself to be inflicted. There can be no doubt that new and thinly peopled settlements, in which there is a large demand for additional labour, possess great advantages over a densely populated country, such as Great Britain and Ireland, for the reception of convicts after they have undergone their punishment. In this country, men regaining their liberty on the expiration of a penal sentence, often find great difficulty in obtaining an honest livelihood. In the general competition for employment, character,

* Since these sheets have gone to press, the Home Secretary (Mr. Cross) has announced in the House of Commons that the convict establishment at Gibraltar is to be broken up at once, and the prisoners brought home to be located in various English convict prisons.

naturally and properly, secures a preference to men untainted with crime; and the discharged convict is liable to be
thrown back upon a criminal course of life from the inability
to procure employment by which he can honestly maintain
himself. In the colonies, on the other hand, where labour is
in great demand, this difficulty is not experienced, and the
opportunity is afforded to the convict, on the termination of
his sentence, of entering on a new career with advantages
which he could not possess in this country, and of his becoming a useful member of society." This reasoning was no
doubt sound. The colonies might be unsuited for the enforcement of purely penal labour, but they were "admirably
adapted for the reception of criminals, whom it is desirable,
both for their own sake and that of society, to remove, after
their punishment has been completed, from being again
brought into a criminal course of life in this country by the
difficulties and dangers to which they are unavoidably
subject, but from which in the colonies they are in a great
measure exempt."* Accordingly, in this third stage the
convicts, including all male adults fit for the voyage, were
sent out to Van Diemen's Land, not as transported criminals,
but simply as exiles. On arrival they remained in the hands
of Government till they were engaged by settlers, when the
conditions of hiring were much what they had been in the
days of probation. The object being to assimilate the position of the exile to that of the assigned servant, except when
assignment was open to objection. Great things were expected of these exiles. Chastened and toned down by their
home discipline, it was hoped that their behaviour would be
the admiration of all beholders. This expectation was not
entirely borne out by the results. In spite of many flourish-
ing statements to the contrary, the conduct of these exiles was
not altogether exemplary; so much so, that the conditional
pardons with which they were first provided, had to be
altered to tickets-of-leave; substituted because, as holders of
the latter, they might still be subjected to some discipline
and restraint. But the blame did not arise in actual error
in the system, but only that too much was expected from it.

* Earl Grey: Colonial Policy.

The authorities had not yet learnt that no amount of penal discipline will ever change the criminal's character. He may promise to be good in future; his punishment may leave behind it a certain terror, which while it is remembered may keep him out of mischief, but the man remains at heart much the same.

Nevertheless, this method of ultimately disposing of the convict population was, as far as it went, distinctly successful. That it did not go farther, and that it is not still the custom, is probably the fault of the colonists themselves. Within a year or two of the establishment of the system, Van Diemen's Land waxed virtuous, and would have no more convicts, whether whitewashed or not, at any price. But a more detailed reference to this will be reserved for the next chapter.

FLANK GATES AT MILLBANK.

CHAPTER XXIII.

PENAL SERVITUDE.

THE changes introduced by Sir George Grey, to which I have referred at the close of the last chapter, remained in force, with certain important alterations, for a number of years following. They were modified to meet changing circumstances, but this was effected without attracting much attention. The years were eventful; the country was busy; war with a great power; India for a time in jeopardy; the map of Europe in process of alteration—grave questions like these closely occupied the public mind. It might have been, too, that people were a little sick of secondary punishment, and were content to leave the problem in the hands of officials

whose duty it was to deal with it. The management of
prisons, as I have had occasion to point out on an earlier
page, is rather a dull theme; and its discussion, where it
can be, is avoided. How long this indifference might have
continued it is impossible to conjecture, but all at once there
fell upon us a panic that must still be fresh in the minds of
most of us. It is only when touched by the sharp sense of
personal insecurity that people are universally roused to take
an interest in such affairs. The moment came at length when
—in presence of a real or imaginary danger—we woke to the
fact that our penal system was all a mistake.

It was in the winter of 1862 that robberies with violence
—garrote robberies, as they were called—suddenly increased
to such an alarming extent, and were accompanied with such
hideous details of brutality, that general consternation prevailed. The streets of London were less safe, said the leading
journal, than Athens in the throes of revolution and under
no government at all. Ours was the most insecure capital
of Europe. No man could walk abroad, even in crowded
thoroughfares, without feeling that he carried both his life
and his money in his hand. Both might be wrested from
him by an insidious malefactor before the victim was even
conscious of his danger. On all sides instances of these
treacherous assaults multiplied; and though varying somewhat in their method of execution, each and every one of them
belonged unmistakably to the same class of crime. One day we
heard that a young lady of fifteen had been attacked in
Westbourne Crescent in the afternoon. She was half throttled,
and a pistol held to her head, while they rifled her pockets,
and tried to tear off her necklace, and the pendants from her
ears. Her head was to have been shorn, too, of its magnificent
hair, which, as one of the ruffians cried, would certainly fetch
a goodish sum; but just then the sound of approaching
wheels frightened these human vultures from their helpless
quarry. Next a poor old woman, a feeble tottering creature
advanced in years, was knocked down and wantonly maltreated
for the half-dozen coppers she carried in her pocket.

These attacks were made at all hours and in all neighbourhoods. Daylight was no protection, nor the crowds in a

thoroughfare. One gentleman was felled to the ground in the afternoon near Paternoster Row, another in Holborn, a third in Cockspur Street. Later on, at night, the dangers of course multiplied a hundred-fold. Poor musicians, tramping home after performing in some theatrical orchestra, were knocked down and robbed of their instruments as well as their cash. It was a service of danger to be seen taking the money at the door of any entertainment. A gang of garroters, for instance, had their eye on Michael Murray all night as he stood at the door of the Teetotal Hall in Chelsea, and as soon as he left for home, they followed with stealthy step till they overtook him in Sloane Square and knocked him down, having first throttled and rifled him. If you stood still in the street, and refused to stand drink to any man who accosted you, he would probably then and there give you a hug. Those who took a delight in attending public executions did so at their own peril. A Mr. Bush, who was standing in front of the Old Bailey when Cooper was hanged, was hustled by several men, who first forced his hands up over his head, then unbuttoned his coat and stole his watch.

In every case, whether the victim resisted or was resigned, he was nearly certain to be shamefully ill-used. Now and then the biter was bit, as when three men fell upon a certain foreign gentleman who carried a sword, and was a master of the art of self-defence; or when another, who knew how to hit out, was attacked by two ruffians, both of whom he knocked down. But as a general rule the victim suffered tortures. When down on the ground as often as not he was kicked about the face and head, usually with savage violence, his teeth were knocked down his throat, his eyes closed, and he was left insensible, streaming with blood. In most cases there was every appearance that the outrage was deliberately planned beforehand. There were accomplices—women sometimes; and all were banded together like Hindoos, as *The Times* put it, sworn to the practice of "Thuggee." For months these crimes continued to be prevalent. Every morning's news chronicled "more outrages in the streets;" more and yet more; till, as the fogs of November settled down on the devoted heads of the honest inhabitants of London, men's

hearts failed them for fear, and life in sequestered street or
retired suburban villa seemed hardly worth an hour's purchase.
Every journal teemed with complaints; *Punch* took up the
question with grim humour; at the theatres audiences roared
at Mr. Toole, then shuddered to think they had still to get
home after the play was over.

At length the horrors of garroting culminated in the
arraignment of a crowd of such offenders in one batch at the
Central Criminal Court. There were seven-and-twenty of
them. The cases of all bore a certain family likeness; though
differing somewhat in detail, there was in each the same
insidious method of attack, followed by the same brutality
and wanton violence. Speaking to the most hardened, the
judge, Baron Bramwell, said, as he passed sentence, that it
was his belief that they were "utterly destitute of morality,
shame, religion, or pity, and that if they were let loose they
would do what any savage animal would do, namely, prey
upon their fellows." Therefore he was resolved to keep them
out of mischief as long as he possibly could. All got heavy
sentences, ranging from "life" downwards, and all were
consigned to Millbank, where they are still well remembered—
strong, able-bodied, determined-looking scoundrels; quite top-
sawyers in the trade of thieving, ready for any kind of daring
work, treating their incarceration with the utmost contempt,
as indeed they might, for it was nothing new to them. One
or two had graduated in crime during the days of the Penitentiary; but neither Mr. Nihil nor any one else had succeeded in reforming them. One had actually at one time
been an officer, a warder, in this very prison. Formerly a
soldier in the Marines, Leat's career had been rather
chequered. He had been present at the siege of St. Jean
d'Acre, and was at that time servant to an officer in the
fleet, through whom he obtained his situation at Millbank,
from which he was soon dismissed for drunkenness. After
this he went rapidly to the bad; was caught, and sentenced for obtaining goods under false pretences, next for
robbing a lady at Richmond Park, and now for the third time
he entered prison as a garroter. Although they maintained
throughout, from the moment of their capture, in the dock

and after sentence, an insolent and defiant demeanour, yet
in the prison these murderous rogues conducted themselves
fairly well; only two of them got into serious trouble. These
were Dixon and another, Needham, who together made a
vigorous attempt to escape. Dixon cut out, by means of a
sharpened nail, the panel in his cell door, unbolted it, got out,
and then set Needham also free. Their idea was to surprise
the officer as night patrol, and seize his keys. With this
object they concealed themselves behind a passage door, and
as he appeared struck him behind the ear. Fortunately the
blow fell light, and the officer turned to grapple with the
prisoners.

Such were the men, and such the work they did. Was it
strange that the public should complain of a system of penal
repression which left us to the tender mercies of ruffians like
these? We had abandoned transportation—and what had we
got in exchange? A system which as now administered had
"completely failed." * " It may have been a necessity, but it
clearly has not been a success. We may perhaps be compelled
to retain, or even to extend it; but its administration must be
altered. As it is it has no terrors whatever for the evil-doer,
while it gives but little protection to society." † So spake
The Times; and, as may be supposed, it spared no pains to
support its views with tangible evidence. Its columns teemed
with letters on the subject, and special correspondents visited
the chief convict establishments to spy out their nakedness
and report their inefficacy as places for the punishment of
criminals. Convicts, it was agreed on all sides, quite scoffed
at the terrors of penal servitude. Bar the loss of actual liberty,
which is doubtless the dearer to a man the closer he approaches
to a lower species of animal, the convict prison was made so
comfortable to the convict that he was loath to leave it, and
hardly dreaded to return. Well-housed, well-fed, with labour
just sufficient to ensure good digestion and a healthy circulation
of the blood; debarred only by a fiction of the luxuries he
chiefly loved; let loose from prison as soon as he chose to
evince signs of amendment, a convict was altogether master
of the situation. So said the critics. Penal servitude was

* *Times,* Dec. 6, 1862. † Ibid.

like going down into the country after "the season." A little
slow, perhaps; but very healthy and re-invigorating after a
racket in town—just the discipline, in fact, to which men
careful of themselves are ready to submit for a time, so as to
issue forth afterwards braced and strengthened for a fresh
campaign of pleasure. In these retired residences there was
rest for the tired thief, for the burglar whose nerves had
suffered, for the playful miscreant who had been able only to
half kill his victim, and who wished to recruit his strength.
Here they found congenial society, such as a man meets at
his club: others of his own set, with whom he could chat
about the past, or concoct new plans for the future. His
creature comforts were well looked after; he never worked, as
free labourers did, in the rain; and if by mischance he did
wet his feet, there were dry stockings for him on his return to
his cosy well-warmed cell. If he had any special "whims"
which called for gratification, an attentive official almost forestalled his wish. The leading feature of the whole system was
to keep the convict comfortable and contented.

All this, and more, the panic-stricken public, speaking
through the press, threw in the teeth of the authorities. Reform
was called for loudly; trenchant and immediate reform. If
the system of penal servitude was at fault, then must we recur
to transportation beyond the seas. It is almost amusing to
notice how, in their terror, those who were most urgent in
their cry for renewed transportation, forgot the complete
collapse of that method of punishment only a few years before.
Blinded by what they deemed a pressing danger, they ignored
past experience; the evils of assignment had faded from
memory, and likewise the atrocities of the probation-gangs.
All that was present and plain was, that far away from
England lay other lands, whereon the sewage might be shot
as heretofore; and that such a removal of the criminal classes
would rid the mother country of its ruffians and all its alarm.
But no sooner was this proposal formulated than difficulties of
execution came at once to the front. The colonies, Queens-
land among others, which had been declared most anxious to
receive convicts, entirely repudiated the idea, and asked very
pertinently whether they might be permitted in return to·

transport their own malefactors to the British Isles? Then the geographers began to search out new countries suitable for penal settlements. One suggested the Falkland Islands; another, New Guinea, while Labrador by many was felt to be just the place for colonization.

Happily none of these suggestions went beyond the merest proposals. Had practical effect been given to any scheme for the re-establishment of penal colonies, it would have been met at once by the objection of expense. Of the excessive costliness of transportation there is no manner of doubt. In 1843 in Van Diemen's Land alone the expenditure on convicts was £300,000, and years of patient economy only brought it down to £240,000 in 1848. This sum was but a fraction of the whole outlay; in addition, the home depôts, those still retained in Australia, Gibraltar, and Bermuda, had to be paid for. So that speaking roughly, the convicts as a body cost half a million of money. To-day we manage the whole of our convicts for £350,000, while the value of the work done, as measured, amounts to £220,000.* There is thus some tangible return for all the outlay; but in a young penal settlement the money is simply poured into a sieve. By-and-by, perhaps, by the creation of new markets and new dependencies, the mother country may benefit to some extent; but these are but indirect gains after all, and the time of fruition may be indefinitely delayed. However much, then, the public might clamour for a renewal of transportation, that it was clearly impracticable was evident to all who approached the question with calmness and deliberation. Yet the difficulty remained. Penal servitude was felt to be inefficient—what remedy was to be applied? Here obviously was work for a Royal Commission; and a Royal Commission composed of capable and experienced men

* Here are other figures, taken from Colonel Jebb's report of 1851:
1 Gross cost of transportation, with convict prisons in Great Britain and Ireland, Bermuda, Gibraltar, and Western Australia £587,294
Net cost, after deducting value of labour 419,476
2. Gross cost of an assumed maximum of 17,250 males, and 1200 female convicts at home, and at Gibraltar, Bermuda, and Western Australia... 370,750
Net cost, after deducting value of labour 195,700

was thereupon appointed, which in truth did excellent service. Of the labours of this commission, and the conclusions arrived at, I shall speak by-and-by more at length; let us pause now for a moment to consider what was the real meaning of this penal servitude, which was so much abused on every side. Did it indeed deserve to be called inefficient, if not entirely a failure?

Some years had elapsed since transportation had quite come to an end; since Van Diemen's Land, following suit to New South Wales, elected to forego the advantages of cheap labour, rather than be inundated any longer with our convicts. After two years' suspension, transportation thither had been resumed in 1850 in a modified form. The men sent out were those, who having been subjected already to penal discipline at home, were deemed to be purged and purified. But the people of Van Diemen's Land would not have them at any price, nor in any shape or form. Although pains were taken to explain that these were well-disposed "ticket-of-leave men," not convicts, their reception was violently opposed. A struggle ensued, but in the end the Imperial Government gave way, and the last convict ship sailed for Van Diemen's Land in 1852. While we cannot withhold approval of the course the colony adopted, there is no doubt that it was almost suicidal. Mr. Trollope, who visited Van Diemen's Land, now known as Tasmania, in 1871, describes in graphic language the consequences to the colony of its magnanimous conduct. Absolute stagnation and want of enterprise everywhere apparent, the skeletons of great works in ruins, others half finished doomed to decay for want of hands, land relapsing into uncultivation, towns deserted, grass growing in the streets—the whole place lifeless and inert. Possibly, if the question were again put, the answer would be in different terms. But in 1850 the discomforts entailed by transportation were so recent and disagreeable, that these colonists could not be brought to believe that by a better system of administration such evils might be altogether avoided.

Nor were the people of Van Diemen's Land singular in their resolve. Even before they had in plain language so declined, other colonies had displayed a similar unmistakable reluctance to become receptacles for convicts. As early as 1848, Earl Grey, in search of new fields for transportation, had addressed a circular to all colonial governors, pointing out in persuasive periods, the advantages to be gained by accepting this valuable labour which, nevertheless, no one cared to have. Strange to say, only one colony—that of Western Australia—replied affirmatively to this appeal. At the Cape of Good Hope, the appearance of a convict ship in 1849 produced a tumultuous and indignant protest.* At other places the bent of the colonial mind made itself equally unmistakable, so that it was at length openly announced in the House of Commons, that unless our colonial possessions grew more amenable, transportation must cease.

As all these various questions covered a period of several years, it can hardly be said that the crisis which necessitated change came suddenly or all at once. The Government was loath to surrender till the very last the idea of maintaining the existing system or something like it, but they were not without fair warning that they were building on hopes delusive and insecure. And it is evident that throughout the period of doubt, they gave the question the most anxious care, although the evident disposition was more towards tinkering up what was rickety and useless, than substituting a radically new plan. To this, no doubt, they were in a measure forced. The mere idea of retaining a large mass of

* It was in September, 1849, that the *Neptune* convict ship reached Cape Town from Bermuda. The moment her arrival was signalled, the church bells began to toll half-minute time, and a public notice was put forth by the anti-convict association, calling on the people to be calm. At the same time the municipal commissioners addressed the Governor, Sir Harry Smith, begging that the *Neptune* might be forthwith ordered to leave the shores of the Cape. "The convicts," they said, "must not, cannot, and shall not be landed or kept in any of the ports of the colony." Sir Harry's answer was that he must carry out his orders; upon which the people drew a cordon round the ship and cut off supplies from Government House, so that His Excellency could get no meat, and had to bake his own bread. Finally, he agreed to compromise, and the *Neptune* was allowed to remain in the Bay till a vessel could be sent home for instructions. The authorities at home considered the opposition at the Cape too serious to be resisted, and directed the *Neptune* elsewhere.—*Annual Register.*

convicts at home was hailed by the public with alarm; and it became almost an axiom that offenders sooner or later, but as a rule inevitably, must be banished from the country. This was the underlying principle of every scheme. The convicts must be removed to a distance, not necessarily as a punishment—it might be as a boon to themselves—but in any case as a benefit to their country. In point of symmetry the method is undoubtedly admirable; theoretically perfect now as it was then. The assisted emigration of discharged prisoners supplies the easiest means of providing them with that honest labour which is supposed to preserve them from a relapse into crime. But whether as freemen, exiles, or convicts in chains, they were all indelibly branded with the stigma of their guilt, and we cannot even now find a country ready to receive them. At the time of which I am writing the resolute attitude of all the colonies, save one, compelled us to reconsider our position. We were forced, in fact, though sorely against the grain, to make the best of a bad bargain and keep nearly all our convicts at home. These might be taken in round numbers to average some eight thousand— the largest proportion in England, a few hundreds only at Bermuda and Gibraltar. What was to be done with them ?

Fortunately a solution of the difficulty was not far to seek. It was to be found in the new prison at Portland, which had been called into existence as part of Sir George Grey's scheme to purify "probation;" and the nucleus or germ thus supplied was capable of indefinite development as needs might arise. It would be incorrect to assert that the Portland Breakwater owes its origin to this vexed "convict question," inasmuch as years before, in 1843, that is to say when "probation" was still in full swing of supposed success, the Select Committee on Harbours of Refuge had warmly advocated the construction of some such work in Portland Bay. The objects of this great national undertaking—now in the lapse of years become an actually accomplished fact—were to secure a naval station in war, and at the same time to " afford shelter and safety to the commercial marine in the long line of coast extending from Plymouth and Torbay, to Portsmouth and the Downs." Materials for the work lay close at hand.

Portland quarries were filled with vast heaps of refuse stone exactly suited for the work; this stone was the *débris*, the inferior strata which had in all cases to be first removed before the "best bed" was reached, wherein lay that superior quality of which St. Paul's, Whitehall, and other edifices are a standing advertisement to this day. All this had been fully discussed by the Select Committee; and the Portland works were finally decided just before this convict difficulty cropped up. But here indeed was an additional and a stronger argument to recommend the undertaking. Two birds would in fact be killed by the same stone. The convicts otherwise redundant would be profitably employed, and a great harbour would be constructed at a distinct saving to the public. No wonder that Sir James Graham grasped at Portland as a drowning man might at a straw. But in reality he found a substantial life-buoy rather than a straw, and by means of it came safe to shore.

The execution of the scheme was entrusted to Colonel Jebb of the Royal Engineers, who was already well known in connection with prison building and generally with penal legislation. He had for some years past been associated with the two official inspectors of prisons; after that he had assisted in the superintendence of Millbank, when constituted a convict depôt, and he had been in reality the moving spirit of the commissioners who built the "model" prison at Pentonville. In those early years he gave undoubted earnest of his energetic character and great powers, a promise hereafter more than fulfilled. Colonel Jebb's task was in the first instance to provide accommodation of some sort on the island of Portland wherein the convicts might be securely lodged immediately adjoining their works. He describes, in a memorandum dated 1847, the style of place he proposes to build. Naturally, he says, when the works on which the prisoners are to be employed are likely to be completed within a limited time, something less costly than a substantial prison would suffice. Safe custody, and the due enforcement of discipline must of course be secured; but these might be obtained without any very extravagant outlay. He suggested, therefore, buildings on wooden frames, with corrugated iron partitions; the whole

so constructed as to be easily taken to pieces and removed to
another site if required. In these buildings the convicts might
be kept safe and separate, at the probable cost of little more
than £34 per cell. Similar prisons might be run up anywhere,
so that the whole number of convicts for whom accommodation
was required might be housed for a couple of hundred thousand
pounds. Colonel Jebb accompanied this proposal with certain
figures as a set-off against this outlay. He assumed that the
maintenance, including every item of the whole number, would
amount to £158,000, but their earnings would be £180,000.
The balance gain was therefore of £22,000—a sufficient interest
on the original cost of the prison buildings. These figures
were speculative of course, nor were they found exactly accurate
in practice, although there is no great difference in the balance
gain. The cost of maintenance proved undoubtedly higher
than thus estimated, but *en revanche* the earnings were also
considerably more.

Three years later, in March, 1850, Colonel Jebb reports
to the Secretary of State that he has provided room for 840
prisoners at Portland. "The main buildings consist of four
large open halls, eighty-eight feet long by twenty-one broad,
having four tiers of cells on each side." The interior of the
halls were well ventilated, and could be warmed; the cells
were seven feet by four, and furnished with hammock,
tables, shelves for books, etc. "The cells are divided by
partitions of corrugated iron, and are sufficient to secure the
effectual separation of the men at night, and to admit of their
taking their meals in them, and reading or otherwise occupying themselves after working hours, till they go to bed." In
addition to the cell accommodation there was of course full
provision for officers' quarters, chapel, kitchen, wash-houses,
stores, and so forth. Moreover ample space was reserved
"within the boundary wall for the erection of additional
buildings, so as to increase the number of convicts to 1200
or 1500, if it should be found necessary or desirable." Everything was now in fair working order. The foundation stone
of the breakwater had been laid in July, 1849, by Prince
Albert, who visited the prison and presented a Bible and
Prayer-Book for use in its chapel; but till then, and during

the first year of the occupation of a "bleak and barren rock" the convicts were chiefly employed in setting things straight within the prison walls. They had to level parade grounds, make roads and reservoirs, fit gates and doors, paint and clean up the whole establishment. As soon as practicable they were turned on to the breakwater works. "The stone," says Colonel Jebb, "is to be removed from the quarries by means of several lines of railways, which are arranged in a series of inclined planes from the summit to the point where the breakwater joins the shore. The waggons will be raised and lowered by wire ropes, working on 'drums,' placed at the head of each 'incline,' the loaded train in its descent drawing up the empty one from the breakwater."

In the general detail of work, the share that fell upon the convicts was the plate-laying, levelling, forming embankments and excavations, getting out and stacking the stone, filling the waggons, sending them down and bringing them back from the incline. Some 500 were so employed during the first year, 1849, and their earnings were estimated at about £15,000.

Portland when thus fairly launched became the starting-point for the new arrangements. Other prisons were needed, and they must be built like Portland. But time pressed, and anything actually available at the moment was eagerly pressed into the service. Down at Dartmoor, on the high lands above Tavistock, was a huge building which had been empty now for five-and-thirty years. Its last occupants had been the French and American prisoners of war, who had been confined there down to the peace of 1814. Ten thousand, some said twelve thousand, had been accommodated within the walls— surely there must be room there for several hundred convicts? Colonel Jebb, hearing that Captain Groves from Millbank was staying down at Plymouth, begged him to run over to inspect Dartmoor. The place was like a howling wilderness; the buildings in places without roofs; the walls in holes, if not in ruins. But a few repairs would soon make the place habitable, said Captain Groves; and accordingly a batch of convicts, under Mr. Morrish, now one of the directors of convict prisons (1884), were sent down to commence operations.

In a short time Dartmoor prison was opened. Then other
receptacles were prepared. The hulks had been pressed into
the service, and were employed, but only as a temporary
measure, at the various dockyards to house the convicts till
proper buildings on the new plan could be erected. There
were ships at Woolwich, and others at Portsmouth. At
the first station the old *Warrior*, and the *Defence*, took
the able-bodied, while the *Unité* served as a hospital; at
Portsmouth there were the *York, Briton, Stirling Castle,*
till 1852, when the new convict prison was occupied. Soon
after this, in 1855, contracts were entered into for the erection
of a large prison at Chatham, which was completed in 1858,
and to which all those at the Woolwich hulks were in course
of time transferred. The intention at both these stations was
to devote a mass of convict labour to further the dockyard
extensions. At Chatham the object in view was to construct,
high up the tortuous Medway, a chain of artificial basins
capable of containing our fleet. Hither beaten ships might
retire to refit; while new ironclads, built in the dock close by,
might issue thence to retrieve disaster. From the first the
work was of an arduous character. The battle was against
the tide and the treacherous mud. But the whole of St.
Mary's Island has been reclaimed; marsh has given place to
solid ground; the three basins are completed, and with the
barracks, store-houses, and other buildings will be fully
incorporated within the limits of Chatham Dockyard. At
Portsmouth, a feat has been accomplished, not exactly similar,
but wonderful also in its way.

So much for the framework—the bones, so to speak, of the
new system; let us see next something of the living tissues
with which it was filled up.

Speaking broadly, it may be laid down that the plan of
treatment inaugurated by Colonel Jebb and his colleagues,
was based on persuasion rather than coercion. This, indeed,
they openly allowed. They were not advocates for a "purely
coercive and penal discipline." They conceived that there
was sufficient punishment without that; the convicts suffered
enough in the "long periods during which they remained
under penal restraint," and there was further discomfort in

"their eventual deportation to a distant colony,* and the somewhat severe restrictions to which they are subjected when they gain the boon of a ticket-of-leave." The directors of convict prisons hoped, therefore, to accomplish their object by reward and encouragement rather than by strictness and terror. They desired to put it plainly before every convict that if he would but continue quiet and obedient, he would be sure to benefit in the long run. It was really worth his while to be good, they said. "It will convince us that you are on the high road to reform, and the sooner we are convinced you are reformed, the sooner you will be set at large." Everything was made to depend on conduct—good conduct—in other words, the mere formal observance of rules, a submissive demeanour, and a readiness to echo—but with hypocritical hearts—the lessons the chaplains taught. The word "industry" was tacked on to "conduct," but only in a subordinate sense, and so long as the convict was civil he might be as lazy as he liked.

Precise rules provided the machinery by which a due estimate of each man's conduct was to be obtained. Every governor of a prison kept a character-book, in which he was to enter concisely his observation upon the character and conduct of every prisoner, so as to be thus enabled to reward him by classification and good-conduct badges, and more especially "to report with confidence whenever he may be called upon in conjunction with the chaplain to assist the authorities in determining the period of detention of the different prisoners." The same rule went on to say, "He (the governor) shall take every opportunity of impressing on the prisoners that the particulars of their conduct are thus noticed and recorded; and that whilst no effort at good-conduct and industry on the part of a prisoner will be disregarded by the authorities of the prison, every act of wilful misconduct and punishment will be equally noted, and will tend to prolong the period of his detention under penal discipline." The governor's opinion was to be endorsed by that of the chaplain, and even the subordinate officers were

* These regulations were drawn up at a time when transportation was still practised, though only to a limited extent.

called upon to record their views of the demeanour of the
prisoners they especially controlled. The whole object of
this classification and this supervision was to "produce on
the minds of the prisoners a practical and habitual conviction
of the effect which their own good conduct and industry will
have on their welfare and future prospects."

These extracts from Colonel Jebb's earliest reports will be
sufficient to indicate the bias of his mind. He too, like others
who had gone before, was hopeful of reformation by purely
moral means. As he has himself declared in one of his
reports, he thought he might more surely gain the great
end he had in view by leading than by driving. Upon this
principle the whole system of management was based. There
can be no question that those who were its authors took their
stand upon the highest ground. They were called upon to
inaugurate a new order of things, and they did so to the best
of their ability, in the most straightforward, conscientious
fashion. The glaring evils of transportation, as it had been
administered, were then still staring them in the face.
"Speaking humanly," says Colonel Jebb,* "the demora-
lization of every individual sentenced to transportation
was certain. No matter what might have been his previous
character, what the amount of his constitution, or what the
sincerity of his efforts and resolutions to retrace his steps, he
was placed within the influence of a moral pestilence, from
which, like death itself, there was no escape." The necessity
for great and radical changes was imperative; and these
changes were carried out in the manner I have described.
Great results were expected to follow from them.

In the first year or two everything appears *couleur de rose.*
"As a body the men show a spirit of willing and cheerful
obedience. The strictest discipline is maintained with a very
small proportion of punishment. The industry of the working
parties is remarkable." Again, the same report asserts that
"any candid and dispassionate inquiry into the condition and
prospects of the convicts who have passed through periods of
penal and reformatory discipline at Pentonville and Portland,
will prove beyond doubt that, to say the least of it, the

* General Report of 1861.

majority of those now serving are likely on their release to be
respectable in their station of life, and useful to those who engage their services; thus realising the anticipations of the
Pentonville commissioners, that a large proportion of our
convicts would be qualified on their discharge to occupy an
honest position in their own or any other country."

This was in 1852. The system was to have ten years to
run—ten years of trial, so to speak—before it was attacked
with the shower of obloquy to which I have referred at the
commencement of this chapter. What had happened in the
interval? Was the method of management preserved intact?
Had it deteriorated, or had other causes interfered to pave the
way to failure? I will endeavour to answer these questions in
a few words.

Not only was all the fair and soft treatment with which
the system had started in effect maintained; if anything it was
altogether over-done. The tenderness and considerateness of
the authorities grew and increased till at length it knew no
bounds. Far-seeing and able as was Sir Joshua Jebb, however skilful and capable as an administrator, on one point he
was weak. It was an amiable weakness, but it did both
himself and his system incalculable harm. He had formed
too high an opinion of the criminal class; he was too hopeful,
too ready to accept the shadow for the substance, to be
satisfied with promise rather than performance, and to view
the outward whitewashed semblance of purity for the radical
transformation of the inner man. This was the key-note of
the system, and this as time passed grew and gained strength,
till at least there was some semblance of truth in the allegations so freely cast in his teeth. It became known, and this
beyond contradiction, that the diet in those days was far too
generous; that the care taken of the convicts was tender to
the extent of ridiculous coddling; that the labour exacted was
far below the amount that each might reasonably be expected
to perform. These facts, which are more or less proved by
the evidence before the commission of 1863, are fully borne
out by the traditions of the department itself. Old officers
tell me that in all the prisons discipline was almost a dead
letter. The convicts themselves ruled the roast. They did

not break away, because there were troops at hand who would
shoot them down; but otherwise they did just what they
pleased. Their warders, taking their cue from the supreme
power, sought to humour them into obedience by civil speeches
rather than by firmness and resolution. The officers were
afraid to enforce their orders, and the convicts saw that they
were afraid. Men who are over-fed, if they are also idle, are
sure to prove saucy and run riot. Some of the scenes at the
convict prisons were disgraceful, almost rivalling at times, but
without the fearful consequences, the anarchy and disorder I
have described in chapter x.

That the convicts were thus as a body insolent and insubordinate, was undoubtedly due to the petting and
pampering they received. But another, and a potent cause
too, was the unsettled, dissatisfied spirit evoked in the whole
mass by several successive alterations in the law—alterations
which it was absolutely necessary to introduce, but which none
the less produced unevenness of treatment between various
classes of prisoners.

The first change was in 1852, when transportation was
found to be at its last gasp. Some substitute was needed
because there were thousands awaiting removal, and yet no
outlet for them. "After much anxious consideration it was
determined by the Government to commute their sentences to
imprisonment in this country for certain proportionate periods
—three years for seven years, and so on." * At the same time
a new style of punishment was invented, to describe which the
words "penal servitude" were coined, and passed current in
the language. Of course those under the first system were to
leave prison at the end of their commuted terms; but they
went out as ticket-of-leave men, and not absolutely free; while
those who were sentenced, after 1853, to the new punishment,
remained within the walls to the last.

Here, then, an invidious distinction was clearly instituted,
although the evil effects thereof were not for some time
apparent. But as the years rolled by, numbers of the "transportation men" were set at large as holders of tickets-of-leave.
Their conduct was not quite blameless, and there was soon

* Sir Joshua Jebb: Report of 1857.

an indignant outcry at their premature release. Of course every offence committed everywhere was fastened upon them, and the system which permitted them to be out and at their mischievous work. Sir Joshua Jebb was of opinion that more was made of the matter than the occasion justified. He considered that "into this outcry was enlisted all the disappointment that had been felt, and all the alarm which had been excited at the bare idea of the discontinuance of transportation, which necessarily involved the release at home of so many rogues who had hitherto been finally got rid of."

Immediately following this outcry, however, came a fresh consideration of the question, and a fresh Act of Parliament, making further and new provisions. Of this the prominent feature was the extension of the terms of penal servitude which a judge might pass, to correspond with the former terms of transportation. By the same Act the method of granting tickets-of-leave was fully "recognised and recommended, so that a measure which had been adopted as a convenience, or necessity, in commuting a sentence of transportation into one of which a portion should be imprisonment, and the remainder on license, became part and parcel of our penal administration." The actual consequences of these changes were that in all the prisons there were convicts serving side by side under these different conditions. "Some with remissions under the old Transportation Act; some without remission, sentenced between 1853 and 1857; others with remission under the Act of 1857." No doubt, then, those in the second category had some sort of grievance, and the temper of the convicts was not, in these days, such that they exhibited longsuffering patience under even more trivial trials.

Many prescriptions were tried to remedy the discontent—increased food, greater privileges, more persuasive talk. But to a prisoner such substitutes are mere dross compared to the true gold of freedom to pass beyond the prison walls. Nothing would keep the malcontents quiet; and where a few are evilly disposed among a crowd of men, others without just cause of complaint are soon sucked in and go with the stream. After festering and rankling below the surface for some time, the mischief came to head in an outbreak at Portland in 1858, where the convicts threw down their tools and in a body struck work.   By-and-by a much more serious mutiny occurred at Chatham.   But both were happily checked without bloodshed, and by the mere exhibition of armed force.

Finally, in 1862, the "garroters' panic" broke upon un-protected London.   Then it was that the last new system of secondary punishment—the system which had grown by slow degrees out of the remnants of "transportation," and which was now ten years old—was arraigned to show cause why it also should not give place to something more satisfactory to all concerned.

CHAPTER XXIV.

GENERAL CONCLUSIONS.

It cannot be said that the verdict of the commissioners appointed to report in 1863 was unfavourable to the system they were called upon to review. On the contrary, they declared that the general impression that the punishment as administered under Sir Joshua Jebb was not of a sufficiently penal character, was erroneous. The commissioners could not admit that the system was really at fault. The life of the prisoners, they said, was extremely monotonous. "Having been used in most cases to constant change and excitement, they are debarred from all pleasures and amusements, they are compelled to pass their time in a dull unvarying routine of distasteful labour, and at the close of each day's work they return to the cheerless solitude of their cells." No doubt they did less work than many a free man gladly performed of

2 G

his own accord; but the convicts' labour was nevertheless not light, and they all hated it most cordially. Again, they were not really too indulgently treated. If, for instance, they took shelter from a light shower of rain, it was only because there was a difficulty in the prisons of drying rapidly a quantity of wet clothes. The commissioners were not even sure that the convicts' diet was excessive, although satisfactory evidence was put before them that convicts were better fed than paupers in workhouses or than numbers of the free labouring poor.*

But having made these admissions, the commissioners could not deny that "the system appears to be not sufficiently dreaded by those who have undergone it, or by the criminal classes in general." The number of re-convictions, they thought, proved this; moreover, "the accounts given of penal servitude by discharged convicts, and the fact that they generally come back so soon† to their original haunts, tends to prevent its being regarded with fear by their associates. Indeed, in some (though doubtless exceptional) cases, crimes have been committed for the sole purpose of obtaining the advantages which the offenders have supposed a sentence of penal servitude to confer." The system could not, therefore, be called perfect. It had failed to some extent —but how? The commissioners attributed its shortcomings in a minor degree to defects in the discipline maintained, but thought the blame lay really in the shortness of the terms of imprisonment awarded in the courts of law.

To speak first of the latter point; the commissioners reported that there had been a notable reduction for some years previous in the length of sentences, and to make them still lighter came the remission of time granted under the new rules.‡ It was a curious fact that the late increase of crime

---

* Mr. Harries, an official at Gwydyr House, supplied long and valuable tables to prove this, which will be found in an appendix to the report of 1863. His statement may be briefly summed up in the facts: 1. That in prison a man got 377 ounces of food weekly, costing 4s. 1d.; while, if free, he would have to support himself and family on 8s. a week. 2. Lunatics and paupers could be fed at the rate of 2s. 4d. per week.

† By obtaining an early release on ticket-of-leave.

‡ The Act of 1857.

had corresponded in point of date with the discharge of
prisoners who were first sentenced for short terms under the
Act of 1857, and was probably mainly attributable to their
release from custody.* And they had come out unchastened.
"The discipline to which convicts are subjected does not
produce its proper effect in short periods of punishment."

Next as to the discipline. It was clearly a mistake to lay
so much stress on conduct only. It was wrong, too, that the
convicts should be allowed to earn enormous "gratuities,"
or sums to be handed over to them upon discharge. Many
left prison with £30, £40, sometimes £80, in their pockets.
The effect of this was to make a sentence of penal servitude
an object of desire, rather than of apprehension. Besides,
the longer a man's sentence—presumably, therefore, the
greater his crime—the greater the sum he was entitled
to take away with him. Again, the measures to keep the
prisoners under coercion were far too mild. Punishment
did not follow fast enough on acts of violence and aggravated
misconduct. The infliction of corporal punishment was too
restricted, and the "cat" used too light. There should be
more power to use it and greater promptitude in its infliction. Then came the work and the diet; but on these points
the committee spoke with less confidence. Last of all, there
was an entire absence of supervision of those who were at
large on ticket-of-leave.

Having enunciated these propositions, the commissioners
went on to recommend certain important changes in the
manner of carrying out penal servitude, chief among which
were :

1. That in future no sentence should be passed of less than
seven years.

2. That re-convicted criminals should be treated more
severely than others.

* This increase was incontestable—1860 showed no increase or
decrease on previous years, but in 1862, convictions in England rose
from 12,066 to 15,312; and sentences to death or penal servitude in
England increased from 2,267 to 3,196. Robberies of violence rose
from 32 in 1860 to 97 in 1862, and burglaries in the same time rose
from 179 to 259.—*Parliamentary Record on Penal Servitude*, 1862.

3. That convicts, after enduring separate imprisonment for nine months, should pass on to public works, where they might be permitted to earn by industry and good conduct an abridgment of a part of their imprisonment.

4. That all males, if possible, should be sent to Western Australia during the latter part of their sentences, " it being highly desirable to send convicts, under proper regulations and without disguise, to a thinly peopled colony, where they may be removed from their former temptations, where they will be sure of having the means of maintaining themselves by their industry if inclined to do so, and where facilities exist for keeping them under more effective control than is practicable in this country with its great cities and large population.

5. That all who were unfit to go, and, gaining a remission of sentence, were discharged at home, should while on licence be subjected to close supervision by the police.

Such was the substance of the report. But it is right to mention here that the commissioners were not quite unanimous in the conclusions arrived at. Two of them, Mr. Henley and the Lord Chief Justice, would not sign the report. Mr. Childers put his name to it, but under protest. He could not agree to the proposals as to transportation. His view was the Australian one, and he was of opinion that " the measures recommended—while costly to the country and odious to her colonies—would at best afford only a brief delay in the solution of a question daily becoming more difficult."

But by far the most important of the dissentient voices was that of Sir Alexander Cockburn, the Lord Chief Justice, who appended to the report a long memorandum giving his reasons for not concurring in it. After a careful perusal of this, the reader would, I think, be ready to concede that the Lord Chief Justice went nearer the mark than his colleagues. They hesitated to admit that our penal system was defective. Sir Alexander Cockburn had no sort of doubt of it, and maintained that the same impression was pretty generally abroad. But if there were faults in it, said the commissioners, then the administration of the law was to blame, it was too lenient. To this the Lord Chief Justice would by no means agree. The leniency of the judges, as it had shown itself of late, was nothing. "The spirit in which the law is administered," he observed, "is not the growth of yesterday. It has arisen gradually out of the more humane and merciful disposition of men's minds in modern times, whereby punishments inflicted without scruple in former days would now be regarded cruel and inhuman." No; the inefficacy of penal servitude did not lie in the shortness or inequality of sentences, but in the manner in which the punishment is inflicted. "Moderate labour, ample diet, substantial gratuities, are hardly calculated to produce on the minds of the criminal that salutary dread of the recurrence of the punishment which may be the means of deterring him, and through his example, others from the commission of crime."

And then the Lord Chief Justice goes on to put forth the following pregnant sentences, which I quote in full. In taking up the question of punishment, he says, "it is necessary to bear in mind what are the purposes for which the punish- ment of offenders takes place. These purposes are twofold : the first, that of deterring others exposed to similar temptations from the commission of crime ; the second the reformation of the criminal himself. The first is the primary and more im- portant object : for though society has, doubtless, a strong interest in the reformation of the criminal, and his consequent indisposition to crime, yet the result is here confined to the individual offender ; while the effect of punishment as deterring from crime extends, not only to the party suffering the punish- ment, but to all who may be in the habit of committing crime, or who may be tempted to fall into it. Moreover, the refor- mation of the offender is in the highest degree speculative and uncertain, and its permanency in the face of renewed temptation exceedingly precarious. On the other hand, the impression produced by suffering inflicted as the punishment of crime, and the fear of its repetition, are far more likely to be lasting, and much more likely to counteract the tendency to the renewal of criminal habits. It is on the assumption that punishment will have the effect of deterring from crime, that its infliction can alone be justified ; its proper and legiti- mate purpose being not to avenge crime but to prevent it.

"The experience of mankind has shown that though crime will always exist to a certain extent, it may be kept within given bounds by the example of punishment. This result it is the business of the lawgiver to accomplish by annexing to each offence the degree of punishment calculated to repress it. More than this would be a waste of so much human suffering; but to apply less, out of consideration for the criminal, is to sacrifice the interests of society to a misplaced tenderness towards those who offend against its laws. Wisdom and humanity no doubt alike suggest that, if consistently with this primary purpose the reformation of the criminal can be brought about, no means should be omitted by which so desirable an end can be achieved. But this, the subsidiary purpose of penal discipline, should be kept in due subordination to its primary and principal one. And it may well be doubted whether, in recent times, the humane and praiseworthy desire to reform and restore the fallen criminal may not have produced too great a tendency to forget that the protection of society should be the first consideration of the lawgiver."

I have dwelt thus at length upon the committee of 1863 because upon the recommendations put forward in its report are based the outlines of our system of secondary punishment as it exists to the present day. Nearly all the reforms and changes indicated have been by this time brought about. There is no longer a wasteful superabundance of food in the prisons; the gratuities have been cut down to the more modest sums of two and three pounds. Convicts are not, it is true, still sent to Western Australia; but that is simply because we do not need to send them—there or anywhere else.* The law for the supervision of convicts at large upon tickets-of-leave has been elevated almost to a science under the recent searching acts relating to habitual criminals.

But one other, by far the most important improvement that followed this report, was the adoption of the "mark system"; in other words, of a method by which remission was

* We have indeed learned to do without this forced emigration as an opening for convicts on discharge from prison; and this is to a large extent due to the praiseworthy action of the Discharged Prisoners' Aid Society, 39, Charing Cross.

to be regulated, not by conduct as heretofore, but solely by labour actually performed. For it must be understood that the commissioners unhesitatingly accepted the principle of remissions. In this they were at issue with the Lord Chief Justice, who thought that no prisoner should escape one particle of the whole sentence laid upon him by the judge. "It was most material," he said, "to the full efficiency of punishment that its infliction should be certain." The door was opened to doubt and uncertainty the moment you allowed the precise term of the sentence to be interfered with. The objection was cogent if the remissions were to be granted in a haphazard, capricious fashion and not by regular rule. But surely if the scale were drawn up on a regular plan and worked without deviation, a sentence with remission might be just as certain as one without. The former might, perhaps, be shorter than the latter—our judges being perfectly aware of the possible remission would regulate their sentences in proportion to this abridgment.

On the other hand, there was a clear and distinct gain to be expected from the practice of remitting sentences. This was fully recognised by the commissioners. "The hope of earning some remission is the most powerful incentive to industry and good conduct which can be brought to act upon the minds of prisoners." The commissioners perhaps laid more stress on good conduct than was absolutely imperative, although they pointed out, very pertinently, that "good conduct in a prison (apart from industry) can consist only in abstaining from misconduct, which gives no just claim for reward." But this harping upon good conduct was a weak point in their armour which the Lord Chief Justice quickly discovered. He would not admit the necessity for thus coaxing convicts into obedience by promising them an earlier release if they behaved well. That was no argument, he said, for remissions. Discipline ought to be strong enough to be independent of such questionable support. "I can see no reason to think," he goes on—"considering the powers of coercion, discipline, and reduction of diet, possessed by the prison authorities—that, by the application of firmness and determination with a sufficient force of officers, convicts, especially if not massed in too great numbers, but judiciously distributed, may not be kept under perfect control and discipline."

No doubt the commissioners over-estimated the necessity of remission as a means of ensuring good conduct; but they were clearly in the right in recommending the principle as a certain incentive to industry. The experience, both of this and of other countries, has demonstrated that it is impossible to compel convicts to work hard by mere coercion, the attempt to do so having invariably failed, while it has produced a brutalising effect on their minds and increased their previous aversion to labour. On this ground the late Captain Maconochie many years ago recommended that the punishment to be inflicted on criminals should be measured, not by time, but by the amount of labour they should be compelled to perform before regaining their freedom; and he devised an ingenious mode of recording their daily industry by marks, for the purpose of determining when they should have a right to their discharge.*

Captain Maconochie himself experimented on his own suggestions, in Norfolk Island, but not with any great success. The state of Norfolk Island, indeed, was never such as to encourage experiments of any kind. It was really reserved for the officials who superintended the working of transportation in Western Australia† to give the system its first practically successful trial. There a convict was allowed to earn by each day's labour a number of marks, and as soon as they amounted to a total previously calculated according to his sentence, he was granted a ticket-of-leave. Industry now became the test, and not good conduct; the latter was only recognised by making misconduct carry with it a forfeiture of some of the marks already earned by industry.

The convict's early release was no longer a matter of certainty provided only that he avoided certain acts of rebellion, but it was made contingent on something he had to earn. His fate rested in his own hands; it was not to depend

* Report, p. 27.

† Captain (now Colonel) Sir Edmund Henderson was the Comptroller-General of Convicts in the colony.

upon the opinion others formed of his character. The success which was shown to have attended the adoption of this principle in Western Australia has been equally apparent in this country. The mark system, which I shall describe directly, is the keystone, the mainspring of our present method of dealing with our convicts, and the valuable results which have grown out of it are nowadays clearly apparent.

Perfect, however, as is the mark system in theory, it is possible that in practice it might have been less successful had not its introduction been accompanied by a new and stringent discipline.

In 1864, with other alterations came also the appointment of a new band of administrators—those for the most part who had gained their experience in Western Australia; and with this new blood came new vigour into the working of the machine. They administered, naturally, to the legacy left them by their predecessors, taking up the system as they found it; but upon this they soon grafted many new and salutary reforms of their own. More especially was it evident that from henceforth there would be no more ill-advised pampering of criminals.

I will here describe briefly what this new discipline really is. It may be said to be based primarily on the rule laid down by the Lord Chief Justice to which I have already referred : it is intended to be deterrent rather than reformatory, to affect more the criminals *in posse* than *in esse*. Not that reformatory efforts are slackened. They are merely subordinated. "Reformation," says a high authority, "is an object which for every reason we are bound to follow strenuously ; but it must not be effected in such a manner as to interfere with the deterring principle, because punishment is primarily to prevent crime by the warning held up to those who might, but for such influences, fall into it."* The new system is essentially one of insistance rather than entreaty ; but it cannot be called harsh, though it is undoubtedly stern.

A convict sentenced to penal servitude passes through

---

* An Account of the Manner in which Sentences of Penal Servitude are carried out in England. By Col. Sir Edmund Du Cane, C.B., R.E., Surveyor-General of Prisons.

three stages.   In the first he endures nine months' "separate"
confinement in one of the London prisons—either Millbank or
Pentonville; which is supposed to be about as much of that
severely penal discipline as a human being can safely bear.
Thence he proceeds to "the works"—to one or another of
the Government prisons in the country, according to his
physical fitness for the *travaux forcés* in progress at each.
These prisons are at Chatham, Dartmoor, Portsmouth, and
Portland.   The work at each varies slightly in severity as it
does in character.   At Chatham and Portsmouth, the bulk of
the prisoners are engaged in excavating, digging, and moving
clay, which is laborious in the extreme; at Portland till lately
the work consisted principally in quarrying, removing, and
building up afresh the stone in the breakwater and on
the fortifications; at Dartmoor the reclamation of waste land,
and its subsequent tillage, finds employment for all hands.
Here, at these large establishments, the convict for the first
time finds himself under the operation of the mark system.
His sentence is represented by a certain equivalent—thus, five
years means 9300 marks, seven years 13,680, ten years 21,300,
and so on.   The following simple formula will explain how
these sums have been arrived at:

$$6 \ (S \times 365 - 270) = M.$$

where S is the sentence in years, and 270 represents the
days spent in separate confinement, when the convict earns
no marks.   The 6 represents the minimum of daily marks;
but the maximum he may earn is eight, and he can thus
overhaul his time, so to speak, day by day, till he reduces
it by one-fourth.   His daily industry is measured by the
official under whom he works, and duly entered in the "Party
Mark-Book," a book closely inspected by the superior officers
as a guarantee of fair play to the prisoner.   But the prisoner
is also allowed to know how he stands, and he has in his
possession a card on which the marks as they accrue are
carried to his credit, and he can appeal if he thinks they have
not been awarded fairly.

Marks, marks, marks—these are in truth the subject of a
convict's dreams and of every waking thought.   He jealously

guards what he has got, and as strenuously he seeks to add to
his store. These marks are a bribe which persuade him to
work by the convincing argument of personal advantage. He
gains thereby not the promise of money in sums—which it
was both unfair to grant and demoralising to him to receive—
but the priceless boon of a speedier return to his home beyond
the walls. By this device many of the evils urged against
"forced labour" are to a great extent removed. It has been
said that no man will try his best who is forced to work. This
was one of the arguments against the system of assignment,
as tending to show that the convict servants were nearly
valueless. But by the mark system, over and above the
ordinary stimulus given to industry, there is the still greater
inducement to show skill, aptitude, and intelligence; for, it
being the convict's great aim and object to gain marks, it
follows also that it is his desire to gain them as easily as he
can. Hence he realises readily the privilege of being raised
above the level of the unskilled labourers around him, who are
committed to a regular routine of only the same monotonous
and irksome toil. Hence, also, if he knows a trade or handi-
craft, he grasps eagerly at any chance of being allowed to
follow it; and if actually so selected, he is careful to put forth
his best abilities for fear of relegation to the severer labour
from which he has but just escaped. In the same way those
who know no trade are disposed to give their best endeavours
to learn one; and, without exception, all who are still in the
heavy "gangs," will labour on with alacrity, hoping thereby
to establish some sort of claim to pass on afterwards to lighter
and more agreeable work. The impetus thus given to intelligent industry and to cheerful alacrity only those who are in
daily observation of it can fully appreciate. But it may be
seen also in the results accomplished, in the style of work
which can be undertaken and successfully carried out; but of
these I will speak more at length further on.

But, however gained, the convict in course of time comes
to the day when his card is full. Here and there men
forfeit the whole of their remission; but as a general rule—
some sooner, some later—are granted the great boon for
which they have hopefully toiled on. They are released

from prison, as it is called, "on licence";—that is to say,
they have the Queen's licence to be at large before their
sentences have expired. This is, in common parlance, the
ticket-of-leave. But, though free from prison restrictions, the
condition of a licence-holder is far from one of absolute
freedom. He is held strictly under the supervision of the
police. They know beforehand that he is coming, and they
have photographs of his appearance. He is bound to report
his arrival in the police district where he means to reside,
and he cannot move thence without police permission, and
even with that he is only passed on to another police district.
With all this his demeanour is attentively observed : any
suspicious conduct, such as habitually associating with improper characters, being without ostensible means of livelihood,
being found in suspicious "situations," failing to report
himself and his whereabouts at proper intervals—any of these
may lead to the revocation of his licence and his return to
the prison whence he came, there to remain till his old sentence
is entirely expired.

These then are the three stages. First, separate confinement; secondly, hard labour on the public works; last of
all, release with a ticket-of-leave. I have, I trust, explained
the nature of each phase of treatment so as to be perfectly
intelligible to the general reader; and I think it must be
abundantly evident that the way of transgressors, now more
than ever, is hard.

I have now brought—though, I fear, in but a desultory
and incomplete fashion—the history of penal legislation down
to our own times. I have tried to trace the successive steps
taken in this country to solve that most difficult of social
problems—the satisfactory disposal of criminals. I have
shown how prison reform began with Howard; how it was
carried on at Millbank, the great national Penitentiary; and
how it fared amid the changes and vicissitudes of the passing
years. I have described how transportation was first adopted,
how it flourished, and how it failed. I have endeavoured to
explain how, piece by piece, bit by bit, the blocks which were
amorphous and incongruous, have been hacked and hewed and
hammered, till from them we have built up something of a

symmetrical system—a system so far satisfactory that in ten years there has been no call for further change. When, in 1871, an international prison congress assembled in London, many of the philanthropists who came to us from abroad were not a little astonished to find we had any system at all. Each had come armed with the peculiar method of treatment his own country favoured, and each was eager to press it on our acceptance. Yet the actual fact was, all the measures recommended had been in some way or other tried by us already. So far from being without a system, we had probably experimented more than other people; and that which remained to us was just what we had found to be practically possible, and at the same time suited to our needs. Further improvement may still be required as occasion arises; but meanwhile, it is some consolation to know that our present system will stand the two principal tests by which such matters are commonly judged. The first of these is the inquiry how far it has succeeded in diminishing crime; the second, whether its working is economical and followed by positively remunerative results.

But it behoves us to be most cautious in adopting the first-mentioned test. No doubt the severity or mildness of penal treatment plays a certain part; but that part is constantly over-estimated, and we are apt to attribute to it results that are more properly traceable to other causes. It has been well pointed out by a writer who speaks with authority, that "The prosperity of a country, the facilities for getting a living honestly, the condition of education, moral and literary, the efficiency of the police—all contribute to affect the statistics of crime."* Nevertheless, on two important occasions—in 1830 and in 1862—it was shown that the prevalence of crime was undoubtedly in a measure due to the immunity enjoyed by offenders; and therefore our most modern system must not be robbed entirely of its contribution to bring about that diminution in crime which beyond question has become apparent in recent years. It would be unprofitable to seek to allot to each of the causes already enumerated its relative contribution to the general result attained; but it must be remarked that one,

* Sir Edmund Du Cane.

at least, of them is likely ere long to be much more widely
operative. The future progress of education in this country
under the late Acts may reasonably be expected to affect
appreciably our criminal statistics. And this not alone from
the increased enlightenment of the various candidates for prison,
but because the would-be, or rather the possible, criminal will
now be subjected to reformatory treatment at an age when he
is susceptible of cure. I have adverted in an earlier page * to
the great fundamental error which has hitherto underlaid all
so-called systems by which the reformation of offenders has
been essayed. I have said that we have always commenced
too late. It is far different when the same engines of education and persuasion are turned upon the young. It is through
them that we should look to bring about a reduction of crime;
because, by reforming them, and by teaching them that it is
to their own manifest advantage to be honest, we shall
probably check recruiting for the ranks of the "dangerous
classes."

On the second test, however, of the value of our penal
system, we are furnished with evidence that is far more
tangible and satisfactory. The results obtained speak for
themselves. We have been forced to keep our convicts at
home, and we have made the most of the bargain. At the
four principal stations where convict labour has been massed
for years, the works executed by it will last long as monu-
ments of the system which has called them into existence. At
Portland the convicts have quarried in all 6,000,000 tons of
stone, sufficient to construct a breakwater "nearly two miles
in length, and running into water fifty or sixty feet deep;"† and
they have built the barracks and the principal part of the almost
impregnable fortifications by which the island of Portland is
defended.

In executing these works, the convicts carried on all the
mechanical operations; they quarried, dressed, and placed the
stone; they cast and forged iron-work, and acted as carpenters,
fitters, and smiths. All the extensive plant used on the works
was kept in repair by them; they made all the cranes and
derricks in the quarries, and laid the rails by which stone was

* Page 158.   † Paper on Convict Labour, by Col. Du Cane.

removed in waggons. At Chatham the dockyard extension works, already referred to, include a " Repairing Basin" with an acreage of twenty-one acres; the "Factory Basin" of twenty acres; the "Fitting-out Basin" of twenty-eight acres. The bottom of these basins is twelve feet below the old river-bed, and thirty-two feet below the level of St. Mary's Island. The surface of the latter, once a marsh intersected by creeks and nearly submerged at high tide, has been raised eight feet; and the whole island has been surrounded by an embankment nearly two miles in length, which has been principally executed by convict labour. "In carrying out these works," says Sir Edmund Du Cane,* "the prisoners have been employed in excavating, pile-driving, and concreting for the foundations; bricklaying, concreting, stone-dressing, and setting in connection with the construction of the basin walls and entrances; removing the earth from the area of the basin by means of waggons and incline planes, barrow roads, barrow lifts, and tipping waggons; loading and unloading materials; plate-laying; attending standing and locomotive engines. At Portsmouth similar operations have been performed by prisoners in making the large extensions of that dockyard, besides a vast quantity of preliminary work, such as demolishing the old fortifications." Some three hundred millions of bricks, all made by convicts, have been used in the foregoing works. Work of a still higher value, pecuniarily, has been accomplished by convict labour, in the building of new prisons and adding to the old prisons. Since 1863, upwards of four thousand new cells have been constructed, and a number of accessory buildings, officers' quarters, and so forth. The figures given by Sir Edmund Du Cane on this head are very satisfactory. The cost of these constructions was £311,200; the lowest contract price would have been £553,200; hence there has been a saving of £242,000 by employing convict labour.

Other works of vast importance have been initiated since 1871. A new prison has been built at Borstal near Rochester, intended to house the convicts employed in constructing the

* Manner in which Penal Servitude Sentences are carried out in England, p. 66.

forts, recommended by the Royal Commission on defences in 1859, and which are to protect Chatham from a southern attack. A smaller prison has given facilities for the erection of store-houses and magazines at Chattenden, on the left bank of the Medway. The new prison for separate confinement at Wormwood Scrubbs has been nearly completed, as described in the opening pages of this work. Finally, the year 1883 saw the commencement of a large enterprise at Dover, where a convict prison has been commenced, and where extensive harbour improvements will shortly be undertaken. A portion of the convict labour available in Scotland, is also to be applied to the enlargements of Peterhead and other northern ports.

There are those who in spite of such valuable results are still disposed to find fault with our system. Some regret transportation because it had at least the merit of removing a mass of criminals permanently from this country; others hanker after perpetual solitary imprisonment. I would remind the former that transportation is hardly feasible now, for reasons already given—not the least important of which is its excessive costliness; besides which, with modern facilities for travelling, the permanency of the removal is by no means assured. Besides, if the state for the public protection charges itself with the retention of a number of persons, it is surely the wiser and more practical plan to keep them and make them work for their living at home, instead of giving their labour gratis to far-off possessions, few of which are grateful, even if they do not indignantly reject the proffered boon. The latter objectors are, I think, blinded by their own superabundant goodness of heart. Their reiterated recommendations of the cellular system—of uninterrupted solitary confinement, that is to say—are based, first upon the *ignis fatuus* of prison reformation of character, and next upon their dislike to our convict system, which they call a method of congregating together masses of criminals little less demoralising than the oldest forms of association. In neither case, I apprehend, are they drawing just conclusions from premises that are sound. Not only, as I have already tried to prove, is protracted cellular imprisonment impossible on account of its fatal consequences, but (I am quoting again from Sir Edmund Du Cane) "perpetual seclusion in a cell for years, with no communication with his fellows, is (for a prisoner) an artificial state of existence so absolutely opposed to that, which nature points out as the condition of mental, moral and physical health, and so absolutely unlike that which he is prepared to follow on his discharge from prison, that it cannot be expected to fulfil the required object."* Moreover, that which these philanthropists are pleased to stigmatise as the "corrupting gang system," is but a partial association after all. The prisoners work together, it is true, and so gain the solace of companionship; but this privilege does not extend to free, unrestricted intercourse with one another. At labour they are compelled to work in silence, not absolute of course, but at least protracted conversation is out of the question, and by the very character of the labour exacted there is little leisure for it. And when not thus at labour and under an officer's eye, they are alone, locked up in separate cells. Hence the contaminating influences cannot be said to be very largely operative.

This, with other alleged shortcomings of our present convict system, was, however, fully discussed by a Royal Commission, which sat under the presidency of the Earl of Kimberley in 1878, "to inquire into the working of the Penal Servitude Acts." This commission examined a variety of witnesses, including several ex-convicts,† and came to the conclusion that "the system as at present administered is on the whole satisfactory; it is effective as a punishment, and free from serious abuses." "We believe," said the commissioners, "that a sentence of penal servitude is now generally an object of dread to the criminal population." At the same time they recommended certain minor reforms, chief among which was some plan for the separation of the less hardened from the habitual offenders. This suggestion was at once

---

* An Account of Penal Servitude. Although, as I have said, the effect of penal systems in diminishing crime is problematical, it may be mentioned here that in Belgium, where the cellular system partly holds, recommittals to prison are at the rate of 78 per cent.

† Among others the author of the well-known work, "Five Years' Penal Servitude."

adopted by the directors of convict prisons, and a " star class,"
as it was styled, was formed, into which were drafted "all
prisoners not versed in crime." Great pains are taken to
eliminate the black sheep. Whenever a prisoner is supposed
to be convicted for the first time, he becomes the subject of a
special investigation. Careful inquiries are made as to his
antecedents and character. The police, the clergyman of the
parish, all persons who would be likely to know him are
written to, and if the result is satisfactory, the prisoner is
admitted into the " star class." There he remains throughout
his sentence; certain special wards and special employments
are allotted to him and his fellows, so that he may escape the
contamination of the worst criminals. For the very worst
there is also a special treatment, and they are subjected to a
second term of "probation," or strictly separate confinement.
Finally, for all prisoners alike the former practice of allowing
free inter-communication at exercise has been discontinued.

Perhaps the most important of the recommendations of
Lord Kimberley's commission was that some system of independent inspection should be instituted in the convict prisons.
This has also borne fruit, and every prison is regularly inspected by one or more gentlemen, unpaid and non-official
visitors, who, without interfering with the administration,
exercise a general supervision over the prison and its inmates.
The recommendation was made with the hope of " conducing
to public confidence " in the convict system, and "as a
valuable safeguard against abuses creeping into it." There
is every reason to think indeed that this most desirable end
has been attained, and that the convict prisons where penal
servitude is enforced are as perfect as they can be made.

APPENDIX.

───◆───

SALARIES OF OFFICERS—1817.

Governor	. £600 a year.	
Matron	. 250 ,,	with percentage.
Chaplain	. 400 ,,	
Secretary and Accountant	. 300 ,,	
Surgeon	. 400 ,,	(medicines provided).
Master Manufacturer	. 200 ,,	with percentage
Steward	. 150 ,,	

INFERIOR OFFICERS.

MALES.		NO.
Taskmasters, each .	. £60 a year, with percentage .	. 4
Turnkeys ,, .	. 50 ,, ditto and rations .	. 20

FEMALES.		NO.
Taskmistresses, each .	. £60 a year, with percentage .	. 2
Turnkeys ,, .	. 50 ,, ditto and rations .	. 10
Nurses ,, .	. 50 ,, with rations .	. 2

SERVANTS.

Lodge Porters .	. £50 a year, with rations	. 3
Messenger .	. 50 ,, ditto . .	. 1
Patrols .	. 50 ,, ditto . .	. 4
		46

Total Male Officers . 32 | Total Female Officers . 14

DAILY RATIONS.

1 lb. bread (whole meal).
¾ lb. of beef or mutton without bone.
1 lb. of sound potatoes.
Salt and pepper; also coals and candles.

───────

Governor, Chaplain, Surgeon, to be married men.
Outer Lodge Porter, ditto.
Porter at Lodge of Female Pentagon, ditto.
Secretary not to live in the Prison.

PERCENTAGE.

Three-fourths, or 15s. in the £, or 9d. in the shilling, to the Establishment; one-eighth, or 2s. 6d. in the £, or 1½d. in the shilling, to Prisoner; one-twenty-fourth, or 10d. in the £, or ½d. in the shilling, to the Manufacturer, Matron, Taskmaster, Taskmistress, and Turnkey of the Subdivision.

As the earnings varied considerably, the average annual amount received by each officer was about £10.

THE FIRST COMMITTEE OF MANAGEMENT appointed by the Prince Regent in Council at the Court of Brighton, on the 12th February, 1816, was composed of—

> The Right Hon. Chas. Abbott, *Speaker of the House of Commons.*
>   "   George Rose.
>   "   Charles Bathurst.
>   "   Charles Long.
>   "   Richard Ryder.
> Sir William Curtis, Bart.
> Sir James Shaw, Bart.
> Sir Benjamin Hobhouse, Bart.
> John Fane, Esq.
> Wm. Morton Pitt, Esq.
> George Peter Holford, Esq.
> Edward Bootle Wilbraham, Esq.
> Davies Giddy, Esq.
> George Byng, Esq.
> William Mellish, Esq.
> Charles Wetherall, Esq.
> Charles Shaw Lefevre, Esq.
> Rev. Archdeacon Pott.
> Rev. Archibald Cambridge.
> Rev. John Thos. Becher.

CHARLES DICKENS AND EVANS, CRYSTAL PALACE PRESS.

www.ingramcontent.com/pod-product-compliance
Lightning Source LLC
Chambersburg PA
CBHW031814270326
41932CB00008B/425

9 783744 756532